# PLAYING GOD:
Fifty Religions' Views on Your Right to Die

# PLAYING GOD:

Fifty Religions' Views on Your Right to Die

by Gerald A. Larue, Th.D.

## MOYER ▲ BELL

Wakefield, Rhode Island & London

Published by Moyer Bell

---

**LIBRARY OF CONGRESS
CATALOGING IN PUBLICATION DATA**

Larue, Gerald A.

Playing God: fifty religions' views on your right to die

p.cm.

1. Euthanasia—Religious aspects. I.Title.

R726.L373        1996                    95-9666
179'.7—dc20                                  CIP

ISBN 1-55921-145-8

---

Printed in the United States of America
Distributed in North America by Publishers Group West, P.O. Box 8843, Emeryville, CA 94662, 800-788-3123 (in California 510-658-3453) and in Europe by Gazelle Book Services Ltd., Falcon House, Queen Square, Lancaster LA1 1RN England.

# Contents

# Introduction

Dramatic changes have occurred in health patterns in the last ten years. The right of terminally individuals to refuse heroic medical treatment has been affirmed and reaffirmed in state after state and has been endorsed by practically every religious group. Living Will and Durable Power of Attorney for Health Care forms are widely distributed and can be purchased in many stationary stores.

On December 1, 1991, the Patient Self-Determination Act (PSDA), the first federal law to address end-of-life decision-making, became effective throughout the United States. The act requires that all federally funded health care institutions, including hospitals, skilled nursing facilities, Health Maintenance Organizations (HMO's), home health agencies, and hospice programs, as well as Medical and Medicare programs, inform patients at the time of admission of their right to prepare and sign advance directives for health care by the institution, and to have their documented wishes carried out. *Hemlock Quarterly* of January 1992 summarized pertinent information in the act:

> *Information:* Before or at admission, the patient must be informed, in writing, of his/her right under that state's law to accept or refuse treatments while he/she is competent and to make decisions about the health care he/she will receive if he/she loses competence. Handouts given to the patient must include an explanation of exactly which state statutes or what case law for that particular state allows as well as a description of the institution's policy as it affects the patient's right to refuse treatment through advanced directives.

1

*Documentation:* Every new patient must be asked before or at admission if he/she has prepared a Living Will and/or a Durable Power of Attorney for Health Care. The response, and a copy of the documents, if they exist, should be a permanent part of the patient's medical record and be made known to all personnel who will be involved in the care of the patient.

*Non-discrimination:* Members of health care staff are forbidden to alter in any way or to determine a patient's care on the basis of whether or not he/she has prepared a Living Will or conferred a Durable Power of Attorney on another individual.

*Education:* Health Care facilities must provide inservice education for members of their staffs, and public programs for members of the community they serve, about the PSDA and current right to die laws applicable in their state.

These important changes are designed to put individuals in charge of their own life and death.

Steps are still needed to protect patient rights on those occasions when paramedics respond to emergency situations. Paramedics are trained to immediately initiate procedures designed to maintain or restore heartbeat and breathing to those who would otherwise die. They do not have time—nor can they take time—to determine whether the patient has signed a Living Will or Durable Power of Attorney for Health Care directive. Some communities are proposing that individuals who do not want heroic procedures to be initiated wear easily identifiable bracelets that will serve as do-not-resuscitate (DNR) guides for paramedics. To this end Montana has authorized the department of Health and Environmental Sciences to adopt a standard means for identifying individuals' wishes regarding life-sustaining procedures or do-not-resuscitate in emergency situations. A similar law is due to be passed in New York. DNR bracelets are being produced by the Medic-Alert Foundation International (2323 Colorado Avenue, Turlock, CA 95380, 800-432-5378).

*Hemlock Quarterly* for July 1991 reported the following:

1. Opinion surveys taken among health care personnel indicate strong support for physician-assisted euthanasia. For example, of 498 doctors polled by the journal, *Physician's Management*:

2

- 88% said that they would honor a patient's or relative's request to discontinue life support.
- 10.7% said they would write a prescription for a fatal drug dosage for an AIDS patient, if asked.
- 9.4% said that at certain points in their careers they had taken an action resulting in a patient's death.

2. The American Board of Family Practice reports that 91% of doctors it interviewed believe that a terminally ill patient has the right to choose to die. Asked if a patient with an illness that will permanently impair his or her quality of life has the right to choose to die, 81% said yes. (The board did not specify what it meant by the term "right to choose to die.")

3. The 1991 Roper poll of 1500 persons living in the states of Washington, Oregon, and California resulted in the following:

- 67% of Protestants, 66% of Catholics and 88% of Jews who were questioned supported legalized voluntary medically-assisted euthanasia for the terminally ill who suffer distressing pain.
- 57% of both Protestants and Catholics, and 85% of Jews voted in support of allowing doctors to legally prescribe lethal drugs so that terminally ill persons could commit suicide.
- 52% of Protestants, 48% of Catholics, and 71% of Jews said that doctors should be permitted legally to give terminally ill patients who wished to die lethal injections.
- Of those interviewed, 57% of Protestants and Catholics and 67% of Jews also supported the need to change laws to legalize medically assisted death for the terminally ill who request it.
- 68% of Protestants, 67% of Catholics, and 75% of Jews supported the right of assigned Attorneys for Health Care to make decisions for the administering of lethal drugs on behalf of terminally ill persons in accord with the terms of the agreement.

Democratic decision-making requires an informed public. The polls demonstrate a broad, general awareness of euthanasia issues. As we develop more medical technologies to prolong the life of terminally ill persons, more and more families face hard decisions concerning the care of loved ones. Television, movies, documentaries, news commentaries, and talk shows have brought before the viewing public the dilemmas of the terminally ill and those around them as they confront painful death or the prolongation of life of those in persistent vegetative states. Magazine articles and newspaper stories often augment the information flow. Men and women are better informed today about end-of-life problems than ever before in history. In a democratic country they have the right to demand the freedom to make their own choices.

Proposition 119 in the State of Washington and Proposition 161 in the State of California, both defeated by small margins (8%), received wide media attention. These initiatives served to educate the public about the growing concern of many people about their right to choose the time and manner of their deaths. Moreover, the initiatives provided many voters with the opportunity to make known to legislators their feelings, beliefs and intentions.

The enormous amount of attention and positive response to Derek Humphry's book, *Final Exit*, underscores the widespread interest in active euthanasia and the right of self-determination for terminally ill people. *Final Exit* was on *The New York Times* bestseller list for fifteen weeks and sales hit 500,000 copies. It has been translated into eight different languages and, like many controversial documents, was banned for a time in Australia and New Zealand.

In this book I present—without comment—the points of view of clergy and denominations. (Some responses are lengthy and others are short.) However, because the relationship of the Holocaust to euthanasia, Geronticide, Slippery Slope and other issues are being critically debated I have taken the liberty of responding to and, I believe, clarifying some aspects of these subjects. In doing so, I have not made direct or specific reference to any of the materials submitted by any religious group.

**References**

Humphry, Derek, *Final Exit*, Eugene, Oregon: The Hemlock Society, 1991.
Humphry, Derek, *Let Me Die Before I Wake*. Eugene, Oregon: The Hemlock Society, 1984.
Shneidman, Edwin S., *Death: Current Perspectives* (3rd edition) Palo Alto, California: Mayfield Publishing Company, 1984.

# Acknowledgments

It is important to recognize the many persons who have cooperated in making this book possible. During the mid 1980s, a suggestion by Derek Humphry, founder and former executive director of the Hemlock Society USA, of a need for a book dealing with the attitudes of religious groups to euthanasia resulted in a book called *Euthanasia and Religion*. Recently he has brought to our attention changes in health care and their impact on society in general and on religion, and he suggested the need for this new volume. I am most appreciative of our long association and friendship. My admiration for Derek's integrity, courage and commitment is exceeded only by my deep feelings for him as a person.

The Leonard Davis School of Gerontology in the Andrus Center at the University of Southern California is a wonderful environment for research. The personnel in the school's Administrative Office never cease to be of help. The door to the office of the Director, Dr. David Peterson, is always open and he is continually supportive. Marie Bergara, Pauline S. Abbott, May Ng and Joyce K. Kinjo have rescued me from a multitude of technical problems and I am most grateful to them.

From time to time, students have called my attention to some important document or article and their input has been helpful. Research papers by Tammy Anderson, Marcia Briggs, Paula Davis, Justin Nast, Joyce Riley and Alex Sassani have been helpful in providing insight into specific issues.

However, one person stands out: Maria Cristina Corpus, a graduate student in Gerontology from The Philippines. Cristina has been involved in this book from the beginning. Her steadiness, wonderful organizational skills, and patient, careful interpretation of my sometimes imperfect directions have helped my work load and made possible the organization of a mass of materials shared by various religious groups. I cannot find adequate words to express my appreciation, so I will simply say thank you, Cristina.

Personnel in denominational and church headquarters, scholars and researchers in religion, and ethicists and clergy have been generous in providing documentation, articles and sermons as well as responding to direct questions. I am most appreciative of their openness and willingness to share. I have tried to be faithful in presenting these opinions and beliefs and, should I have erred in any way I can only express my apologies now.

Cheryl Smith, former Staff Attorney, and Diana Smith, Staff Librarian, of the Hemlock Society USA in Eugene, Oregon, have provided me with important documents and news clippings that would otherwise have been unavailable to me. I thank them for the ways in which they have remembered me and forwarded these important materials. Scott Judd has earned my thanks as he has been responsible for the final preparation of the manuscript and subsequent production of this book. My student aide, Jennifer Sherwood, helped in the final preparation of the manuscript. And thanks to my editor, Jennifer Moyer, and indexer, Patricia Gross.

Finally, I thank my wife, Emily Perkins Larue, my most constant supporter. She placed my study off limits to her wishes to enjoy an orderly household. She has tolerated the piles of books and papers that surround me when I am engaged in a project and has never failed to offer words of encouragement for my work. Throughout our mutually hectic schedules, the warm tie of love that binds us has made it possible to share each other's woes and bear each other's burden. Who could ask for anything more?

*Gerald A. Larue*
Huntington Beach, California

# Foreword

The chapters that follow contain reactions from various religious groups to euthanasia and, in particular, to physician-aid-in-dying or physician-assisted suicide. In some instances a denomination has produced what might be recognized as an "official statement" which describes the position held by the majority in that particular religious group. Such statements tend to be products of long and careful study, analysis and reflection on the relationship between faith positions, scriptural interpretations, or traditional patterns of thought and the problems raised by modern medicine and the efforts to legalize physician-assisted death. These documents are designed to provide guidelines as opposed to must-be-followed orders. On the other hand, the guiding and authoritative statement produced in Rome, in May 1980, by the Sacred Congregation for the Doctrine of the Faith is to be followed and adhered to by all Roman Catholics.

Several religious groups have not produced statements. In these cases, I have consulted with denominational theologians, philosophers, clergy and others who have been wrestling with the issues involved. For example, the multifaceted discussions that have been taking place within Judaism are briefly presented. But now, still another dimension has been added to the discussion.

Initiative 119 provoked discourse within the synagogues and churches in the state of Washington. Through the generosity of rabbis and ministers I have been able to include materials that were produced and shared with congregations in that state. Thus, in addition to "official" statements outlining denominational guidelines and commentaries produced by scholars in institutions of learning, I have included the comments of clergy who work directly with congregations and with families who face life and death issues. In this way the practical is combined with the theoretical or academic.

In still other reports, I have relied upon individuals who are, in a sense, accepted spokespersons for their particular religion. Dr. Hassan Hathout, who is both a medical doctor and an Islamic scholar, presents the position of Islam. Christian Science is represented by a statement provided by the office of the Christian Science Committee on Publication for Southern California and so on. Some clergy have refused permission to publicize and share their positions regarding physician-assisted suicide or euthanasia. For example, Roman Catholic priests who digress from their church's stance have refused to let me put in print their identities along with their concerns and the basis for their theological disagreement with the position of the church. The same is true of some members of ultra-conservative or orthodox denominations and fundamentalist churches. These persons do not wish to become estranged from their fellow clergy nor are they prepared to face confrontation and perhaps condemnation by denominational authorities. Without permission to identify such individuals, all I can do is to make the unsupportable and rather weak statement that "they are there." Despite the impossibility of presenting many of the challenges entertained by some clergy, out of this present study a number of other important facts have come to light.

- There is no single religious position concerning euthanasia and/or physician-assisted suicide or euthanasia. Nor is there a Christian or Jewish, much less a Judeo-Christian, point of view or conclusion concerning euthanasia and physician-assisted euthanasia. The differences in points of view that emerge in the following chapters make it clear that no one can claim that "this is what a Christian believes concerning euthanasia," or, "this is the Jewish position on physician-assisted euthanasia." Even as a denomination may produce a statement outlining its position opposing physician-assisted euthanasia, the clergy in the field may argue that men and women in terminal pain and suffering have the right to choose for themselves their way of death without condemnation. This divergence in thinking is made as clear in the section on Judaism as it is in the section on the Episcopal Church. These theologians and academicians are not without compassion; they tend to deal in a most professional and academic way with traditional ethics and biblical interpretations. The dying person wants to be right with his or her God. In such contexts local clergy often move away from academic theology toward practical theology. They give their support (and, in a sense, provide divine approval) to those who seek to take steps to end their miserable suffering and their lives.

- Despite the theology that finds some sort of spiritual merit in suffering, whether it be a mystical identification with the suffering of Christ or benefits related to karma concepts, there are clergy who deny the validity of such claims. They find suffering to be without any real merit spiritual or otherwise. Suffering is recognized as debilitating and dehumanizing both spiritually and physically. It tears at the souls of loved ones who can only stand by helplessly as the patient cries out for release. It tortures the one who is in interminable pain. Permitting suffering to continue during the brief period of life remaining to the dying person invalidates claims to the highest human ethic of love, compassion and caring. Insisting that suffering is a requirement of God can raise questions concerning the interpretation of the deity as a loving, caring, father figure. Compassionate responses that endorse physician-assisted euthanasia or suicide to end suffering and terminate life fly in the face of traditional theology and call for reconsideration and reevaluation of those theologies that find merit in pain.

- Practically every theology speaks of the sanctity of human life. Again, modern medicine, with its capacity to prolong life without enhancing the quality of life, raises questions about the traditional theological interpretation of the sanctity concept. Whether or not a religion truly testifies to a belief in the sanctity of human life by insisting that a dying person be compelled to live out a life of bitter suffering to the last breath, rather than choosing to be eased out of pain by lethal injection is now being questioned. Clergy are moving away from what might be labeled "standard" interpretations to a differing perspective testifying to the sanctity of the life of a terminally ill person in intractable pain.

- The standard accusation—that physician-assisted euthanasia is tantamount to "playing God"—also is called into question. Chaplains, among others, are asking whether or not the churches or synagogues, in their response to modern medicine's ability to continue to keep terminally ill persons alive, might be the ones who are truly playing God. The refusal of support by religious groups of so-called "heroic" medicine, and the endorsement of what is often called "voluntary passive euthanasia," constitutes a first step in abandoning the playing God role. The disease is allowed to run its course without medical interference and the person is allowed to die. A second step, according to some clergy, is to support the personal autonomy of a terminally ill person as a God-given right and in the name of a merciful and compassionate God, to provide a ministry that supports the individual's right to choose a quick, painless and dignified death. In such a situation, euthanasia becomes an act performed in the name of a merciful and compassionate God rather than an act that usurps the intent of the deity.

These are demanding and progressive concepts. To insist that the person committed to a faith position is required by that faith system to die amid pain and suffering, or should one choose not to die "naturally," to be exposed to divine and social condemnation and rejection is, for many, both troubling and unsettling. Throughout history, religious groups have been compelled to come to terms with changing times. It can be anticipated that as modern medicine and medical science continue to hone the skills that extend life and forestall the process of dying for the terminally ill in intractable pain, that compassionate clergy will adapt their theologies to meet human needs. Such adaptations enable them to fulfil their roles as caring and compassionate servants of the deity. As in the past, it can be anticipated that religious officialdom will conform after the changes have taken place in the front lines where people live, suffer and die.

These are drastic and demanding times for the study of faith and culture. The following chapters will illustrate the ways in which various religious groups are wrestling with issues of death and dying. It is clear that some faith systems appear to be adamant and unyielding in their condemnation of euthanasia. On the other hand, there are religious groups that support the individual's right to request physician-assisted euthanasia and who press for changes in the law to accommodate and legalize medical response to such requests. Some denominations have made alterations in their positions; others continue to struggle with ways to come to terms with both the benefits and the problems growing out of modern medicine. The following chapters provide insight into what is taking place.

## A NOTE ON THE TEXT

To indicate the many and lengthy extracts from individuals from religious groups, the type is indented and rag right. Text written by the author is set in the usual manner, flush left and right.

# Chapter 1

## Determining Death

There was a time when death was easily defined as "not living" or as "lifeless." Lack of heart beat and the cessation of breathing followed by physical decay were the basic criteria for determining when a person was dead. Cessation of breathing was often determined by putting a feather beneath the nose and on the lips of the victim where the slightest breath would cause it to move. The heart was checked by placing one's ear on the patient's chest and listening for the heartbeat. Little was known about comatose states in which breathing can be so shallow that it is almost undetectable and heartbeat so faint that it cannot be heard. So mistakes were made. Some persons were buried alive, a fact that was discovered when, after coffins were disinterred and opened, it was found that the cloth linings had been ripped to shreds by the "corpse" on awakening in the grave. Some people made desperate attempts to avoid such happenings. For example, in some family sepulchers, a rope was attached to a bell that hung outside the family crypt. The free end of the rope was put in the coffin, so that should life return, the person in the coffin could signal that event.

These patterns belong to another age. Today, cardiopulmonary resuscitation (CPR), which is the administration of lifesaving measures involving external cardiac compression massage and mouth-to-mouth resuscitation, can restore effective heartbeat and breathing to a person who has collapsed from cardiac arrest. The development of such emergency techniques has restored life to individuals who would, in other times, have been presumed to have died.

In other cases, persons who have experienced extreme hypothermia (lowering of body temperature) and who betray all the signs of death have been resuscitated even after a considerable period of time has elapsed. In other times, these persons would have been considered dead. A few years ago, hypothermia was used in hospitals as a surgical procedure in rapid (eight- to ten-minute) heart operations to virtually stop blood flow. Today in open heart surgery, heart/lung machines keep the blood flowing and only mild hypothermia is employed (body temperature is reduced from 98.6 degrees F or 37 degrees C to about 82 to 88 degrees F or 28 to 31 degrees C). The concern is with minimizing damage to ·the heart muscle during heart operations that can last several hours.

Patients under the influence of barbiturates or anesthetizing or paralyzing drugs may show the classical signs of death but still be alive. Barbiturates are a group of sedative drugs that function by depressing activity within the brain. They have been used under strict controls as anti-anxiety drugs, sleeping drugs and anticonvulsants. Taken without medical control, in large quantity and with alcohol, they can bring an individual to a near-death state and, in some cases, can produce death. Anesthetizing drugs are used in hospital settings to control or abolish pain during surgical procedures by depressing the activity of the central nervous system. In the medical setting they produce a coma effect. Cocaine, once used as a local anesthesia for minor operations, has now degenerated into a street drug. In its purified form, known popularly as "crack," it can produce seizures, cardiac arrest, coma and death. In the coma state, with breathing and heart rate reduced, a person could mistakenly be considered dead and therefore beyond the remedial care that could sustain life.

The definition of death is clouded further by those patients who can breath and maintain heartbeat but who are labeled "brain dead." Brain death refers to the loss of cognitive and awareness functions. The lower brain stem that maintains respiration and heartbeat may continue to function and keep the body alive, but the part of the brain that controls the senses no longer functions. The question arises: Is that person "alive?" How can "brain death" be determined for sure?

The complexity of defining death is compounded still further when surgical hypothermia is employed. By cooling the blood (normal temperature is 98.6° F) to about 60° F all blood circulation is halted, there is no heart beat, and no breathing. (*The American Medical Association Home Medical Encyclopedia, Vol. 1*, p. 563). A recent television documentary recorded an operation on a brain aneurysm that involved heart stoppage for eight minutes. When the operation was completed, the blood temperature was brought back to normal, the heart was induced to begin its regular function and the patient recovered without any apparant damage to the brain. Was the patient dead for 8 minutes?

In response to the need for definitions medical criteria have been developed. In 1968 the Ad Hoc Committee of the Harvard Medical School to Examine the Definition of Brain Death published its findings. These findings have been widely adopted, with minor variations, as guides in determining when a patient has suffered irreversible loss of brain activity. They are:

- Unreceptivity and unresponsivity, which implies total un- awareness of external, even the most painful, stimuli, which evoke no vocal (not even a whimper or a groan) or other response (such as a grimace) including quickening of respi- ration or limb withdrawal.
- No movements or breathing after the respirator has been turned off for a three-minute period and no effort to breath spontaneously.
- No reflexes such as non-pupil response to bright light, no evidence of swallowing, yawning, vocalizations, etc.
- A flat (isoelectric) electroencephalogram.

The procedures, conducted by a physician, should be repeated and record no change within a twenty-four hour period. If all criteria are met, the patient is, for all practical purposes, presumed to be, medically speaking, dead. The criteria exclude two types of cases: hypothermia, and cases where the presence of central nervous system depressants such as barbiturates are discerned. The norms, now generally adopted in medical care and in the Uniform Determination of Death Act, which in modified form has been legislated in many states, are developments from the "Harvard criteria." The Uniform Determination of Death Act came into being in 1981 through the cooperative efforts of a number of groups, including the American Medical Association and the American Bar Association. The act provides that an "individual who has sustained either (1) irreversible cessation of circulatory and respiratory functions, or (2) irreversible cessation of all functions of the brain, including the brain stem, is dead."

One might think that the above definitions would pretty well settle the issue, but this is not so. Moral and ethical concerns arise in the cases of individuals who are not dead, but may be unconscious and unable to supply their own nourishment. At this point definitions of the states of unconsciousness can be most important.

Coma is to be separated from brain death. A person in coma is in a state of unarousable unresponsiveness exhibiting no response to external stimuli. But the coma state is not permanent; it will resolve itself into some other state. In some cases the person revives, as if from sleep, even after long periods of time, sometimes months. In other cases the person sinks into deeper coma where some automatic responses are noticeable such as coughing, yawning, blinking, and roving eye movement, all of which indicate that the lower brain stem is functioning. Or the person may slip into a condition of unresponsivity known as the persistent vegetative state (PVS), which is deeper than coma and in which the upper part of the brain, the cerebrum, and in particular its outer layer, or cortex (the part of brain that is responsible for those activities that we recognize as peculiarly human) is permanently impaired or inoperative. The lower brain stem that controls involuntary functions such as breathing, blinking, waking-sleeping cycles, etc., may still function. In this state, the person is considered brain dead, or has experienced cerebral death. This was the condition of Nancy Cruzan.

Nancy Cruzan was injured in an automobile accident in 1963. Medical doctors pronounced her brain dead. Because intravenous feeding had been introduced, the woman was kept "alive" receiving nourishment through feeding tubes for seven years. Finally, after receiving court orders, the family was able to have the feeding and hydration tubes removed. The removal of the essential life-support tubing could be labeled "allowing to die," inasmuch as no further efforts would be made to sustain life. Although her body stopped receiving nourishment, Nancy Cruzan did not die immediately. She died slowly. After a period of twelve days, through lack of nourishment, her heart gave out. In actuality, Nancy Cruzan died from starvation and dehydration. It is assumed that she suffered no physical or mental pain, but the family that was by her bedside throughout the dying ordeal obviously felt pain.

Moral and ethical considerations have been raised concerning Nancy Cruzan's death. Could it be said that she truly died seven years before the life sustaining equipment was removed and "nature was allowed to take its course?" Would it have been more ethical and more compassionate to administer a single lethal dosage of medication to enable Nancy Cruzan to die quickly rather than to die slowly by starvation and dehydration? Can starvation and dehydration really be considered "normal" or "nature's way" for human beings to die? On the other hand, would prolonging her persistent vegetative state for many more years (she appeared to be physically healthy) have been the highest expression of moral concern?

14

The situation might have bean eased if the physicians had not initiated the feeding regimen in the first place. But is there really any moral difference between not starting a life-sustaining procedure and withdrawing the same procedure after it has been started? Chances of recovery from a vegetative state have been estimated at less that one percent during the first six months, and as practically or almost never after a one-year period. In Nancy Cruzan's case, after seven years, there was absolutely no hope of recovery. Are medical doctors, whose aim is to do all they can to help their patients recover from accidents and illnesses so that a normal life might be lived, to be so severely handicapped that once they have begun life-sustaining procedures they cannot stop these same procedures except by virtue of court procedures? At some point, legalized physician assisted euthanasia for persons who, having signed either a Living Will or a Durable Power of Attorney for Health Care form in which they have expressed their wishes for the abandonment of life-sustaining treatment should they become like Nancy Cruzan, can be recognized as a viable alternative to the prolongation of life or to death by slow starvation.

In hospital situations, patients who would normally exhibit all of the classical signs of death do not die because they are kept alive by respirators and heart-lung equipment. These machines can sustain vital signs even after true death has occurred. If these persons have signed valid organ transplant forms that state that in the case of persistent vegetative state they wish to have their organs transplanted so that others may live, at what point can these persons be considered to have died? For example, an individual in a PVS has had the heart removed for transplantation but the circulation of the blood and breathing functions are still maintained by machines, say for a period of forty-eight hours, so that the kidneys may be kept healthy for removal to help another waiting patient. Is the person without the heart "alive" during the forty-eight-hour period or can it be presumed that death occurred when the individual entered the persistent vegetative state? The definition of death becomes most important in such an instance.

Belief systems may also enter into efforts to define death. For example, Roman Catholicism (along with other Christian groups) teaches that a person is both body and soul. In the words of Vatican II, "Though made of body and soul, man is one. " (Pastoral Constitution on the Church in the Modern World, 14). Reference is often made to the Book of Wisdom (3:1-3), which is not accepted as authoritative Scripture by Protestants:

But the souls of the just are in the hand of God,
and no torment shall touch them.
They seemed, in the view of the foolish, to be dead;
and their passing away was thought an affliction
and their going forth from us, utter destruction.
But they are in peace.
(The New American Bible)

Roman Catholic theologians claim that the individual is dead when the soul leaves the body and in this sense the soul is equated with life. Just when the soul-departure occurs is open for discussion. Is the concept of the soul related to the higher cortical functions of the brain—to those functions that characterize uniquely the human being? When these functions are permanently damaged and no longer function, has the soul left the body? Is the soul related to breath as it is in so many biblical passages so that when a person stops breathing the soul departs? Then what if the person is resuscitated? Does the soul return? Or is the soul associated with a life-principle that signifies that so long as the person is breathing and the heart is beating, the soul remains in the body and departs only at death of the total organism? Is there then, a theological definition of death acceptable to all Christians and does it differ from the Buddhist or Hindu belief systems?

Religions that postulate an afterlife or reincarnation deny the finality of death. Life continues in another dimension or is continued in another existence. Pseudo-scientific denial of death is also expressed in cryonics, which involves the freezing of a dead body for possible revival in another time when the cures for the disease that caused death and the necessary skills to reconstitute a frozen body into a living organism have been mastered.

At present, the Harvard criteria, in its varying forms, provides the only medical guide for determining when a person is brain dead. On the other hand, apart from those whose life-functions are sustained by machinery, the old criteria still apply. A person is dead when the heart stops pumping the blood, the lungs stop pumping air and the processes of decay begin. Of course the medical definition of death does not touch on the issue of quality of life.

## SANCTITY OF LIFE/QUALITY OF LIFE

Two themes appear repeatedly in the discussion of euthanasia and religion. They are sanctity-of-life and quality-of-life issues. Sanctity of

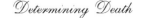

life refers to the preciousness of life or the sacredness of life, and implies the absolute inviolability of human life. For western religion, the concept of sacredness is usually supported by reference to the deity: "God gave life and only God should take life." Or life is seen as a loan from God, a loan to be recalled in God's time and in accord with God's will. To interfere with the divine timing by shortening the life-span is to assume jurisdiction over that which belongs to God alone and such an act is labelled "sin."

Sanctity-of-life concepts can also rest on a non-theological basis. The life of an individual is seen as a one-of-a-kind absolutely unique product of nature. Each person with his or her unique DNA (deoxyribonucleic acid), which is the principle carrier of genetic information, and with his or her own personal experiences, is a never-to-be-duplicated life-form to be respected, protected and nourished. To violate the person is to violate the sanctity of that special life. Many in the medical profession who subscribe to the sanctity-of-life doctrine actually practice something else. Anacephalic infants, born without complete brains, cannot survive for more than a few days. These unfortunate infants are placed in isolation and allowed to die of starvation. Because the infant cannot possibly live, it is neglected or abandoned. All that is done is to provide for the infant a bed in which to die. From time to time, the life-support systems, including naso-gastric or intravenous feeding and hydration tubes, of a permanently comatose person are withdrawn. If the patient does not die immediately, he or she is allowed to perish slowly by starvation and dehydration, a process that can take days or weeks. Just how such behavior can be said to give recognition to the sanctity-of-life principle is not explained. By removing the feeding tubes, the doctors do not deliberately kill the patient, they simply let the person die. They are "letting nature take its course" or they are "letting God call the patient home." They are not interfering with divine purpose or intent, nor do they express disdain for the uniqueness of life. On occasion, a doctor will administer a mega-dose of morphine in full awareness that the medication will kill the patient. The action is justified as an effort to control pain. Here again, the doctor can argue that the concern was with the quality of life and the sacredness of life. Death was simply a byproduct of that concern.

Not all patients receive the same treatment. Not every patient is simply permitted to die. Some who suffer heart failure are subjected to resuscitation techniques that restimulate the heart. Others who suffer heart failure will not receive the same attention. These latter persons have been placed in DNR (Do Not Resuscitate) or "slow code" categories. Should they suffer heart failure, nothing is done to revive them or whatever resuscitation patterns are initiated are so slowed and delayed that there is no hope for restoration of heart beat. In other words, the medical profession practices and endorses a selective interpretation of the sanctity-of-life idea. It would appear that some lives are deemed to be more sacred than others and should the heart of one of these patient's stop functioning, it is reactivated. These lives appear to be "worth" preserving. Others are allowed to die. Who makes the decision and on what basis?

The person earmarked for DNR will be the one who has little potential for living a life of quality if revived. The person whose chest is thumped and pumped and who is jolted by electric shock when the heart stops beating is, obviously, one whose life is considered to be sacred and whose heart should be reactivated. Medical decisions may be made on the basis of statistical prognosis. Certain diseases at a particular stage of development provide little or no hope of cure or of alleviation of suffering. The physician's familiarity with the progress of an illness, plus knowledge of the patient's health patterns and potential for recovery, may also affect treatment patterns. Quite often the patient and the patient's family are involved in the decisions to employ the DNR code.

On occasion decision-making can be cluttered with legal processes. For example, in 1979, Brother Joseph Fox, an 83-year-old Marianist Brother, suffered cardiorespiratory arrest after a routine hernia operation and the administration of ten mg. of valium. Heart massage restored his heartbeat but, during the arrest, insufficient oxygen reached his brain and Brother Fox suffered massive brain cell destruction. He was reduced to a chronic vegetative state and able to perform only the most primitive digestive processes. He could not move, speak, hear, think or recognize anyone. The Marianist Brothers, acting in accord with the Vatican Declaration, requested that the respirators sustaining his life be removed and that Brother Fox be permitted to die naturally. The Nassau Hospital officials refused the request and the Nassau County District Attorney, pressured by right-to-life groups, warned that anyone who disconnected the life-support equipment would be prosecuted for homicide. Here it would seem the sanctity of Brother Fox's life was a supreme concern in the mind of the District Attorney and right-to-life groups.

The Marianist Brothers petitioned the court. They pointed out that Brother Fox had said that he never wanted to be reduced to a vegetative state. The court upheld their appeal. Here it would seem that quality of life was the concern of the Marianist Brothers, Brother Fox and the court.

The District Attorney appealed to the Appellate Court and again the Marianist appeal was supported. The District Attorney then turned to the New York Court of Appeals, the highest court of the state. During the appeal, Brother Fox's heart failed and he died. What becomes clear is that for the Marianist Brothers, the sanctity-of-life doctrine was augmented by the quality of the life that remained for Brother Fox. Their interpretations supported Brother Fox's right to die "naturally," free from the life-sustaining respirator. In the mind of the District Attorney and right-to-life groups, sanctity-of-life required the sustaining of Brother's Fox's life as a permanently comatose patient.

For some, the idea of sanctity-of-life is reinforced by the commandment "Thou Shalt Not Kill" (5th in Roman Catholic reckoning, 6th in Protestant lists). The commandment reads literally, "You shall not commit homicide," and refers, therefore, to only one form of killing. Anyone who reads the Bible will be aware that a variety of killings are justified and that the deity is often involved in sending death or determining the time of death.

What is most important in the appeal to the Bible as the authority for decision-making regarding suicide or euthanasia, is that nowhere in the Bible is suicide or assisted suicide condemned. Indeed, as Arthur J. Droge and James D. Tabor have shown in their careful analysis of all relevant biblical passages, there is no condemnation of, or negative comment on, what they prefer to call "voluntary death." (*A Noble Death*, Harper, 1992, p. 58.) What remains, then, for those who seek sanctity-of-life support in the Bible is the interpretation of passages that recognize God as the giver of life and therefore automatically the determiner of the time of death.

The quality of life issue arises when a terminally-ill patient is in intractable pain or when a patient is reduced to a persistent vegetative state or when an anacephalic infant is born. One asks, "What is the quality of life for this person?" Theologically, it can be argued that no matter how brief the life span (as in the case of the anacephalic infant), how cognitively impaired the person may be (as in the case of Brother Fox), or how racked with pain the existence of a patient may be, regardless of how minimal the quality may be, that life is sacred and is to be prolonged until "natural death" occurs. Realistically any estimation of the quality of life for these individuals must judge it to be minimal and perhaps even absent. To recognize the absence of quality is to render a negative evaluation that must be coped with by loved-ones, care-givers and perhaps the public at large in the cases of the anacephalic infant and the person in a persistent vegetative state. In the case of the terminally ill patient in intractable pain, the suffering individual is also involved in making an evaluation of the quality of life. Beyond the issues of quality and sanctity, the public and perhaps the family may be troubled by other issues such as financial costs and the energy and time demanded of hospital personnel in treating such cases.

The agony endured by those who love and care for the patient can be heart-breaking as they sit and wait for nature to take its course. In the case of the cognitively-aware patient in intractable pain partially controlled by drugs that affect the patient's ability to function mentally and socially, the suffering of both patient and family can be devastating. Not everyone knows how to respond compassionately. One well-meaning clergyman, deeply committed to the sanctity-of-life doctrine, informed me that he comforted his wife who was ravaged by cancer that had attacked her internal organs with the reminder that "Jesus had suffered even more" and that she should "try to identify with Jesus' pain." Even the sedatives used to numb her agony constituted a weakening of faith inasmuch as Jesus refused the sedative (wine mingled with myrrh) which was offered to him on the cross (Mark 15:23). I must admit that I was shocked, angered and dismayed at the way in which theology seemed to assume more importance than an empathetic response to the woman's pain. Fortunately, the majority of clergy are not so theologically hidebound.

The sanctity-of-life issue must be reduced to simple practicalities. Which testifies most to the sanctity-of-life: the refusal to end life quickly by a medically provided lethal injection for an anacephalic infant, for a permanently vegetative loved one or for a beloved family member terminally ill and crying out for release, or the insistence that these lives be lived out to the bitter end when nature or God terminates the life? In such cases, is physician-assisted euthanasia the greatest evil or is it the most compassionate statement of reverence for life and for the quality of life? Obviously, each individual must make the decision for himself or herself. Some doctors, acting in accord with the expressed wishes of the patient and with the support of the patient's family, are presently making these decisions, either secretly and illegally or under the guise of providing pain control. In some cases family members, acting in accord with the continuing request of a suffering, terminally-ill loved one, have assumed responsibility for the patient's death. Often the act remains a family secret. In other cases, arrests and courtroom trials have ensued which have resulted in a variety of sentences ranging from imprisonment to probation to exoneration.

It is clear that the efforts to preserve life in each and every instance are not valid. Quality of life, potential for survival, and potential for cure all need to be involved. What to do in those instances where the prognosis is completely negative remains a problem. Removal of life support equipment, benign neglect and abandonment, and the administration of drugs that reduce the person to semi-consciousness are inadequate answers.

Clearly the issue is far too complex to do more than raise basic questions for consideration in this book. As the literature relating to euthanasia continues to expand, the various sanctity-of-life arguments will expand accordingly. Helga Kuhse concludes her thoughtful analysis of the subject (*The Sanctity-of Life Doctrine in Medicine*, Oxford, 1987) with these words:

> When we refrain from preventing the deaths of handicapped infants, comatose patients, and the terminally ill and suffering, by classifying the means necessary for keeping them alive as "extraordinary," "not medically indicated," "disproportionately burdensome," and so on, we are resorting to an equally spurious device in order to preserve our sanctity-of-life ethics unscathed. If we want to go beyond definitional ploys, we must accept responsibility for making life and death decisions on the basis of quality or kind of life in question: we must drop the "sanctity-of-life" doctrine and work out a quality-of-life ethic instead. (p. 220)

## THE SLIPPERY SLOPE THEORY

From time to time, those who express concern about the potential deleterious effects of legalizing or endorsing medically-assisted voluntary euthanasia warn about the "slippery slope." According to this theory, once medically assisted euthanasia is legalized for the terminally ill who request it, legalized killing of other groups will automatically follow and even become compulsory. These "other groups" would include the physically and mentally handicapped, the elderly, the impoverished, those who depend on welfare for survival and, perhaps, even members of some specific ethnic, racial, political or religious group. Validation of the "slippery slope" argument is supposed to be found in Nazi Germany, where, according to this interpretation, a progression of persecution and death-camp killing was apparent.

How does one respond to such warnings? To begin, it is important to be aware of the legal restraints in proposed legislation for physician-assisted euthanasia. Every possible safeguard against abuse has been introduced. At no place within the proposed legislation is there any hint of bias or prejudice against any group of people. What is proposed is *voluntary* euthanasia, something that never happened in Germany. Before these terrible scenarios are introduced, the proposals for legislation should be examined as indeed, they have been by medical persons, lawyers, clergy and others who have contributed to the wording and who support the concept. Active, voluntary physician-assisted euthanasia is not a nightmarish notion conjured up by some depraved group of people; it is a response to deep concerns for human well-being and human rights. At the same time, it is important to acknowledge the presence of bigots and racists and organized hate groups in America (and elsewhere in the world). Certainly if such people should ever take control of the nation, they could, possibly, initiate a program similar to that enacted in Nazi Germany. The very recognition of the existence of such persons and groups in a free, democratic society in itself should provide some degree of protection against them.

It is imperative that there be continuing education on the constitutional rights of all persons. The laws that permit hate groups to exist are the same laws that protect us from abuse by such organizations. We are a nation under law. Bigots and hate groups are free to be what they are and to express their distasteful ideas. However, under law, they do not have the right to act out their hatred and bigotry by oppressing others or curtailing the freedom of others. Freedom loving people must be always on guard. In the television program, "Hate on Trial," hosted by Bill Moyers, white supremist Tom Metzger uttered this chilling warning:

> I have planted my seeds. They're already in the ground. We're embedded now, don't you understand? We're in your colleges. We're in your armies. We're in your police forces. We're in your technical areas. We're in your banks. (Rosenberg, p. F. 13)

If there is danger of a slippery slope in euthanasia, it resides in the virulent thinking of zealots whose proclaimed biases and attitudes threaten the very freedom we cherish.

The slippery slope argument implies that once the right to voluntary medically-assisted euthanasia is legalized, it will become incumbent upon the handicapped, the frail elderly and others to rid society of their presence. They will recognize themselves as societal burdens, no longer contributing to human welfare while demanding from society excessive energy, time and money for their upkeep. The fact is, such an attitude is now present in some segments of our society and, in some cases, it does lead to suicide, not only by the frail and handicapped, but by those who are poverty stricken or too poor to afford the excessive costs of medical treatment. At this point, social restraints become essential. These restraints grow out of religious and social teachings about the value and sanctity of human life, the love of persons for each other, the compassionate response of humans to others in need of help.

It has also been implied by some who argue against legalized euthanasia that the weak, the infirm and the frail elderly will be coerced, persuaded or cajoled into accepting euthanasia. They will be made to feel useless in a society where the work ethic is dominant and where those who do not produce may be viewed as drains on the vitality of society. They will be persuaded that, inasmuch as they serve no further useful social purpose, it is incumbent upon them to die. Perhaps there will always be those few who seek to dismiss the value of human life and who stand willing to rid society of persons they consider to be useless. It is possible to extend the current "no deposit, no return" mentality to humans. There may also be those few who will seek to be rid of some feeble elder whose continuing existence delays the distribution of inheritances. But to allow fear of such persons to be the basis for ignoring the rights of terminally ill persons who may be in pain, or in a vegetative state, to have their wishes to die fulfilled, seems to be unethical and undemocratic. Leon R. Kass, a medical doctor has commented:

> Everyone—even those in favor of euthanasia—recognizes the possible abuses, among them the coercion of consent and the slide into killing the weak and the unwanted without their consent. To ally these fears, partisans of euthanasia point to the Netherlands, where for over a decade physicians have been practicing mercy killing with the acquiescence, if not the whole-hearted support, of the law and the larger society. If Holland, without doubt a highly civilized, liberal, and humane nation indeed, in World War II a bastion of principled de- cency against the unspeakable assaults on human life opts for mercy killing and practices it without abuse we can take heart

and proceed gently into that good night. Let us look to the
Dutch [pp. ix-x].

The slippery slope argument rests on fatalistic assumptions. It
reflects the belief that the future is inevitable and that we have absolutely
no control over private or public destinies. The implications are that the
predictions of "the worst possible scenario" are not simply possible or
even probable, but are assured. There is no recognition that in a
democratic society we have open to us choices concerning the future.
The slippery slide into some sort of compulsory euthanasia as opposed
to voluntary euthanasia is not part of that preference.

The slippery slope argument reflects lack of faith in the validity of
the democratic system, and in the power of our free society to control by
law those who would prey upon the weakness of others or force their
particular notions on others. It reflects uneasiness about the ethical and
moral qualities of modern humans and would seek to limit human
compassion and human autonomy by reacting primarily to fears of what
might happen. The so-called domino effect does not operate automatically. Because one action is taken, it does not follow that another more
drastic step need follow. Our way of life, with its multiple varieties of
human responses that enhance human freedom to make personal
choices, invalidates the arguments of those people who would forecast
doom at every step.

But what of the references to what happened in Nazi Germany? There
a socially advanced nation was transformed politically, morally and ethically,
almost overnight. Could the slippery slope that some find in that nation's
history be a forewarning of what could happen elsewhere?

There are two generally quoted bases for the idea of the slippery
slope in Nazi Germany. The first comes from a guilt statement by Pastor
Martin Niemoller, published in the foreword of his book *Exile in the
Fatherland* (Grand Rapids, Michigan: Eerdmans, 1986, p. viii). Niemoller wrote:

First they came for the Socialists and I did not speak out
   Because I was not a Socialist.
Then they came for the trade unionists, and I did not speak out—
   Because I was not a trade unionist.
Then they came for the Jews, and I did not speak out—
   Because I was not a Jew.
Then they came for me—
   And there was no one left to speak for me.

The second basis for the slippery slope idea in Nazi Germany comes from the observations of Dr. Leo Alexander, the Austrian-born psychiatrist, who taught medicine at Harvard and Duke Universities. As a consultant at the trials of Nazi war criminals, he was shocked and dismayed by what he learned of the evil practices done under the name of medicine in Nazi Germany. In 1949, he wrote in an article titled "Medical Science Under Dictatorship" in *The New England Journal of Medicine* (Vol. 39, pp. 46f):

> Whatever proportions these crimes finally assumed, it became evident to all who investigated them that they had started from small beginnings. The beginnings at first were merely a subtle shift in emphasis in the basic attitude of physicians. It started with the acceptance of the attitude, basic in the euthanasia movement, that there is such a thing as life not worthy to be lived. This attitude in its early stages concerned itself merely with the severely and chronically sick. Gradually, the sphere of those to be included in this category was enlarged to encompass the socially unproductive, the ideologically unwanted, and finally all non-Germans. But it is important to realize that the infinitely small wedged-in lever from which this entire trend of mind received its impetus was the attitude toward the nonrehabitable sick.

It is most important to recognize two aspects of these important reports. The first is that what took place in Germany occurred under a dictatorship, not in a democratic setting. So long as the ethnic diversity in America provides opportunity for persons of different racial, religious and ethnic backgrounds to live and work together in freedom and in peace, the patterns of Nazi Germany will remain foreign. If America should ever move towards the kind of dictatorship that Hitler brought to Germany, then our accepted standards of ethical and moral behavior may well be scrapped. Meanwhile, within our democracy the progression described by Dr. Alexander cannot take place.

The second aspect lies is what B. F. Skinner has called the need for countercontrols. In the essay "Compassion and Ethics in the Care of Retardates," (*Cumulative Record: A Selection of Papers*, Appleton-Century-Crofts, 1972) he pointed out that "The trouble arises because those who exert control are subject to little or no countercontrol" (p. 286). Countercontrols serve to curb violent action and remind those to whom authority and power are given that there are limits on what they may or can do. These same countercontrols serve as the social and ethical reminders that help to curb behavior. Our social countercontrols exist in part in the ballot box where we can vote out of office persons who do not properly represent us or who violate the will of the people; and where we can introduce initiatives supported by signatures of thousands of individuals. Our countercontrols include the media in which investigative reporters call our attention to the acts of those who misuse public trust, where letters to the editor and articles and essays inform us and prompt us to respond. Our countercontrols include the right of public to protest in rallies. In Germany, as the Nazis assumed control of the nation, there were no valid countercontrols. The church was, for the most part, silent or cooperative. Hitler's propaganda machine educated others to his point of view and dissenting voices were outshouted or silenced. Ultimately, the countercontrol had to come from the outside at the cost of millions of lives. In a democratic system of government countercontrols are always present.

Law in a democratic society develops out of the diversity of community. Where there are "bad" laws, the conscience of members of the community move them to disobey those laws or to seek to change them. In Europe, there were those who rebelled against Nazi regulations and who, disregarding their own welfare, gave protection and succor to Jews who would otherwise have been placed in work camps or put to death. In America, the legalized restrictions of African-American rights that grew out of the slavery mentality were finally challenged and changed. The challenges came from members of both the black and the white communities who were appalled at the indignities suffered by Americans simply on the basis of their darker skin pigmentation. Laws that impacted on the role of women began to change when women were granted full citizenship status and given the right to vote in 1920. The embarrassment of the people of the United States over the undemocratic imprisonment of Japanese-Americans during World War II has been publicly acknowledged. Today our democratic culture is still evolving as citizens become aware of limitations placed on women by males in control of business and the work forces. The humane reactions of concerned and aware persons serve as ever-growing counterforces to practices (whether they are legalized or are reflections of unthinking, but nevertheless demeaning, attitudes) that interfere with human rights or that endanger the lives, property and rights of citizens whether they are healthy or ill, rich or poor, old or young.

It is important to note that despite the implications for Nazi Germany embodied in the Alexander statement, there never was "a slippery slope." As Daniel Callahan has noted:

The Nazi experience is only partially relevant. Theirs was not a move from legal voluntary euthanasia to involuntary killing. They never had the first phase at all, but went straight to the killing. ("Can We Return Death to Disease?," *Hastings Center Report*, Special Supplement, January/February, 1989, p. 4 ff.)

The so called "euthanasia" program, first proposed by Hitler in 1935, initially to get rid of the physically and mentally handicapped, provides an example of "technological barbarism" which can never be linked to present day "good death" (euthanasia) proposals. Hitler's program began on September 1, 1939 with the enactment of his decree called "Order for the Destruction of Lives Which are Unworthy of Being Lived" (*Vernichtung lebensunwerten Lebens*). As the Fuhrer's psychopathic feelings of insecurity grew, the definition of the "unworthy" expanded. Consequently, some who were labeled "the unfit and unworthy" died in concentration camps like the one at Auschwitz where they entered through a gate bearing the deceptive, mocking, cynical promise that "work makes free" (Arbeit Macht Frei). Some, like the Gypsies, were slaughtered because their dark skins threatened Hitler's concept of a racially pure Aryan Germany (estimates range from 70,000 to 500,000 Gypsy deaths). Ultimately more than eleven million persons were killed.

The murderous slaughter of six million Jews was a genocide resulting, in part, from centuries-old suspicion and raw hatred present in German anti-Semitism. In 1543, Martin Luther spelled out his personal hatred of the Jews, "in a scurrilous pamphlet entitled "On the Jews and Their Lies," which was widely circulated in Germany for centuries right up to and including the time of Hitler (Waite, p. 249). In crude language, Luther described the Jews as gluttonous, lazy people who "fleece us of our money and our goods." It was Luther's policy for dealing with the Jews that "Hitler would carry out in every detail." What was Luther's final solution?

First, to set fire to their synagogues or schools . . .

Second, I advise that their houses also be razed and destroyed.

Third, I advise that all their prayer books and Talmudic writings, in which such adultery, lies, cursing and blasphemy are taught, be taken from them . . .

Fourth, I advise that their Rabbis be forbidden to teach henceforth on pain of loss of life and limb . . .

Fifth, I advise that safe-conduct on the highways be abolished completely for the Jews . . .

Sixth, I advise that . . . all cash and treasure of silver and gold be taken from them . . .

Seventh . . . let whosoever can, throw brimstone and pitch upon them, so much the better . . . and if this be not enough, let them be driven like mad dogs out of the land . . . (Waite, p. 250).

One need only look into the history of the Jews in Europe to see how difficult their life was for centuries before Nazism. At one time Jewish separatism had been encouraged by rabbis concerned with preserving the Yiddish language and protecting congregants from the progressive influence of German culture. During the late 19th and early 20th century, a reverse trend toward emancipation and assimilation had developed among Jews in both Germany and Austria so that assimilated urbanized German Jews often thought of themselves more as Germans than Jews. Nevertheless, there was a malevolent anti-Semitism alive in central Europe. Clearly, the fate of six million Jews was not based on their inability to produce or to work but grew from a virulent hatred spawned hundreds of years earlier that came to full maturation under Hitler. Hitler boasted in 1908 that he was an anti-Semite. The tangible manifestation of Hitler's personal bigotry—the holocaust—came much later (Waite, pp. 186-191).

The Holocaust and Nazi Germany's cruel treatment of those considered to be undesirables cannot be used legitimately or honestly to support a simplistic argument linking slippery slope and euthanasia. Maltreatment of Jews preceded Hitler. Hitler's elimination-of-the-Jews policy was an overt expression of a current feeling that had festered for centuries in Europe and indeed is still present in parts of Europe and in the United States.

The slippery slope pattern cannot develop in America, so long as the government is of the people, for the people and by the people, and so long as the national ethic endorses the right to life, liberty and the pursuit of happiness for all citizens.

It should be noted that the governing assembly of the Evangelical Lutheran Church in America, meeting in Kansas City, Missouri in August 1993, overwhelmingly repudiated Martin Luther's anti-Jewish tirades and recognized their contribution to the persecution of Jews during the Nazi regime.

## GERONTICIDE, HEALTH RATIONING AND EUTHANASIA

Where do ideas like geronticide come from? What is the basis for them? What is their purpose? Obviously, they are related to the increasing numbers of elderly people in our society. The intent appears to be to frighten the elderly into believing there is some sort of sinister plot designed to kill them should they become incapacitated or incompetent. The purpose may also be to cloud the issue of physician-assisted euthanasia by suggesting that there may be a hidden agenda.

Some who protest against physician-assisted suicide have attempted to link active voluntary euthanasia to the notion of elder killing or geronticide. According to Stephen G. Post, Geronticide is, "the direct killing . . . of the severely demented elderly" (*Infanticide and Geronticide*, p. 317). Post's article reveals clearly that the equation of euthanasia and geronticide is entirely in his mind. He wrote:

> Advocates of active euthanasia insist that only those persons who freely request death should be killed. Yet if voluntary active euthanasia is to be permitted, why not non-voluntary? Killing the severely demented elderly patient would not be involuntary, that is, against the will of the patient, because the patient does not have those capacities necessary for volition. Restrictions could be developed to prevent the slide toward *in*voluntary euthanasia. But *non*-voluntary active euthanasia might be more difficult to discourage, because it does not have the coercive quality of *in*voluntary actions. (p. 323)

Having created this mythical Why Not? nightmare, Post notes that of those whom he imagines would support geronticide, "Conceivably, the severely demented would be better off dead, and society would then be relieved of a significant burden." (p. 324). Post then argues that demented persons should not be considered as "mere shells," but simply as "different;" that societal and religious prohibitions against killing "innocent human life" provide protection for all of us, and that killing the severely demented might serve as a signal to the elderly "who become highly reliant on care givers that it is better to be dead than to be a social burden." (p. 326). He concludes by commenting that he does not "reject 'quality of life' decisions to withhold or withdraw treatments" (p. 327), which could be interpreted as providing a basis for selective geronticide inasmuch as the patients for whom he would advocate withdrawal of life support equipment could also be viewed as "mere shells."

## Demographic Data

At the beginning of the twentieth century life expectancy at birth was about 47.5 years. Today, as we approach the end of the century, life expectancy at birth is in the 70s, a change that is due in part to the defeat of many childhood diseases that once plagued the nation, as well as to the development of new cures and treatments that can prolong life and forestall death. As a consequence of the tremendous growth in medical and pharmaceutical technology and cure, the number and proportion of the population aged 65 and over has shifted rapidly. Between 1959 and 1980 the population in the United States of those aged 65 and older more than doubled, growing from 12.3 million to 25.5 million. Among those aged 85 and over there was an increase from 577,000 in 1959 to 2.2 million in 1980. It is estimated that by the year 2030 over twenty percent of the population will be over 65 years of age and those over 85 will make up almost three percent of the population. The pattern is the same for Canada (Vezina, p. 14). Because those over 85 years of age are at the greatest risk for chronic illness, or tend to become functionally dependent, they have increased needs for medical, social, and support services. It is estimated that the health care costs for older Americans, which today is about $162 billion per year, is likely to double in the coming decade. Of the nine million Americans who today require long-term care, approximately six million are over age 65. It is estimated that at least a half-million nursing home patients in the United States are incapacitated in some way by dementia. Alzheimer's disease, which today costs society about $88 billion per year, could affect as many as five million persons by the year 2000, unless some medical cure or formula that retards the progress of the disease is found. These statistics, considered in isolation, are frightening and provide part of the basis for notions about geronticide.

It is notable, though, that the vast majority (over ninety percent) of elderly people are self-sufficient, in reasonably good health, and are not in institutions. As the Honorable Monique Vezina, Canada's Minister of State for Seniors noted:

> It is worth keeping in mind that 90 percent of people over the age of sixty-five live quite independently in the community outside of an institution. We need to take note of all those people aged sixty-five, seventy, seventy-five, and often eighty or more who are keeping active, exercising, getting involved, and meeting the challenge. (p. 15)

In other words, to consider the health needs of elderly persons on the basis of the unhealthy minority is the grossest form of stereotyping and ageism. To combine visionary nightmares of geronticide with efforts to legalize voluntary physician-assisted euthanasia is unethical and distorts the deep compassionate concerns of those who support the right of individuals to choose the time of their dying.

Several important factors need to be considered in response to Post's essay. The first is that voluntary active euthanasia proposals are laced through and through with protective language to guard against any form of involuntary or non-voluntary euthanasia. Second, Alzheimer's disease, which he lists as an ailment that could result in placing the elderly in the "mere shell" category, is under study with research into causes, control, and cure conducted by major gerontological and medical centers. The research is bringing us closer and closer to an understanding of that disease, as well as to an understanding of Parkinson's and other ailments that affect the elderly. Indeed, it is now clear that one potential for aiding those suffering from Parkinson's may lie in the use of fetal tissue from abortions that until now were discarded and which, under Presidents Reagan and Bush, were barred from use in government supported research. Thus, many of the so-called empty shells of Post's imaginative geronticide may be cured or may have the effects of the invasive illness diminished or forestalled.

## Health Rationing

What is obvious and most troubling is that, in the United States, health rationing that impacts directly on the lives of the elderly is presently in effect. The United States and South Africa are the only first world countries without a National Health Insurance program that protects the health of all citizens. Therefore, approximately 37.5 million persons in the United States are without health insurance. When the underinsured are included, this number rises to some 70 million. The uninsured include young and old—men, women and children in poverty or living barely above the poverty level. These persons are barred from adequate health care. Many are older persons, for whom the Medicare system provides only limited protection. When catastrophic illness occurs, the financial resources of the older person can be completely drained. Even under normal conditions, the costs that must be born by the older person beyond that which Medicare covers can be burdensome. Some Health Maintenance Organizations (HMO's) participate in the Medicare program and insure health care for the elderly, but HMO's require that all services be rendered by their institution and participating doctors. One may not select a physician or medical expert outside the HMO plan. Medicaid, which covers drastic illness, kicks in only after the elderly person has been reduced to poverty level. Therefore, in one sense, by virtue of inadequate health coverage for the elderly, a form of geronticide is being practiced. Unless ailing older persons can find ways to pay for health services or to obtain help in times of health crises, they must go untreated.

Emergency hospitals in cities like Los Angeles (the Los Angeles County University of Southern California Medical Center is the largest emergency department in the nation) keep patients waiting hours and even days before receiving treatment. Some elderly needing help become discouraged and leave without being treated. They give up and put off seeking medical help until their condition worsens. Governmental cutbacks in hospital funding further ration medical services not on the basis of age, but by lack of funds to provide service.

The State of Oregon has taken steps to address their particular medical needs. They have established a priority list of 709 illness in which medical procedures are ranked according to their social value and medical effectiveness. The state will pay for the first 597 illnesses on the list; the plan does not cover ailments that will improve on their own, conditions where home treatment is effective, cosmetic surgery, and conditions where treatment has been found to be generally non-effective or futile (although comfort care is provided). As Daniel Callahan has noted, the Oregon plan is not an age-based system and therefore avoids the need to set age-based limits (p. 91). A summary of the Oregon Health Plan is given in Appendix V.

Callahan has stated that quality of life is more important than age. Using age as a determinant for deciding who will or will not have access to medical resources dehumanizes a significant segment of our population. On the other hand, he believes that aged patients, who suffer from numerous chronic illnesses or are in a persistent vegetative state, should not receive interventions that simply prolong their lives. They should receive comfort and be permitted to die. Callahan opposes voluntary physician-assisted euthanasia.

Of these issues, only the notion of geronticide bears directly on euthanasia. However health costs, the aging of the population, and concerns over health coverage do impact on the elderly. Unlike younger members of the population, elderly life trajectories are limited. There is no hope for future careers that will increase income or provide company health insurance. The elderly are necessarily concerned with the immediate present and with a short-term future. How will their health needs be met? How will incapacitating illness of body or mind be treated? What are their rights as citizens to have their personal wishes respected should they choose to request or reject physician-assisted euthanasia? Elder rights are an important ethical concern.

## SUICIDE AMONG THE ELDERLY

Some elderly persons commit suicide. When life reaches a stage where its quality has diminished to the point of insignificance, where the future appears to offer no hope for change from the bleakness of the presence, where existence has become meaningless, some older persons find ways and means to take their own lives.

In 1988, according to the United States Bureau of Census, the elderly represented 12.1 percent of the population, but accounted for 21.3 percent of suicides (J. L. McIntosh, p. 61). In addition to the clearly defined suicides, it is estimated that many more commit suicide by passive or covert means such as refusing food, drink, and medications (N. J. Osgood and Thielman, 1990). In addition, suicide attempts by older people often go unreported. It is estimated that as many as 10,000 over-age-60 suicides are committed each year in the United States but that 4,000 may be unreported (Stillon, McDowell and May, 1990). Reasons for non-reporting may include the wish to avoid stigmatizing the family of the deceased, efforts to protect life insurance benefits, the practice of certifying suicide only when suicide notes are found, even though suicide notes are lacking in the majority of cases, and finally, because we tend to accept the death of older persons as "natural" or accidental (Miller, p. 2).

The suicide rate for those aged 65 and over is fifty percent higher than that of the younger population. Older persons are far more successful in committing suicide than younger persons. The ratio of successful suicides among the over-65 age group are four to one, while among the younger population the ratio is estimated to be as high as two hundred to one (Stillwell, McDowell and May, 1989). Further, older people seem to choose more violent lethal methods of self-killing such as the use of guns or jumping from high places. Motivations for suicide among the elderly include:

Issues of health, including impaired vision and hearing, loss of mobility, continuing pain, suffering and physical weakness.

Financial issues, including loss of income necessary for a comfortable life, and loss of home and possessions.

Loss of independence and the need to rely upon others for the basic requirements for survival.

Loss of social roles in family, employment and community which have previously given meaning and purpose to life.

Cognitive impairment and the awareness of the possibility of increasing impairment through developing Alzheimer's disease or other forms of dementia.

Stress augmented by the loss of significant others, particularly a spouse, and corresponding feelings of loneliness and abandonment.

Feelings of uselessness, of being a burden to one's self and others and a desire to be done with the boredom of living.

In some cases, negative responses to life may be augmented by the misuse or abuse of alcohol, medications or drugs.

Fear (in some cases almost terror) of the indignity of being reduced to the conditions the elderly person has observed in some nursing homes where patients sit mindlessly day after day only partially aware of the world around them.

Whether are not these responses to life are justified or should be alleviated by counseling, it is important to recognize that they exist.

What is most distressing in suicide attempts are the instances where the effort is botched and the person ends up in worse condition. The bullet does not kill, but destroys part of the brain, rendering the person comatose or brain dead. The leap from a high building smashes bones but does not kill. The side effects of overdoses of medications add complications to the older person's already complicated life.

The ways in which clergy and congregations deal with the needs of aging parishioners, and the ways in which they respond to attempted or successful suicides will vary. Obviously if the suicide is successful, there is little merit in condemning the victim or the family. Some attention to causes might result in programs that will alleviate depression, anxiety and fear among the elderly. On the other hand, it must be recognized that the older person who commits suicide has made a decision and acted upon it. He or she has expressed autonomy over life and death and has chosen the moment and the means of death. Because such choices are not uncommon, and because there are occasions when the chosen means of dying are ineffective and produce additional problems for the victim, family and society, the importance of physician-assisted suicide, at least for the terminally ill in continuing pain, needs to be considered and evaluated as an alternative. Such an alternative does not constitute or endorse geronticide, nor does it signify public acceptance of suicide as the only answer to the problems of aging. What is recognized is the freedom of choice in matters of dying and death. With the greying of the generation of baby-boomers, freedom to make such a choice may assume new importance.

## EUTHANASIA, AUTONOMY AND MORAL SANCTION

The word euthanasia is formed from two Greek terms: *eu*, which means "good," and *thanatos*, which means "death." Therefore, in its simplest meaning, euthanasia signifies a good death. Just what might comprise a good death and how a good death may be experienced can be debated. Consequently, the term euthanasia has assumed several dimensions.

Many would suggest that a good death is one that came about without extended suffering and pain, perhaps a death that occurs during sleep. Others would introduce the notion of "quality of life" and ask, "can existence reach a point where the quality of living is so reduced that death—one would hope a good death—is to be preferred over living?" They point out that modern medical technology, with its potential of prolonging the dying process, can keep comatose persons alive for extended periods of time. Although the patient may not be in pain perhaps choosing death is better than choosing mere existence. Edwin S. Shneidman comments on the concern with the quality of life and death in the introduction to the third edition of *Death: Current Perspectives:*

> Certainly one of the most refreshing currents in the changing thanatological wind is the increasing emphasis on a "humanistic" approach to death—an approach that seems to parallel the humanistic trends in other sectors of society today. This new approach is seen, for example, in an increasing concern that the dying individual live as fully and as richly as possible until death and that communication with the dying be tailored to specific human needs, and in the recognition of a need for special therapies to help those who have suffered the loss of someone close. Indeed, this humanistic trend in the treatment of the dying and those immediately affected by

35

death is causing a complete reexamination of the premises on which we have traditionally based our views of death and dying (p.3).

The humanistic concern that Professor Shneidman refers to has had a long history affecting the concern for "a good death." Consequently, the term euthanasia refers to the act or the effort to bring about a good death, a painless death, a merciful death. In recent years, several facets of euthanasia have been recognized. They are voluntary and involuntary euthanasia, active and passive euthanasia.

Voluntary euthanasia refers to the act of inducing a merciful death in accord with the wishes and desires of the subject. For example, when Derek Humphry's wife, Jean, was in intractable pain from cancer and there was no hope for recovery or for adequate control of pain, Derek, at her request, provided the lethal medication that ended her life and her suffering. Actually, Derek Humphry engaged in an act of assisted suicide, but the intent was to provide a merciful death. This was voluntary euthanasia. (See Derek Humphry, *Jean's Way.*)

Involuntary euthanasia would be the bringing on of the death of a suffering person without that person's permission. There have been a number of such cases reported in the news media. The person who causes the death acts out of compassion and love and ends the life of a loved one who may not be able to communicate. The act may be performed in the belief that this is what the person would have desired. Certainly the desire to terminate the pain or the apparent meaninglessness of the person's existence is involved. In other words, the act is performed without malice. Such actions may be labeled murder or homicide and when they become known the perpetrator is arrested and tried in a court of law.

Both of the above cases involve what has been called active euthanasia. Something is deliberately done to extinguish life. When the act is performed at the request of the dying person, it is labeled active voluntary euthanasia. If performed without the request of the victim, the act constitutes active involuntary euthanasia, the providing of a good or merciful death without the clear acquiescence of the victim. Most religious groups oppose active euthanasia.

Passive euthanasia refers to what has been called "letting the patient die" or "pulling the plug." Life-support systems are removed from a terminally-ill patient and the patient dies as a consequence of the removal. There are those who debate whether or not there is really any difference between active and passive euthanasia; both involve decisions and actions that bring on the death of the person. Where the life-support machinery is removed at the request of the patient, the act in known as voluntary passive euthanasia. When the life-support equipment is removed without a statement from a patient the act is called involuntary passive euthanasia. Involuntary active euthanasia is against the law. There are instances, however, where the courts permitted the cessation of treatment to allow the patient to die. Their decision was based on evidence that the patient who was incapable of expressing wishes had in the past expressed to friends and family his or her wishes regarding the withdrawal of life-support equipment, permitted the cessation of treatment to allow the patient to die. Most religious organizations support passive euthanasia, which is often described as the abandonment of heroic means to sustain life.

In recent years, to enable persons to make known their wishes before they become terminally ill and perhaps incompetent and unable to express their wishes, two documents have come into being: the Living Will and the Durable Power of Attorney for Health Care. Each is designed to provide means for an individual to express his or her wishes regarding terminal illness and death. One or the other is supported by legislation in most states. An example of each is provided in Appendix VII. Each is designed to provide the individual with as much autonomy as possible over the means of dying and death. Neither provide for active voluntary euthanasia, and, for many, this omission needs to be remedied.

What is now in contention is known as physician-assisted euthanasia or physician-assisted suicide. There are those who believe that the proper person to assist the terminally ill to end their suffering and their lives is the medical doctor. The physician has access to lethal medications. He or she has the proper instruments and the required knowledge for making a lethal injection or for provision of the right amount of a poison to bring about death. The difficulties with procuring and determining proper amounts of lethal medication by lay persons has been discussed by Derek Humphry both in *Final Exit* and *Let Me Die Before I Wake* (both published by and available from The Hemlock Society USA).

Efforts to legalize physician-assisted euthanasia are underway in several states. The first attempt, Proposition 119, in the state of Washington, was defeated by an eight percent margin in November, 1991. 701,818 persons voted for the Initiative (46.4%) and 811,104 voted against (53.6%). In California, in November 1992, the Humane and Dignified Death Act (Initiative 161) was also defeated by an eight percent vote when 4,562,010 people (46%) supported the Initiative and 5,348,947 people (54%) opposed it. In Oregon, Ballot Measure 16, the physician-assisted suicide law was passed on November 8, 1994 by a 2% margin with fifty-one percent (615,789) supporting the measure and forty-nine percent (583,651) opposing. What these figures have made clear is that there are millions of people supporting the right to have medical assistance that would enable them to die with dignity.

## AUTONOMY AND PHYSICIAN-ASSISTED SUICIDE

The right to make decisions for oneself is a prized freedom. Certain restrictions may be imposed upon persons who are under age and listed as dependents, or who are confined in prison, or found to be mentally incompetent. For all others, the privilege of making choices that determine the course of life is a given, unless those choices injure or infringe upon the rights of others.

When physical infirmities incapacitate individuals and they become physically dependent upon others, freedom of movement may be restricted but there should not be any impairment of the right to choose. One of the most important choices for the terminally ill may be whether or not to continue to live with pain and disabilities until the disease causes death. Those who are mobile are free to move about and may discover ways to take their own lives; those who are bedridden and perhaps connected to life-sustaining machines cannot make such choices.

Pro-choice supporters of physician-assisted euthanasia believe that means should be provided for competent, clear-thinking adults who may be bedridden with terminal illnesses so that they are free to choose to live or die. If, after careful weighing of alternatives and conversations with significant others, the individual should choose the time to die, then the means to execute that choice should be freely available. Friends and relatives who might be willing to provide assistance are untrained in the use and administration of lethal drugs and could botch the job. The logical person to assist the ailing individual is his or her medical doctor. Should the physician be persuaded that, given the situation of the patient, the disease is terminal and the request is rational, then, after proper steps are taken to make sure all legal prescriptions are in order, the doctor should be free to act with the assurance that there will be no prosecution for compliance with the patient's wishes. Autonomy is a key issue in debate concerning physician-assisted euthanasia.

There are, of course, medical personnel who have expressed unwillingness to participate in ending the life of a patient. They object on the basis of personal moral, ethical, or religious grounds. It is clear from the reports provided by different religious groups in this book that some physicians, committed to a faith position, would not be willing to participate in an act of physician-assisted euthanasia. The right to make such choices without being condemned for their decision is theirs as free citizens and as persons committed to a particular ethical position. On the other hand, should physician-assisted euthanasia be legalized, it should equally be the right of physicians as free citizens and as persons committed to their particular ethical stance to choose to participate in an act of euthanasia without condemnation or legal prosecution. In either case, it would be incumbent upon physicians to make clear to their patients their standing on this important issue.

Some hospitals might also determine that physician-assisted euthanasia not be performed on their premises. They have the right to make such a decision; it is their responsibility to make their position clear to all patients at the time of admission.


## EUTHANASIA AND HOSPICE

Some respondents to my questions about religious practices suggested that the hospice concept offers an alternative way of dying that makes euthanasia both unnecessary and undesirable. There can be no argument that the hospice movement provides the terminally ill of all ages with a supportive, caring environment that enhances feelings of personal worth as well as the potential for a gentle and dignified death. However, it is important to note that those who support medically-assisted aid-in-dying also support the hospice concept as an alternative way of dying.

The most famous hospice, St. Christopher's Hospice, located in South East London, was opened in 1967 by Dame Cicely Saunders. Its name is from the ancient word hospice (from the Latin *hospitium*: hospitality) which described medieval resthouses for travelers, and from Christopher who was the patron saint of travelers. The purpose of St. Christopher's is to provide "whole person" care to terminally ill patients. The "whole person" concept gives recognition to the fact that because the patient's illness affects not only the dying person but also a larger circle of family and friends, it is imperative that the larger group be included in the care-giving.

The hospice team consists of physicians, nurses, social workers, physiotherapists, chaplains and volunteers, each of whom has received special training. This group functions as a multidisciplinary care unit whose aim is to provide patients with the individualized attention needed for the living of a full life, however short, and with the assurance that their families will be given needed support in the future.

At present St. Christopher's has four wards with sixty-two beds; during a year it admits over 900 patients to its home and site care programs. With a home care center, a bereavement counseling service, a nursing home for elderly residents, a study center that provides courses and conferences for those involved in palliative medicine and care for the dying, a nursery for staff children and neighborhood children, St. Christopher's has become the model to be copied as closely as possible by the more recent hospice centers that continue to develop in Europe and America.

Since 1970, when the hospice concept was introduced in America, more than 1000 hospice programs have been created. Some hospices are, like St. Christopher's, located in separate buildings or units. Some are associated with hospitals, some are independent of hospitals. Costs for care in hospice units approximate those of hospitals'. Payments are made by the patient's family, by some (not all) insurance companies, by some state governments, or are embraced in HMO programs.

The bulk of hospice work is related to home care. In home care, the family is the primary caregiver and hospice views both the patient and the family as the unit of care. The hospice team provides both emotional and physical support and may include the patient's own doctor, the hospice doctor, nurses, social workers, therapists, psychiatrists, chaplains and volunteers. Emotional support includes empathetic listening and counseling. Physical support extends from assistance with patient care to occasional full take-over of responsibilities for a day each week.

Hospice recognizes three major goals. The first is to ease the physical discomfort of the patient by keeping the person as pain free and as alert as possible. No efforts are made to effect cures and no artificial life-support systems, no chemotherapy, no blood transfusions are involved. Medical procedures are intended only to provide physical relief and the only drugs or technologies employed are those designed to ease pain. Whenever possible, pain management is under the patient's jurisdiction and is generally administered by the patient himself or herself on the basis of personal need. The medication maintains patient comfort and contributes to a peaceful death and at the same time eases family tensions occasioned by watching a loved one in excruciating pain.

The second precludes the employment of rescue techniques once the patient stops breathing allowing death with dignity. Hospice stresses the quality of life by keeping the patient alert, able to enjoy visitors and environment without being desensitized by pain and anxiety. Hospice units welcome visitors of all ages and in some locales, pets are permitted. Obviously pets are not prohibited in home care setting. The underlying idea is that the individual, as a social being, can only fully manifest personhood in the presence of others. Thus the world of hospice is composed of young and old, healthy and ailing, frail and strong, just as is the normal world of healthy, mobile human beings. The emphases are on palliative care and on creating an environment that seeks to enable the ill to recognize their unique personal worth. In the words of Dame Cicely Saunders, "You matter because you are you, and you matter to the last moment of your life."

Finally, hospice is designed to assist a patient achieve a peaceful death. Again, because the term "patient" is interpreted to include the dying person's family and friends, recognition is given to the needs of these others in adjusting to impending death. The work of hospice begins before the patient's death and extends beyond it.

There can be no quarrel with what hospice seeks to provide. Unfortunately hundreds of thousands of persons in the United States are without the needed medical coverage or are without the necessary funds, or live in areas where there are no hospice programs. In addition, despite hospice claims regarding pain control, there are a few invasive diseases that resist pain medications or are so severe that the suffering person is reduced to a stupor or even unconsciousness in the desperate efforts to control the pain. One could wish that hospice care was open and available to all and that each suffering terminally-ill person had the right and the opportunity to choose the hospice way of dying. Realistically, the wish remains a wish, and for some, the right to choose medically-assisted death provides an option that can be accepted or refused.

Scott Judd, who was a staff member of the National Hemlock Society, has commented:

> Many Hemlock chapters are supported by hospice nurses and volunteers, and at least one local chapter of hospice that I know of has voted on a stance of no stance on the issue of aid-in-dying. Though the leadership remains predictably opposed, it may be worth emphasizing the slowly emerging "inside-out" support from the hospice community.
>
> There has always been a friendly alliance between many

hospices in America and The National Hemlock Society. A considerable number of Hemlock members work as volunteers in hospice: One leading California Hemlock member was for some years chairperson of her local hospice.

The liaison has always been strongest on the West Coast. From what I can observe this is because hospice groups there are more likely to be set up and run by people with a humanitarian motivation, while on the East Coast the hospices are more likely, but not exclusively, to be founded by religious people.

Sometimes hospice staff call Hemlock and report that a patient of theirs is inquiring about euthanasia. We are asked to send our literature directly to this person. On the other hand, Hemlock members sometimes call headquarters and ask for the name of their nearest hospice. We stock informational materials on hospice for these occasions.

In 1983 I spoke to a world conference on hospice in Montreal, Canada, (apparently the first pro-euthanasia person invited to do so) and found during the question period that hospice people believed that only fear of pain drives people to ask for euthanasia. They reiterated Dame Cicely Saunders's view that pain management was now so sophisticated that euthanasia was unnecessary and irrelevant. I explained that 10 percent of terminal pain is still uncontrollable. But, more important, it is the symptoms of their illness and the side-effects of many drugs that propel people to accelerate their end.

Both hospice and Hemlock provide valuable services to different types of people with varying problems. It is quality of life, personal dignity, self-control and choice that we in the euthanasia movement care most about, things that are too intimate for hospice, for all its noble efforts, to be able to supply.

## REFERENCES

## THE SLIPPERY SLOPE THEORY

Alexander, Leo, "Medical Science Under Dictatorship." *The New England Journal of Medicine.* 1949. Vol. 39, p. 46f.

Callahan, Daniel, "Can We Return Death to Disease?" Hastings Center Report, Special Supplement, January/February, 1989, pp. 4–6.

Kass, Leon R., "Foreword," in Carlos F. Gomez, *Regulating Death*. New York: Free Press, 1991, pp. ix–xi.

Niemoller, Martin, *Exile in the Fatherland*. Grand Rapids, Michigan: Eerdmans, 1986.

Rosenberg, Howard, "Free Speech Includes 'Hate'," *The Los Angeles Times*. February 5, 1995, pp. F 1, 12, 13.

Skinner, B.F., *Cumulative Record: A Selection of Papers*. Third edition. New York: Appleton-Century-Crofts, 1972.

Waite, Robert G.L., *The Psychopathic God Adolph Hitler*. New York: Basic Books, 1977.

## EUTHANASIA, AUTONOMY AND MORAL SANCTION

Admiraal, Pieter V., "Euthanasia Applied at the General Hospital," *The Euthanasia Review*, Vol. 1, No. 2, 1986, pp. 97–107.

Admiraal, Pieter V., "Drug Combinations are Superior," *Hemlock Quarterly*, No. 31, April, 1988, p. 3.

Angell, Marcia, "Euthanasia," *The New England Journal of Medicine*. Nov. 17, 1988, Vol. 319, No. 20.

Cohen, Cynthia B., editor, "Casebook of the Termination of Life-Sustaining Treatment and the Care of the Dying." *A Report by The Hastings Center*. Bloomington: Indiana University Press, 1988.

Colt, George Howe, *The Enigma of Suicide*. New York: Summit Books, 1991.

Gomez, Carlos F., *Regulating Death*. New York: The Free Press, 1991.

Lynn, Joanne Lynn, *By No Extraordinary Means*. Bloomington: Indiana University Press, 1989.

Martocchio, Benita C., *Living While Dying*. Bowie, M.D.: Robert J. Brady Co., 1982.

Prado, C.G., *The Last Choice*. New York: Greenwood Press, 1990.

Sobel, Harry J., editor, *Behavior Therapy in Terminal Care*. Cambridge, Mass. Ballinger Publishing Co., 1981.

Toufexis, Anastasia, "Killing Psychic Pain," *Time*, July 4, 1994, p. 61.

Vaux, Kenneth, editor, *Who Shall Live?*, Philadelphia Fortress Press, 1970.

Veatch, Robert M., *Case Studies in Medical Ethics*. Cambridge, Mass.: Harvard University Press, 1977.

## GERONTICIDE, HEALTH RATIONING, AND EUTHANASIA

Callahan, Daniel, "Evaluating the Oregon Priority Plan." *Journal of the American Geriatrics Society*, Feb. 1991, pp. 622–623.

McIntosh, J.L., "Epidemiology of Suicide in the United States," in A.A. Leenaars, ed., *Life Span Perspectives of Suicide: Time-Lines in the Suicide Process*. New York: Plenum Press, 1991, pp. 55–69.

Miller, M., *Suicide After Sixty: The Final Alternative*. New York: Springer Publishing Company, 1979.

Osgood, N.J. and S. Thielman, "Geriatric Suicidal Behavior: Assessment and Treatment," in S.J. Blumenthal and D.J. Kupfer, eds., *Suicide Over the Life Cycle: Risk Factors, Assessment and Treatment of Suicidal Patients*. Washington, D.C.: American Psychiatric Press, 1990, pp. 341–379.

Pawlson, Gregory, "The Oregon Experiment," *Journal of the American Geriatrics Society*. Feb., 1991, pp. 620–621.

Post, Stephen G., "Infanticide and Geronticide," *Age and Society*, Vol. 10, 1990, pp. 317–328.

Stillwell, J.M., E.E. McDowell and J.H. May, *Suicide Across the Life Span: Premature Exits*. New York: Hemisphere Publishing Corporation, 1989.

Vezina, Monique, "Are We Ready to Meet the Challenge?," in *Long-Term Care in an Aging Society*, ed. by Gerald A. Larue and Rich Bayly. Buffalo, New York: Prometheus Books, 1952, pp. 13–17.

# Chapter 2

---

# Judaism

---

Discussion regarding euthanasia in Judaism generally focuses on one of two basic legal categories: that of *goses* or *gosses* and that of *terefah*. *Goses* refers to a person in the final stages of life; *terefah* is concerned with a person suffering from an incurable terminal illness.

In an article published in the Spring issue of *Judaism* in 1975, Teodoro Forcht Dagi noted that the Talmud makes reference to Proverbs 31:6, "Give strong drink to one about to perish . . . ," and to the discussion in Hillel relating this verse to a criminal about to be executed. He wrote, "The range of acts which halakhah permitted, and even required, indicates that the deontological codification had a strong sense of mercy and deep sensitivity to suffering." In the passage from Proverbs and its interpretation he found "a precedent . . . for relieving the suffering of one about to die." He continued:

> Medically speaking, the Talmud recognized a state of moribundity called *goses*. A patient was called *goses* when he could no longer swallow his saliva (*Even Haezer*, cxxi, 7). It is generally assumed that this state would last no more than three days (*Yoreh Deah*, cccxxxix. 2). According to some authorities, even if a patient cannot swallow his saliva, if he can be kept alive for more than three days, he is not *goses* (Rabbi David Bleich, New York, personal communication). Even in this state, however, the patient must be considered a living being, and does not give up any of his rights as a living Jew. Whoever removes the pillow from under the head of a patient who

45

is *goses*, or does anything at all which hastens his death, is considered criminally culpable of having shed blood (*Yoreh Deuh*, cccxxxix. 1). Jakobovits discusses Isserles' amplification of the point forbidding the removal of a pillow from under the head of a *goses*. (Jakobovits: *Jewish Medical Ethics*, pp. 122-3) "It is forbidden to cause the dying to pass away quickly; for instance, if a person is in a dying condition for a long time and he cannot depart, it is prohibited to remove the pillow or the cushion from underneath him following the popular belief that feathers from some birds have this effect."

Other sources also concur that the life of a dying person must be seen as so delicate that it is threatened by even the smallest movement. Any threat to the thread of life is clearly prohibited. There is some qualification, however; according to the *Sefer Hasidim*, one is prohibited from committing an action which would extend the dying process (*Sefer Hasidim*, nos. 234 and 723).

Active euthanasia is thus prohibited, and one who kills a dying person is subject to the laws dealing with simple murderers (cf. *Sanhedrin* 78a, and Jakobovits, *Op. cit.* p. 306, notes 44-77). Jakobovits indicates the possibility that passive euthanasia, as we have described it, might be acceptable where death is imminent, but his position is complicated by Bleich's restraint that if it is possible to keep a patient alive by some means for more than three days, even in the absence of the ability to swallow, he cannot be considered *goses*. In short, while halakhah considers the matters of euthanasia and the dying patient at some length, it clearly prohibits active euthanasia, and gives no clear warrant permitting the withdrawal of life-supporting measures in the dying patient. The notion of brain death is altogether absent, although it must be noted that the condition of being unable to swallow one's saliva is equivalent to brainstem death in modern medical parlance, and destruction of the gag reflex. This degree of central nervous system death is not far removed from the definition of brain death now becoming more commonly accepted in medical circles. Consciousness *per se*, however, is not considered grounds for determination of the medical state. Death can be declared only when respiration ceases, and interference with the dying process previous to that is governed by the principles we have just mentioned.

Both by Jewish law and by secular law, the physician is advised to desist from active euthanasia. If it could be shown that a patient would die within three days in the absence of the initiation of a new therapy (the first component of passive euthanasia) *and* the patient were already *goses*, a strong case might be made for therapeutic reticence. If the patient were not *goses*, however, or if it were not certain that he would die within three days, even this warrant would be lacking. The discontinuation of a respirator is quite problematical, and appears to be absolutely prohibited under extant interpretations of halakhah. The consideration of passive euthanasia, then, at least according to halakhah, is perhaps different in principle from the consideration of active euthanasia, but not far removed in practice. Secular law seems more comfortable with some forms of passive euthanasia. The discontinuation of life support and the reluctance to initiate new therapy is not uncommonly discussed in daily medical practice. Both courses are essentially legitimatized in practice.

The Jewish position regarding active euthanasia appears to be clear. Immanuel Jacobovits, whose work is often cited (*Jewish Medical Ethics*, N.Y.: Bloch, 1959, pp. 123-124) wrote:

It is clear, then, that, even when the patient is already known to be on his deathbed and close to the end, any form of *active euthanasia* is strictly prohibited. In fact, it is condemned as plain murder. In purely legal terms, this is borne out by the ruling that anyone who kills a dying person is liable to the death penalty as a common murderer. At the same time, Jewish law sanctions, and perhaps even demands, the withdrawal of any factor—whether extraneous to the patient himself or not—which may artificially delay his demise in the final phase. It might be argued that this modification implies the legality of expediting the death of an incurable patient in acute agony by withholding from him such medicaments as sustain his continued life by unnatural means. . . . Our sources advert only to cases in which death is expected to be imminent; it is, therefore, not altogether clear whether they would tolerate this moderate form of euthanasia, though that cannot be ruled out.

His position is reaffirmed by Elliott N. Dorff of the University of Judaism, Los Angeles. In a chapter entitled "The Jewish Tradition," in *Caring and Curing: Health and Medicine in Western Religious Traditions* (Ronald L. Numbers and Darrell W. Amundsen, eds.), Dr. Dorff commented on both active and passive euthanasia:

> Jewish sources have classified active means of euthanasia as murder, even when the motivation of the perpetrator was benign. They have, however, allowed passive euthanasia when a cure is no longer possible. Although the sources have not put it in quite this way, the general princIple is that Jews are commanded to cure, but not to perpetuate life beyond its natural bounds. Two Talmudic passages and one thirteenth-century responsum described situations in which it was permissible to let nature take its course. The principle embodied in these sources was later incorporated into the glosses of Rabbi Moses Isserles on the *Shulhan 'arukh* (sixteenth century) as follows: "One in a dying condition is considered a living being in all respects. Whoever closes the eyes [of the dying person] is regarded as one who sheds blood. . . . *Gloss*: . . . It is likewise forbidden to do anything to hasten the death of one who is in a dying condition. For example, if one has been in a dying condition for a long time and could not depart, we may not remove the pillow or the mattress from under him just because some say that there are feathers from some fowl which cause this prolongation of death. Similarly, we may not move him from his place. . . . However if there is anything which causes a hindrance to the departure of the soul, e.g. if near the house there is a knocking sound of a wood cutter, or there is salt on his tongue, and these hinder the departure of the soul, it is permitted to remove it, for there is no direct action involved since he merely removed the hindrance."
>
> The thirteenth-century source actually *prohibited* any action that might lengthen the patient's agony by preventing his quick death, and it forbade those attending at the moment of death to cry, lest the noise restore the soul to the deceased. Some later authorities even prohibited the use of medicines to "delay the departure of the soul." Modern technology has obviously made these questions considerably more complicated by enhancing the ability to maintain many bodily functions artificially, thereby blurring the distinction between life and

death. Contemporary rabbis therefore differ markedly on many of the particular questions that have arisen in this regard. Whatever their differences, they all attempt to balance the tradition's underlying principles of respect for life against the permission, and perhaps the obligation, to let nature take its course at some point.

Judaism thus has had a long history of dealing with medical questions. Its answers have been informed by its fundamental theory of the body as the creation and property of God on loan for the duration of life. Although the following Mishnah is written as a warning to witnesses in capital cases and not in a medical context, it offers a fitting expression of the sacredness of life within Judaism that makes concern for the well-being of the body a matter of divine import: "Only one man was originally created in order to teach the lesson that if one destroys a single person, Scripture imputes it to him as if he had destroyed the whole population of the world. And if he saves the life of a single person, Scripture imputes it to him as though he had saved the whole world. (*Sanhedrin* 4:5)"

With regard to the use of *terefah*, rather than *goses* as the operative legal category in discussing terminal illness, Dr. Elliot Dorff has written an extensive commentary, "A Jewish Approach to End-Stage Medical Care," which was published in *Conservative Judaism* (Vol. XLIII, No. 3, Spring 1991, pp. 3-51). He points out that:

Because we can maintain people on life-support systems, and because we still cannot accurately predict the moment of a person's death, the only way to use the category of *goses* at all in these matters is to define a *goses* not in terms of the remaining hours of his/her life, but rather as anyone who has been adjudged by the attending physicians to have an irreversible, terminal illness. Some Orthodox and Conservative rabbis in recent years have moved in this direction.

There is, however, a better way in Jewish law to conceive of most of the cases with which we are concerned. As Daniel B. Sinclair has pointed out, however we define the category of *gesisah*, all agree that the person in that category is still considered alive. Therefore, any withholding or withdrawing of treatment from such people always comes with not a small amount of ambivalence and guilt. The *halakhic* category which describes these situations much more accurately and appropriately, he suggests, is that of *terefah*, a person with an incurable disease. Such a person is, according to medieval authorities, a *gavra katila*, an already dead person, and consequently one who kills him or her is exempt from human punishment although subject to divine and extra-legal penalties.

When applied to animals other than human beings, the term *terefah* refers to one suffering from a fatal organic defect, such as a pierced windpipe or gullet. It is presumed that a *terefah* animal will die within twelve months. A human *terefah* is also defined on the basis of medical evidence—specifically, as Maimonides says, "it is known for certain that he had a fatal organic disease and physicians say that his disease is incurable by human agency and that he would have died of it even if he had not been killed in another way." Since the death of a *terefah* is inevitable, evidence of *tarfut* is equivalent to evidence of death, and therefore, according to the Talmud, the deserted wife of a *terefah* may remarry. According to most authorities, twelve months must elapse before permission to remarry may be granted, analogous to the presumption regarding animal *terefot*. *Tosafot*, however, argue that fundamental physiological differences between humans and other animals (and, I would add, the expenditure of considerably more human energy and resources in caring for sick humans) often enable people to survive for a longer period. These factors underscore the fact that for all of these authorities, the twelve-month period with regard to humans is only an estimate, and the crucial factor in the definition of *terefah* is the medical diagnosis of incurability. As Sinclair says, then: "The outstanding feature of the category of human *tarfut* for the current debate concerning the treatment of the critically ill is the exemption of the killer of a *terefah* from the death penalty. This feature focuses attention upon the fact that a fatal disease does detract from the legal status of a person, and also introduces a measure of flexibility into the issue of terminating such a life. This is in direct contrast to the category of *goses*, which is based on the premise that a *goses* is like a living person in all respects. Indeed, almost all the laws of the *goses* confirm his living status and, as already observed, can only be appreciated against the background of the domestic death-bed. The *terefah* category adopts a different perspective (the effects of the critical illness upon a person's legal status), and as such, it is much closer to the current debate on the termination of the life of a critically ill patient." (*Tradition and the Biological Revolution.* Edinburgh: Edinburgh University Press, 1989, p. 22)

This is not, at course, to say that an incurably ill person is totally equivalent to a dead person. On the same page of the Talmud on which Rava says that "all admit that the killer of a *terefah* is exempt from human legal proceedings, he also asserts that one who has illicit sex with a terminally ill person is liable. As the Talmud goes on to explain, the liability derives from the fact that the sexual act performed with an incurably ill person will still produce pleasure, while the same act with a dead person would not do so since, as Rashi says, all of a dead person's warmth and moisture (humors) have been lost. One must also note that the exemption from prosecution stems from two converging reasons, only one of which is relevant to our concerns. The factor discussed in the Talmud is that the expected death of the person makes his testimony irrefutable (*edut she'i atah yakhol lehazimah*); it is only explanations in Rashi and other medieval sources which add the consideration that the incurably ill person is considered as if already dead (*gavra ketila*).

Moreover, while one may be *exempt from punishment* (*patur*) for intentionally killing an incurably ill person, one is still forbidden to do so (it is *not muttar*); indeed, one is still, according to Maimonides, subject to divine sanction and to extra-legal sanctions by the court or king. With regard to all people guilty of bloodshed who, for some reason, cannot be convicted of a capital crime under the usual rules, the king may, if it is necessary to reinforce the moral standards of the society, execute them on his own authority. If he chooses not to do so, he should, says Maimonides, "flog them almost to the point of death, imprison them in a fortress or a prison for many years, or inflict [some other] severe punishment on them in order to frighten and terrify other wicked persons" who specifically plot to commit bloodshed in a way not subject to court action.

In sum, then, as Rashi is careful to say, the *terefah* is considered a dead person (*gavra ketila hashiv lei*); that is, the incurably ill person is made *analagous* to a dead person, *not equated* to one. This makes the entire category of *terefah* exactly parallel to the state of health which concerns us. The

Talmud records a disagreement as to whether an incurably sick animal can or cannot live for another twelve months, and this resembles the ambiguity of the situation each moment with regard to incurably sick humans as well. Interestingly, in one place in the Talmud, it is the self-same Rava who claims that the *terefah* can live a year, and in another Rava is identified with the reverse position. *Tosafot* therefore describe this as one of several discussions in the Talmud in which names have been reversed when recorded in different places, and they claim that the correct version is the one in which Rava claims that a *terefah* can live an additional year. Critical students of the Talmud might have yet another answer. For me, though, the very existence of this confusion in the Talmud concerning the status of the *terefah* is just right: we are confused as to how to think of an incurably ill person, especially in the last stages of life, now more than ever. . . .

The intriguing question, then, is whether there might also be grounds to override the general prohibition against killing an incurably ill person to permit withholding or withdrawal of life-saving machines or medications, at least in some cases.

The law of siege may well provide such a precedent. The *Tosefta* describes a case of a group of travelers threatened by brigands. The latter demand that the travelers give up a specific person in their group to be killed. The *Tosefta* permits the group to hand over the individual. Later sources understandably qualify this provision. According to one view, the specified individual may be delivered only if the whole group is otherwise faced with certain death. Another interpretation maintains that the designated person may only be handed over if he or she is guilty of a capital crime. Maimonides and most commentators after him rule according to the latter reading.

What if the designated person was a *terefah*? R. Menahem Meiri says: "It goes without saying that in the case of a group of travelers, if one of them was a *terefah*, he may be surrendered in order to save the lives of the rest, since the killer of a *terefah* is exempt from the death penalty."

Meiri specifically does *not* extend this to a *goses*. This is surprising, for a *goses* is typically closer to death than is a person who has just been diagnosed as having an incurable illness. Nevertheless, one can understand R. Meiri's reasoning: the *goses*, after all, is a living person in all respects, and hence any complicity in his/her death would be tantamount to murder. The *terefah*, on the other hand, is, as it were, already dead, and hence killing a *terefah* does not entail capital punishment. These facts mean, for R. Meiri, that in a case in which many lives might be saved as a result of the death of a *terefah*, the latter's life does not possess the same value as that of the other, viable persons.

Put another way, the Talmud establishes the general principle of the sanctity of each and every human life by posing the rhetorical question, "How do you know that your blood is redder? Perhaps the blood of the other person is redder!" As Rabbi Joseph Babad says, the Meiri is effectively asserting that a *terefah* is one exception to this tenet of the equality of all human lives; that is, a *terefah*'s blood, is less "red" than that of a viable human being.

A somewhat different approach has been proposed by Rabbi Irving Greenburg in the article "Towards a Covenantal Ethic of Medicine" (in *Jewish Values in Bioethics*, ed. by Levi Meier, N.Y. Human Sciences Press, 1986, pp. 124-149). The covenantal approach affirms that human beings, created as God's partners in "completing creation," enjoy an unusual ethical freedom. In making ethical judgments, one must first look to tradition for applicable wisdom and precedents, thereby maintaining continuity with Judaism. However, inasmuch as human beings are created in the divine image, they share in divine power to the extent that they have the God-given individual privilege and ability to make and act on their own ethical decisions. Therefore, although tradition may continue to contribute to ethical decision making, an individual patient has the autonomy and the ultimate authority to decide in quality-of-life issues. That is to say, the patient may make a legitimate decision that is contrary to rabbinic tradition.

In response to a query concerning physician-assisted euthanasia, Professor Dorff wrote as follows:

The Jewish tradition permits (and, on some readings, requires) removal of medications and machinery which impede the natural process of dying of a person who is in the last stages of life. On some interpretations, this would include anyone with an incurable, terminal illness. Judaism does not, however, permit actively causing the death of a person. In other words, it equates active euthanasia with murder. Such action would be prohibited to anyone, whether physician, family member, or anyone else.

Obviously, the intention of a person who commits active euthanasia is radically different from that of one who commits murder. In the former case, the person acts out of compassion and seeks to end the incredible suffering of a patient in the last stages of a disease, while the motive for murder is radically different. Judaism clearly understands that suffering and it requires that every step short of bringing about the death of the patient be taken to alleviate it. Consequently, in recent decades Jews have been active in the hospice movement. With the increasing sophistication of medicine in depressing pain, the sanctity of life can now be preserved together with compassion without engaging in active euthanasia.

Reconstructionist Rabbi, Dr. Rebecca Alpert, presented the Reconstructionist position on euthanasia as follows:

The general tendency of Reconstructionist Judaism is to begin with the sources and to be guided both by them and by contemporary sensibilities. There are several areas where Reconstructionist thinking takes traditional sources in new directions.

First is the concept of *gosses*. It has struck many of us that the category may be useful in defining stages at the end of life. In contemporary situations, the concept of a three day period of dying is no longer relevant. We should be able to use the concept of *gosses* for someone who is consciously in the end stages of the process of dying, whether in a persistent vegetative state, or in a hospice program. This gives us an interesting opportunity to help people understand how to live while dying, while at the same time to face the inevitability of death of themselves or a loved one.

As I have studied the literature on helping people to die, I have come across an often overlooked midrash on the death of Rabbi Judah, that counters the idea that "active" euthanasia is not permitted. The story is told that while Rabbi Judah the Prince was on his death bed, his disciples stood around and prayed for him, that his soul not depart. His female servant, understanding the situation, dropped a pitcher on the floor above them. When the rabbis heard the noise they stopped their prayers, and that moment, Rabbi Judah died. The story viewed the servant's action as praiseworthy.

I think we are less inclined, from the Reconstructionist point of view, to make a strict distinction between active and passive euthanasia. As I understand both the medical and ethical perspectives, there is little basis for the differentiation. A positive reading of the Rabbi Judah story would definitely support the view that Jews may take a positive attitude in helping/allowing someone to die, and not prolonging death.

There is still a problem, however, with physician assisted death when a person is not *gosses* (in its expanded definition). Certainly, every attempt should be made to ensure a good end to life for an individual, as free from pain and suffering as is possible. We should use all resources at our command to help people face death. But Jewish teaching would err on the side of life, and would not encourage people to seek to end their lives.

Yet even this idea would not be held to hard and fast. Jewish teaching also reminds us that we may not judge others until we have stood in their place, and we must therefore be sympathetic with those for whom life is too much to bear.

A Reconstructionist perspective also demands that we look at these situations on a case by case basis, as does Jewish law. We cannot expect to have uniform answers, for all situations demand a careful understanding of the situation as it has evolved in the life of a family or community.

## JEWISH RABBIS AND PROPOSITION 119

When Proposition 119 was proposed in the State of Washington, a number of rabbis prepared statements for their congregations supporting the initiative.

Rabbi Norman D. Hirsh wrote in the Temple Beth Am Seattle, Washington *Bulletin* for October 21, 1991, that he supported Initiative 119. He said:

I support the initiative because there are cases when there is no hope for cure, when the doctors cannot control the pain, when the pain and price for the patient and family are so great that the merciful and wise course of action is for the patient to be able to choose under strict condition to ask the doctor for help in ending his or her life. Are the safeguards of Initiative 119 sufficient? I think probably so. Although I fear there will be some abuses.

The teaching of Judaism which guides me in this matter (and other teachings will guide others) is that the human being is a co-worker with God (*Shabbat* 119b). I believe this means a significant and radical use of human freedom. Using mind and skill, and motivated by love and compassion, researchers and doctors have become co-workers with God to preserve and prolong life. But this wonderful achievement has also opened up new problems. Now, in this time of medical achievements in prolonging life, we must again become co-workers with God (whose plan includes both death and life) in order, when appropriate, to make it possible to end life. Again, our motivation is love and compassion. In a medical setting we have exercised human freedom resolutely to prolong life. Sometimes in a medical setting human freedom needs to be exercised resolutely to bring life to an end. With proper reluctance and safeguards, a terminally ill person should be able to choose to do that. We should not make an idolatry out of prolonging life.

Rabbi Earl Starr of Temple De Hirsch Sinai, Seattle, Washington, also supported Initiative 119. In a personal statement, he wrote:

Judaism values the human life, the sanctity of every being and the primacy of the soul.

The rabbis have discussed in ancient and modern times in varying degrees the problems and issues before us.

We are not God and we are not trying to make God's decisions, but, we also believe that as theology advances, so must we continually reevaluate every case of life and death.

It is our duty to do all in our power to improve the quality of life and to rely on our knowledge, hearts, and minds toward this goal. We have progressed in our attitude toward providing heroic methods in prolonging life when it is painfully clear that the person is physically dead. Science has also provided many medications for alleviating pain.

Now we are asked to consider another step. Initiative 119 would make the following available to the people who voluntarily (and let us stress the word voluntarily) wish it: 1. Life-support procedures would be withdrawn, or 2. A licensed physician could voluntarily facilitate death by the most compassionate, painless, appropriate means.

To say that this is a serious matter would be a gross understatement. I support this Initiative because, in my 34 years in the rabbinate, the questions have been posed so many times. When a family or individual wishes to hold on until the last possible moment, that is their voluntary decision. But, when an individual does not wish to—there is no choice. We must allow a person to die with dignity and remove the guilt from the family that often arises.

We must also protect the doctors and give sanction to their actions when the patient asks for expertise and help. Speaking personally, I am certain that I would want to make my own choice and have made that abundantly clear to my family.

Life is a gift—death is a part of life.

Rabbi Anson Laytner is director of the Seattle Jewish Federation Community Relations Council and the Washington Association of Jewish Communities. He produced an essay titled "A Liberal Jewish View on Initiative 119, the 'Death With Dignity' Initiative." It reads:

Modern medicine offers wonderful cures and dramatic interventions which can add years to life and restore life to those who would have died in previous generations. At the same time, as population ages and people with chronic diseases survive, we end up living longer, sicker lives. Where twenty years ago, one might have died quickly or at home, today one dies in intensive care, hooked to machines and surrounded by doctor specialists.

Dying used to be leave-taking of friends and family, an asking for and granting of forgiveness, a time for reviewing one's life and for the use of rituals to aid the dying and the family. Today it is drugs and machines with the patient unconscious or heavily sedated. No rituals mark the passage from life to death. Worse, often, as a patient dies, the hospital staff will burst into activity in a last ditch effort to resuscitate the patient.

Death today represents a failure of modern medical technology rather than a natural part of life.

Modern medicine ignores the dying process. It has the knowledge and techniques to prevent onset of dying but no rituals to help deal with the lingering type of death that the technology brings. It offers the ability to sustain a person on life-support machinery indefinitely, but not a lot of instruction on when to stop intervening and let a person die.

French historian Phillipe Aries has written: "Death has been made into a series of little steps which finally makes it impossible to know which step was the real death, the one in which consciousness was lost or the one in which breathing stopped. All of these little silent deaths have replaced and eased the once great dramatic act of death." Today death is a process, not an event.

The issue of what to do with the terminally ill is the question before us. . . . The subject is not only medical, nor is it a matter solely for our secular courts to decide. Furthermore, the problem affects not just the patient, but also the patient's family and friends and those who treat the patient. The issue of life and death goes to the core of what religiously based moral values are all about. Since we are Jews, the answers lie not just within our own individual consciences, but also in Jewish tradition and law.

While Rabbi Levy has given traditional perspectives on Initiative 119, I will strive to reconcile Jewish tradition and halakha with support for 119.

There is a basic difference in our approaches: for the Orthodox, decisions are made on the basis of judicial precedents within the halakha, i.e. it is a matter of law and legal interpretation done by the qualified authority, the rabbi; but for the non-Orthodox, the halakha is a guide, with a vote but not a veto, and it is balanced by the individual conscience. The spectrum of opinion in non-Orthodox circles runs from those who give greater credence to halakha than to conscience to those who favor conscience over halakha. Personally, I fall somewhere in the middle. Let me also state at the outset that I am no expert either on biomedical ethics or on the halakha related to this issue. The opinions I present are my own and I strongly encourage people here to consult their own consciences and rabbis for guidance on this crucial subject.

According to Jewish tradition, the sanctity of life takes precedence over almost all other values. We should do everything in our power to sustain life because life, even our very bodies, are on loan to us from God. Even if a person may live but an additional hour *hayyei sha'a* we must help him or her; such is our reverence for life. This is our common point of departure. The difficulties come in applying this principle to the specifics.

Tradition teaches that nothing positive may be done to encourage death in a dying person, called a *goses*, who is treated, in every respect, as a living human being. On the other hand, a *goses* should not be kept from dying when all hope for recovery is past (Ket. 104a, Isserles to SA YD 339.1, SA EH 121.7, SA CM 221.2), nor should medicine be used to hinder a *goses'* departure (Eger to SA YD 339.1). The common point to these laws is that at the critical point where no hope for recovery exists, a person, the *goses*, is allowed to go. To hasten death is wrong and suicide is considered a sin (AZ 18a, Sem. 2.2, SA YD 345.2). Euthanasia is likewise prohibited. It is seen as the equivalent to murder in all but the most extreme situations, the Holocaust, for example.

If there is a principle to which most *poskim*—those rabbis with the stature to make definitive rulings—will agree, it is that one doesn't have to continue providing a patient with futile treatment that merely prolongs death. But all would also say that nothing active must be done to hasten death. *If a distinction may be made, and it is the very one that medical technology has made so hard to draw, it is between sustaining life and prolonging death.* The first, according to our tradition, is obligatory; the latter is not.

The problem before us is two-fold: medical technology has increased our abilities to intervene in the dying process and prolong life in some form, but also that we know less than previous generations about when death occurs, again because our technological abilities can extend life in some form to the point where the distinction between life and death becomes blurred.

In the past, what separated a *goses* from the dead was evidence first of breathing, and later, of a heartbeat. Today there are competing definitions of, or criteria for, death. Even modern Orthodox authorities are divided on if and when to turn off life-support machinery. The Israeli Chief Rabbinate, and more significantly Rabbis Moshe Feinstein and Tendler, rule it is permissible under specific modern medical conditions that describe brain death; but Rabbis David Bleich and Jacob Levy say no, basing themselves on the presence of heartbeat.

The crisis for us as Jews revolves around the fact that the traditional ways of defining the states of death no longer apply, the definition of a *goses* is too narrow and too difficult to apply in the modern medical context. To give an example, according to the halakha, someone with cardiac arrest should be considered a *goses* and it is forbidden to move the *goses'* body lest it hasten death. But if CPR is administered—which means moving the body—the person may be restored to life. So what does one do?

There are at least four routes to resolve the current dilemma. First, one may follow the direction of either of the Orthodox rabbis mentioned above—or any other Orthodox rabbi—and guide one's practice accordingly.

Second, one may follow those who are attempting to reinterpret the definition of *goses* since the traditional definition is irrelevant. Rabbi Elieser Waldenberg of Jerusalem redefines a *goses* as one having an irreversible loss of basic physiological functioning. Under his definition, all forms of life-support would be considered as impediments to dying. Thinkers such as the former chief rabbi of England, Immanuel Jakobovitz, and Conservative rabbis Seymour Siegal and Elliot Dorff also have advocated this idea. It is my personal choice as well.

Third, one may explore new halakhic categories which might offer greater latitude. Basing himself on the work of Tel Aviv University law professor Daniel Sinclair, Rabbi Elliot Dorff recently has written a Conservative responsum advocating reliance on the legal category of *terefah*, one suffering from a fatal illness. In Jewish law, a *terefah* is considered as one already dead, and under certain circumstances, the life of a *terefah*, like that of a fetus, is worth less than the life of the fully alive. Applying this to our issue, Sinclair and Dorff hold that it is permissible to remove life-support systems in certain cases. This is a provocative, even radical idea, but I personally find the use of the category not genuinely applicable to the issue of death and dying.

Lastly, an even more revolutionary idea from maverick Orthodox thinker Rabbi Yitz Greenberg, Conservative Rabbi

Daniel Gordis, and Reform Rabbi David Ellenson among others: They suggest that the gulf between traditional teachings on death and dying and modern medical technology is so great that we should disregard the old criteria and seek a new, non-legal approach instead. They advocate that instead of relying on Jewish case-law, with the rabbi as final arbiter of what is moral, we should use the teachings of tradition to better understand our covenantal relationship with God. If we understand our role in the larger picture, we can then draw conclusions for the field of Jewish medical ethics. In this construct, the rabbi would serve as a resource for the traditional values and approaches for the patient, family and medical personnel. But the power to decide, based on the I-Thou nature of the covenantal relationship, would reside with the patient, and between the patient and God. This is a completely non-halakhic even anti-halakhic approach which could turn Jewish discussion of the issue of death topsy turvy. Personally, I prefer the middle ground mentioned above.

Let me conclude with some specific points relating to Initiative 119.

First, according to our tradition, the individual Jew has a high degree of, but not total, autonomy to choose which form of treatment shall be used to preserve his or her health (TB BM 85b). Also, when a life is in doubt, one is told to err on the side of leniency by listening to the patient rather than the doctor (TB Yoma 83a). Then there is the principle, mentioned earlier, about sustaining life but not prolonging death. What this means is that a Jew may decide whether to opt for aggressive medical treatment or not; he or she may choose hazardous therapies, or not; he or she may choose to die in a hospital or in a hospice. It all depends on what the individual is comfortable with. It means that if a procedure offers little chance of curing a person, it need not be done; further, if a therapy proves ineffective, it may be stopped. It means, according to some authorities, that it is permissible to ease a person's pain with drugs, even if it has the double effect of shortening that person's life. It can mean, if hydration and nutrition are considered as medicine and if normal food and water are offered, that these procedures may be terminated if the patient shows no sign of improvement. In this case, what would result is a bodily systems failure which the feeding tube was seeking to circumvent. It can mean that a person in a persistent vegetative state or irreversible coma may be taken off hydration and nutrition as long as normal food and water were continued to be offered because the procedures were shown to be not beneficial to the patient's recovery.

Choice by the individual Jew is the key to all of the above possibilities. Therefore it is incumbent on each individual, especially if you are concerned with how you will be treated, to fill out a living will and provide for durable powers of attorney, specifying which medical treatments one requests and which one wishes to refuse. There is even a living will for traditional Jews which empowers the rabbi to decide on behalf of a patient in accordance with his interpretation of the halakha. I cannot stress the importance of doing this enough. Do it as you do your material will and your ethical will. It is important for you, for the well-being of your family and friends, and for the well-being of the physicians and hospital staff who will care for you.

Lastly, some words about aid-in-dying, without a doubt the most controversial aspect of the Initiative. I have wrestled long and hard with this concept, and I will continue to do so. Clearly, Jewish tradition is against suicide and euthanasia and killing in most cases. If anything, our tradition would be more tolerant of the suicide of a terminally ill person on the grounds of mental despondency than it would be of a physician or someone else providing euthanasia, even if it was done at the request of the terminally ill person and with the best of intentions. I do not know if I would choose it for myself if I became terminally ill. I think not. I also don't think that I, as a rabbi, could counsel someone to avail themselves of it, or for a physician to offer it. But at the same time, I have complete sympathy and understanding for someone with a debilitating terminal illness who chooses this route.

I do not know if it is morally right to ask the physician to do this deed, even though participation would be totally voluntary on the physician's part. Although physicians today do provide aid in dying unofficially, through the so-called double effect of offering pain-killing drugs which also limit a patient's breathing ability, to make aid in dying an optional part of a physician's role is hard for me as a rabbi to endorse.

For me, one of the most troubling parts of the aid in

dying provision is that one may choose to die at any point after one has been diagnosed as having six months left to live. Thus, one may be near death's door and receive aid in dying, something I find less objectionable and even understandable, but one may yet be superficially very healthy and still choose aid in dying. The latter strikes me as wrong. But I would have less difficulty understanding suicide by such a person possibly even a guided suicide such as the Hemlock Society offers than voluntary euthanasia. The actual difference may be slight in fact, the result would be the same but to me it is significant. It goes back to the principle of sustaining life, but not prolonging death. I hold that for non-traditional Jews, one should hold onto life as long as possible, but that once death is inevitable, nothing should be done to hinder death from occurring, and that the patient, the family, the rabbi and the physicians should work together well before the fact to ensure the dying patient as quick and as painless and as meaningful a passage as is humanly possible. At the same time, I would have *rahmanus* on any Jew whose situation compelled him or her to choose aid in dying over a lingering and perhaps painful death. Ultimately, such matters are between the individual and God; no other mortal can or should stand in God's place to judge a person in such a situation.

But Initiative 119 is not a Jewish initiative; there are people of other faiths whose religious views run the gamut from official opposition to 119 to official support for it. Although our tradition opposes aid in dying, far be it from us to impose our religious views on people of other faiths. Therefore I support passage of Initiative 119, even with its aid in dying provision, for exactly the same reason as I support the abortion initiative, Initiative 120: religious freedom of choice. Although I don't think I would counsel aid in dying, I believe it important for those who do accept and advocate the concept that providing aid in dying not be a criminal act. The beauty of 119's aid in dying provision is that it is completely voluntary, for the dying patient, for the physician and for the hospital. Let each person and let each faith choose, by the means appropriate to each, that which is morally right for them.

## HUMANISTIC JUDAISM

Unlike other Jewish groups, Humanistic Jews do not rely on tradition to form ethical judgments. According to Dr. Sherwin Wine, the founder of the movement and the Rabbi of Birmingham Temple in Farmington Hills, Michigan, although Humanistic Judaism has "no official position on euthanasia . . . there is a general consensus." The following statement represents Rabbi Wine's personal opinion (reprinted from *Humanistic Judaism*, 1991).

The right to die. Is it a human right? Is it an absolute right?

We are celebrating the two hundredth anniversary of the American Bill of Rights. The Bill of Rights does not mention the right to die. Nor did the Founding Fathers discuss it.

Yet millions of people today are talking about the right to die. Part of the reason is the highly publicized activity of Michigan's own Dr. Kevorkian. Only recently he assisted two sick and unhappy women to commit suicide.

Most of the reason lies elsewhere. Human life is getting longer and longer. Aging brings with it the lingering diseases of decay and humiliation. Millions of unhappy disabled people inhabit nursing homes, unable either to live or to die.

Medical technology makes terminal illness less terminal. Thousands of people are now attached helplessly to machines. Their dependency and helplessness deprives them of dignity. But the machines whir on, indifferent to their humiliation.

The most important reason is the way people today view suffering. At one time people accepted suffering as the normal human experience. In a survival culture, dominated by notions of sin, men and women accepted pain as an inevitable human fate. But the modern world has changed our expectations. Today most of us believe in the right to happiness. We demand more of life than suffering and continuous pain. What used to be tolerable is now intolerable. What used to be meaningful is now meaningless. Many of us would rather be dead than helplessly disabled.

As a result, the right to die has now appeared on the civil rights scene. Some right to die advocates are absolutists. They maintain that every human being has the right to be the absolute master of his existence. If he wants to live he has the right to live. If he wants to kill himself, for whatever reason, he has the right to kill himself. No one has the right to tell him what to do with his life. Absolutists even believe that a person has the right to demand of others, especially physicians, compassionate assistance for whatever decision he makes. The right to die, therefore, means the right to assisted suicide.

Opposed to the absolutists are the moderates, who hold the belief that every human being has the right to be the master of his life, but not absolutely. After all, most human acts have social consequences and many of them are the result either of madness or momentary depression. Moderates maintain that people have the right to commit suicide in some cases, but not in all cases. The right to die is not absolute.

For moderates the right to suicide is a function of the quality of life. If a person is suffering from a terminal illness and is no longer able to control his bodily functions, then he has the right to die. If a person is suffering from a terminal illness and is experiencing intolerable pain then he has the right to die. If a person is afflicted with a chronic disabling sickness and is totally dependent on other people and machines for his survival then he has the right to die.

And he has the right to die with dignity. Modern medicine should be his friend, not his enemy. To preserve a life that is all suffering and no happiness, against the will of the sick person himself, is an act of cruelty, not mercy. Compassion would dictate that the physician assist the helpless victim to die as painlessly as possible. The purpose of medicine is not preservation of life. It is the preservation of meaningful life. And for many people, life has no meaning if it is deprived of pleasure and autonomy.

Moderates believe that the quality of a person's life is to be determined not only by the subjective judgment of the person but also by the external judgment of caring professionals. Assisted suicide should not be arranged at the whim of the person requesting it. It also needs the balance of outside opinion. Legitimate complaints have to be distinguished from temporary depression. And the hope of recovery is not only a function of the patient's mood but also depends on the medical facts. Hospitals and health care institutions need to establish committees to consider requests and to judge their appropriateness. These committees need to include physicians, social workers and ethicists. If a request is approved, the medical profession has a moral obligation to assist the petitioner in the act of suicide. Euthanasia (dying easy) is a right for many of the helpless and the hopeless.

The problem with the intervention of Dr. Kevorkian is the absence of any external balance to the personal decision of the women he assisted to die. Enduring chronic pain may not be a sufficient reason to justify medical support for death. The petitioners needed the objective consideration of outside people. The haste with which the suicides were conducted is not only a condemnation of a social system that equates endurance with meaningful life, but also an indictment of the eagerness of Kevorkian to publicize an important issue.

As you have already surmised, I am a moderate. I thank Dr. Kevorkian for dramatizing an issue we need to confront. But I also hope for more rational procedures to provide compassionate medical assistance. Human life may not be sacred when it has lost meaning. But it is important enough for us to be careful when someone asks to die.

## RIGHT-TO-DIE IN ISRAEL

The *Jewish Exponent*, published in Philadelphia, Pennsylvania, reported in the May 8, 1992 issue that Israel's right-to-die movement is gaining acceptance. The report reads as follows:

The society was founded by Tel Aviv attorney Yitzhak Hoshan who, four years ago, gained considerable notoriety when he represented the family of a gravely ill man, the late Gideon Nakash, which unsuccessfully attempted to force a local hospital to comply with his wish that he be allowed to die.

Even after Nakash died, his widow went on to sue the hospital for taking undesired "heroic measures" to keep her husband alive, though she eventually decided to drop the case.

Nevertheless, the actions of Nakash's widow clearly had an impact because similar requests are now routinely, if quietly, honored in most Israeli hospitals, despite the fact that euthanasia, passive or active, remains illegal in this country.

Since three bills to legalize euthanasia in certain circumstances failed to gain Knesset approval in the 1980s, the Society for the Right to Die With Dignity sees little immediate chance for legislative initiatives and concentrates on educational activities instead.

For example, it urges people to sign a living will, in which they ask doctors to avoid "artificial measures" to keep them alive should they be mortally ill or severely injured and unable to express their own wishes.

Physicians, at least in public, have reacted cautiously to this document. Professor Mordechai Ravid of Meir Hospital said that the living will would cause him to ponder the matter from a philosophical viewpoint, but would not alter his approach.

"Medical considerations," he declares, "will determine which measures I take, and for how long, to try and save a patient's life. After all, if I decide to withhold some treatment it will be my responsibility, and if I am brought to trial, it won't help me to say that I was simply fulfilling the wishes of my patient."

People typically prepare a living will and join the society after watching what happens to their parents. This was the case with Kivka Hochhoieser, whose father, after a stroke, "became a different, feebleminded person who finally had to be put in a mental hospital.

"I saw the people there," Hochhoieser recalls, "eating cigarettes they picked up from the floor because they had no idea what they were doing. Sometimes they had to be tied up, and often they couldn't even identify their own beds; it became necessary to forcibly remove them from the beds of others.

"Finally, most were unable to control their bodily functions and, since the staff couldn't constantly clean up after them, the stench was terrible."

# Chapter 3

# The Roman Catholic Church

Here can be no question that the most important Roman Catholic document dealing with euthanasia is "The Declaration on Euthanasia" by the Sacred Congregation for the Doctrine of the Faith, 1980. Every article dealing with euthanasia written by a Roman Catholic scholar, theologian, or ethicist since that time refers back to the Declaration. It is reproduced at the end of this chapter.

On May 26, 1988, Joseph Cardinal Bernadin addressed the Center for Clinical Medical Ethics at the University of Chicago Hospital. His topic was "Euthanasia: Ethical and Legal Challenge." After noting the pluralistic nature of American society and the freedom of individuals to accept any given religion or no religion, the Cardinal raised the question as to how public policy decisions are made and "how do we determine which aspects of our life, whether social or personal, are subject to public policy decision?" He believed that key factors should include "public peace, the essential protection of human rights, and commonly accepted standards of moral behavior in a community." He asserted that with regard to euthanasia, "Long ago our predecessors determined that the taking of innocent life was contrary to the public good even if it is done to alleviate pain or suffering." This "decision," he noted, "is being challenged on two fronts. First, does the state have any interest in this matter, or should it be left up to the individual? Second, is euthanasia truly contrary to the public good?"

He suggested that the movement to legalize euthanasia derives from three sources. The first is medical. Modern technologies, he said, "Have given physicians previously unknown capabilities" to heal and preserve life, a good that "has not been an unmixed blessing. . . . This possible domination of technology over the proper course of life has left many people fearful of being kept alive in an inhumane fashion. . . . The fear, then, of the pain and discomfort of a life prolonged inappropriately has led to an erosion of the natural instinct to preserve one's own life.

"The second cause of the movement towards euthanasia involves two aspects of the legal dimension of our society." The first is concerned with the numerous lawsuits and settlements involving the medical community that have raised fears in that community. "The result has been that, in certain critical decisions involving living and dying, many perceive that the focus of concern may no longer be the good of the patient as that has been traditionally understood by our Judeo-Christian moral tradition. Instead, the concern will be whatever will best protect the physician and the health care institution from legal action." The second is related not only to the people's fear of technology but also the fear of "losing a fundamental right, the right to self-determination." Cardinal Bernardin commented on the decline of the sense of community and "the rise of an exaggerated concept of individualism" which "replaces concern and responsibility of the *common good*. . . . And in the light of this momentum, it is understandable that persons who ask family and friends to keep them from an unseemly death would think that those fulfilling this wish should not be prosecuted for doing a 'good deed'."

The Cardinal's third point relates to the social fixation "on youth and beauty" with the result that, "Those who are older and not so healthy may question whether they ought to continue living. And those who are younger and supposedly healthy may reject those who remind them of their own human frailty." He continued:

> Likewise, our society is raising profound questions about the ultimate meaning of life. While it had once been assumed that pain and sacrifice were part of the human experience and contributed to the meaning of life, many would question that assumption today. An ethos of instant gratification does not suffer pain or sacrifice easily. A world whose meaning is centered in a seemingly unlimited present moment may interpret death as a purely human event, devoid of any relationship to a divinity who sustains a truly endless eternity. . . .
>
> These three aspects of our culture, and others, are the context of the current discussion of euthanasia. A culture that does not prize the wisdom of aging and feels intimidated by ill health will be less likely to oppose the ending of an aged or

infirm life. A culture that is devoid of a vision of values that transcend time and individual choice will be more likely to feel no discomfort with an immediate solution. And a culture of youth and immediacy will be uncomfortable with the allocation of precious fiscal and health resources to those who are marginal or sick.

His basis for opposing euthanasia rests in his affirmation of a "Consistent Ethic of Life" grounded "in the Judaeo-Christian heritage" and the "religious tradition" that life is sacred "because God is its origin and destiny." Also stemming from this ethic is the belief that "human life is social in nature." Consequently, "we have the *positive* obligation to protect life" and "we have the *negative* obligation not to destroy or injure human life directly, especially the life of the innocent and vulnerable." Therefore, "Euthanasia is wrong because it involves a direct attack on human life. And it is a matter of public policy because it involves a violation of fundamental human good. . . .

> We are saying that those whose lives have, in fact, entered the dying process should be helped to live the remainder of their lives with full human dignity and with as little pain as possible. We also are saying that those measures which we would consider to be ethically extraordinary need not be used to prolong life. We also are saying that, when considered on a case by case basis and in the light of our ethical principles, there are situations when we can withdraw what have become useless and burdensome measures.
>
> In this nuanced context, we are opposed to creating *a priori* categories of persons whose lives no longer need to be protected, where life is no longer seen as being sacred and inviolable. Once we begin saying that a certain category of persons or a specific individual—for whatever reason, and whether the person is conscious or unconscious—no longer possesses human dignity, then we have assumed a prerogative which only belongs to God. Human rights may then be given or withdrawn as arbitrarily as they were in the Third Reich of yesterday or in South Africa today. The dignity of innocent life is absolute; it cannot be violated.

Cardinal Bernadin then stated that inasmuch as humans "are meant to live in community," therefore, "The state has a moral and legal interest in protecting innocent life from the moment of conception to natural death." This means that "As citizens and leaders in our society, we must engage our legislatures and judicial system in a dialogue to find ways to ensure that appropriate medical decisions are made by patients and their surrogates in consultation with the physician and others. If this process is improved, fewer physicians and health care institutions may feel a need to refer these decisions to the courts out of fear of legal liability."

The Cardinal pointed out that "we are not morally obliged to do everything that is *technically* possible. In other words, there are cases where we would not be obliged artificially to provide nutrition and hydration." He raised the question about the equitable distribution of health care money. "Are we, in fact, spending too much on the elderly, or are we spending too little on all health care? To say it another way, are we spending too much of our financial resources on certain patients, or are our overall allocations for health care too limited? . . . I mention this, not to confuse the discussion about euthanasia, but to point out that the legalization of euthanasia is not the proper way to solve the problem of inadequate care for the poor and the unborn."

He called on religious leaders to engage in dialogue with "philosophers, anthropologists, and legal scholars to discern how we can preserve the rights of the individual without eroding or destroying our social nature." In conclusion, he stated:

> In dialogues such as this, we need to confront the issue directly and help form a national consensus in favor of the presumption that the State has a compelling interest in opposing euthanasia. The basis for such a consensus is already present in our land. It is our task to bring it to the fore so that it truly can be said that, as citizens, we are entitled to life and need not fear that innocent life will ever be taken.

When Initiative 119, which called for physician-assisted euthanasia, was placed on the ballot in the State of Washington, in 1991, the Roman Catholic Church produced a variety of printed materials opposing the Initiative. For example, Archbishop Raymond G. Hunthausen of Seattle, Archbishop Thomas J. Murphy of Seattle, Bishop William S. Skylstad of Spokane, and Bishop Francis E. George of Yakima signed the following statement requesting readers to vote against the Initiative:

To our Sisters & Brothers in Washington State:

On November 5, 1991 citizens of our State will be voting on Initiative 119. Each of us will be answering a critical question which will affect the way we view and treat terminally ill people: "Should physicians be allowed to assist in the suicide of their patients?"

The significance of that question has deliberately been clouded by euphemisms and slogans which hide the stark reality and implications of I-119. The real issue at hand is whether we, as a society, will endorse suicide, assisted suicide and the direct taking of a life as an appropriate means of dealing with dying people.

After praying about and discussing the issues which I-119 present, we firmly conclude that I-119 does not promote or enhance human dignity. Our opposition to this effort to legalize medical killing flows from our conviction that life is sacred and that God alone is the true sovereign over life. Our dignity and worth are simply innate to our relationship with God and not dependent on our social usefulness.

I-119 has been marketed as a vote for "choice," a choice about controlling one's death. In an imperfect health care system with diminishing financial resources we ask what kind of choice is I-119 really proposing? How many people, upon learning of a serious illness or disability, will feel they have an "obligation" to remove themselves from this life? Is this a humane response to the reality of sickness? Is this a signal to the frail among us that their lives are simply not worth living? Is this what we want enshrined in public policy?

We believe the merciful response, albeit the more challenging, is one in which society assists persons with terminal illness and their loved ones to live as fully as possible the time they have left together; one in which society helps assume the burden of providing physical comfort and care, including management of pain; one in which society surrounds a dying brother or sister with compassion and care.

I-119 does present a choice. But what does this kind of choice say about us as a people? We would be misled if we think compassion provides an easy means to take life. Should not our concern help to prevent desperate, lonely or forgotten people from reaching for suicide as an attractive alternative?

We believe, as others do, that compassionate people will create other choices.

We ask you to join us in saying no to legalized medical killing. No to physician assisted suicide. No to I-119.

Your brothers in Christ

A special supplement of the magazine *Commonweal*, August 9, 1991, Vol. 68, No. 14, which dealt solely with the Washington Initiative, was also distributed. It contained articles by Albert R. Jonsen, Carlos F. Gomez, Leon R. Kass and Daniel Callahan, each of whom presented a different argument against the Initiative. Jonsen, who is professor and chairman of the department of Medical History and Ethics at the University of Washington, attacked the "safeguards" in the Initiative. He wrote:

> These safeguards are, however, only relatively conservative. Like most Natural Death legislation, they require witnesses unrelated by family or financial interest and the written declaration by two physicians that the patient is in a terminal condition, that is, the reasonable medical judgment that death will result within six months. However, there is no mention of presence or evaluation of pain and suffering, no reference to stability of the patient's request over time, no requirement for psychological evaluation (safeguards that are mentioned in reports of the Dutch tolerance of active euthanasia). The patient must simply be diagnosed as being in a terminal condition and make an uncoerced request for aid-in-dying. Most important (and most different from the Dutch practice), Initiative 119 appears to remove the aid-in-dying decision and execution from all legal oversight.

He then went on to predict a dire "moral cataclysm:"

> There will be a flood of persons seeking aid-in-dying, coming from all over the United States and Canada, since only in Washington will their desire to end their lives be honored without fear of prosecution. Hospitals will have to decide not only what stance they will take, but how to inform patients of their position (in accord with the new patient self-determination provisions of Medicare) and even how the new law will affect their admissions and credentialing policies. Phy-

sicians will have to form their consciences and, if they choose to provide aid-in-dying, learn how to do it (as new "medical service" it will, like all others, require standards and training: it is not so easy to effect a "dignified and humane" death). Professional groups will be faced with the task of establishing appropriate self-discipline and surveillance, since, like other medical services, aid-in-dying falls within professional self-regulation. Third party payers will have to decide whether aid-in-dying is a covered and reimbursable medical service. Legal authorities, since they seem to have no jurisdiction, will have to determine how they deal with suspicious cases and allegations of abuse. Above all—and this is the properly "moral" aspect of the cataclysm—all persons will be presented with the opportunity to relieve themselves and their families and the society of the burdens of their own final illnesses. This is not, I think, an unambiguous opportunity: its implications go far beyond the beneficent promotion of autonomy and the relief of pain and suffering.

Carlos Gomez, who is a resident in internal medicine at the University of Virginia Health Sciences Center, raised questions concerning the validity of using Holland's medically-assisted euthanasia program as a model for what could happen in Washington. He questioned the accuracy of reports about deaths from Holland and suggested that the boundaries of the law were often exceeded there. Having raised this concern for control, he stated:

> This raises, finally, the question of how well this practice can genuinely be regulated, and what this society would accept as a tolerable degree of assurance that its most vulnerable people—the weak, the unconscious, the demented, the socially stigmatized and marginalized—would be well protected from an unwanted death.

He then commented:

> To construct this matter of euthanasia as merely a question of patient autonomy is, I believe, to give short shrift to those who cannot be truly autonomous. The fact that these people are voiceless—that they do not vote, do not write or read articles, cannot advance their own interests—makes them par-

ticularly worthy of our concern. The practice of euthanasia—at least as currently envisaged for the state of Washington, would place these patients at intolerable risk.

Leon R. Kass, Addie Clark Harding Professor for the College and the Committee on Social Thought at the University of Chicago, dramatically raised the specter of the worst possible scenario as he conjured up the following:

> It is naive and foolish to take comfort from the fact that the currently proposed change in the law provides "aid-in-dying" only to those who request it. For we know from long experience how difficult it is to discover what we truly want when we are suffering. Verbal "requests" made under duress rarely reveal the whole story. Often a demand for euthanasia is, in fact, an angry or anxious plea for help, born of fear of rejection or abandonment, or made in ignorance of available alternatives that could alleviate pain and suffering. Everyone knows how easy it is for those who control the information to engineer requests and to manipulate choices, especially in the vulnerable. Paint vividly a horrible prognosis, and contrast it with that "gentle, quick release:" which will the depressed or frightened patient choose, especially in the face of a spiraling hospital bill or children who visit grudgingly? . . . Will we not sweep up, in the process, some who are not really tired of life, but think others are tired of them; some who do not really want to die, but who feel that they should not live on, because to do so when there looms the legal alternative of euthanasia is to do a selfish or cowardly act? Will not some feel an obligation to have themselves "eliminated" in order that funds allocated for their terminal care might be better used by their families or, financial worries aside, in order to relieve their families of the emotional strain involved?
> Euthanasia, once legalized, will not remain confined to those who freely and knowingly elect it—and the most energetic backers of euthanasia do not really want it thus restricted. Why? Because the vast majority of candidates who merit mercy-killing cannot request it for themselves: adults with persistent vegetative state or severe depression or senility or aphasia or mental illness or Alzheimer's disease; infants who are deformed; and children who are retarded or dying. All

incapable of requesting death, they will thus be denied our new humane "assistance-in-dying." But not to worry. The lawyers and the doctors (and the cost-containers) will soon rectify this injustice. The enactment of a law legalizing mercy killing (or assisted suicide) on voluntary request will certainly be challenged in the courts under the equal protection clause of the Fourteenth Amendment. Why, it will be argued, should the comatose or the demented be denied the right to such a "dignified death" or such a "treatment" just because they cannot claim it for themselves? With the aid of court-appointed proxy consenters, we will quickly erase the distinction between the right to choose one's own death and the right to request someone else's—as we have already done in the termination-of-treatment cases.

Clever doctors and relatives will not need to wait for such changes in the law. Who will be around to notice when the elderly, poor, crippled, weak, powerless, retarded, uneducated, demented, or gullible are mercifully released from the lives their doctors, nurses, and next of kin deem no longer worth living?

Daniel Callahan, Director of the Hastings Center, discussed social dimensions of aid-in-dying. He argued:

. . . We should as a society say no, and decisively so, to euthanasia and assisted suicide. Initiative 119 should be defeated. If a death marked by pain or suffering is a nasty death, a natural biological evil of a supreme kind, euthanasia and assisted suicide are wrong and harmful responses to that evil. To directly kill another person in the name of mercy (as I will define "euthanasia" here), or to assist another to commit suicide (which seems to me logically little different from euthanasia) would add to a society, already burdened with man-made evils, still another.

Euthanasia is mistakenly understood as only a personal matter of self-determination, the control of our own bodies, just a small step beyond the removal of legal prohibitions against suicide. Unlike suicide, euthanasia should be understood, as of its nature, a social act. It is social because, by definition, it requires the assistance of someone else, as the expression "aid-in-dying" itself makes clear.

Legalization would also provide an important social sanction for euthanasia, affecting many aspects of our society beyond the immediate relief of suffering individuals. The implications of that sanction are profound. It would require the regulation and oversight of government. It would add to the acceptable range of permissible killing in our society, still another occasion for one person to take the life of another.

We might decide that we are as a people prepared to live with those implications. But we should not deceive ourselves into thinking of euthanasia or assisted suicide as merely personal acts, just a slight extension of the already-established right to control our bodies and to have medical treatment terminated. It is a radical move into an entirely different realm of morality: that of the killing of one person by another. . . .

We cannot, I believe, transfer our sovereignty to another without contradicting it. A sovereignty that can legally and morally be given away is fragile and contingent, not sovereignty at all. To allow another person to kill us is the most radical relinquishment of sovereignty imaginable, not just one more way of exercising it. Our life belongs no longer to us, but to the person into whose power we give it. No person should have that kind of power over another, freely gained or not. No defender of civil liberties and the right of self-determination should want to see that possibility made available.

Does it not make a difference that the absolute power is given, not to subjugate another (as in slavery), but as an act of mercy, to bring relief from suffering? This might matter but for one crucial consideration. The suffering of the person to be killed is subjective, unmeasurable by and intangible to an outside observer. However, real and intense to the person himself or herself, it cannot be gauged from the outside by any objective standard. We know that pain and suffering can vary enormously from one person to another, even those with identical medical conditions. To legalize euthanasia would thus be to authorize one person to kill another based on indeterminable, variable, and subjective expressions of suffering. I can think of no other area of medical practice where equally drastic, irreversible actions are taken on the basis of unmeasurable symptoms. There is no way for the doctor to distinguish between the reasonableness of one person who suffers greatly, but wants to continue living, and that of another person with similar suffering who wants to be dead. It is not the suffering as such that makes the difference, I believe, but the attitude taken toward it. In saying this I do not deny the reality of suffering. I am only underscoring how inaccessible the intensity of suffering can be to the external observer, and also how it must express the meaning given to it, not merely its brute psychological intensity. . . .

There is a related problem worth considering. If the act of euthanasia, conventionally understood, requires the request and consent of the patient, it no less requires that the person to do the killing have his or her own independent moral standards for acceding to the request. The doctor must act with integrity. How can a doctor who voluntarily brings about, or is instrumental in, the death of another legitimately justify that to herself? Would the mere claim of self-determination on the part of someone be sufficient—"it is my body, Doctor, and I request that you kill me?" There is widespread resistance to that kind of claim, and doctors quite rightly have never been willing to do what patients want just because they want it. There is surely a legitimate fear that, if such a claim were sanctioned, there would be no reason to forbid any two competent persons from entering into an agreement for one to kill the other. Perhaps it arises out of a reluctance to put doctors in the role of taking life simply as a means of advancing patient self-determination, quite apart from any medical reasons for doing so.

The most likely reason for resistance to a pure self-determination standard is that we have, traditionally, defined the appropriate role of the physician as someone whose duty it is to relieve suffering. It has thus been customary, even among those pressing for euthanasia, to hang on to some part of the physician's traditional role. That is why a mere claim of self-determination is not enough. A doctor will not cut off my healthy arm simply because I decide my autonomy and well-being would thereby be enhanced. But the additional requirement that the physician also be relieving suffering carries with the problem mentioned above. How can a physician determine, much less diagnose in any traditional medical sense, genuine and unrelievable suffering?

The doctor will not be able to use a medical standard.

He or she will only be able to use a moral standard. Faced with a patient reporting great suffering, a doctor cannot, therefore, justify euthanasia on purely medical grounds (because suffering is unmeasurable and scientifically undiagnosable). To maintain professional and personal integrity, the doctor will have to justify it on his or her own moral grounds. The doctor must believe that a life of subjectively experienced intense suffering is not worth living. He must believe that himself if he is to be justified in taking the decisive and ultimate step of killing the patient; it must be his moral reason to act, not the patient's reason (even though they may coincide). But if he believes that a life of some forms of suffering is not worth living, then how can he deny the same relief to a person who cannot request it, or who requests it but whose competence is in doubt? This is simply a different way of making the point that there is no self-evident reason why the supposed duty to relieve suffering must be limited to competent patients claiming self-determination. Or why patients who claim death as their right under self-determination must be either suffering or dying.

There is, moreover, the possibility that what begins as a right of doctors to kill under specified conditions will soon become a duty to kill. On what grounds could a doctor deny a request by a competent person for euthanasia? It will not do, I think, just to specify that no doctor should be required to do that which violates her conscience. As commonly articulated, the argument about why a doctor has a right to perform euthanasia—the dual duty to respect patient self-determination and to relieve suffering—is said to be central to the vocation of being a doctor. Why should duties as weighty as those be set aside on the grounds of "conscience" or "personal values?". . . .

Pain and suffering in the critically ill and dying are great evils. The attempt to relieve them by the introduction of euthanasia and assisted suicide is even greater. Those practices threaten the future security of the living. They no less threaten the dying themselves. Once a society allows one person to take the life of another based on their mutual private standards of a life worth living, there can be no safe or sure way to contain the deadly virus thus introduced. It will go where it will thereafter.

A Pastoral Letter titled "Living and Dying Well" was issued by the Bishops of the Oregon Catholic Conference and the Washington State Catholic Conference on October 10, 1991. The letter dealt with such issues as "Making End-of-Life Decisions," "Christian Perspectives," and "Suffering and Pain in Human Life." Concerning physician-assisted suicide, the Bishops wrote:

> "Physician-assisted" suicide or direct killing through lethal injection is becoming a national issue with a local focus for those of us in the Pacific Northwest. This particular issue assumes greater importance with the actual filing of the 'death with dignity' initiative in Washington (Initiative 119) and the introduction of euthanasia legislation (S.B. 1141) in Oregon in 1991. We in the Pacific Northwest are particularly vulnerable because of our initiative and referendum process, liberal beliefs and the large number of unchurched. Autonomy is a strong social value for us. In this regard, it is important to recognize that giving someone else power over one's own life denies autonomy in the most basic way. As ethicist Daniel Callahan, director of the Hastings Center, has said: "To allow another person to kill us is the most radical relinquishment of sovereignty imaginable, not just one more way of exercising it."
>
> In our judgment on the morality of euthanasia and in our discussions about why introducing euthanasia would be bad public policy, we need to be clear about what we are discussing. Many people today do not carefully distinguish between directly causing another person's or one's own death and refusing inappropriate medical treatment at a time of grave illness or approaching death.

The Bishops concluded their statement with a challenge to the community:

> Euthanasia is a lethal, violent and unacceptable way of terminating care for the infirm. The challenge and task for the community is to show the sick and the dying that they are not abandoned by the human community or by God. The demand for euthanasia will increase if structures of support and skills to care for the sick and dying do not keep pace with the demand.

At this time, we call for increased public support for hospice and home care programs based on a philosophy that rejects the active taking of life. We implore the medical community to educate caregivers to provide better pain management to ease the suffering of the dying. We ask parishes to develop support groups for terminally ill patients and their families, to help persons find meaning in suffering, and to educate the faithful about the issues surrounding death. We commend Catholic and other hospitals for their innovative programs of community outreach and training of pastoral and other care-givers. At this time, it is important that persons of faith reach out to others of good will to reject public policy initiatives that will change fundamental law in this area.

As a community, we are challenged to remember the call to "Choose life." Christ, through his life, death and resurrection to new life has given new meaning to existence. Death is not the ultimate evil. Jesus' exercise of power is one of healing, liberation, and restoration to wholeness. The Church is the continuation of Christ's presence and must express the healing and redemptive love that was characteristic of his ministry. Christians are called to be faithful stewards in caring for that gift.

Prayerful and reverent dialogue about life is part of the Christian tradition. In our religious conversation, we discover God's presence in the activities of life. Death is an integral part of our life experience, and our discussions should consider it thoroughly. We need to share our hopes and fears, our faith and our feelings with one another in the prayerful atmosphere that enables us to be educated in faith as well as in fact.

As Christians, we are called to express our belief that human life is of God. We are called and redeemed by God, and our faith in the resurrection is stronger than our fear of death. As human persons, we share in the actions of all humankind. The offenses of others are as much a shame to us as their achievements are a matter of pride. Resisting those who would dismiss the value of human life and kill their brothers and sisters is a matter of conscience. For death to have true dignity, life must have full integrity. . . .

Not everyone is prepared to accept the motives of those who respond to cries from the terminally ill for release from suffering. In

*Healthcare Ethics* (third edition), Roman Catholic writers Benedict M. Ashley, and Kevin D. O'Rourke discuss and reject the distinction often made between "active" and "passive" euthanasia. They begin their comments with a quotation from the Declaration on Euthanasia which is appended to this chapter. (For the sake of clarity, the bracketed supporting references in their statement have been eliminated.)

> By euthanasia is understood an action or omission of an action which of itself or by intention causes death in order that all suffering may be eliminated." (SCDF, 1980a). This statement of the Church emphasizing that euthanasia may result from an act or an omission of an act calls into question the distinction between *active* and *passive* euthanasia, which we used in previous editions of this book (2nd ed., p. 379). With others, we equated passive euthanasia with allowing to die when there was no moral obligation to prolong life. Thus we considered active and passive euthanasia to be morally different. However, we now perceive that the term *passive euthanasia* was used by many to signify withholding treatment *regardless* of moral obligation to prolong life. Therefore it seems more accurate to consider euthanasia, whether active or passive, as bringing about that death by positive action (inducing death) or by omission (withholding treatment), when there is a moral obligation to prolong the person's life. Thus, as we use the term in this edition, the distinction between active and passive euthanasia does not constitute a moral difference. Active and passive euthanasia are both violations of another person's humanity. Using the term euthanasia with this connotation corresponds more exactly to the terminology of the recent Church teaching, and it also obviates the objections raised by some ethicists that if passive euthanasia is acceptable, active euthanasia should be acceptable as well. However, we continue to maintain that a clear moral distinction exists between euthanasia and allowing to die when there is no longer any moral obligation to prolong life. The reasons that justify the decision that there is no longer a moral obligation to prolong life are discussed in the next section.
>
> When persons freely choose to die and ask to be killed, they are not only committing the crime of suicide but also compounding it by making another a partner in the crime. To yield to such a request is false compassion. To have true com-

passion for the person who has made such a decision is to realize that the person feels hopeless, alienated from community, and doubtful of God's love. Mercy entails staying by such a person's side and through friendship helping him or her to recover hope. The mercy killer in such a case is really adding a final rejection to the many rejections that have already driven the person to that point of despair.

On the other hand, if the sufferer is no longer really free to make a truly human decision but is pleading to be put out of the pain or depression that has taken away his or her capacity to think straight, the mercy killer is simply a murderer putting to death someone no longer able to protect himself or herself.

If the motives of the mercy killer are examined, their claim that they did it for the sake of the victim cannot be easily accepted. The real motive may well be that the relative did not want to accept the responsibility of helping the dying person to the end. Often the killer says, "I loved my mother, I couldn't bear to see her suffer!" It is true in such a case that the killer could not bear to see her suffer, but the quality of that love is no so certain. No doubt, however, sometimes mercy killers are themselves not free enough from tortured feelings to make a sane decision. Medical personnel hardly have such excuses. By consenting to help their patients die, they may simply be evading the painful and threatening task of adequate spiritual care for the dying.

As for the type of euthanasia used by the Nazis, in which patients were put to death without their consent because they were senile, insane, or defective, or as genocide, few in the United States today would defend such a practice, but some are beginning to discuss the morality of euthanasia for people in a comatose condition (Humphry, 1982; Scott, 1983).

Generally, the medical profession has rejected euthanasia absolutely (AMA, 1988b), as is evidenced by the Hippocratic Oath as well as by more recent codes of medical ethics, such as The Geneva Declaration (1957) and the Helsinki Statement of the World Health Organization (1964). However, the tendency of the medical profession in the United States to prolong the act of dying even after the patient does not benefit from life-prolonging therapy has caused many people to opt for euthanasia as a certain manner of ending life when medical therapy is no longer beneficial. The fear of prolonged dying has also led to creation of the living will, and when the living will proved to be unsatisfactory, to creation of the durable power of attorney for incompetent people. Although the living will and durable power of attorney are not unethical and may even be helpful in some cases, they do not of themselves eliminate the decision-making problems that arise at the time of death. As we discuss next, ethical treatment of patients at the time of death depends on a clear understanding of the ethical norms for withholding and withdrawing life support from persons with fatal pathology. Generally, the Christian churches have rejected euthanasia.

On the other hand, the Bishops of Pennsylvania recognize the anguish of the family of a patient in a vegetative state. Their carefully worded statement is marked by clear definitions. The focus is given in the title: "Nutrition and Hydration: Moral Considerations" (*Origins*, January 30, 1992, Vol. 21, No. 34). Having considered whether or not the person in a vegetative state can experience pain or discomfort, they conclude that "the present consensus argues against the existence of such pain, mental or physical." They then turn their attention to the family and caregivers:

> There is no doubt that a family undergoes considerable pain as it watches a loved one who remains for months or years in the persistent vegetative state. It is not at all unusual that members of that family find themselves at times wondering if death would not be a better alternative for the one who is afflicted. This feeling can and does arise out of love, compassion and concern for the sick person. It is also almost always influenced as well by the internal struggle experienced by those who are well. They experience the pain of loss as the person they love is now removed from conscious communication with them. They experience their own exhaustion if they are very directly involved in the care for the patient. All of these are emotions that one would expect to find in such a situation. The family members, however, must be careful not to allow their own fears or frustrations to become the basis for the moral decision making that now falls to them. They must exercise for the one who is ill the same stewardship of life that is the obligation of each of us in our own regard. The desire

to escape from our own burdens cannot become the source of a decision which would end the life of someone else.

There are, of course, other far less worthy motives which can inspire people to decide to terminate nutrition for the unconscious patient. Anger, spite, greed, culpable lack of concern and a host of other motivations can also be part of our human decisions. For this reason it is also desirable that the benefit of the doubt be given to the continued sustenance of the life of the unconscious person.

We must, however, take into real account situations in which the family has reached the moral limits of its abilities or its resources. In such a situation they have done all that they can do, and they are not morally obliged to do more. They would then have reached the limits of ordinary means. However, in the society in which we live this does not present a fully convincing argument. Resources are available from other sources, and these can often be tapped before a family reaches dire financial straits. Such assistance has been and continues to be available.

As the Bishops turn to the subject of euthanasia, their focus is still on those in a vegetative state:

It would be unwise to complete our consideration of these questions without addressing the question of euthanasia. The word once referred to the effort to help make one's dying process easier. It has come finally to refer to some sort of intervention which actually brings about death.

After defining euthanasia in accord with the Declaration on Euthanasia (see p. 74), the Bishops continued:

Etymologically speaking, in ancient times *euthanasia* meant an easy death without severe suffering. Today one no longer thinks of this original meaning of the word, but rather of some intervention of medicine whereby the sufferings of sickness or of the final agony are reduced, sometimes also with the danger of suppressing life prematurely. Ultimately, the word *euthanasia* is used in a more particular sense to mean 'mercy killing,' for the purpose of putting an end to extreme suffering, or saving abnormal babies, the mentally ill or the incurably sick from the prolongation, perhaps for many years, of a miserable life, which could impose too heavy a burden on their families or on society.

It is necessary to state clearly in what sense the word is used in the present document.

By *euthanasia* is understood an action or an omission which of itself or by intention causes death, in order that all suffering may in this way be eliminated. Euthanasia's terms of reference, therefore, are to be found in the intention of the will and in the methods used.

Alleviation of suffering through the purposeful destruction of the life of the sufferer is clearly contrary to true Christian respect for life and Christian love of neighbor. Yet in our own time this solution is proposed more and more frequently and even by doctors, whose very profession should be geared to the preservation of life. It has been said that in the Netherlands as many as one-sixth of all deaths are attributable to euthanasia.

The movement toward murder as a solution to problems has already begun in the societal attitude toward the killing of the unborn. It is rapidly entering into the realm of the "hopelessly" ill. It can just as easily be extended to include the seriously handicapped, either physically or mentally. In none of these cases is it a question of the good of the patient, but more a question of the exercise of a questionable autonomy founded in equally questionable "rights" of the individual. Decisions such as this are all too easily based on the desires or fears or even inconvenience of others and the patient's wishes may not even enter into the question. That is certainly the case with abortion and can just as easily become the case with the incurably ill. In both cases the decision is based on an attitude that there is such a thing as a human life not worthy to be lived. Those who are defective in some way are destroyed rather than cared for. It is an attitude which easily dehumanizes not only the victim but the perpetrator as well.

In 1986 the Council of Ethical and Judicial Affairs of the American Medical Association stated that "it is not unethical to discontinue all means of life-prolonging medical treatment" for patients in irreversible comas. This statement has the weight of whatever prestige that council holds, even though it was not the decision of a referendum of the members and does not tell us anything about how many of the members would support it. Nor should one be misled into thinking that the statement is based on the fact that such patients are suffering some sort of severe pain caused by the care that is being given them. This has already been discussed above, with the conclusion that there is usually no excessive pain due to such feeding. In fact, that same council in 1990 said:

One aspect of the debate about stopping treatment in persistent vegetative states focuses on a concern that the afflicted person will experience suffering after treatment is stopped (e.g., will experience dyspnea after removal of a respirator or face discomfort associated with starvation and dehydration after removal of a feeding tube). The most obvious contradiction to this projection is that, by definition, in persistent vegetative states both the person's capacity to perceive a wide range of stimuli and the neocortical or higher brain functions that are needed to generate a self-perceived affective response to any such stimuli are destroyed. Pain cannot be experienced by brains that no longer retain the neural apparatus for suffering."

But if the pain of the inability to breathe or the pain of starvation and dehydration cannot be felt, then there is no reason at all to support the contention that the removal of nutrition and hydration is being done out of concern for the sufferings of the patient. It must, therefore, be based upon something else and what is that something else if not the decision that the life of this particular patient is not worth living? Sad to say, the intent is not to relieve suffering but rather to cause the patient to die. Nor can it be argued that it is merely the intention to "allow" the patient to die, rather than to "cause his death." The patient in the persistent vegetative state is not thereby in a terminal condition, since nutrition and hydration and ordinary care will allow him to live for years. It is only if that care is taken away and barring any other new disease or debilitation that the patient will die. It is the removal of the nutrition and hydration that brings about the death. This is euthanasia by omission rather than by positive lethal action, but it is just as really euthanasia in its intent.

There is a vast difference between allowing a terminal patient to die and doing something to hasten the death. We find no moral problem in those situations in which treatments are withdrawn because they have become an excessive burden rather than a benefit to the terminal patient. We find no moral problem in the withdrawing even of nutrition and hydration from the patient if the supplying of them is futile or excessively burdensome. It is morally wrong, however, to take these extreme cases and make them the norm for all cases of persistent vegetative state patients, when treatment or care will allow that patient to continue to live and will do so without a burden of excessive pain or suffering. In such cases their removal is tantamount to passive euthanasia (killing by omission).

Much of the contemporary discussion seems to have lost sight entirely of the difference between allowing to die when no treatment or care can any longer save the patient and murder by omission. Recalling the moral truth that one is not obliged to employ means that are either futile or too burdensome but must never intentionally act against innocent human life, we see a clear moral distinction between intending and allowing. The latter is permissible in some circumstances those involving extraordinary means the former is always immoral and therefore forbidden.

## Conclusion

As a general conclusion, in almost every instance there is an obligation to continue supplying nutrition and hydration to the unconscious patient. There are situations in which this is not the case, but those are the exceptions and should not be made into the rule. We can and do offer our sympathy and support to those who must make such hard decisions in those difficult cases. We cannot and do not offer our support to those who are willing to remove from patients the means of sustaining nourishment on the ground that their lives are not worthy of our continued care and concern.

Respect for personal autonomy is a basic principle of medical ethics. This principle reinforces the duty of hospital personnel to secure the consent of patients or their surrogates before initiating or discontinuing treatment. It does not reduce them to mere functionaries who can do no more than carry out the orders of the patient or the patient's surrogate. The purpose of medicine is no more the mere satisfaction of patients' or surrogates' desires than the purpose of teaching is to give students only what they explicitly desire to learn. As a student of medicine the physician has a knowledge of health and the effects of disease. As a professional the physician is dedicated to keeping patients healthy or at least to relieving their suffering. When there are alternative treatments or courses of action, the physician will lay out the advantages and disadvantages of the various choices, and shows respect for the autonomy of patients not by merely acceding to their wishes but by telling them the truth and enabling them to make the right decisions. Neither the patient nor the surrogates of the patient have the moral right to withhold or withdraw treatment that is ordinary. Neither does the physician have the right to do so simply because the patient or the surrogates ask or demand this. In this perspective the physician responds to patient desires only if those desires accord with the proper professional and moral judgment as to what will promote the health, preserve the life or prevent the suffering of the patient. The physician's duty has not been properly done if there has been no effort to persuade the patient to follow the proper course of action. If the patient decides to refuse excessively burdensome or futile treatment, the physician may properly comply with that request. If the patient decides to refuse ordinary treatment, there may in some instances be little that the physician can do to prevent this, but there remains at least the duty to attempt to persuade the patient otherwise or, failing that, for the physician to remove himself from the case so as not to be guilty of complicity in suicide.

It is important to recall that historically the practitioners and researchers in medical science have steadfastly and in some cases heroically striven to offer the very best of care to their patients. If some solution to a medical problem were not available, they gave their time, energies and sometimes even their lives and fortunes to find it, to invent it, to discover some way to preserve their patients' lives and alleviate their suffering. It is our hope that medical science will remain faithful to this wonderful heritage which has been of inestimable advantage to humanity. Using the talents that God has given them, those who have dedicated their lives to providing health care to their fellow human beings need to know that their work is respected and valued by all of us. The fact that there remains so much to do, even though so much has already been achieved, should not discourage them nor deter them from the search for further solutions to problems that we still face. New procedures may have to be found to resolve difficulties of suffering and discomfort. Cost-effective and affordable treatments and care need to be developed so that the burden of caring for the ill will not impoverish families nor add unreasonably to their burdens. Diagnostic methods should be studied so that we can begin to ascertain with better certainty the pain that may actually be suffered by the unconscious. The tradition of health science shows that physicians and nurses have not avoided solving problems which human sickness and disease have presented in the past. We are confident that that same tradition will inspire present and future health care providers to do the same.

We ask also that those in the judicial and legislative fields bring their expertise to bear on these cases and that they will do so with full attention not only to the law alone but to the basic norms of morality and full respect for human life which ought to supply the proper basis for good law. Because of new circumstances generated by medical and scientific advances, there has been serious interest in advance medical directives such as the living will and durable power of attorney. It is quite reasonable to want to leave instructions regarding one's own health care in the event of incapacitation. It is not necessary to submit to procedures which are truly extraordinary or futile. But we caution all those involved in legislation and judgment that laws must have their true foundation in those same principles which guide our moral decisions. Recent court opinions have come very close to agreeing that simply because the patient wishes, nutrition and hydration can be discontinued, even when there is not a question of something that is overly burdensome or simply futile to the patient. The law and legal decisions should never be such as to encourage the removal of the essential means of life and thus yield to a clear intent to bring about death and not merely to the willingness to yield to the fact of human life that all must die and that the day will come for each of us when this is inevitable. The laws must be just and must be based on unequivocal principles which identify the taking of innocent human life and make it illegal, with full recognition that it is already immoral. We should be most cautious and develop these principles very carefully since many of the arguments we have heard in favor of the removal of nutrition and hydration from one group of patients, those in the persistent vegetative states for example, could easily be applied in the cases of other groups such as the retarded, the elderly, the incurably crippled and any other whose diseases modern medicine has not yet been able to cure. Naturally, it would be irresponsible to stand by idly and let such a tragedy occur.

Finally, we appeal to those whose loved ones are in this sad state of unconsciousness. We ask them to allow their pain to give life to an even greater desire to serve those whom they love. We offer our support, our consolation and our sympathy, and we offer also our prayers and our spiritual support. We ask them to trust in the mercy and goodness of God in this situation just as they must do in every situation in life. We join with them in accepting the joy and the burden of stewardship for God's gift of life. We pray that they and we alike may hold lovingly to the gift of life itself, so that when the time comes for us to leave this world and enter into the fullest love of God, we may bring with us that deepest love of life which begins here and finds its fulfillment there.

When the Roman Catholic Church in California prepared to confront the Humane and Dignified Death Act (Initiative 161), some of the articles referred to above were circulated. In addition, new materials were produced. The Rev. Jeremiah J. McCarthy, Academic Dean and Professor of Moral Theology at St. John's Seminary in Camarillo, California, commented that accounts of the use of Dr. Jack Kevorkian's "suicide machine" to take the life of Janet Adkins amplified concerns about euthanasia. In his letter, he wrote that:

In the Roman Catholic community, the response has been one of forthright objection to such a practice. The argument against "physician-assisted-suicide" turns on the following elements:

(1) "Physician-assisted suicide" constitutes a directly intended effort to end the life of a human being. As such it meets the definition of euthanasia explicated in the 1980 *Declaration on Euthanasia*, namely an "action or omission which

91

of itself or by intention causes death in order that all suffering may in this way be eliminated." An intervention of this nature is a direct assault on human life, and in the words of the *Declaration*, "an offence against the dignity of the human person, a crime against life, and an attack on humanity."

(2) A second, compelling argument against this practice is the violation of the physician's covenant of trust. If the first duty of a physician is "to do no harm," then an action such as "assisting" a patient to die harms the integrity of the medical profession as an instrument of healing, and severely compromises the patient's expectation that the physician is committed to the principle of "beneficence," that is to seek the patient's good.

(3) While the means that are adopted to ease a patient's suffering through direct assistance in suicide are not defensible, closer examination must be given to the issue of a patient's suffering. The issue that requires careful discussion is the issue of pain management. There is an ethical alternative to the practice of "physician-assisted suicide." That alternative is an ethics of compassionate care. Once again the *Declaration* is helpful in its articulation of a response to the needs of a suffering patient whose pain management may require medications which run the risk of shortening the patient's life. May such medications be used, and if so, how is such a justification different from "physician-assisted suicide?"

In responding to issues of this kind, the *Declaration* underscores the importance of a spiritual reflection on the meaning of suffering for the Christian. A careful distinction is made between, on the one hand, an acceptance of suffering as a "sharing in Christ's Passion," and, on the other hand, imposing a "heroic way of acting as a general rule." An application of the principle of prudence indicates that the use of medications to alleviate pain is appropriate even though such medications may cause as "a secondary effect semiconsciousness and reduced lucidity." Quoting Pius XII, the Declaration re-affirms the use of painkillers, even if they may shorten the patient's life if "no other means exist, and if, in the given circumstances, this does not prevent the carrying out of other religious and moral duties." The Declaration adds that "death is in no way intended or sought, even if the risk is reasonably taken; the intention is simply to relieve pain effectively, using for this purpose painkillers available to medicine."

In summary, the objection to physician-assisted suicide is based on the violation of the dignity of the human person, the erosion of the trust that is constitutive of the physician-patient relationship, and the public policy implications of an erosion of the sanctity of life principle through physician-assisted suicide.

## DECLARATION ON EUTHANASIA

### Congregation for the Doctrine of the Faith, 1980

*Introduction*

The rights and values pertaining to the human person occupy an important place among the questions discussed today. In this regard, the Second Vatican Ecumenical Council solemnly reaffirmed the lofty dignity of the human person, and in a special way his or her right to life. The Council therefore condemned crimes against life "such as any type of murder, genocide, abortion, euthanasia, or willful suicide" (Pastoral Constitution "Gaudium et Spes" no. 27).

More recently, the Sacred Congregation for the Doctrine of the Faith has reminded all the faithful of Catholic teaching on procured abortion.[1] The Congregation now considers it opportune to set forth the church's teaching on euthanasia.

It is indeed true that, in this sphere of teaching, the recent Popes have explained the principles, and these retain then full force[2]; but the progress of medical science in recent years

---

1. *Declaration on Procured Abortion,* 18 November 1974: *AAS* 66 (1974), pp. 730-47.

2. Pius XII, *Address to those attending the Congress of the International Union of Catholic Women's Leagues,* 11 September 1947: *AAS* 39 (1947), p. 483; *Address to the Italian Catholic Union of Midwives,* 29 October 1951: *AAS* 43 (1951), pp. 835-54; *Speech to the Members of the International Office of Military Medicine Documentation,* 19 October 1953: *AAS* 45 (1953), pp. 744-54; *Address to those taking part in the Ninth Congress of the Italian Anaethesiological Society,* 24 February 1957: *AAS* 49 (1957), p. 146;

has brought to the fore new aspects of the question of euthanasia, and these aspects call for further elucidation on the ethical level.

In modern society, in which even the fundamental values of human life are often called into question, cultural change exercises an influence upon the way of looking at suffering and death; moreover, medicine has increased its capacity to cure and to prolong life in particular circumstances, which sometimes give rise to moral problems.

Thus people living in this situation experience no little anxiety about the meaning of advanced old age and death. They also begin to wonder whether they have the right to obtain for themselves or their fellowmen an "easy death," which would shorten suffering and which seems to them more in harmony with human dignity.

A number of Episcopal Conferences have raised questions on this subject with the Sacred Congregation for the Doctrine of the Faith. The Congregation, having sought the opinion of experts on the various aspects of euthanasia, now wishes to respond to the bishops' questions with the present Declaration in order to help them to give correct teaching to the faithful entrusted to their care, and to offer them elements for reflection that they can present to the civil authorities with regard to this very serious matter.

The considerations set forth in the present document concern in the first place all those who place their faith and hope in Christ, who, through his life, death and Resurrection, has given a new meaning to existence and especially to the death of the Christian, as Saint Paul says: "If we live, we live to the Lord, and if we die, we die to the Lord" (Romans 14:8; cf. Philippians 1:20).

As for those who profess other religions, many will agree with us that faith in God the Creator, Provider and Lord of life—if they share this belief—confers a lofty dignity upon every human person and guarantees respect for him or her.

---

cf. also *Address on "reanimation"* 24 November 1957: *AAS* 49 (1957), pp. 1027–1033; Paul VI, *Address to the Members of the United Nations Special Committee on Apartheid,* 22 May 1974: *AAS* 66 (1974), p. 346; John Paul II, *Address to the Bishops of the United States of America,* 5 October 1979: *AAS* 71 (1979), p. 1225.

It is hoped that this Declaration will meet with the approval of many people of good will, who, philosophical or ideological differences notwithstanding, have nevertheless a lively awareness of the rights of the human person. These rights have often in fact been proclaimed in recent years through declarations issued by International Congresses[3]; and since it is a question here of fundamental rights inherent in every human person, it is obviously wrong to have recourse to arguments from political pluralism or religious freedom in order to deny the universal value of those rights.

## I. The Value of Human Life

Human life is the basis of all goods, and is the necessary source and condition of every human activity and of all society. Most people regard life as something sacred and hold that no one may dispose of it at will, but believers see in life something greater, namely a gift of God's love, which they are called upon to preserve and make fruitful. And it is this latter consideration that gives rise to the following consequences:

1. No one can make an attempt on the life of an innocent person without opposing God's love for that person, without violating a fundamental right, and therefore without committing a crime of the utmost gravity[4].

2. Everyone has the duty to lead his or her life in accordance with God's plan. That life is entrusted to the individual as a good that must bear fruit already here on earth, but that finds its full perfection only in eternal life.

3. Intentionally causing one's own death, or suicide, is therefore equally as wrong as murder; such an action on the part of a person is to be considered as a rejection of God's sovereignty and loving plan. Furthermore, suicide is also often a refusal of love for self, the denial of the natural instinct to

---

3. One thinks especially of Recommendation 779 (1976) on the rights of the sick and dying, of the Parliamentary Assembly of the Council of Europe at its 25th Ordinary Session; cf. SIPECA, no. 1, March 1977, pp. 14-15

4. We leave aside completely the problems of the death penalty and of war, which involve specific considerations that do not concern the present subject.

live, a flight from the duties of justice and charity owed to one's neighbor, to various communities or to the whole of society although, as is generally recognized, at times there are psychological factors present that can diminish responsibility or even completely remove it.

However, one must clearly distinguish suicide from that sacrifice of one's life whereby for a higher cause, such as God's glory, the salvation of souls or the service of one's brethren, a person offers his or her own life or puts it in danger (cf. John 15:14).

## II. Euthanasia

In order that the question of euthanasia can be properly dealt with, it is first necessary to define the words used.

Etymologically speaking, in ancient times *euthanasia* meant *an easy death* without severe suffering. Today one no longer thinks of this original meaning of the word, but rather of some intervention of medicine whereby the sufferings of sickness or of the final agony are reduced, sometimes also with the danger of suppressing life prematurely. Ultimately, the word *euthanasia* is used in a more particular sense to mean "mercy killing," for the purpose of putting an end to extreme suffering, or saving abnormal babies, the mentally ill or the incurably sick from the prolongation, perhaps for many years, of a miserable life, which could impose too heavy a burden on their families or on society.

It is therefore necessary to state clearly in what sense the word is used in the present document.

By euthanasia is understood an action or an omission which of itself or by intention causes death, in order that all suffering may in this way be eliminated. Euthanasia's terms of reference, therefore, are to be found in the intention of the will and in the methods used.

It is necessary to state firmly once more that nothing and no one can in any way permit the killing of an innocent human being, whether a foetus or an embryo, an infant or an adult, an old person, or one suffering from an incurable disease, or a person who is dying. Furthermore, no one is permitted to ask for this act of killing, either for himself or herself or for another person entrusted to his or her care, nor can he or she consent to it, either explicitly or implicitly. Nor can any authority legitimately recommend or permit such an action. For it is a question of the violation of the divine, and offence against the dignity of the human person, a crime against life, and an attack on humanity.

It may happen that, by reason of prolonged and barely tolerable pain, for deeply personal or other reasons, people may be led to believe that they can legitimately ask for death or obtain it for others. Although in these cases the guilt of the individual may be reduced or completely absent, nevertheless the error of judgment into which the conscience falls, perhaps in good faith, does not change the nature of this act of killing, which will always be in itself something to be rejected. The pleas of gravely ill people who sometimes ask for death are not to be understood as implying a true desire for euthanasia; in fact it is almost always a case of an anguished plea for help and love. What a sick person needs, besides medical care, is love, the human and supernatural warmth with which the sick person can and ought to be surrounded by all those close to him or her, parents and children, doctors and nurses.

### III. The Meaning of Suffering for Christians and the Use of Painkillers.

Death does not always come in drastic circumstances after barely tolerable sufferings. Nor do we have to think only of extreme cases. Numerous testimonies which confirm one another lead one to the conclusion that nature itself has made provision to render more bearable at the moment of death separations that would be terribly painful to a person in full health. Hence it is that a prolonged illness, advanced old age, or a state of loneliness or neglect can bring about psychological conditions that facilitate the acceptance of death.

Nevertheless the fact remains that death, often preceded or accompanied by severe and prolonged suffering, is something which naturally causes people anguish.

Physical suffering is certainly an unavoidable element of the human condition; on the biological level, it constitutes a warning of which no one denies the usefulness; but, since it affects the human psychological makeup, it often exceeds its own biological usefulness and so can become so severe as to cause the desire to remove it at any cost.

According to Christian teaching, however, suffering, especially suffering during the last moments of life, has a special place in God's saving plan; it is in fact a sharing in Christ's Passion and a union with the redeeming sacrifice which he offered in obedience to the Father's will. Therefore one must not be surprised if some Christians prefer to moderate their use of painkillers, in order to accept voluntarily at least a part of their sufferings and thus associate themselves in a conscious way with the sufferings of Christ crucified. (cf. Matthew 27:34). Nevertheless it would be imprudent to impose a heroic way of acting as a general rule. On the contrary, human and Christian prudence suggest for the majority of sick people the use of medicines capable of alleviating or suppressing pain, even though these may cause as a secondary effect semiconsciousness and reduced lucidity. As for those who are not in a state to express themselves, one can reasonably presume that they wish to take these painkillers, and have them administered according to the doctor's advice.

But the intensive use of painkillers is not without difficulties, because the phenomenon of habituation generally makes it necessary to increase their dosage in order to maintain their efficacy. At this point it is fitting to recall a declaration by Pius XII, which retains its full force; in answer to a group of doctors who had put the question: "Is the suppression of pain and consciousness by the use of narcotics . . . permitted by religion and morality to the doctor and the patient (even at the approach of death and if one foresees that the use of narcotics will shorten life)?" The Pope said: "If no other means exist, and if, in the given circumstances, this does not prevent the carrying out of other religious and moral duties: Yes."[5] In this case, of course, death is in no way intended or sought, even if the risk of it is reasonably taken; the intention is simply to relieve pain effectively, using for this purpose painkillers available to medicine.

However, painkillers that cause unconsciousness need

---

5. Pius XII, *Address* of 24 February 1957; *AAS* 49 (1957), p. 147.

special consideration. For a person not only has to be able to satisfy his or her moral duties and family obligations; he or she also has to prepare himself or herself with full consciousness for meeting Christ. Thus Pius XII warns: "It is not right to deprive the dying person of consciousness without a serious reason."[6]

## IV. Due Proportion in the Use of Remedies

Today it is very important to protect, at the moment of death, both the dignity of the human person and the Christian concept of life against a technological attitude that threatens to become an abuse. Thus, some people speak of a "right to die," which is an expression that does not mean the right to procure death either by one's own hand or by means of someone else, as one pleases, but rather the right to die peacefully with human and Christian dignity. From this point of view, the use of therapeutic means can sometimes pose problems.

In numerous cases, the complexity of the situation can be such as to cause doubts about the way ethical principles should be applied. In the final analysis, it pertains to the conscience either of the sick person, or of those qualified to speak in the sick person's name, or of the doctors, to decide, in the light of moral obligations and of the various aspects of the case.

Everyone has the duty to care for his or her own health or to seek such care from others. Those whose task it is to care for the sick must do so conscientiously and administer the remedies that seem necessary or useful.

However, is it necessary in all circumstances to have recourse to all possible remedies?

In the past, moralists replied that one is never obliged to use "extraordinary" means. This reply, which as a principle still holds good, is perhaps less clear today, by reason of the imprecision of the term and the rapid progress made in the treatment of sickness. Thus some people prefer to speak of

---

6. Pius XII, *ibid.*, p. 145. Cf. *Address* of 9 September 1958: *AAS* 50 1958, p. 694.

"proportionate" and "disproportionate" means. In any case, it will be possible to make a correct judgment as to the means by studying the type of treatment to be used, its degree of complexity or risk, its cost and the possibilities of using it, and comparing these elements with the result that can be expected, taking into account the state of the sick person and his or her physical and moral resources.

In order to facilitate the application of these general principles, the following clarifications can be added:

- If there are no other sufficient remedies, it is permitted, with the patient's consent, to have recourse to the means provided by the most advanced medical techniques, even if these means are still at the experimental stage and are not without risk. By accepting them, the patient can even show generosity in the serve of humanity.
- It is also permitted, with the patient's consent, to interrupt these means, where the results fall short of expectations. But for such a decision to be made, account will have to be taken of the reasonable wishes of the patient and the patient's family, as also of the advice of the doctors who are specially competent in the matter. The latter may in particular judge that the investment in instruments and personnel is disproportionate to the results foreseen; they may also judge that the techniques applied impose on the patient strain or suffering out of proportion with the benefits which he or she may gain from such techniques.
- It is also permissible to make do with the normal means that medicine can offer. Therefore one cannot impose on anyone the obligation to have recourse to a technique which is already in use but which carries a risk or is burdensome. Such a refusal is not the equivalent of suicide; on the contrary, it should be considered as an acceptance of the human condition, or a wish to avoid the application of a medical procedure disproportionate to the results that can be expected, or a desire not to impose excessive expense on the family or the community.
- When inevitable death is imminent in spite of the means used, it is permitted in conscience to take the decision to refuse forms of treatment that would only secure a precarious and burdensome prolongation of life, so long as

the normal care due to the sick person in similar cases is not interrupted. In such circumstances the doctor has no reason to reproach himself with failing to help the person in danger.

## Conclusion

The norms contained in the present declaration are inspired by a profound desire to serve people in accordance with the plan of the Creator. Life is a gift of God, and on the other hand death is unavoidable; it is necessary therefore that we, without in any way hastening the hour of death, should be able to accept it with full responsibility and dignity. It is true that death marks the end of out earthly existence, but at the same time it opens the door to immortal life. Therefore all must prepare themselves for this event in the light of human values, and Christians even more so in the light of faith.

As for those who work in the medical profession, they ought to neglect no means of making all their skill available to the sick and the dying; but they should also remember how much more necessary it is to provide them with the comfort of boundless kindness and heartfelt charity. Such service to people is also service to Christ the Lord, who said, "As you did it one of the least of these my brethren, you did it to me." (Matthew 25:40)

*At the audience granted to the undersigned Prefect, His Holiness John Paul II approved this Declaration, adopted at the ordinary meeting of the Sacred Congregation for the Doctrine of the Faith, and ordered its publication.*

Rome, the Sacred Congregation for the Doctrine of the Faith, 5 May 1980.

Franjo Cardinal Seper
*Prefect*
Jerome Hamer, O.P.
*Titular Archbishop of Lorium*
*Secretary*

# Chapter 4

# The Greek
# Orthodox Church

The Rev. Stanley S. Harakas is Professor of Orthodox Christian Ethics at the Holy Cross Greek Orthodox School of Theology and the author of *Contemporary Moral Issues* (Light and Life Publishing Company, 1982). In his response to the questionnaire (See Appendix VIII) Professor Harakas warns, "It should be made very clear that [the following] responses, though they reflect the mind and the sense of the Orthodox Church in general, cannot be understood as official, but that they do in some way come to a reflection of the official position of the Orthodox Church."

Professor Harakas believes that:

> . . . the Orthodox Church would sanction the removal of the life-support system. The reason for this is that K. is already dead. The machines are simply keeping the dead body "functioning." That makes clear the ethical and the theological grounds. Our church simply would not want to see the inordinate continuation of biological function after the person is dead. We would make that judgment on the basis of the physician's opinion that the brain is "gone."

The Orthodox Church would not sanction active euthanasia, which Professor Harakas notes is "correctly identified as suicide" (see the questionnaire in Appendix VIII). He writes:

> There is clear canonical teaching in the Orthodox Church and moral teachings that prohibit taking of life in this fashion. It would

simply be self-murder and would be understood as sin since it violates the commandment that we are not to murder or kill.

Nor would the Orthodox Church sanction assisted suicide: "This is essentially an act of murder," states Rev. Harakas. And even should M. request help, "Our Church would clearly identify this as homicide or murder or even compassionate murder if such a term is admissible, but it would be something violated by the fundamental moral code 'Thou shalt not murder.'"

In Orthodox thinking (which accepts a belief in a soul, afterlife and divine judgment), because active euthanasia would be considered suicide, "The person who committed this act would not have a chance to repent of a very serious sin. It would probably mean eternal condemnation." Burial rituals might also be affected. "If the act of 'active' euthanasia were understood clearly as an act of suicide, the church cannot by Canon Law bury the individual, unless it is shown through competent medical certification that the person was mentally ill in doing the act. The chance is that a person who had announced previously the intention to commit 'active' euthanasia would not be buried from the church.

"In reference to so-called 'passive' euthanasia, allowing to die, our publications indicate that this is not an appropriate thing to do, especially if it is done in council with the family and the priest. Under 'active' euthanasia as indicated, it would be considered a form of suicide and therefore would be condemned, and persons would be urged not to do such a thing."

Some dimensions of the theological and biblical bases for the Greek Orthodox position are provided in Professor Harakas' book *Contemporary Moral Issues*. He recognizes changes in the ways in which persons view death and dying and provides information concerning "The Traditional View" and "The Orthodox Response" (pp. 166ff):

### The Traditional View

The traditional view in Western Civilization is that death is an enemy, an evil which is resented, fought against and battled, even though it is seen as inevitable. Death is darkness. It is the end of life on earth as we know it. It is the conclusion of our efforts, our hopes, our dreams, our expectations, our existence as earth-borne beings. That is why, considered in itself, death is evil. The Fourth Horseman of the Apocalypse is a powerful biblical symbol of the evil of death.

*"And I saw, and behold, a pale horse, and its rider's name was Death, and Hades followed him; and they were given power over a fourth of the Earth, to kill with a sword and with famine and with pestilence and by wild beasts of the earth."* (Revelation 6:8)

That is why St. Paul could write, without threat of opposition, that "the last enemy to be destroyed is death" (1 Cor. 15:26).

But death is one thing and dying is another. In the experience of dying, dying is conceived as a different kind of process, depending on the overall view of life which we may have. In history, dying and its meaning are conditioned by the way we respond to the fact of death. It was Freud who said, "The goal of all life is death."

There are three basic responses to death which have served to dictate how we die. The first is fear. This is the view which dominates the thinking about dying in history. Death is recognized as the end, the tragedy that it is, and people approach the end with the agony of self-extinction. They battle it with a fierce clinging to life, in spite of its unavoidability.

The second basic response to death belonged in the past to a small group of philosophers. Epicurus rationalized death out of existence: "Thus that which is the most awful of evils, death, is nothing to us, since when we exist, there is no death, and when there is death, we do not exist."

The philosopher and essayist Montaigne continued this tradition of whistling in the dark by saying it even more sharply. "Of all the benefits which virtue confers upon us, the contempt of death is one of the greatest." Contempt for death makes dying appear easier. For then it is as if it is nothing — not enemy, not tragedy, not pain, not suffering. Consequently, it is a non-thing which is neither to be feared, respected, nor regarded.

The third basic response is the Christian response. Orthodox Christianity — unlike Western Christianity — does not view physical death as a natural result of living. Rather, because death is the consequence of humanity's sin, it is not natural to us. For Orthodoxy, death in its ultimate sense is a perversion of our nature: it is a destructive extension of sin in our lives. "Therefore, as sin came into the world through one man, and death through sin, and so death spread to all men because all men sinned. . ." (Romans 5:12)

Yet, Christians hold also that the power of death over us has been destroyed, essentially, by the saving work of Jesus Christ. Thus, even though death continues to be evil, dying takes on new meaning. The Christian no longer fears dying, even though death is a fearsome thing. He knows and trusts in "our Saviour, Christ Jesus, who abolished death and brought life and immortality to light through the gospel" (1 Timothy 1:10). Together with Saint Paul, every Christian facing his or her own death can repeat the words of the Prophet Isaiah, "Death is swallowed up in victory," as well as the words of Prophet Hosea, "O death, where is thy victory? O death, where is thy sting?" (I Corinthians 15:55-56). The Christian knows the evil and the tragedy of death, but meets and overcomes it through sharing in the resurrected Christ's victory over death.

In discussing the issue of the right to die, Professor Harakas notes that although the Orthodox Christian tradition does not provide specific guidance, "We have several basic ethical traditions in Orthodoxy upon which we are able to draw" (pp. 171 f):

The first is that God is the author of life and that we have the responsibility to defend, protect and enhance life as a basis for living God's will. God is the giver of life, and "in his hand is the life of every living thing and the breath of all mankind" (Job 12:10). To wrongfully take the life of an innocent person is murder and is condemned as a sin (Exodus 20:13).

On the other hand, "it is appointed for men to die once" (Hebrew 9:27). Physical death is inevitable, yet it is something which comes normally *in spite* of our efforts to preserve life. There is something which rings of the barbaric in calls for the "elimination" of human life. That is why *the Orthodox Church completely and unalterably opposes euthanasia.* It is a fearful and dangerous "playing at God" by fallible human beings.

But modern medicine has perhaps gone to the other extreme. It is able now to "preserve" lives which God struggles to take! The various substitute organs devised by medical science are good and useful as therapeutic means. When, for instance, an artificial lung or an artificial kidney is used during an operation, it permits treatment of the diseased natural organ by the surgeon. Often these artificial mechanical organs are used over a period of time so that the patient's life is maintained while the weakened organism is allowed time and energy to recuperate. Sometimes, such as with kidney machines and artificial lungs, almost permanent use of the machine is required. In all these cases, life is enhanced and preserved. Normally speaking, the use of such methods is a necessary and useful step in the therapeutic process whose goal is the restoration of health and life.

When the time comes that the bodily functions do break down completely and irrevocably, and machines continue to keep "a dead body functioning as if it were alive," then, "The Church holds that there comes a time to die." Indeed there is a service (in the prayer book) designed for this very situation. When ordinary medical efforts are incapable of sustaining life, and when the body literally struggles to die, the Church prays as follows:

> . . . *Thou has commanded the dissolution of the indescribable bond of soul and body, O God of Spirits, and has ordered them to be separated by Thy divine will. The body is thus to be returned to the elements from which it was made, and the soul is to proceed to the source of its existence, until the resurrection of all. For this reason we implore Thee, the eternal and immortal Father, the Only-begotten Son and the All-Holy Spirit, that Thou bring about the peaceful separation of the soul of Thy servant* (name) *from his/her body.*

In such a situation there are "clear Orthodox Christian guidelines" available. They are as follows:

1. We have the responsibility, as a trust from God, to maintain, preserve and protect our own lives and those lives entrusted to us;
2. In case of illness, we are obligated to use every method available to us to restore health, both spiritual and medical;
3. Life is so precious and to be so respected that even

when health cannot be fully restored, it should be protected and maintained;

4. When, however, the major physical systems have broken down, and there does not seem to be any reasonable expectation that they can be restored, Orthodox Christians may properly allow extraordinary mechanical devices to be removed. When the body is struggling to die, when its numerous physical systems break down, when it cannot be reasonably expected that the bodily systems will be able to regain their potential for life, the Orthodox Christian is no longer obligated to combine the use of extraordinary mechanical devices;

5. The decision should never be taken alone. It should be shared by the family, if possible. And, certainly, it should be made on the basis of expert medical opinion in consultation with the physician in charge of the case. It should also be made with the advice, counsel and prayer of the priest.

This action should never be confused with euthanasia, which brings to an end, deliberately and consciously, a life which is capable of maintaining itself with normal care. It is one thing to kill and murder; it is quite another to "allow the peaceful separation of soul and body."

But Greek Orthodoxy is not out of touch with modern dilemmas, and euthanasia must be considered. Here Professor Harakas looks at the teachings of the Church fathers, provides some guidelines for the present, and leaves the question open as far as the future is concerned. He writes (pp. 174ff):

A partial answer to this question is to be found in the Orthodox perspective of death. The fathers tell us that death is an unnatural wrenching of the soul from the body leading to the destruction of the psycho-somatic unity that constitutes the human person. Here man is a microcosm, uniting in himself the material and spiritual realms of God's creation. In addition, he bears the imprint of image and likeness to God, and in this resemblance, Adam, the first man, enjoyed immortality. But through the Fall, man rejected God, the only source of authentic life, destroying the likeness and fracturing the image. He strove to make his own life apart from God and, thus, chose death.

Nevertheless, God did not desire that His creation remain in its fallen state, and in His great mercy, He sent His beloved Son into the world to transform and unite all things in Himself. By His Life, Death, and Resurrection, Christ Jesus restored the image and likeness in man to its original wholeness. All aspects of human existence were thereby transformed including death which through the Resurrection has become a passage into eternal life.

As a consequence, Christians should cherish their life on this earth as a most precious gift from God entrusted to them for a time, never forgetting that this life has been bought with a price and already been made new in Christ. At the same time, we must accept the inevitability of our physical death, not in despair, but with anticipation of the Last Day when we shall all be raised up in a transfigured flesh.

A further inference from this conception of life and death is that we do not deliberately contribute to the death of others. Therefore, euthanasia being a deliberate taking of human life, does not constitute a viable alternative for the Orthodox physician or patient.

## SOME GUIDELINES

While the Church suffers with those who are in grave distress, she cannot so betray her commitment to the preservation of human life. Yet, the Church is not insensitive to the needs of those who suffer and in its concern stresses the Christian obligation to relieve pain and make the patient as comfortable as possible. The use of pain killers, such as morphine, is permissible; where they may constitute an undefined effect on the length of the patient's life, no serious attention need be given, when the motive is the comfort and overall well-being of the patient.

Those experiencing great physical pain are also reminded that even suffering has acquired new meaning by our Lord's own passion and has become a means to an enhanced communion with God and an opportunity for spiritual growth.

At the same time, the Orthodox Church parts with those members of the medical profession and others who refuse to acknowledge the inevitability of physical death and advocate the use of "extraordinary measures," at whatever material and psychological cost, to keep a patient alive when there is no hope of restoration to a meaningful, functional existence. The Church which prays for the "quick and painless death" (Prayer for the Separation of Soul and Body) of the terminally-ill patient, considers this kind of treatment not only a poor use of scarce medical resources, but a denial of the will of God.

We must remember, of course, that there are no final, clear-cut answers: Today's "extraordinary measures" fast become tomorrow's regular life-saving procedures. And any life-death decisions to withhold treatment must be considered on an individual case by case basis in consultation with the patient or his next of kin, his physician and spiritual advisor.

He summarizes the Church's position as follows:

The Church, therefore, distinguishes between euthanasia and the withholding of extraordinary means to prolong life unable to sustain itself. It affirms the sanctity of human life and man's God-given responsibility to preserve life. But it rejects an attitude which disregards the inevitability of physical death. The only "good death" for the Orthodox Christian is the peaceful acceptance of the end of his or her earthly life with faith and trust in God and the promise of the Resurrection.

On May 15th, 1984, Father Harakas participated in a Medical Ethics Symposium at Booth Memorial Medical Center in Flushing, New York. Father Harakas' panel comments were titled "The Terminally Ill: Morality, Economics, Physician's Responsibility." He proposed certain guidelines for ethical decision-making concerning the care of the terminally ill, which included the traditional belief "that active life-taking of the innocent is immoral and that active taking of one's own life is wrong . . . that life itself is one of the supreme values, that death is evil and that, by and large, that which promotes life and staves off death is good." Further, he added that "the intrinsic value of each person" is a primary value. He expressed concern that ignoring traditional values might have a negative effect on "the self-understanding of the medical profession . . . as the chief healing agent in our society." Indeed, the abandonment of therapeutic efforts for the terminally ill may well foster such a utilitarian approach to life itself that it will provide a "wedge" which will undermine the respect for the human dignity of persons, precisely in the name of so-called "death with dignity."

In conclusion, Professor Harakas provided some guidelines for the approach to the question of the treatment of the terminally ill:

1. Basically, all persons, including the patient, the family, society as a whole, and the medical community ought to function within a fundamental bias toward the protection and conservation of life, and to function in ways which restrain and limit death. For the physician, this necessarily means that the traditional bias toward healing and therapy must remain primary.

2. In facing illness, we are obligated to use every method available to us to restore health. The principle that life is so precious that it is to be respected and cared for even when health cannot be fully restored should be protected and maintained as ethically valid.

3. When, however, the major physical systems have broken down, and there does not seem to be any reasonable expectation that they can be restored, that is, when over-arching evidence supports a prognosis that the patient is terminally ill, the practitioner, the individual patient, the family and all others associated with the situation are not morally obligated, and ought not to feel obligated, to expend energy, time and resources in a misdirected effort to fend off death.

4. The moral responsibility then changes in this measure: That the concern for the alleviation of pain and suffering, and the personal dimensions of the patient's life receive primary attention. This means that there is a change in moral priorities. For the physician and the medical team, the concern for the broadly understood personal life of the patient assumes the central place, and the medical efforts assume the character of care, rather than therapy.

5. In a sense, this also addresses the issue of the expenditure of money. The expenditure of money on unnecessary and inappropriate therapeutic efforts in order to convince self, family, legal community, or medical peers that we are doing everything possible is morally unfitting. On the other hand, the expenditure of money to provide "a good dying" is both appropriate and fitting and ethically indicated. Ethically speak-

ing, of course, there is the question of proportionality. But, by and large, it does not seem to me that the *amount* of money spent is the critical factor. The moral responsibility remains, in any case. Were it, for example, cheaper to actively seek therapy for the terminally ill patient, than to provide the appropriate care required for a "good death," it still would not be right to do it.

6. Finally, it should be emphasized, that nothing indicated in what has been said above permits or advocates the active taking of a human life, even when it is experiencing terminal illness. Rather, just the opposite. A terminally ill person remains a person, within a family, part of the human race, a child of God. Active taking of a life in such a case continues to fly in the face of the moral bias for the protection and continuation of life whether it be done by another person, on his or her initiative, or on the initiative of the terminally ill person.

# Chapter 5

---

# The Russian
# Orthodox Church

---

In 1985, Professor Thomas Hopko, of St. Vladimir's Seminary of the Orthodox Church in America, responded to my questionnaire (see Appendix VIII) on behalf of the Russian Orthodox Church, and the Very Reverend Archpriest A. Mileant of the Protection of the Holy Virgin Russian Orthodox Church in Los Angeles wrote a letter that covered some of the issues.

Professor Hopko wrote, "We do not find it ethically imperative to keep certain bodily functions acting when a person cannot recover."

The Rev. Father Mileant commented, "We consider that human life is a gift of God, which no one has the right to forcibly take away; however, in our teaching it is not necessary to take 'heroic' measures to prolong the life of a terminally ill patient; in this case, we leave the decision to God who gives life and permits illness."

The Church does not sanction active euthanasia. Father Mileant wrote, ". . . if a person is in great pain and requests to be allowed to die sooner (or his relatives so request), we do not consider it possible to accede to his request, because we believe that suffering is often sent by God for the remission of our sins and the salvation of our souls; so if God has sent someone pain which cannot be alleviated by normal means (pain-killer shots, etc.), we must resign ourselves in the knowledge that this pain is necessary and inevitable." Professor Hopko wrote:

> Here we say that the person must and with God's help can,
> bear what needs to be borne, and in so doing, will give glory
> to God and encouragement and inspiration to others. No one

has the right to take their life in a direct, active manner. The "active struggle" in our view is critically important. People vary greatly in what they consider to be "unbearable." Suicide is no answer.

Indeed, assisted suicide or any form of what was labeled in the questionnaire as "compassionate murder" is eschewed because "It would be a crime and a sin."

The Russian Orthodox Church believes in a soul, in afterlife and in divine judgment. Professor Hopko states, "We believe the person will answer to God and his fellow creatures for actions done in this life. The refusal of life here leads to the conclusion that 'life' would be rejected 'there.' It is not the case of God punishing people for what they have done, as much as the 'imminent punishment' inherent in the evil act, with the concurrent rejection of God's mercy and forgiveness for if there is no 'wrong' there is no need for mercy."

Father Mileant expanded on these ideas:

Concerning the life beyond, we firmly believe that a person has an immortal soul. After his death, his body dissolves, but the soul continues to think, feel and move, as it did in his earthly life.

We believe in only two conditions of the soul, or rather two places where the souls go after death, depending on God's decision; these two places are heaven and hell. We do not admit a medium condition, or purgatory, as in the Roman Catholic faith. We consider it to be a human invention. Nothing is said about it by the Fathers of the Church antiquity, or in the Bible; our Lord Jesus Christ also said nothing about it. We believe what is said in the Holy Scriptures, i.e., the existence of heaven and hell; and only God has the authority to imprison a person in hell or take him out of it.

We also do not admit that a soul sent by God to hell will always remain there. We admit that a soul can be liberated from hell by God's mercy, by the prayers of the Church, or by the good deeds performed in his memory by his relatives and friends. However, we do not know who will be saved and who will be condemned; only God has that knowledge of human souls; we therefore pray both for the righteous (they may have some sins we do not know about) and for the sinners (as God may know of some good deeds of theirs that are unknown to us). For this reason we pray basically for all, and firmly believe in the great power of Church prayers.

Distinction is made in the funeral rituals for those who end their own lives. "If the person himself willed death and participated in it consciously," Professor Hopko wrote, "we do have a service, but it is brief and not the one for whom 'God has taken.'"

Concerning counseling by the Church, Professor Hopko commented:

> We would try to determine if really, barring a miracle (which
> can happen with or without the system), the person would
> not recover and is merely not even being kept "alive" but kept
> with certain bodily functions activated—and would counsel to
> allow nature to take its course, hoping to remove any feelings
> of guilt on the part of those deciding to "pull the plug."

If active euthanasia were being contemplated, he stated that here they would "try to help the person to believe that their struggle and pain has meaning for themselves and others. The depth of the person's faith and convictions in a 'crucified God' are crucial in the counseling approach."

In 1989, Father John Breck, Professor of New Testament and Ethics at St. Vladimir's Orthodox Theological Seminary published a paper that had been presented to members of the Orthodox Christian Association of Medicine, Psychology and Religion in Bethesda, Maryland on Jan. 13, 1989. The article was titled "Selective Nontreatment of the Terminally Ill: An Orthodox Moral Perspective" and appeared in *St. Vladimir's Theological Quarterly* (Vol. 33, No. 3, 1989, pp. 261-272). The article addressed "the issue of selective nontreatment of the terminally ill, including handicapped new-born infants, so-called 'defective neonates'." Father Breck commented:

> It is now possible to maintain biological existence artificially
> for prolonged periods of time, even when there is no hope for
> a cure. This fact obliges us to reopen the question of the rela-
> tion between the "sanctity" and the "quality" of life, and it
> raises ancillary issues such as the allocation of limited resources
> and the potential financial burden upon the patient and his or
> her family. As a result, three lines of ethical reasoning have
> emerged. The first, known as "vitalism," holds that biological

life should be sustained at all costs and by any means available. While this sounds like a noble defense of the "sanctity of life" principle, it is in fact a form of biological idolatry, which places the abstract value of sustained physical existence ahead of the personal needs and ultimate destiny of the patient. The second line of reflection, supporting various forms of "euthanasia," argues that terminally ill patients should be allowed to choose the time and the way by which they will die; it thus promotes what it terms "death with dignity." As recent ethical debate has shown, however, the slogan "death with dignity" can be used to justify a multitude of attitudes and practices that have little regard for the patient's ultimate physical or spiritual welfare. And insofar as it encourages any form of active euthanasia, it unwittingly fosters the ultimate "death with *indignity*" by promoting homicide or suicide. The third view, much more in keeping with a Christian perspective, maintains that at some point in the dying process, nontreatment (the withdrawal of life-support systems) may be morally appropriate, thereby allowing the patient to die a "natural" death.

Yet even this last line of reasoning raises a host of vexing questions. Does the choice of "selective nontreatment," popularly referred to as "pulling the plug," merely "allow nature to take its course"? Or does it amount to an illicit form of euthanasia? In other words, is selective nontreatment ever morally justified, given the fact that its purpose is to hasten the patient's death, even if from natural causes? And what of the differences between various forms of nontreatment: is a moral distinction to be made, for example, between turning off a respirator and withdrawing a feeding tube? Finally, can the "benign neglect" of nontreatment be ethically condoned as truly "passive"? Or does nontreatment, by virtue of its intentionality, always amount to active intervention, a form of euthanasia that qualifies as homicide if not murder?

Questions of this kind usually arise in regard to patients who are in the late states of potentially fatal diseases such as cancer. They apply equally, however, to those newborn infants who, because of genetic anomalies, fetal alcohol/drug syndrome, birth trauma or some other reason are classified as terminally ill "defective neonates." In all such terminal cases the basic question to be resolved is this: what are the limits to which medical technology should be employed to sustain biological existence? To determine the criteria for establishing such limits, we have to begin with the Orthodox understanding of human nature and the purpose of human life. . . .

Orthodox theology understands life as a divine *gift*, to be received with an attitude of responsibility and thanksgiving. God has chosen us not for death, but for life, whose *telos* or ultimate goal is eternal communion with the Persons of the Holy Trinity. This suggests in turn that we should conceive and manage our life from the perspective of *stewardship*. Although a free gift, like the talents in Jesus' parable human existence involves responsibility towards God, to serve His glory and the salvation of His world. Ultimately, human life finds its meaning in *celebration*. Created in the divine image and called to assume the divine likeness, we are to make of our existence a continual *anaphora*, an "offering up" of ourselves and of the cosmos as a whole. In this movement of the heart towards divine life, this transfiguration of the fleshly body into spiritual body, death stands as the last enemy. Indeed, its destructive power has been overcome by the greater power of the Cross; yet it remains the ultimate obstacle between ourselves and the fullness of the new life in Christ inaugurated at our baptism and brought to completion in the Kingdom of God.

In fact, from a Christian perspective, our true death and rebirth occur at the moment we are plunged into the baptismal waters and, in the name of the Holy Trinity, are raised up and united to the communion of saints, both living and dead, who constitute the Body of the glorified Lord. Therefore it might be argued that because of the Cross of Christ, physical death no longer threatens us; it has lost its sting. The last enemy has been transformed into a welcome passage leading to everlasting life and joy.

As true as this may be, however, the "last enemy" continues to hold sway over us in the form of the *dying process*. Anticipation of prolonged and meaningless suffering, more than the event of death itself, is the chief cause of anxiety and despair for the terminally ill. To determine the limits of selective nontreatment, it is necessary to understand the meaning of suffering in Christian experience and the extent to which suffering possesses redeeming quality.

The spiritual exploits of the desert fathers and other Christian ascetics testify eloquently to the reality of "redemptive suffering." Certain forms of physical and mental suffering, distinct from but often associated with pain, can further our spiritual growth in at least three ways. In the first place, suffering makes undeniable the reality of our own sin, weakness and inadequacy. Unlike Job, our patience is limited, and suffering presents us with the constant temptation to "curse God and die." Second, once our inability to save ourselves becomes apparent in the midst of suffering, we can—like Job—obey the God-given impulse to throw ourselves on the divine mercy as our only source of hope and strength. Then again, by forcing us to choose constantly between God and despair, suffering can attain the quality of an ascetic discipline, conquering passions of both flesh and spirit.

Not all suffering, however, is redemptive. Beyond a certain point it becomes dehumanizing, breaking down the will and thwarting the best intentions of the heart. Such suffering can be produced by factors exterior to us and beyond our control: torture, excessive physical pain due to an illness, or mental anguish brought on by external threats. Researchers are now becoming aware, however, that other forms of suffering can be equally degrading and devoid of "redemptive" quality. . . .

Finally, we must admit that suffering often includes an element of the *absurd*. We cannot simply assume that "God wills" tragedy in human existence. In John 9, Jesus affirms unequivocally that suffering and guilt are by no means necessarily connected. God *allows* tragedy, yes. In the prayer of the Optino Fathers we beseech God to "teach me to treat all that comes to me throughout the day . . . with firm conviction that Thy will governs all . . . In unforseen events, let me not forget that all are sent by Thee." Yet it is unthinkable that the God of mercy and compassion should will—in the sense of want or desire—torture, terrorist bombings, or horrendously destructive earthquakes such as we have experienced in recent times. If we affirm that "nothing occurs apart from the will of God," then we must likewise insist upon a fundamental distinction between what God *wills* and what He desires and intends. God does not desire that His creatures, however rebellious they may be, should be victims of dehumanizing suffering. Yet in the unfathomable mystery of the divine economy, He may indeed "will" such experiences.

117

All we can know in this regard, however, is in fact all we *need* to know about the mystery of human suffering. That is, that despite the element of the absurd inherent in it, God *accompanies* us in our suffering; He knows and shares it to the full. As the Suffering Servant, He has the power to transform meaningless anguish into a truly *redemptive* experience. There where the person is rendered incapable of sensing that redemptive quality because of the intensity of mental or physical pain, the possibility remains for "vicarious redemptive suffering" through the anguish of Him who is forever "the Crucified One" (Mark 16:6), as well as through the presence, intercession and love of others who share the burden of the afflicted person.

Thus, when viewed in the perspective of Christ's own sacrificial passion and death, *all* suffering is potentially redemptive. . . .

Applying these thoughts regarding human life and suffering to the situation of the terminally ill, we can suggest certain guidelines that may serve the health care professional and all those who accompany the dying patient.

First, it is necessary to pass beyond the dichotomy between "vitalism" on the one hand and, on the other, euthanasia performed to ensure "death with dignity." The former is manifest idolatry, which denies that the ultimate meaning and end of human life lies beyond the horizon of biological death. The latter is in effect an oxymoron, inherently contradictory in that there is no such thing as a "good death." Death is and will always remain tragic in its very essence. Christian hope is rooted not in the prospect of death but in its defeat, its annihilation through the instrument of death itself. "By death He has trampled down death!" Euthanasia, then, whether active or passive, voluntary or involuntary, provides no solution to the problem of dying, other than to hasten its inevitable outcome.

The ultimate criterion for determining whether selective non-treatment might be appropriate in any given situation must be the *spiritual welfare* of the patient. This implies that the principles of "sanctity of life" and "quality of life" must no longer be seen as mutually exclusive. The sanctity of human existence is not necessarily preserved by sustaining biological functions, nor is its quality assured by pulling the plug or by administering a lethal injection. What indeed is the "quality" of life of a comatose patient?

. . . given the transcendent dimension of human existence, respect for the sanctity of life must always include consideration of its *spiritual quality*. This means that we need to take with utmost seriousness the Church's traditional prayers for the peaceful separation of soul and body. When a patient is irreversibly comatose (insofar as that can be determined) or suffering from intractable pain despite medication, then ethically responsible medical care will *not* retain as its primary goal perpetuation of that state.

Medical treatment should always prioritize the patient's needs. While appropriate care and nourishment are required to prevent infection and limit physical deterioration, the first consideration in the case of the terminally ill should be to relieve physical and psychological pain and distress. A "good death" is attainable only through the process of "good dying." The primary goal of the medical team, then, should not be to prolong the life of the dying patient. It should be rather to alleviate suffering so that the patient is able to rely to a maximum degree on his or her spiritual resources. The "peaceful separation of soul and body" requires sufficient freedom from pain and other forms of suffering so that appropriate preparation for death can be made. It is no infringement of the principle of the sanctity of life to administer medication adequate to this task, even if that medication has as its secondary effect the consequence of hastening the patient's death.

No one but the dying patient himself can determine whether his suffering has redemptive quality. If he is comatose or in great, unrelieved pain, then it is wholly appropriate to withdraw life-support systems and give adequate pain-killing medication, orally or through injection.

Today, however, the courts are dealing with an extension of this principle that raises a very serious ethical issue: whether or not to withhold food and water from a dying patient. Is there a moral difference between removing a respirator and removing a feeding tube? To the minds of many, there is not, and the courts seem increasingly to reflect this conviction. Again there arises the issue of voluntary and involuntary procedures. A terminally ill person may refuse food and water, or proxies may decide to withhold nourishment from a patient who is comatose or incompetent. The problem in the second instance is that we simply do not know what the comatose patient experiences in such a case. Some comatose persons are able to hear and understand everything spoken by those at the bedside, even though they are incapable of active communication. To the degree that any comatose patient might be sensate, removal of the feeding tube could well produce the agony of starvation. Until medical science is able to determine precisely what *this* particular patient is actually experiencing in the way of pain and receptivity of external stimuli, it would be morally wrong to deprive him of food and water. . . .

What, then, is the Church's responsibility in assisting the terminally ill patient through the dying process? We may note the following considerations, but the list could be greatly expanded.

1. First, we must recognize that the dying process is a natural phenomenon in the fallen world and demands appropriate respect and attention from everyone who is directly involved with the patient. Intercessory prayer, unction services, and frequent visits to the dying person should become a part of the life of the Christian community to which he or she belongs. One of the greatest causes of anxiety and depression among the terminally ill is loneliness and isolation. To minister in such situations, family, friends and the medical staff must overcome a natural tendency to "shy away" from impending death, in order to reach out to the patient with understanding, compassion and love.

2. The church community can create a network of resource persons—medical personnel, priests, ethicists, etc.—who can offer support and advice in making crucial decisions regarding the treatment or non-treatment of the dying person. This could be especially beneficial in cases where the attending physician wants to enact procedures which the patient or his representative opposes.

3. The Churches at the national and local levels should encourage development of *hospice* programs, to provide a level of care for the terminally ill that preserves and enhances the spiritual dimension of human life and the dying process. Such programs have already proven their worth by relieving terminally ill patients of the anxiety surrounding death and provid-

ing a supportive environment where they can function creatively and in peace. Whether through institutions or home-care, the hospice programs offer by far the best alternative to hospitalization. And by significantly reducing levels of pain and anxiety, they go far towards refuting arguments for active euthanasia.

4. The Churches could support as well certain carefully drafted forms of "natural death" legislation, guaranteeing that the terminally ill patient will not be used for experimental purposes or subjected to the consequences of a physician's vitalist philosophy. Together with this, they might also encourage uniform legislation regarding "living wills," whose only function would be to prevent non-beneficial or "extraordinary" procedures from being imposed. This should be recommended to protect the financial stability of the patient's family as much as to insure the rights of the patient himself regarding his treatment.

5. The Churches should definitely militate, through preaching, teaching, and other appropriate means, against an attitude, prevalent in the United States today, that makes a mockery of the Hippocratic Oath and of the medical profession in general. This is the attitude which holds that medical treatment is neither a right nor a privilege, owed or accorded by society to its members, but is a *service* rendered to those who have the means to pay. The U.S. is the only major industrial democracy in the world today which does not have comprehensive medical insurance for all its citizens. In Western Europe it is said that the measure of a country's level of civilization is the way it cares for its sick and its aged. On both counts our country belongs at best to the Third World. Only the Churches have sufficient power of moral persuasion to convince the public and our legislators that comprehensive health care is even more crucial to our national welfare than a sound defense or economic policy. It is up to the Churches, then, to press vigorously for quality medical care that is affordable and available to all.

6. Finally, priests and pastors should proclaim through their sermons and through the entire liturgical life of their communities that God is Lord of both life and death. He alone is the ultimate source of hope for the terminally ill. And

we are all, without exception, "terminally ill." Once we can assume that perspective, then perhaps we will be able to request, with conviction and unfailing hope, that He will grant to each of us the grace of a truly Christian ending to our life, one that is painless, blameless and peaceful.

In February, 1992, Father Breck responded to the issues raised in the questionnaire (see Appendix VIII). He wrote:

The Orthodox Church(es) are still struggling with the question of euthanasia, but something of a consensus has long been evident, at least with regard to the larger issue involved. In a word, the Orthodox position is opposed to any form of active euthanasia, including physician-assisted suicide. This prohibition is grounded in a very strong respect for the principle of "sanctity of life" (which governs as well the Church's attitude toward abortion).

Although no official position has been articulated regarding passive euthanasia (as you define it in question #1), there is increasing acceptance among Orthodoxy of the removal or withholding of life-support systems in cases of terminal illness (diagnosed as having less than six months to live). As for intractable pain with a terminal illness, most would accept today the administration of morphine in adequate dosages to control the pain even if that had the secondary effect of closing down the respiratory system and provoking death. This "principle of the double effect" is questioned by many of us; but the Orthodox stance would (or should) also be opposed to "vitalism": a sort of bioidolatry that means keeping a terminally ill person alive at all costs and by all means even when they are in PVS or irreversible coma. In the example of "K," brain-death would justify removal of artificial life-support systems. We have prayers for the dying that request "a peaceful separation of soul from body." This sounds highly dualistic, but its aim is to affirm that life ultimately comes from and belongs to God; and through our prayers for the dying patient we are surrendering the person into the hands of God in view of eternal.

Regarding "M" and active euthanasia: the Church would not sanction her taking her own life, even in case of great pain. Hospice programs in England and elsewhere have shown that pain-management can be effective if proper drugs are used (the frequent American practice of allowing painkilling injections only every few hours, irrespective of how often they may actually be needed, is simply barbaric often justified on the absurd grounds that the terminally ill patient may become addicted...). Pastoral care, provided by the priest but also by friends and family, is crucial here in accompanying the dying person through the period of suffering. Orthodoxy stresses the redemptive value of suffering, seeing it as a participation in Christ's own suffering and sacrificial death. Nevertheless, it is clear that there are levels of physical pain that become simply dehumanizing. When this seems to be the case, then the practice of "snowing"—increasing medication in sufficient dosages to relieve the pain, even if that may hasten death—may prove acceptable. Each case, however, must be evaluated individually, taking into consideration the physical, emotional and spiritual state of the patient.

This means, then, that physician-assisted suicide or homicide committed by the physician would not in any circumstance be acceptable from an Orthodox point of view. Such, in any case, is the prevailing attitude in the U.S. In France, on the other hand, certain Orthodox physicians are admitting the frequency of this practice by some of their colleagues. And some of them are raising the question as to when and under what conditions it might be permissible to use active means to end a patient's life. For the time being, this is restricted to the question of removing a naso-gastric tube from a PVS patient. But the debate is bound to take in other cases as well, especially in light of the situation in Holland and Germany ("Sterbehilfe") today.

The Orthodox very firmly believe in "soul" as well as in afterlife (eternal life in the kingdom of God or in eternal alienation from God). We tend to view divine judgement as the person's ultimate rejection of God's love, therefore a voluntary and willful exclusion from participation in divine life, to which each person is called and for which each person has been created. If a person committed suicide because of unbearable pain associated with terminal illness, the Church would most likely invoke "economia," and permit a liturgical burial otherwise excluded in cases of suicide, unless the indefinable "insanity" can be invoked—of course insanity is not listed in the DSM III). As for a physician or other who assisted in the suicide, the Church would call them to repentance and to genuine contrition. And with regard to the ultimate consequences of their act, only God can determine that, since he alone is Judge.

The Orthodox Church does not bury persons who commit suicide unless, as noted, "insanity" can be established. I'm presently working on this issue for our bishops, trying to broaden the definition of "insane" by reference to the neuropsychological correlates of suicide. But even if formal burial is refused, memorial services may be held for suicide victims, and this because we feel their ultimate fate lies entirely in the hands of a merciful and all-loving God. (Refusal to bury suicide victims is pedagogical: I lived in Alaska for three years, and I often heard Native friends and parishioners say, "Father, if I thought the Church would bury me, I'd kill myself tomorrow . . ." Their depression was usually caused by alcoholism; and when they did commit suicide, means were often found to justify liturgical burial.)

Since K cannot respond to any external stimuli, the question, of course, concerns those who might be in a position to withdraw life-support systems. In the first place, we would want to be very sure that according to sound medical opinion recovery is impossible. If the patient is in PVS or irreversible coma (to whatever extent those can be distinguished), then I personally would recommend withdrawal of what have usually been regarded as "extraordinary" means, including ventilator. Washington Initiative 119 wanted to include PVS among terminal illnesses, and allow removal of nasogastric tubes in all such cases. Frankly, I'm still struggling with this painful question and don't know where it will lead. Recent research has shown that in dying patients, continued hydration can in fact increase gastric and respiratory distress (this is why so many dying patients can be observed pulling out the tubes). But in cases of coma or PVS, withdrawal of the naso-gastric tube represents a form of active euthanasia: the person will inevitably die, and in a very short time. Karen Ann Quinlan survived over 9 years after removal of the respirator because of the feeding tube; but would one want for oneself or a loved one those nine years of comatose semi-existence? This remains the most difficult and heart-rending of all of these questions.

Scripture references tend to focus on God as creator and author of life as sovereign Lord over all human existence, and as the merciful Father who calls all persons to eternal life through Jesus Christ. They are legion.

# Chapter 6

## The Orthodox Church in America

Accsording to the Rev. Dennis R. Rhodes, Archivist for the Orthodox Church in America, the following "Resolution on Human Life" was passed in November, 1980:

The Orthodox Church In America, meeting at its Sixth All American Council in Detroit, Michigan, solemnly reaffirms its commitment to the divine purpose and value of human life:

1. that every human being, male and female, is made in God's image and likeness for everlasting life.

2. that every human being, male and female, must be given the opportunity to develop and fulfill his or her life as perfectly as possible, according to the will of God.

3. that attempts, however subtle, to reduce the differences between men and women to purely physical or biological factors, devoid of spiritual, moral, psychological and theological significance are to be rejected.

4. that value and spiritual well-being of the human person and human life is of supreme importance, having precedence in every instance over purely economic, political, corporate or ideological interests, purposes and goals.

5. that marriage is to be upheld as a sacred mystery to be entered into and developed as a gift from God, for His glory and the good of His creatures.

6. that the family is a foundational reality of human life,

whose value and integrity is to be protected and defended at all costs.

7. that children are to be received as a gift of God, to be cared for lovingly, joyfully, and sacrificially by every means possible.

8. that the wilful abortion of children is an act of murder and the sinful character of that act always remains, even when contraception has taken place in the most tragic circumstances. To protect the life of the unborn all legal means should b employed, including the adoption of a human life amendment to the United States Constitution.

9. that human life in all of its forms is sacred, and every means must be used for its preservation, protections and defense: political, economic, legal, moral and religious.

10. that while, in some cases, the artificial prolongations of a person's biological life in this world may be inconsistent with the proper understanding of human life, it is to be clearly distinguished from euthanasia with horror as any other form of deliberate murder.

11. that the showing of violence by the media in a crude and senseless form is harmful to human society, and should be curtailed.

12. that the degradation of sexual life, marriage and family life, particularly as it is often portrayed in the media as farcical and enslaving, is to be forcefully condemned.

13. that sexual activity outside of commitment of marriage fornication, adultery, homosexual relationships, are to be rejected as abnormal and destructive to human life made by God's image and likeness.

The Orthodox church in America pledges its support to all efforts to protect and preserve the dignity and sanctity of the human person and the human community in the name of the Kingdom of Justice, Peace and Joy revealed in the Christian Gospel.

# Chapter 7

# American
# Carpatho-Russian
# Orthodox Greek
# Catholic Church

Bishop Nicholas of the American Carpatho-Russian Greek Catholic Church, Johnstown, Pennsylvania, provided the following information regarding the Church's position on suicide, mercy killing and bodily integrity:

## SUICIDE

No believer is permitted to take the life of another and likewise cannot take his own life. Suicide is murder, self-inflicted and therefore a grave sin. Committing suicide signified a loss in the perception of the goodness of our heavenly Father and shows patience, hope and faith in God has been lost. A person of faith, regardless how great the difficulties he or she faces, must never resort to suicide as a so-called solution to problems in life. Orthodoxy denies Christian burial of one who knowingly commits suicide. Only when a physician certifies that such a sad victim of circumstances has indeed lost sanity entirely does the church permit the final obsequities be celebrated with recourse to the diocesan hierarch, mandatory in such cases.

## MERCY KILLING

The Orthodox Church has since time immemorial honored life and exalted the faithful believer as a child of God. Those who themselves plan and others who participate with them in the destruction of life place themselves outside the salutary grace of Christ and His Church. If the victim has given advance consent to such a heinous practice, Christian burial is excluded and no memorials or Divine Liturgies may be celebrated for the repose of such a soul unless it may be medically proven the individual in question was totally depraved and psychologically and spiritually bereft of normal good reason. Anyone who participates in assisting such a person is placing himself beyond the ability of the Church to redeem him and is guilty of actual murder. The ordinary canonical and Scriptural penalties are to be invoked in such cases which provide for a denied Christian burial, sacramental participation unless and until necessary remorse and repentance are evidenced in the Sacrament of Reconciliation in which absolution can only be granted with the express consent of the hierarch of the diocese.

## BODILY INTEGRITY

Faithful believers must be desirous of preserving their bodily integrity. Our heavenly Father has created us in His own image. Although sin has destroyed our likeness to Him, it is our Christian vocation which prompts us to restore it in the life of the Church. Except for extreme medical reasons, it is not permitted an Orthodox believer to submit to vasectomies and tubal ligations for the express reason of inhibiting procreative ability. This violates the image of the body of man and woman as we received it from our Creator and which we are called upon in our Orthodox Christian vocation to return intact and integral, if this is His will, at the time of departure from this vale of tears. Only in those cases where professional physicians warrant such procedures to avert life-threatening circumstances, are they accepted by the spiritual life of the Church of Christ.

# Chapter 8

---

# The Lutheran Churches

---

## THE LUTHERAN CHURCH, MISSOURI SYNOD

The Lutheran Church Missouri Synod is one American Church group that has actively been studying the relationship between faith and conduct as related to euthanasia. At the 1971 convention, in resolution 9-07, the church affirmed its belief "that the world is God's creation" and "that human life is God's gift" and that, therefore, "human life must be treasured, supported and protected." The affirmations went on to state:

> We encourage all people to avoid perverting God's will by resorting to indiscriminate termination of life, either directly through such acts as abortion or euthanasia or indirectly through the improper use of drugs, tobacco, and alcohol, or any of God's means for sustaining life.

In 1975, the Convention was presented with Resolution 8-10, which never materialized "since it failed to receive action before adjournment." Because the motion was recorded in the Convention Proceedings, however, it did serve to alert the Lutheran membership of the continuing concern about euthanasia. The resolution read, in part:

> WHEREAS, God created men in His image and gave them life; and
> WHEREAS, The world belittles the value of human life through perverting God's will by prematurely terminating life

through such acts as indiscriminate abortion, euthanasia, and the improper use of drugs, tobacco, and alcohol. . . .

(It should be noted that, "In Session 7 the committee deleted 'indiscriminate' before 'euthanasia'."

At the 1977 Convention, a resolution "To Affirm the Sacredness of Human Life" (3-30) was formally adopted. It read:

WHEREAS, Life is a gift from God and comes into being by an act that shares in the creative powers of God Himself; and

WHEREAS, Scripture teaches that suffering has a purpose of God; and

WHEREAS, Life and Death belong in the realm of God's providence; and

WHEREAS, Scripture teaches that suffering has a positive purpose and value in God's economy and is not to be avoided at all costs (2 Cor.1:5-7; 2 Cor.4:7-11; Heb.12:5-11; Rom 8:16-18; 28, 35-39; Phil. 3:10; Col. 1:24); and

WHEREAS, we sing of the positive purposes of suffering in our worship (TLH, 523, 528, 533, et al.): and

WHEREAS, The Commission on Theology and Church Relations (CTCR) and its Social Concerns Committee (SCC) currently have a study in progress regarding the question of euthanasia; and

WHEREAS, The willful taking of the life of one human being by another is contrary to the Word and will of God (Ex. 20:13); therefore be it

RESOLVED, That the Synod affirm that human life is sacred and finds meaning and purpose in seeking and following God's will, not in self-centered pleasure, a concern for convenience, or a desire for comfort; and be it further

RESOLVED, That the Synod affirm the positive benefits of suffering, so that God's children may be comforted in Christ Jesus and have their sights focused more firmly on eternal values; and be it further

RESOLVED, That the Synod unequivocally declare that the practice known as euthanasia, namely, inducing death, is contrary to God's Word and will and cannot be condoned or justified; and be it finally

RESOLVED, That the CTCR and its SCC be urged to complete their study as soon as possible.

In October 1979, the Commission on Theology and Church Relations (CTCR) published the "Report on Euthanasia with Guiding Principles" which had been prepared by its Social Concerns Committee (referred to in the 1977 resolution 3-30). This very thorough study opened with a definition of euthanasia which made a distinction between active and passive forms. Active euthanasia was defined as "taking direct steps to end the life of persons who are not necessarily dying, but who, in the opinion of some, are better off dead." It is also described as the deliberate easing into death of a patient suffering from a painful or fatal disease." Passive euthanasia is "the discontinuance or avoidance of extraordinary means of preserving life when there is no prospect of recovery."

But the report continues, "This practice does not, in a proper medical sense, signify euthanasia. Instead, it normally belongs to the responsible care that medical personnel exhibit toward patients that appear to have irrevocably entered the process of dying." The report refers to specific cases, and as support for clearly separating "euthanasia" from "responsible care" noted:

> Other examples of situations which are said to call for euthanasia involve persons suffering from unresponsive, far-advanced cancer with intractable pain, irreversible brain damage resulting in a vegetative state, and individuals with marked senility who suffer from life-threatening illnesses. It is to exceptional cases of this kind that the following statement of the New York Academy of Medicine applies:
>
> > When, in the opinion of the attending physicians, measures to prolong life in which no realistic hope of effecting significant improvement will cause further pain and suffering to the patient and family, we support conservative passive medical care in place of heroic measures in the management of a patient afflicted with a terminal illness.

It should be noted that this statement does not use the term "passive euthanasia." Instead, it speaks of "conservative passive medical care." Here is a reminder that the medical profession is hesitant to use the term "euthanasia" partly because the use of such distinctions as "passive" and "active" euthanasia has tended to blur the ethical dimensions inherent in the possibilities of extending and ending life almost at will. In normal medical parlance the term "euthanasia" stands for "mercy killing." As such this practice plays no rightful role in the profession of healing, and it has no place in the church except for purposes of condemnation.

To confound the whole field of definitions still more, the term "euthanasia" is sometimes modified by such adjectives as "voluntary," "involuntary," and "compulsory." If euthanasia is voluntarily administered by and to oneself, it is a form of suicide. If applied by another with the deceased's consent or cooperation, it is both suicide and murder. If the application of a death-accelerating measure is administered by someone else without the consent of the patient or his family, it is called involuntary. If administered in violation of the wishes of the patient and/or the family, it is known as compulsory euthanasia. In an involuntary and/or compulsory situation it is a form of murder. It is a patient-killer, not a pain-killer. In any form, it is illegal at the present time in every state.

The various semantic distinctions which have been indicated here, especially the use of "passive" or "active" and "positive" or "negative," serve to confuse the unwary and to desensitize those who oppose the legalization of mercy killing disguised as "happy death." In some cases the differentiations made may be well-intentioned. Yet the use of various qualifiers in connection with the term "euthanasia" has created great confusion, thereby raising unnecessary hazards for persons committed to a God-pleasing attitude regarding the issues of life and death.

Properly speaking euthanasia entails direct intervention, the killing of a human being, with or without his knowledge or consent. It may be briefly defined as the administration of a lethal dose to the patient or the deliberate refusal to use even the ordinary means of sustaining life. It is in this "active" sense that the word "euthanasia" will be used in the present study.

In discussing the legal status of euthanasia, the Report states that only in Uruguay are there legal provisions and regulations which permit magistrates to forego punishment where homicide is committed "out of compassion and at the victim's repeated request." In Switzerland and Germany mitigation of punishment is permissible "where the killing proceeds from 'honorable motives.' The legality of acts of omission as a means of hastening death, or removing obstacles to its accomplishment, are still clouded with ambiguities" throughout the world. The Report concludes:

> While the foregoing discussion characterizes the current legal climate with respect to euthanasia and the identification of some of the principal arguments adduced by proponents of change, our own position as Lutheran Christians who seek to bring our conduct into conformity with the divine will cannot, in the last analysis, be settled by purely secular sanctions or from considerations of public policy alone. It is appropriate at this time to include a reminder that resort to euthanasia would be sinful even if the time should come when mercy killing may no longer be defined by society as a crime.

Following a discussion of the meaning and significance of "life and death" in which specific medical problems (Start Birth, Spina Bifida, Advanced Malignancy, Brain Damage) are defined and attention is given to the significance of "ordinary and extraordinary Means," the report turns to "Ethics in Theological Focus." Life "is the Creator's Gift" and "God created human beings to live and not to die. Death in any form is inimical to what God originally had in mind for His creation. Death is the last great enemy to be overcome by the power of the risen Lord (1 Cor. 15:26). To speak of 'death with dignity' or 'merciful release' therefore consists of engaging in unholy rhetoric." The first section concludes with the pronouncement:

> It is within God's purview alone to decide on the moment when the individual is to share that life which lies beyond death in a world restored to a splendor even greater than its pristine purity. Within the context of this certain hope, mercy killing runs squarely against the grain of the will of a gracious Creator. . . .

Other issues considered under the heading of "Ethics" include "Life and Death in View of Redemption" and "Life and Death in the Light of Sanctification." Here, among other topics, the role of medical practitioners and the responsibility of the Christian community are discussed.

The Report provides a recapitulation which concludes:

> While illness and death comprise an intrusion into life, they are allowed to carry on their destructive work under God's

permissive will as reminders that we have here no abiding status and ought to look forward to the "city which has foundations, whose builder and maker is God" (Heb. 11:10). At the same time, pain and dying are experiences which can serve the further useful purpose of recalling people to the awareness that they are not autonomous. Life as a gift from God is an endowment whose disposition lies in the hands of God Himself, working as Creator, Preserver, Savior and Sanctifier.

Against this background the suggestion of deliberately accelerating death runs counter to what the biblical revelation offers by way of both moral principle and spiritual insight into man's nature and destiny as these are woven into the fabric of God's saving intent. This situation calls for increased acceptance of the disciplinary challenges inherent in personal suffering as well as of the opportunities for service to the ill and the dying. Concurrently, the potentials of medical technology in all of its ramifications for good or ill make it imperative for the medical profession to rethink the whole matter of life and death in such a way as to do justice to the will of Him who created life in the first place and who has redeemed it and still keeps sanctifying it.

The report closes with twelve "Guiding Principles" designed "to help individual Christians and groups of the faithful in their response to the issues which confront us in this area." The list includes the following:

1. Euthanasia, in its proper sense, is a synonym for mercy-killing, which involves suicide and/or murder. It is, therefore, contrary to God's law.

2. As Creator, God alone knows with certainty whether a disease or an injury is incurable.

3. When the God-given powers of the body to sustain its own life can no longer function and doctors in their professional judgment conclude that there is no real hope for recovery even with life-support instruments, a Christian may in good conscience "let nature take its course." Guidelines suggest that the patient (if capable of discussing the facts) be involved together with the doctor, the nearest of kin and the pastor.

In a lecture entitled "Decision—Life or Death" given in November 1990 at the Lutheran Home for the Aging, Dr. Samuel H. Nafzer, Executive Director of the Commission on Theology and Church Relations (CTCR) discussed the implications of the 1977 Resolution 3-30 and the 1979 Report on Euthanasia with Guiding Principles. He quoted from a statement made by President Bohlman in the "From the President" column in *The Lutheran Witness* of August, 1990:

> In view of medical technology that allows us to keep bodily functions going even when there is no perceptible brain activity, what is "death" and when does it actually occur? When a patient's comatose condition appears to be irreversible, but death is not imminent, must the provision of food and water by artificial means be continued indefinitely? How extensively should the state regulate that decision? Is it proper for Christians to prepare legal documents authorizing some to "pull the plug" under certain conditions? If so, what are those conditions? (The "living will" laws which now exist in 40 states bear careful scrutiny!)

Later he focused on some specifics.

## LIFE AND DEATH

The commission defines life as "vitality," "a state of existence characterized by active metabolism." "Vegetative life . . . is the simple metabolic and reproductive activity of a human being apart from the exercise of conscious mental or psychic processes." (p. 12)

Death refers to "the cessation of life," "the cessation of all vital functions without capability of resuscitation." The AMA says that "death shall be determined by the clinical judgement of the physician using the necessary available and currently accepted criteria." (p. 15) In this connection the Commission notes the use of "a new criteria for death" called "irreversible coma or brain death" according to these 4 criteria:

1. unreceptivity and unresponsivity
2. no movements or breathing
3. no reflexes
4. flat electroencephalogram (brain-wave test)

## LIVING WILLS

It should be remembered that this report was prepared sixteen years ago; much has happened since then. But already then "Living Wills" had appeared on the scene. In the fall of 1976 the State of California became the first state to enact legislation known as "The Living Will," a written documented and witnessed instruction to the family or heirs of an individual that no extraordinary efforts be used to resuscitate or reestablish his or her respiration or heartbeat in case he/she is afflicted with an apparently fatal terminal disease. The CTCR evaluates such an instrument with these words:

Such a document, certified at a time when the person involved is presumed to be of sound mind, does not request destruction or killing. Instead, it constitutes a request that good medical judgment be exercised. It does not abjure the use of compassionate care and treatment. Euthanasia is not at issue in such cases, for no deliberate attempt to hasten death is involved. It is a matter of providing instruction not to undertake heroic or extraordinary measures in order to sustain some semblance of life. (p. 12)

## ETHICS IN THEOLOGICAL FOCUS

In this section of its report, the Commission reflects on the question of euthanasia on the basis of the Christian faith as confessed in the Apostles Creed. The first article of the Creed teaches that life is the Creator's gift. God created human beings to live and not to die. Had it not been for sin, there would be no death in this world, and the word euthanasia would never have occurred to anyone. Death is an enemy, and mercy killing "runs squarely against the grain of the will of a gracious Creator." The time of one's death, therefore belongs to God's purview alone, when in his permissible will, it is time for the individual to share that life which "lies beyond death in a world restored to a splendor even greater than that of its pristine purity."

The second article of the creed summarizes what the Scriptures teach about God's victory over death in the suffering, death, and resurrection of Jesus Christ. In Christ's work of redemption, Christians find not only a paradigm for meaningful suffering, but also the opportunity to share in Christ's distress (cf. Col. 1:24). Here we come face to face with the paradoxical understanding of life and death which informs the Christian view. One might expect the prospect of eternal life through Christ to lead to attempts to abbreviate the course of an individual's existence here on earth. Such examples are not missing from the course of history (cf. 8th century St. Goar), but one finds no warrants for this sort of action in Scripture. The assurance of life after death offers no excuse for ending life at will by euthanasia. Jesus' healing miracles foreshadow this major paradox of history.

. . . that the mightiest advances in medical care have been made in those cultures which have come most heavily under the influence of the Christian religion with its emphasis on the blessed hope of everlasting life.

In opposition to a secularized view of life and death issues, the Christian religion does not regard the prolongation of life as the most important goal in life. Nor does it regard life in this world as the last chapter in a person's existence. The very idea of desiring to decide life and death issues represent the sin of wanting to take over the role of God in the name of sinful human autonomy. It represents a denial of meaning through redemptive suffering.

The third article brings to light what the Scriptures teach about the work of the Holy Spirit given to a Christian in his baptism. In this connection, the Commission points out how cases of lingering and painful illnesses provide the opportunity for the prayer by the one who is sick as well as for the opportunity for fellow Christians to minister to the one who is suffering and perhaps dying and in so doing to minister to Christ Himself (cf. Matt. 25:40: "Verily, I say to you, whatever you did to one of my brothers here, however humble, you did to me").


## CONCLUDING THOUGHTS

As we continue to wrestle with new aspects of decisions concerning life and death as progress is made in the field of medical science, it is imperative that we let our practices be both informed and normed by Scripture and not by the "spirit of the times." The principles laid down in the Holy Scriptures do not change, although our application of them may need to be discussed in the light of new developments.

The effect of the Cruzan decision will be, I believe, to increase the need felt by many people for "Living Wills." The report of the CTCR clearly does not object in principle to such instruments. As I was working on this assignment, I got a call from a former officer of the Synod who had been a strong supporter of pro-life causes. When I told him what I was working on, he volunteered the information that he and his wife had recently attached a "living will" to their regular will for these reasons: 1) the desire that doctors not employ heroic measures to keep them alive when there is no hope for recovery; 2) economic concerns that their inheritance not be depleted; and 3) in order not to lay a burden of guilt on their children for decisions which they might be forced to make concerning their treatment.

As we address these issues of life and death decisions, we need to be on guard against two errors—that of depreciating life on the one hand, and absolutizing life on the other. We Christians accept and treasure life as a precious gift from God as together with St. Paul we say "To live is Christ." We are being quite faithful to that which the Scriptures teach when we sing

> Praise the Almighty, my soul adore Him
> Yea, I will laud him till Death
> With songs and anthems I'll come before Him
> As long as He doth give me breath.

We treasure this life, we do not take new born babies, baptize them, and quickly dispatch them from this vale of tears to heaven. Instead, we raise up hymns of praise and thanksgiving for life, we prize it, treasure it, and exercise good stewardship over it.

But at the same time, we Christians do not worship life here on this earth as if that is all that there is, for with St. Paul we believe that "to die is gain." We believe that there is life with God in heaven for all those who fall asleep in Jesus. We Christians, although we mourn the loss of loved ones in death, do not weep as those who have no hope. We do not fear pain and suffering as unmitigated evils. We know that death is not the end. With St. Paul we can therefore look death in the eye and exalt: "Death is swallowed up in victory." (1 Cor. 15:54). We can say at the moment of death, "Lord, now let thy servant depart in peace." And we can sing:

> I'm but a stranger here, Heaven is my home.
> Earth is a desert drear, Heaven is my home.
> Danger and Sorrow stand, Round me on every hand.
> Heaven is my fatherland, Heaven is my home.

It is this paradoxical view which informs the decisions which we face regarding life and death issues.

# THE EVANGELICAL LUTHERAN CHURCH IN AMERICA

The Evangelical Lutheran Church in America (ELCA) came into being in 1987 when the American Lutheran Church, The Evangelical Lutheran Church and the Lutheran Church in America combined. The Lutheran Church brought to the union a social statement on Death and Dying which was adopted in 1982. The section on "Euthanasia" reads as follows:

## THE IRREVERSIBLY DYING PERSON

As the final stages of the dying process occur, there comes a time to recognize the reality of what is happening by refraining from attempts to resuscitate the person and by discontinuing the use of artificial life support systems. To try desperately to maintain the vital signs of an irreversibly dying person for whom death is imminent is inconsistent with a Christian ethic that mandates respect for dying, as well as for living.

## BURDENSOME TREATMENTS

In such cases, the issue is whether it is preferable to have a greater number of days that are overshadowed by the rigors of therapy or a lesser number of days that are more peaceful, i.e. whether quantity of life or quality should be accorded priority.

The foregoing should not be taken to imply that chronically ill persons should be allowed to die because their lives are judged to be not worth living or because they are viewed as burdensome or useless to society . . . the Christian response . . . must be a strong presumption in favor of treatment. Exceptions might arise in cases of extreme and overwhelming suffering from which death would be a merciful release, or in cases in which the patient has irretrievably lost consciousness. . . . One may in good conscience refuse burdensome treatments in some situations.

## ACTIVE EUTHANASIA

> Deliberatively administering a lethal drug in order to kill
> the patient, or otherwise taking steps to cause death, is quite a
> different matter. . . . Christian stewardship of life . . .
> mandates treasuring and preserving the life which God has
> given. . . . To depart from this view by performing active
> euthanasia, thereby deliberately destroying life created in the
> image of God, is contrary to Christian conscience.

In discussing the "Theological Perspectives on Death and Dying," various attitudes to death were presented, including death as "natural" (Genesis 25:8), as "tragic" (Psalm 6:4), as "friend" and as "enemy" (I Corinthians 15:56). The Christian concept of "Victory Over Death" (Romans 6:4, 8:38-39) concluded the section. The comments on "Ethical Decision-Making" made the familiar reference to life as a gift from God and called for respect for the integrity of the life process, which includes both birth and death, and for both living and dying occurring within "a caring community." The individual's rights in determining treatment, a call for "truthfulness and faithfulness" in human relations, and the significance of "hope and meaning in life" were all stressed.

If a patient is irreversibly dying with a progressive disease for which no effective therapy exists, "As the final stages of the dying process occur, there comes a time to recognize the reality of what is happening by refraining from attempts to resuscitate the person by discontinuing the use of artificial life-support systems. To try desperately to maintain the vital signs of an irreversibly dying person for whom death is imminent is inconsistent with a Christian ethic that mandates respect for dying, as well as for living." On the other hand, any involvement in active euthanasia is absolutely forbidden:

> Deliberately administering a lethal drug in order to kill the
> patient, or otherwise taking steps to cause death, is quite a
> different matter. This is frequently called "active euthanasia" or
> "mercy killing" (as contrasted with the cases discussed above,
> which involve withholding or withdrawing medical treatment,
> thereby allowing death to occur from a disease or injury).
>
> Some might maintain that active euthanasia can represent
> an appropriate course of action if motivated by the desire to
> end suffering. Christian stewardship of life, however, mandates

treasuring and preserving the life which God has given, be it our own life or the life of some other person. This view is supported by the affirmation that meaning and hope are possible in all of life's situations, even those involving great suffering. To depart from this view by performing active euthanasia, thereby deliberately destroying life created in the image of God, is contrary to Christian conscience.

Whatever the circumstances, it must be remembered that the Christian commitment to caring community mandates reaching out to those in distress and sharing hope and meaning in life which might elicit a renewed commitment to living.

The ELCA in the State of Washington published statements indicating that the Church took a firm stand in opposing Initiative 119. Both statements were signed by Steve Lansing from the Lutheran Public Policy Office of Washington. The first was titled "ELCA Opposes Initiative 119."

The citizens of Washington will be making a decision of great importance on November 5. On that date voters will decide whether Initiative 119, the "Death with Dignity" initiative, will be approved. This measure would permit physicians to deliberately take the life of individuals who meet certain criteria and who have requested aid-in-dying. Aid-in-dying is a procedure which would allow for active euthanasia. Though the methods for carrying out this procedure are not clearly specified in the initiative the most likely alternatives are the administration of a lethal injection or the prescription of an overdose of medication. ELCA social policy is very clear in opposing active euthanasia.

It is important to put this issue in an historical context. In the 1970s there was growing concern that seriously ill people nearing death were having their lives inappropriately extended through the use of artificial life support. This led to the development of Natural Death Act legislation which now exists in all states but Nebraska. Such legislation lays out the conditions in which artificial life support can be withheld or withdrawn. The rationale of such legislation is that once a patient's condition has deteriorated to a certain point it is permissible to allow the natural process of dying to occur and not take extraordinary measures to extend life.

Current law in our state allows an adult person to make a written directive instructing such person's physician to withhold or withdraw life-sustaining procedures in the event of a terminal condition. The directive only takes effect when persons are unconscious or are no longer capable of communicating their decisions to their family or doctor. The directive may be revoked at any time by the patient. Our state's Natural Death Act specifically prohibits any affirmative or deliberate act or omission to end life other than to permit the natural process of dying.

Over the past decade two areas of the Natural Death Act in our state have been the focus of particular debate. One concerns the definition of terminal condition and whether that definition includes patients in a coma or a persistent vegetative state. The second is whether life sustaining procedures include artificial nutrition and hydration. During the 1991 legislative session a broad-based coalition, including the ELCA, supported legislation which addressed these two areas of concern. However, legislative leadership decided no action should be given that the citizens would be voting on Initiative 119.

Initiative 119 does address the definitions of terminal condition and life sustaining procedures although in a manner which many believe is inadequate. However, the basis for ELCA opposition to Initiative 119 is the aid-in-dying provision. The ELCA believes that active euthanasia is not the answer for dealing with the difficult issues surrounding end-of-life treatment and care. Our society must make a commitment to provide end-of-life care which is humane and compassionate. We have excellent models, such as hospice programs, which demonstrate what can be done if we have the will. Active euthanasia serves only to deflect us from reaching out to those in our midst who need our loving attention.

Next month a second informational piece on Initiative 119 will be available to your congregation. That piece will provide more detail regarding the reasons for the ELCA's opposition. At this juncture what is most important is that citizens understand what the initiative would allow and begin to consider the implications of permitting active euthanasia in our state.

The second statement was called "Initiative 119":

Last month your congregation received an informational piece concerning Initiative 119, commonly referred to as the "Death with Dignity" initiative. It was explained that the social policy of the ELCA clearly opposes active euthanasia and thus the ELCA, as an institution, is opposed to Initiative 119. The purpose of this informational piece is to provide more detail regarding the ELCA's opposition.

As noted previously, Initiative 119 creates a procedure called aid-in-dying which would allow for active euthanasia. Obviously this is a difficult and emotional issue. Despite the triumphs of modern medicine new medical technologies do not always cure but sometimes inappropriately prolong the dying process. To use extraordinary measures to maintain the life of an irreversibly dying person for whom death is imminent is inconsistent with a Christian ethic that mandates respect for dying, as well as for living. For this reason ELCA social policy holds that in certain carefully defined circumstances it is permissible to withhold and/or withdraw medical treatment. In such circumstances one is recognizing the limitations of modern medicine and is allowing the natural process of dying to occur.

However, legalizing active euthanasia is a far different matter. The ELCA believes that life is a gift of God and the integrity of the life processes which God has created should be respected. Some would maintain that active euthanasia is an appropriate response if motivated by the desire to end pain and suffering. Yet Christian stewardship of life calls us to preserve the life God has given, be it our own or the life of another person. This view is supported by the affirmation that meaning and hope are possible in all of life's situations. In dealing with difficult medical conditions we must look for other means to address them and not utilize the expedient course of deliberately taking life.

Proponents of Initiative 119 make two primary arguments in favor of legalizing active euthanasia. The first is to claim that the issue is one of personal choice. Personal choice is certainly an important value. But given the stresses and pressures faced by persons confronted with terminal illness to what extent would their choice be free? In a society in which the vulnerable are often cast aside and viewed as a burden the possibility of active euthanasia raises troubling questions. For example, how many people, upon learning of a terminal illness, will feel they have an "obligation" to remove themselves from this life? Would the availability of active euthanasia be a signal to the frail among us that their lives are simply not worth living?

The second primary argument is the need to avoid unnecessary pain and suffering. Clearly minimizing pain and suffering is a laudable goal. However, recent advances in pain management have significantly enhanced the ability of medical personnel to reduce and control pain and further research will result in even greater benefits. Health care professionals knowledgeable about pain management indicate that current techniques have progressed to the point where a very small percentage of patients need experience any appreciable pain and suffering. Our task should be to make pain management services available to all those in need. This is the proper response to pain rather than the premature termination of a person's life.

Even if an individual favored active euthanasia Initiative 119 is not good public policy because it lacks sufficient safeguards. The initiative states that the patient must be competent and that their request for active euthanasia must be voluntary. However, it does not define competency nor provide an adequate procedure for determining competency. Likewise it does not provide for an adequate professional assessment of whether the person's choice is truly voluntary or a reflection of depression. There is no requirement that members of the patient's family be notified if the patient decides to receive aid-in-dying. Further, the patient need make only one request in order for active euthanasia to be performed. It would be much more prudent to require a waiting period and multiple requests from the patient so that there was assurance about the patient's desires. Remember that active euthanasia involves the taking of a person's life and is thus irreversible. Given this fact Initiative 119 should contain much more stringent safeguards.

The difficult issues surrounding death and dying illustrate the fundamental problems afflicting our existing health care system: lack of access, exploding costs and uneven quality of care. It is imperative that our society address these problems and construct a health care system that provides care of reasonable quality to all persons, at an affordable cost. As a part of that health care system we must make a commitment to provide end-of-life care which is humane and compassionate. Hospice programs are an excellent model of a humane and effective approach to end-of-life care. Surely there are other models we can develop which meet the needs of those facing serious medical problems. For the ELCA, active euthanasia is not an appropriate response.

It is important to note that ELCA social policy is not intended to try to bind the conscience of individual Lutherans. Each of us must make our own decision on the issue of whether active euthanasia should be legalized. However, it is hoped that Lutherans will give consideration to ELCA social policy in making their decisions and recognize that such policy has been arrived at through a serious process of study and deliberation.

## OTHER LUTHERAN GROUPS

Pastor Vilis Varsbergs of the Chicago Latvian Zion Lutheran Church wrote:

Our little Church has made no special study and has not adopted any statements concerning euthanasia. If we were to debate this issue with our clergy, I would expect a rather liberal stance, much like what the ministerium of the ELCA would say. Most of our younger pastors are graduates of present-day ELCA seminaries. If our members were polled, I would expect even more liberal attitudes. Passive euthanasia would definitely be accepted by all - and active euthanasia opposed by most pastors. Many lay people would justify suicide and many might even favor medical assistance in dying.

The rationale would be that heroic medical measures interfere with the natural process of dying. Refusing to let persons whom God calls die, doctors play God. In active euthanasia men play God as well and there is the other danger: where and how to draw the line once help in dying is permitted for anyone.

Pastor Les Galland, Business Administrator for the Association of Free Lutheran Churches enclosed a statement from a recent annual conference.

> INASMUCH as the government of the beloved United States has allowed the use of therapeutic abortions as a means of birth control, AND WHEREAS the indiscriminate taking of a human life, including that of a human fetus, is against our understanding of the Word of God, BE IT RESOLVED, That the Annual Conference of the AFLC stands opposed to abortion as a means of birth control. BE IT FURTHER RESOLVED, That each congregation and individual within the AFLC be encouraged to protest in writing to their respective legislative officials.

## STATEMENT OF ISSUES

James M. Childs, Jr., who teaches theology and ethics at Concordia Senior College, Fort Wayne, Indiana touched on basic questions in his essay, "Euthanasia: An Introduction to a Moral Dilemma," which appeared in *Currents in Theology and Mission* (pp. 67-78). Prof. Childs notes that euthanasia is "a borderline situation in which every right and wrong is not evident in every case and most cases fall within the gray area of decision-making. The borderline situation arises as a result of the 'fallenness' of our world in which normal moral laws are confounded by the world's abnormal condition."

For instance, as he discusses indirect euthanasia, he notes that "the use of painkillers that relieve the suffering of the terminal patient . . . may also contribute to hastening his death." He does not challenge the intentions of those who favor indirect euthanasia and he comments: "Behind the judgement of all those who approve indirect euthanasia is the recognition that the prolongation of life without any hope of recovery soon becomes tantamount to violence against life by prolonging the agonies of death." But the problem does not end here:

> Nonetheless, acceptance of indirect euthanasia in principle does not make decisions easy. It has been common to seek help in deciding by making the distinction between ordinary and extraordinary means of treatment. We are normally not obligated to use extraordinary measures that promise no sig-

nificant results. What is ordinary in one case may be extraordinary in another when it cannot contribute to a cure. Things as commonplace as intravenous feeding, oxygen tents and antibiotics can become extraordinary if the situation is so severe as to indicate that they prolong life unnecessarily and that the patient is not even aware of them as an expression of comfort and care. Making such a determination is easier to talk about than it is to do. Withdrawal of oxygen, shutting off a respirator or disconnecting the intravenous tubes are simple, straightforward acts of denying a human being the basic elements of life: air, food, and water. It is at this point that we sense how close the act of omission comes to acts of commission.

Following a discussion of the ways in which various theologians and ethicists have confronted these problems, Childs raises the question "Who Decides?" Here he lists some qualifications for decision making:

First of all, as Christians we do not believe that our lives are ours to dispense with as we choose. God is the creator, preserver and redeemer of our lives. Christian conscience cannot countenance any means of euthanasia that is an act of unfaith which despairs of the Lord's help in time of suffering. At the same time, desperate attempts to cling to life at all costs may also reflect a lack of trust in the promise of life everlasting in the Christ. Secondly, a patient is surely dependent upon the expertise and counsel of his doctors and his decision will be shaped by the information they give. Thirdly, the right of the patient to decide is limited by the rights of others attending him. He cannot expect medical personnel and family to act against conscience, even though he has a legal right to refuse treatment and may even secure a court order to that effect. Fourthly, the patient's right to decide is further bounded by his own condition. When extreme pain and suffering set in, one's capacity to understand and direct one's own situation is greatly affected. Finally, a patient is bound by the law as it impinges on his estate should his act be judged a suicide, and as it impinges on medical staff who may be subject to prosecution for aiding and abetting a suicide or even for homicide.

If a patient is comatose, the decision is to be made by the medical staff, the family, and the clergy. Childs recognizes the assistance that a

Living Will provides in such a situation. He believes that, "The primary concern of Christian ethics is not whether one can justify life-taking under certain conditions, but how one can best act on the positive obligations to love and care for the other person. This is the fundamental thrust of *agape*-love." Because Christians recognize that humans are created in "the image of God for immediate, personal communion and union with their creator," they know that a command implicit in creation and "elsewhere made explicit . . . requires that we do not take life, that we do no harm, that we seek to preserve life, and that we seek to ameliorate all suffering, pain, and disease that is destructive of personal humanity." How does one interpret this belief in terms of the issue of euthanasia?

> If, for example, we are considering the possibility of indirect euthanasia in an apparently hopeless case, we need to interpret how our positive obligations toward human life are applicable to the withdrawal of extraordinary means or even of all means of life support. If our conclusion is that no method we possess can reverse the dying, then the obligation to preserve life ceases to be relevant and gives way to another dimension of our respect and love for lives: the relief of suffering and the opposition to all things which dehumanize and denigrate humanity. Our care for the dying demands that we avoid the sort of medical heroics that will finally become an aggression against life by prolonging the person's dying rather than preserving meaningful personal existence for even a short time. At the same time, the decision to withdraw or withhold certain measures for patients who are even slightly able to sense the presence of our care should not include withdrawing measures that are comforting and that enhance our ability to communicate that care.

Childs cautioned against being too ready to make decisions in such circumstances:

> We need to fight the almost ingrained conviction that if persons cannot care for themselves and be productive in a normal way, they are not fully human, cannot have a meaningful life, and have a questionable right to live. When the dying and the defective reach that conclusion about themselves, it is up to those who care to prove them wrong.

Insofar as active or direct euthanasia is concerned, Childs' position is that of the Lutheran Church. He argues that, first of all, it is wrong in principle in that it is contrary "to a generally formulated absolute which forbids life-taking and commits us to the preservation of life." He does recognize that conflicts of "absolutes" may occur and that feelings of guilt can be developed. His second objection introduces the 'domino' or 'wedge' theories, which imply that excesses may result if "direct euthanasia were to be permitted in principle." He recalls the Nazi experience and quotes a Florida physician-legislator who suggested that the state could save five billion dollars over the next fifty years if all the mongoloids were allowed to succumb to the pneumonia they frequently contract.

His third objection is that "only God can make an end to life." But he comments, "To the extent that it means we can abdicate struggling with responsible decision-making in the care of the dying, I think it is wrong." He recognizes that to rest a case solely on the divine "lordship of life" could mean the refraining from certain life-saving measures. He summarizes his general approach as follows:

> When death is inevitable and meaningful life is not present, an obligation to relieve suffering takes over and we may need to cooperate with the patient's dying. This involves withdrawal of "extraordinary" life-support measures and/or the administration of pain-relievers that may shorten life. This course of action may obtain when a child is born for whom only artificial life support can enable survival and for whom there is no hope of life apart from this. It may also obtain in cases of brain death and/or irreversible loss of consciousness where there can be no hope for the recovery of spontaneous vital function. Finally, it may obtain in a case of a person facing irreversible dying in unrelieved agony.

The moral dilemma of such situations compels Childs to comment that ". . . the extreme situation of conflict that forces us to comprise one absolute demand in favor of another, whether we choose euthanasia or not, is a compromise of tragic dimensions with which we have to contend."

# Chapter 9

---

# The Episcopal Church

---

## THE CHURCH OF ENGLAND

The Church of England is the English equivalent of the Episcopal Church in the United States; both are branches of Anglicanism, which originated in England as the church of England.

In November 1980, the Church of England's Board for Social Responsibility made the following statement:

> The Church of England believes that doctor's duty of care for their patients includes enabling those who are dying to die with dignity; that there is no moral obligation on doctors to hasten or prolong dying by artificial means in every case; that pain killing drugs may be administered even though they might shorten life; and that neither of these two courses should be described as euthanasia. . . .
>
> The fact that distress is not always adequately controlled in hospitals is one reason for current interest in legislation in favour of euthanasia. The Board for Social Responsibility therefore calls upon doctors and nurses to secure the well-being of patients and help those with terminal illness with dignity, and to that end to take adequate steps to control pain.

In 1975 the Church Information Office published a report entitled "On Dying Well: An Anglican Contribution to the Debate on Euthanasia." When the report was discussed at the 1976 General Synod of the Church of England, the majority supported its conclusion that there should be no change in the law to allow euthanasia. However, as the report's title clearly indicates, it is a contribution to the debate; there is no official Anglican 'line' on the subject. In chapter 7 the report offers the following conclusions:

> If all the care of the dying were up to the standards of the best, there would be few cases in which there was even a prima facie argument for euthanasia; better alternative means of alleviating distress would almost always be available if modern techniques and human understanding and care of the patient were universally practised. . . .
>
> In situations in which, for any reason the techniques referred to above are not available (as might happen, for example, in the jungle, in emergencies and accidents, or in war, where medical aid is lacking or insufficient) exceptional cases could conceivably arise in which deliberate killing would be morally justified as being in the best interest of the person concerned.
>
> However, to justify a change in the law in this country to permit euthanasia, it would be necessary to show that such a change would remove greater evils than it would cause. We do not believe such a justification can be given: for
>
> a. such cases are very few, and would be fewer still if medical, and in particular hospital, practices were sounder;
>
> b. a change in the law would reduce the incentive to improve these practices;
>
> c. the legalisation of euthanasia would place some terminal, and even some non-terminal, patients under pressure to allow themselves to be put away—a pressure which they should be spared;
>
> d. it would also, in practice, be likely to result in recourse to euthanasia in many cases in which it was far from morally justified, and performed for unsound reasons;
>
> e. in the rare cases (if such there are) in which it can be justified morally, it is better for medical men to do all that is necessary to ensure peaceful dying, and to rely on the flexibilities in the administration of the law which even now exist (which would have to be subject to rigid formalities and safeguards) for general use:
>
> f. although there may be some patients whose relationships with their doctor would not suffer, we believe that for the great majority of patients their confidence in doctors would be gravely weakened."

# THE EPISCOPAL CHURCH

For a proper perspective on the ways in which the Episcopal Church has been confronting the issue of euthanasia, it is important to compare recent statements of the Church's stand with those issued within the past twenty-five years. In 1985 John K. Martin, Secretary for Communication of the Anglican Consultative Council, reviewed the copies of the reports of the Lambeth Conferences of the Anglican Church and concluded, "As far as I can see there are no statements on this subject (euthanasia)." He commented, "I do know, however, that a number of Churches who are members of the Anglican Communion have expressed their mind on this matter, if not through their synods, then through research and the engagement of their Boards for Social Responsibility."

In 1985 the Rev. David Scott of the Protestant Episcopal Church wrote:

> The Episcopal Church has not formulated and published any official position on the questions surrounding "euthanasia." Therefore, it is impossible to answer the questions as you formulate them, e.g., "would your religious organization sanction. . . ." Your language . . . presupposes a kind of authority of theological teaching and writing which is not relevant in the Episcopal Church. The Episcopal Church has taken specific stands on, for example, abortion. These are published in the Journals of the General Convention of the Church. But even these "official" resolutions are not juridically binding on Episcopalians.

Mrs. G. Nancy Deppen, Consultant for Information and Resource at The Episcopal Church Center in New York, shared a statement reflecting opposition to euthanasia by the General Convention in 1982, which is taken from *Social Policy of the Episcopal Church in the Twentieth Century*, by Weston, under the theme of "Special Causes" (p. 56):

> Another single-occasion action was an expression of complete "opposition to the legalizing of the practice of Euthanasia, under any circumstances whatsoever" by the General Convention of 1952. The statement drew attention to: "a growing movement to legalize the practice of Euthanasia." It also asserted that ". . . this Church believes that as God gives life so only through the operation of the laws of nature can life rightly be taken from human beings." An editorial in *The Living Church*, more than a decade earlier, had vigorously op-

posed proposals to legalize the practice of Euthanasia. By contrast, however, another meeting of the General Convention tabled a resolution against capital punishment.

In the February 21, 1973 issue of *The Christian Century* Dr. Robert M. Cooper, who was at that time Assistant Professor of Ethics and Moral Theology at Nashotah House (Episcopal) in Nashotah, Wisconsin, wrote an article titled "Euthanasia and the Notion of 'Death with Dignity'" (pp. 225ff). He suggested that "the contemporary stress on euthanasia can be seen in part as evidence of our culture's pervasive concern for what is cosmetically pleasing . . . With this concern goes the belief (usually unstated) that pain—*physical* suffering, in this instance—is life's greatest evil."

Dr. Cooper argued that he found "the idea of dignity basically abstract and not particularly Christian." He continued:

First, it is abstract because it operates on the assumption that we know what is a *fitting*, a *worthy* death for a human being, and because it ignores the specificity of the person and deals with him as one human instance under the generalizing concept of "dignity." More fundamental, especially for the Christian, is my second point. We do not yet fully know what it is to be human; and because we do not know, we cannot, or ought not, glibly speak of "human dignity." But most of us are arrogant enough to suppose that we know what is *human* being. Thus we talk readily about "humanizing the structures of government," "humanizing the education system," etc. An article in the *Episcopalian* (October 1972, p. 40) quotes Mrs. Henry J. Mali, president of the Euthanasia Educational Fund and the Euthanasia Society of America, as saying that the aim of both those organizations "is to humanize the treatment of terminal illness, so death may come gently." At the risk of appearing monstrous, I must comment that this view, while indeed humanistic, is not necessarily Christian. "Beloved," we read in the First Epistle of John (3:2, RSV), "we are God's children now; it does not yet appear what we shall be, but we know that when he appears we shall be like him, for we shall see him as he is." For Christians this verse does not function as a counsel of despair but rather as a keynote for reverence and hope. Our faith is that God has shown himself in his

Christ, and that in the Christ we can begin to perceive God's idea of being human.

Dr. Cooper then considered the concept of human suffering. In particular, he referred to a statement he quoted earlier, by Mrs. Mali, "that death may come gently." He wrote:

> This seems to imply that pain, suffering, is undignified. Is it? Clearly, some suffering is undignified, but some is not. Indeed, the bearing of pain is often noble. Christ's bearing of pain, however, takes on transcendent importance for mankind—or so Christian faith holds. Yet multitudes in our society insist that pain is the greatest evil in life; or, put the other way, that pleasure is the greatest good. There are probably those who hold that suffering or pain is the greatest evil who do not, in fact, hold its corollary, that pleasure is the greatest good. I submit that, in either form, this is the view that largely governs our culture and manifests itself everywhere—not least in the arguments of euthanasia.
>
> But the Christian view is that suffering is fundamental to human being, whatever human being is or may turn out to be. The Christian view is that happiness is not the same as pleasure. It is possible to be happy while suffering pain. I think it was C.S. Lewis who pointed out that the martyr slowly burning to death on a griddle may be said to be happy, though it would be crazy to say that he is experiencing pleasure. Pain is not the greatest evil known to man, and pleasure is not his greatest good. Surely the evil greater than pain is to deny that pain, excruciating pain, is radically an ingredient of the human condition.

Dr. Cooper's statements reflect his own opinion and some aspects of the dialogue that took place within the Episcopal Church concerning this issue. On December 18, 1976, Tom Lambert, staff writer for the *Los Angeles Times*, reported on an address given by the Most Rev. Donald Coggan, Archbishop of Canterbury, to the Royal Society of Medicine, and on the responses to the address. The article read, in part:

> The Most Rev. Donald Coggan disputed "the view held by many that Christians believe that life must be artificially pro-

longed under all circumstances . . . just for the sake of doing so."

Coggan quoted the 19th-century poet Arthur Clough: "Thou should not kill, but needst not strive officiously to keep alive."

*The London Times, Daily Mail* and *Daily Telegraph* endorsed parts or all of the 67-year-old archbishop's speech, which presumably reflected the Church of England's views. It also was approved in varying degree by the British Medical Association, Britain's Human Rights Association and the Voluntary Euthanasia Society.

A spokesman for the euthanasia group said, however, that Coggan "does not go as far as we would." The archbishop had warned against legalized euthanasia, and suggested that the issue of a patient's life or death should be the responsibility of his doctors, clergymen and relatives.

The archbishop also was praised editorially for deploying what he called "the conspiracy of silence" which he claimed cloaks the subject of death, and the "charade" in which a terminally ill person is told he is getting better.

Objections were raised in his apparent suggestion that National Health Service doctors' life-death decisions also involve a "responsibility" to the government, the taxpayers and "other patients in the long waiting queue."

"The resources of the national exchequer are not limitless, and the prolongation of the life of one aged patient may in fact entail the deprivation of aid to others and even the shortening of their lives," the archbishop said.

President Sir Rodney Smith of Britain's Royal College of Surgeons described as "unacceptable" the archbishop's suggestion that doctors should consider "the problem of availability of resources" when treating terminally or incurably ill patients. "Knowledge and conscience" must guide the doctors, Smith said.

Mrs. Deppen provided a copy of a resolution passed at the General Convention, held in 1982, pertaining to the Uniform Determination of Death Act. The resolution stated:

RESOLVED, that this Executive Council commends the President's Commission for the Study of Ethical Problems in Medicine, which was charged with developing a uniform determination of death statute; and be it further

RESOLVED, that the report and position of this Commission be circulated throughout The Episcopal Church; and be it further

RESOLVED, that Episcopalians be encouraged to consider and to comment on the proposed Uniform Determination of Death Act (U.D.D.A.):

"An individual who has sustained either 1) irreversible cessation of circulatory and respiratory functions, or 2) irreversible cessation of all functions of the entire brain, including brain stem, is dead. A determination of death must be made in accordance with accepted medical standards."

As the Rev. David Scott pointed out, such resolutions are not binding on Episcopalians. Therefore, it should be expected that the dialogue concerning euthanasia will continue.

In December 1991, Dr. David A. Scott reiterated his earlier comments:

As I indicated in my response to your questionnaire in 1985, it is difficult or impossible to respond to your request for "the position" of The Episcopal Church. Resolutions passed at our General Conventions might be viewed as expressing the mind of the church, but this is open to debate. They certainly do not carry the same official authority as a papal encyclical. In any case, the Standing Commission on Health did address some of the issues you mention in your letter in their "1991 Blue Book Report," a collection of Commission Reports gathered for the delegates to the General Convention.

Dr. Susan R. Hiatt, Professor of Pastoral Theology pointed out that the 1991 General Convention passed two resolutions relating to euthanasia. The first (C-008), "re-affirms a 1982 resolution on Living Wills and urges 'commitment to the concept of allowing peaceful death, enabling patients to maintain control and dignity . . .' and urges 'continued study of issues surrounding the quality of life and terminal care.'" The second, (A-093a), is the one referred to by Dr. Scott and reads as follows:

RESOLVED, That this 70th General Convention set forth the following principles and guidelines with regard to the forgoing of life-sustaining treatment in the light of our understanding of the sacredness of human life:

1. Although human life is sacred, death is part of the earthly cycle of life. There is a "time to be born and a time to die" (Eccl. 3:2). Our Christian faith in the resurrection transforms death into a transition to eternal life: "For as by a man came death, by a man has come also the resurrection of the dead" (1 Cor. 15:21).

2. Despite this hope, it is morally wrong and unacceptable to intentionally take a human life in order to relieve the suffering caused by incurable illness. This would include the intentional shortening of another person's life by the use of a lethal dose of medication or poison, the use of lethal weapons, homicidal acts, and other forms of active euthanasia.

3. However, there is no moral obligation to prolong the act of dying by extraordinary means and at all costs if such dying person is hopelessly ill and has no hope of recovery.

4. In those cases involving persons who are in a comatose state from which there is no reasonable expectation of recovery, subject to legal restraints, this Church's members are urged to seek the advice and counsel of members of the church community, and where appropriate, its sacramental life, in contemplating the withholding or removing of life-sustaining systems, including hydration and nutrition.

5. We acknowledge that the withholding or removing of life-sustaining systems has a tragic dimension but that the decision to withhold or withdraw life-sustaining treatment should ultimately rest with the patient, or with the patient's surrogate decision-makers in the case of a mentally incapacitated patient. We therefore express our deep conviction that any proposed legislation on the part of national or state governments regarding the so-called "right to die" issues, (a) must take special care to see that the individual's rights are respected and that the responsibility of individuals to reach informed decisions in this matter is acknowledged and honored, and (b) must also provide expressly for the withholding or withdrawing of life-sustaining systems, where the decision to withhold or withdraw life-sustaining systems has been arrived at with proper safeguards against abuse.

6. We acknowledge that there are circumstances in which health care providers, in good conscience, may decline to act on request to terminate life-sustaining systems if they object on moral or religious grounds. In such cases we endorse the idea of respecting the patient's right to self-determination by permitting such patient to be transferred to another facility or physician willing to honor the patient's request, provided that the patient can readily, comfortably and safely be transferred. We encourage health care providers who make it a policy to decline involvement in the termination of life-sustaining systems to communicate their policy to patients or their surrogates at the earliest opportunity, preferably before the patients or their surrogates have engaged the services of such a health care provider.

7. Advance written directives (so-called "living wills," "declarations concerning medical treatment," and "durable powers of attorney setting forth medical declarations") that make a persons's wishes concerning the withholding or removing of life-sustaining systems should be encouraged, and this Church's members are encouraged to execute such advance written directives during good health and competence and that the execution of such advance written directives constitute loving and moral acts.

8. We urge the Council on Seminary Deans, the Christian Education departments of each diocese, and those in charge of programs of continuing education for clergy and all others responsible for education programs in this Church, to consider seriously the inclusion of basic training in issues of prolongation of life and death with dignity in their curricula and programs.

Dr. Hiatt referred to the recently enacted health care proxy law of the State of Massachusetts which deals with patient rights in accordance with the national Patient Self-Determination Act, passed in December, 1991. She enclosed a "question from the nationally administered General Ordination Examination, which students planning on ordination in June just wrote in January 1992." Students are asked to imagine receiving a letter from an 88-year-old former parishioner who is alone, in economic straits, in poor physical health, barely able to look after him/herself and asking the pastor for spiritual guidance as he/she contemplates "calling it a day." The examination question challenges students to discuss the issues involved, the ethical and moral bases for their response, the kind of guidance that would be given and what responsibilities the pastor might have in such a case. It is satisfying to know that student clergy are confronting issues of suicide and euthanasia before assuming full pastoral responsibilities.

Suicide and euthanasia have also been discussed in *Episcopal Life*. In the January, 1992, issue, Dana H. Smith, who is Professor of Religious Studies at Indiana University and author of *Health and Medicine in the Anglican Tradition* argued that suicide is not an acceptable option for Christians. The Rev. Charles Meyer, Chaplain and Assistant Vice President for Patient Services at St. David's Hospital in Austin, Texas, and author of *Surviving Death: A Practical Guide to Caring for the Dying and the Bereaved* took the opposite stance.

Dr. Smith's presentation echoed traditional objections to suicide. The first is that suicide is a violation of self, inasmuch as it "represents a presentation of non-negotiable demands by one part of the self; an action that cuts off internal discussion. It is an irrevocable choice that may be made by a small majority." The second objection is that suicide is a violation of community in that "suicide is never a solitary act . . . the social repercussions can be enormous. Legacies of guilt are much harder to live with than legacies of being overburdened." Finally, he notes that suicide has been recognized as an offense against God. He wrote:

This objection has been the central argument against suicide in 20th century theological ethics. God is sovereign, owner and parent. Therefore it is possible to hurt God, to offend him, by taking one's own life rather than living a life of response to God and others. A life of response to God is not a life that is completely under the control of a self. Acceptance, patience and endurance constitute such a life.

Should each of us be willing to surrender our lives to God and for each other? Of course. Does that mean we may rightly choose to refuse treatment? Naturally. But discernment or discovery that the party's over should be distinguished from insisting that I must be in charge. We should preserve "suicide" as a term of moral criticism for persons who, in an act of despair or hubris, hurt themselves, their loved ones or God.

We should be most circumspect about our use of this term of criticism. But we should never concede that an individual's life is simply his or hers to dispose of as he or she sees fit—that any free choice at the end is as good as another. Our engagements with each other and God's investment in us are too profound for that.

Chaplain Meyer's approach to the issues of suicide and euthanasia was to introduce four people: one, in a nursing home for three years, is in a persistent vegetative state; one is in second stage Alzheimer's disease; one has Lou Gehrig's disease, and the fourth, who is now paraplegic and is in the final stages of dying from AIDS. The four share two things: "they are Christians, and they want to die now—by their own hand if they can do it; by the hand of a significant other if they cannot." He wrote:

> Is this a contradiction in terms? Absolutely not. The contradiction is in demanding that these persons must endure their mental and physical suffering to salve the fearful consciences of family, society or health-care practitioners.
>
> The first difficulty with suicide is defining it. Is it suicide to hasten my death if I am diagnosed with a terminal illness (defined in most states as "incurable or irreversible condition")? Is it suicide to withdraw or withhold any life sustaining or life-prolonging treatment?
>
> Many people would say it is in both cases, that there is a moral obligation to keep "life" going as long as possible. It is unthinkable and selfish, they suggest, to "give up too soon" and forgo the chance for further pleasant experiences, family reconciliations, finishing unfinished business or seeing one more sunrise.
>
> The arguments against suicide and assisted suicide may have made sense thirty years ago, before we had the medical technology to prolong dying nearly indefinitely. But those arguments are worthless when placed in the context of respirators, artificial nutrition/hydration, high-tech intensive care units (including neonatal) and the "technological imperative" to use them all.
>
> Usually based on the "sanctity of life" and the "sovereignty of God," arguments against suicide contend that all life is sacred and God is in charge of the universe, therefore no one has the right to take what belongs to God (life), or to usurp God's prerogative to decide how and when we die.
>
> It is interesting that people who espouse these arguments

have no trouble playing God by maintaining futile treatments long after the God they presumably believe in would have called the patient home if allowed to do so.

But the truth is that all life is not sacred and God does not plan our every move, capriciously inflicting us with illness, accident, disease, and misfortune for some insidious and unfathomable reason or purpose. All life is not sacred in the sense of needing vigilant protection and prolongation at all costs. And our lives are as free to end from automobile accidents as they are to end from cancer.

We play God when we medically intervene in the first place, and we must accept the logical endpoint of that intervention—the option to artificially cause or hasten the death of a person whose life we have artificially prolonged often into a state of existence that bears little resemblance to life as the patient previously defined it.

The major issue underlying suicide is suffering, and we have no societal consensus on what that is, much less on how to alleviate it. In the Netherlands, where self-requested euthanasia in terminal illness has been successfully practiced for fifteen years under physician and court supervision, one criterion is that the patient must be in "intractable suffering," suffering unrelievable by any other means than death.

Suffering may be physical, but, as in the four cases listed above, it may also be psychological or spiritual for the patient and the family, including indignity incompatible and inconsistent with the way the person lived. Suicide/assisted suicide/ hastening death may then be seen as the kindest way to relieve suffering—the most loving thing to do for all involved. Arguments decrying such action because "suffering is redemptive" have no understanding either of redemption or of the type of prolonged death possible in our health-care system.

We are a death-denying culture and a death-denying church. Everybody wants to go to heaven, but nobody wants to die to get there. And it is this denial and avoidance of our own inevitable demise that often leads to the refusal to examine and support the need for acceptable conditions under which suicide may be sanctioned.

If we believe what we say we believe every Sunday, then we must find ways to allow persons a way out of the artificially sustained states of existence we have allowed our biomedical technology to create. The same argument can be made for intractable suffering in mental illness, physical and mental disability and genetic anomaly.

Suicide and assisted suicide are two of those exits that ultimately must be viewed with mercy by God, if not by the church.

# Chapter 10

## The Church of Scotland

The 1977 Report of the Church and Nation Committee presented the following reflections and conclusions on euthanasia to the Church's General Synod.

### THEOLOGICAL CONSIDERATIONS

. . . Apart from innumerable difficulties in pursuing euthanasia legislation, the principle behind it cannot be supported theologically. The Christian recognizes no right to dispose of his own life even though he may regard those who commit suicide with compassion and understanding rather than condemnation. Here again Christian belief in God's sovereignty over life could not support the concept of permissibility in law to kill a fellow human being even when he requests it. Furthermore, voluntary euthanasia legislation would weaken the sanctions of law against killing, thereby opening the door to an extension of the law to cover imposed euthanasia. . . .

Christians who cannot accept the defeat of God's purpose but point to and participate in the victory of his love, will always seek new ways out of suffering. Good examples of this can be found in many hospitals and in hospices for the care of the dying which have demonstrated that, given concentration of effort, training and financial provision, dying in hospital need be neither painful nor distressing. It must be said, however, that in the meantime the provision of these is inad-

equate. The same point may be made about facilities for the
mentally handicapped, the brain damaged and the senile. It is
a matter of where society places its priorities. The decision to
kill 'out of mercy' abandons hope. The Christian Gospel of
love seeks God's healing and salvation in the darkest valleys of
despair.

The report then offers observations on the practical difficulties
inherent in euthanasia, in medical, legal and social terms; including:

Medical: . . . there would be many [doctors] who would
resent legislation in an area where experience and compassion
may provide adequate guidelines. Such legislation would be
most unwelcome to many patients and would destroy the relationship of trust which must exist between doctor and patient.

Legal: . . . All of these [legal] questions and many more
would be required to be answered with legal precision in any
legislation which would not create more difficulties and
anomalies than it sets out to resolve. Furthermore, legislation
breeds more legislation, and reasons for euthanasia other than
the good of the particular patient, e.g., the good of society,
might lead to consequences even more abhorrent to the Christian conscience.

Social: Those who work in the field of social welfare are
aware of further difficulties that would inevitably arise in the
realm of personal relationships and particularly in hospitals for
the incurable, the long-term disabled and the aged, which
could well become places of fear, apprehension and insecurity,
thus bringing misery to those very patients who ought to be
the subject of 'tender loving care' and ultimately an 'easy and
dignified death.'

Conclusion: The [Church and Nation] Committee consider that the Church can only express abhorrence of the deliberate termination of life and sees the alternative as 'good
terminal care.' Legislation on the subject would be unacceptable to many doctors; it would from the legal point of view be
difficult to frame, to interpret and enforce, and open to unfortunate projections; and from the theological point of view it is
contrary to Christian Faith and Ethics.

The Gospel tells us of love of God and of neighbor and
the hope of the coming of Christ's Kingdom. In the light of

this our primary calling as Christians is to seek alternatives to euthanasia in adequate concern for those for whom life has become burdensome by reason of age or illness.

Individual pastors of the Church of Scotland have called for use of the Living Will and for passive euthanasia. The Rev. Ean Simpson, minister of Kerse Church, Grangemouth, Stirlingshire, in an address to the General Assembly of the Church of Scotland in 1978, called for respect for differing attitudes toward euthanasia. His comments were published in the summer 1980 edition "The Newsletter of Exit."

Now I well realize that there are patients and doctors who are opposed to euthanasia on principle, and I respect their stand. By the same token, therefore, those of us who are involved, whether as a doctor or a minister, in helping terminally ill people to die peacefully and with dignity have the right to receive similar respect for our wishes. I believe that no person or group of persons, however well-intentioned, should have the right to dictate terms of dying to the incurably ill. If any- one believes on conscience sake that he should die without the merciful help of drugs, then he must be free to do so. But it is quite wrong to demand that others who do not share his belief follow the same course.

Mr. Simpson took issue with the argument that "it is the Christian duty to face maximum pain" and said that he would like to take some of those who propose this idea "to some bedsides where both relatives and staff are nearly driven frantic by the pleas for release from severely ill patients." He added: "To argue that it is the Christian duty to conquer pain is fine when the loved one is going into a gentle, peaceful decline. But the suggestion becomes a mockery of empty words when you are confronted with a man or woman literally screaming for death." He protested that his statements were "not purely an emotional reaction on my part," but were related to the "harsh facts surrounding terminal illness in many cases. Doctors and nurses are helpless and the minister is merely the impotent symbol of a belief that suffering here will be rewarded with glory there. 'Dying well' sounds splendidly admirable in the committee-room, but it has no place in the face of the realities of the hospital ward." The Rev. Mr. Simpson concluded with an appeal for the use of the Living Will. According to Sheila Little, Chairman of the Voluntary Euthanasia Society of Scotland, Mr. Simpson addressed the

General Assembly again in 1980, but apparently his appeal went unheeded and he received no general support for his position.

The Rev. Gavin McCallum, who is a member of Scottish Exit, wrote a brief article in the Spring 1981 edition of that organization's newsletter. He pointed out that "Christ by his teachings and miracles showed that suffering was against God's will and that man must cooperate with God to relieve it." Further, he anticipated that "A time will come for everyone when the body should be allowed to die with dignity, freeing relatives and friends from strain, setting the soul free from an aching body or a sick mind, and allowing the individual to enter into the peace of his Father's House."

Writing in the Summer, 1981, issue of the newsletter of Scottish Exit, the Rev. Alistair Bennett, a retired minister of the Church of Scotland, commented on the use of the Bible as a guide for the ethics of euthanasia:

> There is a gulf of over twenty centuries between then and now, between them and us. The Bible speaks of great moral and spiritual truths but the evaluation of these truths and their implication and application today will be very different from what it was so very long ago. They could not foresee our situation and we can never go back to theirs. Like them we must have the courage to form our own judgements and inti- mate our own behavior, responding to the situation in which we live. The difference will be that we will make our judge- ments enlightened by modern knowledge and empowered by modern technology and threatened by modern population. We would be moral cowards and unworthy descendants if we tried to lean back and expect our ancestors to make our decisions.
>
> In Biblical times, both Old and New Testament, people firmly believed that illness was caused by evil spirits or was a sign of the punishment of God. Like all his contemporaries Jesus shared the same belief. People had little understanding of the constitution or working of the human body and no knowledge whatever of bacterial or viral infection. Birth, ill- ness, age and death were all shadowed by ignorance and super- stition and fear. For us the whole situation has been transformed. The birth and growth of medical knowledge and its prodigious advances in this century have brought astonish- ing new comprehensions and armed us with sweeping new powers which can be blessedly benign or catastrophically ma-

levolent, according as we use them. It is within this age of
change and innovation that we have been born and within it
we are fated to live and die. We cannot turn back the clock.
We must adapt to our environment. This is the human adventure.

But Mr. Bennett is sensitive to the deep spiritual concerns of the
Christian community:

There is one question which is bound to lurk at the back of
the mind of those who have been brought up under orthodox
Christian teaching. What if there is a life to come? Would
anyone who contributed to their own death here be punished
there? The uncertain vision of a life to come, which has so
many versions, should never divert us from dealing realistically
with the actual problems of this present life. Evidence for another life is hard to find, while evidence for the needs of this
life moves urgently in our bodies every day. The distant dream
does not cancel out the dull pain. Will there be punishment?
It is a hypothetical question. No one on earth has the answer.

# Chapter 11

---

# The Presbyterian
# Church (USA)

---

The World Alliance of Reformed Churches appears to have taken no stand on euthanasia. In 1985 the Rev. James E. Andrews, Stated Clerk of the Presbyterian Church (USA), stated his opinion: "The organization would be opposed to the artificial prolongation of life in hopeless situations."

With respect to the second question (see Appendix VIII) Mr. Andrews was unable to provide any estimates of response except to suggest that in the second and third portions of the question the percentages of approving votes would drop appreciably.

He stated, with respect to question three:

> The confessional positions of the member Churches of the
> World Alliance of Reformed Churches unanimously support
> the concept of life after human death. The development of
> thought about medical ethics has not progressed to the point
> of evaluating participation in active euthanasia with regard to
> its impact upon the spiritual state (salvation) of the patient or
> one who participated in the termination of the patient's life.
> These would be dealt with in traditional terms such as suicide,
> and homicide.

It is not in the tradition of the Reformed Churches "to extol the deceased nor to estimate the deceased's spiritual state at death." Funeral services emphasize confidence in the love of God through Jesus Christ. Nor does the World Alliance "participate in the establishment of

170

standards" for counseling in the situations set forth in questions five and six.

The Rev. Thomas McElhinney, a pastor in the Presbyterian Church (USA), made reference in his response to the statement adopted by the 1983 General Assembly of the Presbyterian Church (USA) entitled "The Covenant of Life and the Caring Community." (This statement is discussed below.) Dr. McElhinney indicated that the answer to the first question in the questionnaire would be "yes" and that although the response to question #2 would divided, "most would understand it." Most would tend to condemn assisted suicide, but a sizable minority would accept it. Except for very conservative members, most would agree that the participation in active suicide would have no effect on the afterlife.

Back of the statement "The Covenant of Life and the Caring Community," which was published in *Church and Society* (July/August 1983), was a working committee which prefaced its presentation of the policy statement with material reflecting its research into biblical, theological and ethical issues. The background study covered such items as "Where Are We Coming From?" and considered "The Church as a Covenant People," which presented the biblical foundation for statements about the dignity of human life and the church as a caring community. Another topic included was "Where Are We in the Development of Biomedical Technology?" But the section dealing with "Decision Making at the End of Life," which was published in *Church and Society* and which is reproduced below, is the most significant for the purposes of our inquiry.

In the pre-statement study, it was stated:

> The biomedical implications of the theology of death and eternal life reflected in contemporary theologians are several. (1) We fight with God against the power of death; (2) We hope for a time in history when disease and untimely death will be overcome; (3) We accept death as a part of life experience; (4) We do not live under the dominion of death but live toward the promise of life; (5) We trust the details to God; and (6) In life and death we are with God.

Following this statement, the study turned to "The Ethics of Life and Death." Seven important points were made:

> 1. The direction of Biblical ethics is against taking the life of another even for benevolent reasons. Persons should not

171

be deemed worthless, too old, too weak, unproductive, socio-pathic or a burden, thereby justifying some act of positive "mercy killing," or the more fashionable slow killing by ne-glect. When persons fall into deep sickness, pain, suffering, unconsciousness; when they lie helpless under deep sedation or at the brink of danger in intensive care, they must know that they will not be abandoned.

While the direction of Biblical ethics is against taking the life of another, it in no way claims that it is necessary to pro-long the life—or the dying process—of a person who is gravely ill with little or no hope for cure or remission. Persons who are terminally ill must be able to trust that their dying will not be prolonged by unrequested technological interven-tions. As theologian Paul Ramsey has stated, "We need . . . to discover the moral limits properly surrounding efforts to save life. We need to recover the meaning of only caring for the dying, and the justification—indeed the obligation—of intervening against many a medical intervention that is pos-sible today." The existence of specific medical technology does not require that it be used. . . .

2. Most discussions of ethics in health care addresses the issue of autonomy (i.e., a person's right to make—or at least participate in—decisions related to his/her own body), prima-rily when discussing death and dying. The popular cliches related to this issue are: "the right to die," "death with dig-nity" and the "right to refuse treatment." Although cases (Quinlan, Fox, Saikewicz) which have been prominent in the mass news media and which have focused on these extraordi-nary issues are more dramatic than commonplace, they still necessitate a moral response. *In a pluralistic society where people have different beliefs about life and death, basic Christian respect for persons demands that a person's decisions about death be hon-ored in most instances.* (Emphasis mine: G.A.L.)

The choice of whether or not to undergo further treat-ment, whether or not to consent to experimental therapy, or to donate tissue should be a personal decision. Since the at-mosphere of critical care medicine is highly charged with val-ues such as medical authority, vested interest and patient submission, care should be taken by the physician to converse freely and candidly with the patient. The patient ought to know the options, the pros and cons of each option, the thoughts of the attending clinicians, and then be encouraged to make their own decision. Two extremes must be avoided. The first extreme position paternalistically decides for patients what is best and then announces that decision. This view holds that it is unkind or unreasonable to invite the patient into the debate over options (and that the physician knows best) and so proceeds to make proxy decisions for the patient. The second unfortunate course sets the options and scenarios before the patient like a computer. It gives the probabilities and statistics and then says, "There you are, now decide!" Both of these approaches shrink from the pain and reward of a cooperative judgment. The best course is one which involves coming to a thoughtful medical judgment, sharing this with the patient, reviewing the alternative courses, and inviting the patient's response. The tragedy of patient refusal—or thoughtless acceptance—of procedures and the increased possibility of legal action often arise from failure to respect the patient's humanity and enter into responsible dialogue with them.

Another variation on paternalistic decision making involves the externally imposed judgement about patient's quality of life. If a patient's quality of life is deemed unsuitable or intolerable by members of the health care team, treatment may be terminated—or not initiated—and the patient allowed to die. This judgement about a person's quality of life made by someone other than the patient is far different from an individual's making such a decision about their own life quality. While members of the health care professions are called upon to make quality of life decisions at many levels—and it is unrealistic to deny that such decisions are not necessary—a word of caution is in order to those who make such decisions and to all who may be patients at some point in time. We must take great care not to denigrate the worth or life of others and impose a judgement of poor quality, which might provide justification for stopping treatment or avoiding the patient. . . .

3. The real, almost inevitable danger of reducing human lives to statistic or mechanical processes must be acknowledged. The influences of economic factors often unspoken, loom large. The efforts to place economic values on patients' lives or determine how many treatments an individual deserves. While reprehensible, nonetheless they occur. If medical

care must be rationed (e.g., dialysis after 60 years of age), policies should be made following public deliberation so that those affected will have had a chance to participate. . . .

4. There is a danger and temptation to idolize bodily life by making retention of physical life the only good and primary goal. Jesus touches the subject when he says that "Whoever would save his life shall lose it." Too much effort to defend one's own life, to bury it in a safe place like the one talent man, to refuse to give life away, or to fail to use it up goes against the grain of Christian calling. It is indeed idolatrous to try to keep a person's body alive no matter how empty that life may be. Human beings are transcendent creatures. Real life comes from beyond bodily function. Jesus asks: "Is not life more than food and the body than clothing?" (Matthew 6:25b). Often hospitals and medical personnel are simply engaged in a contest to preserve "life," with little concern for quality or expectation. Sometimes they win the battle, but the patient loses. Clinging to life rather than reaching out to life compounds the tragedy.

5. The affirmation about eternal life that is woven into the Gospel according to John should be emphasized. Eternal life is here and now. According to the Apostle Paul, the light of promise shines in the present moment. Eternal life, not death, is the ultimate reality. That assurance keeps Christians from living all of life being afraid of death. For Christians the adventure is never toward an end but toward new beginnings. Elizabeth Kubler-Ross has written that death is the final stage of growth; it would be more appropriate to affirm that death is another stage of becoming. For Christians, death can be understood as the next chapter in the surprising story of life.

6. Decision making is never sure; deciders are seldom secure. Persons are ambivalent about whether to approach death with dread or hope, whether to resist or to accept. Possibly this ambivalence comes from the built-in will to live and the corresponding will to die. Whatever its origin, ambivalence is woven into the fabric of being itself, and decisions of life and death are met with a kind of frustrating ambiguity. Since life-death decisions can rarely be made with certainty, even when all the evidence is in, decisions must be made with hu-

mility and with a posture of seeking God's forgiveness and acceptance.

7. Finally, the Church is in the world to be an example, not to impose value or beliefs. By its life and its attitude toward life, it can and should bear witness to the faith. The Church in this area, as in many others, must be the community of care, protection and nurture. In this way, the Church can be a model in a pluralistic society for how these decisions ought to be made while preserving and enhancing human dignity and worth.

The preliminary study included as appendices a Living Will, a set of guidelines titled "Directions for my Care, A Christian Affirmation of Life," and a "Form or Declaration Under the Voluntary Euthanasia Act of 1969." The "Directions for My Care" document states:

> If my death is near and cannot be avoided, and if I have lost the ability to interact with others and have no reasonable chance of regaining this ability, or if my suffering is intense and irreversible, I do not want to have my life prolonged. I would then ask not to be subjected to surgery or resuscitation. Nor would I then wish to have life support from mechanical ventilators, intensive care services, or other life prolonging procedures, including the administration of antibiotics and blood products. . . .

The Directions provided for the appointment of a person authorized to act on the patient's behalf.

The Christian Affirmation is addressed to family, friends, physician, lawyer, and clergyman. The first half is a statement of belief in God as creator and sustainer of life, a belief in Jesus Christ as the prefigurer of resurrection who makes possible the anticipated death-resurrection process, and a belief in the worth and dignity of each individual in the conviction that God "has entrusted to me a shared dominion with him over my earthly existence so that I am bound to use ordinary means to preserve my life but I am free to refuse extraordinary means to prolong my life," and in the acceptance of death as "a free human act which enables me to surrender this life and to be united with God for eternity."

The second part of the Affirmation requests that the individual be informed of approaching death in order to prepare for it. It is important that the patient be consulted about all medical treatment, that unbearable pain be alleviated, but that "no means should be used with the intention of shortening my life." Further, the dying person is joined by friends, family, and the whole Christian community "in prayer and mortification as I prepare for the great personal act of dying."

The Declaration Under the Voluntary Euthanasia Act has three parts:

> 1. If I should at any time suffer from a serious physical illness or impairment reasonably thought in my case to be incurable and expected to cause me severe distress or render me incapable of rational existence, I request the administration of euthanasia at a time or in circumstances to be indicated or specified by me or, if it is apparent that I have become incapable of giving directions, at the discretion of the physician in charge of my case.
>
> 2. In the event of my suffering from any of the conditions specified above, I request that no active steps should be taken, and in particular that no resuscitatory techniques should be used, to prolong my life or restore me to consciousness.
>
> 3. This declaration is to remain in force unless I revoke it, which I may do at any time, and any request I may make concerning action to be taken or withheld in connection with this declaration will be made without further formalities.
>
> I wish it to be understood that I have confidence in the good faith of my relatives and physicians, and fear degeneration and indignity far more than I fear premature death. I ask and authorize the physician in charge of my case to bear these statements in mind when considering what my wishes would be in any uncertain situation.

Some details of the study have been presented here because of the sensitivity to differing points of view and the willingness to accept the pluralistic nature of the human community. There appears to be no desire to press the findings or attitudes of the Presbyterian Church (USA) on any other group. Furthermore, the study carefully examines existing policies and attitudes in the medical and religious communities and provides guidelines for the protection of human rights and the recognition that the desires of individuals may differ. Finally, the study makes an effort to deal with the legal dimensions confronting individuals who wish to have a voice in determining how their final days will be spent. It is my feeling that much of what is reprinted here can serve as an example for other religious communities.

The conclusion of the policy statement adopted by the 195th General Assembly of the Presbyterian Church USA and published in *Church and Society*, 1983, was titled "Decision Making at the End of Life." It read as follows:

1. Many members of the Presbyterian Church will face health care decisions toward the end of life which they could not have anticipated and many of those decisions will require judgments that relate to values held by the patient. Therefore, the 195th General Assembly (1983) calls upon its members to:
   a. Select their physicians with regard not only to the skillfulness of the medical care which they can provide, but for their values regarding human life and community, whenever such a choice is available.
   b. Take time to reflect on their own values and discuss these with family members, close friends, and their clergy.
   c. Speak with their physicians about their concerns regarding care and become educated about their condition in order to permit informed decision making.
   d. Provide instructions (and designate two agents to carry out instruction) with regard to extraordinary therapies and treatments to prolong life.

2. The church should be a place where individuals and families can make plans about death, manner of death, living wills, etc. Therefore the 195th General Assembly (1983) calls upon the church:
   a. To request the program agencies to make available information and study tools for use by congregations, regarding options available at the end of life and means of informing health care professionals of their wishes.
   b. To hold seminars utilizing the aforementioned materials and/or qualified resource persons whenever possible.
   c. To advocate that human need and benevolence replace the opportunism and exploitation that so often surround the death experience presently.

3. Harmony and integration should be sought between intensive care, curative hospitals, and hospices so that end-of-life care can be free from jurisdictional conflict and therapeutic and palliative care are available to all.

## Chapter 12

# The United Methodist Church

Claiming no authority "beyond that of a 'good Methodist,'" the Rev. Lord Soper, former President of the Methodist Conference and a recipient of the Methodist World Conference Prize for Peace, addressed the International Conference on Euthanasia and Suicide at Oxford, in September, 1980. He stressed his belief that "the Christian faith is a developing, and not a static thing," and enunciated "the fundamental principles within which I find myself in fervent support of the principles of voluntary euthanasia. . . . Christianity begins in a sacramental view of life."

> When we come to human beings it may surprise some people when I make this the cardinal point: that the sacramental view of life demands that we see human beings in an eternal concept and not in a temporal one. It strikes me as somewhat ludicrous that people who profess their ardent desire to get to heaven use the most scrupulous precautions to keep themselves here on earth.
>
> The fact that lies beyond any doubt is that the way we think of Christian view of voluntary euthanasia must depend ultimately on what we regard as the sacramental view of man. That's where Christianity starts. Now what is the nature of the Christian faith? It is the law of love. The Christian's love is compounded of active compassion. Any expression of the law, as of course dear old Saint Paul knew, must ultimately be set within the general framework of love.

179

Lord Soper continued and explicated his beliefs concerning the "relevance" of voluntary euthanasia:

. . . to remove the fear of dying, not the fear of death, but the fear of all the terrible and nauseating conditions that very often prevail. And when death is coming, not to be kept from that other world in which many a Christian—in fact all Christians—should believe.

This to me is common sense, the common sense that proceeds from the belief above everything else that love is the fulfillment of the law, and must take precedence over every category of law.

The one thing that above everything else I have been taught over the years is that it is idle to talk in terms of sacredness and of love and of compassion until you're prepared to try, however imperfectly, to carry them out within the framework of everyday society.

What we have to do, surely, is to express this within the kind of framework which will exercise an effect in its turn upon those who, at the moment, are largely blinded by prejudice.

If you ask me what is the Christian view with regard to euthanasia I can, without any doubt, recommend it in the terms of my father who, at the end of his life—and it was a very full and in many ways a saintly life—complained somewhat bitterly to me that the doctors were hindering his approach to the celestial world to which he had looked forward for the whole of his life. He wanted to go home. And—in the simplest terms—what right has any of us to prevent somebody who wants to go home from starting on that journey unhindered by all the drugs and stupidities that belong to a materialistic age?

This is an age in which we contrive to believe that the scientific concept of life is the final satisfactory one. It is nothing of the sort.

Jesus said "Seek ye first the Kingdom of God and its righteousness, and all things necessary will be added to that discovery."

In the voluntary euthanasia effort I find one expression of a loving and sacramental concept.

Lord Soper's remarks reflect his own beliefs and cannot be taken as representative of the Methodist Church in Britain or elsewhere. As the heading of this address in the Autumn, 1981 issue of the Scottish Exit newsletter warns us, "Christian Views on Euthanasia Vary Enormously."

In 1980 and again in 1988 the General Conference of the United Methodist Church adopted the following statement which has been published in *The Book of Discipline of the United Methodist Church*, 1988, under item 71H, "Social Principles:"

> Death with Dignity: We applaud medical science for efforts to prevent disease and illness and for advances in treatment that extend the meaningful life of human beings. At the same time, in the varying stages of death and life that advances in medical science have occasioned, we recognize the agonizing personal and moral decisions faced by the dying, their physicians, their families, and their friends. Therefore, we assert the right of every person to die in dignity, with loving personal care and without efforts to prolong terminal illnesses merely because the technology is available to do so.

The Rev. Eugene W. Hibbard, a retired United Methodist Church Minister associated with the Sultan Community United Methodist Church in Sultan, Washington wrote:

> My experience through forty-five years of ministry is that I have not found a single person who has wanted to be a bedridden vegetable. They have prayed that life might end in peace and glory before they become helpless and a burden to others. On speaking with them further I discover that they do not want to go even to a nursing home. A man in my present church has had terrible guilt in putting his wife with Alzheimer's into a nursing home. She is doing well there, for she is not aware of her surroundings and seldom recognizes him.
>
> I personally feel that the freedom to end one's life should be a personal decision and not placed upon the conscience of another. Thus I feel that I have the right to be given the right "pill" when I ask for it. When I am faced with long suffering and a cruel death, yet am unable to choose to ask for a "pill" then we are on another ball field.
>
> This is when doctor assisted granting of the mercy of death comes in. Here is the area that needs a lot of legal

thinking to protect both the patient and the doctor. A doctor needs to be covered by more than his own choice or decision. The patient's wishes, the family, and another doctor's approval needs to be involved. Further, a doctor needs to be protected from a suit filed against him.

The Rev. Arthur D. Campbell, who lives in Seattle, Washington, is also a retired minister in the United Methodist Church. He wrote as follows:

My position was taken from a variety of perspectives. I spoke with my 94-year-old father whose wisdom exceeds mine, and who felt that he would take the choice of ending his life with a physician-assisted process if he were to be faced with a terminal and painful disease. He is also a retired minister, as I am, and so saw no conflict between the faith stance to life and his feeling about the choice of death.

Our faith always holds in balance the respect for life, a reverence for it, with the quality of life. One without the other is contradictory. The right-to-life includes the right to make decisions regarding one's own life. Those decisions include, for me, the right to die in the style that seems appropriate to one's health.

In a television interview in Yakima, prior to my retirement and prior to the election I spoke about a decision our family made regarding a member of the family and assisted that family member with a physician assisted death, and everyone said it was the humane thing to do. However, the family member was our boxer dog Ranger. If it is the humane thing for a pet, why is that different from the human animal? The one element that makes this issue ever more critical is that our dog had no decision in the matter of his death while a man or woman would have.

We are in a time when terms need to be developed consistent with what we are talking about. You use the term "euthanasia," and the term "suicide" is also used. Both of these seem to me to miss what it is that we are talking about.

Jean S. Reis, Administrative Secretary for Resident Bishop Calvin D. McConnell, Seattle Area, Pacific Northwest Conference, graciously provided a copy of the Advanced Edition of the *Daily Christian Advocate*

(DCA) for May, 13th, 1992, which dealt with petitions presented to the General Conference of the United Methodist Church which met during the previous week. On pages 459-460 the DCA published Calendar Item #1363 (Petition CS-10656-3000-R), the action of the Legislative Committee of the General Conference that dealt with the issue of death and dying. The amended version, reproduced below, was passed and appears as the *1992 Book of Resolutions* of the United Methodist Church. Jean Reis noted that "the *Book of Resolutions* carries statements on contemporary issues as adopted by the General Conference. However it is not the 'law' of the church, as is the *Book of Discipline*."

## INTRODUCTION

The United Methodist/Roman Catholic Bilateral Dialogue completed its discussions on end of life bio-medical ethical issues in 1988. Their agreement was published as "Holy Living, Holy Dying," a booklet that includes discussion questions based on the text, and five case studies to use in testing the agreements. The three year dialogue, made up of eight Roman Catholics and eight United Methodists was sponsored by the Bishops' Committee for Ecumenical and Interfaith Affairs of the National Conference of Catholic Bishops and by the General Commission on Christian Unity and Interreligious Concerns of The United Methodist Church. The document was intended for and has been used by local groups, preferably by United Methodist and Roman Catholic congregations together as they struggle with issues related to death and dying. Upon completion of the bilateral dialogue, the United Methodist participants, with the addition of two other United Methodists for special expertise, and based on the original text, rewrote the material for submission to the United Methodist General Conference, 1992. While the outline and much of the content remains the same as that published in the joint agreement, the United Methodist did significantly alter the document in some sections. What follows, therefore, is a statement by United Methodists only and should not be interpreted in any other way. In order to distinguish between the original bilateral text, entitled "Holy Living, Holy Dying," and the later statement developed by the United Methodists alone, the latter document is titled, "Understanding Living and Dying as Faithful Christians." The following proposed resolution on "Understanding Living and Dying as Faithful Christians" was written by United Methodists who served on the United Methodist/Roman Catholic Bi-lateral Dialogue on End of Life Biomedical Ethical Issues. Rev. Janet Lutz, Director of Pastoral Care, Barnes Hospital, St. Louis, MO

Ms. Cathie Lyons, Associate General Secretary, Health and Welfare Ministries Department, General Board of Global Ministries, UMC, New York, NY

Dr. J. Robert Nelson, Institute of Religion, Texas Medical Center, Houston, TX

Bishop Benjamin R. Oliphint, chairperson Bishop of the Houston Area, Houston, TX

Rev. Jeanne Audrey Powers, staff Associate General Secretary, General Commission on Christian Unity and Interreligious Concerns, UMC, New York, NY

Dr. Robert I. Shelton, Department of Religious Studies, University of Kansas, Lawrence, KS

Dr. Richard Tholin, Dean, Garrett-Evangelical Theological Seminary, Evanston, IL

Dr. Wilson Yates, Dean, United Theological Seminary, New Brighton, MN

Additional writers included: Rev. Patricia Brown, Executive Secretary, General Board of Global Ministries, and Dr. Sally B. Geis, Iliff School of Theology, Denver, CO.


## UNDERSTANDING LIVING AND DYING AS FAITHFUL CHRISTIANS


### Part One: Theological and Ethical Affirmation

#### 1. Divine Creation of Human Life

All human life is the gift of God. Distinct from other creatures, we are created male and female in God's image with intellect and free will. Thus endowed with the capacities for knowledge, freedom, responsibility and personal relationships, we are called in community to realize the divine purpose of living, which is to love God and one another. As Christians, we believe that God reaffirms this value of all human life through the incarnation of Jesus Christ and through the empowering presence of the Holy Spirit.

## 2. The Human Condition

Humanity is subject to disease and the inevitability of death. Death as well as life is a part of human existence. Given this relationship, we should be free from either denying or exalting death. Our propensity, however, to distrust God leads us to distort the ordered place and meaning of death. When we do, our fears and anxieties become exaggerated and we are led into despair, believing God has forsaken us.

Our human situation is further exacerbated by our sins of indifference, greed, exploitation and violence, and by the moral failure engendered by stupidity and narrow-mindedness. As a result, we have rendered our earthly environment unhealthy and produced unjust social structures perpetuating poverty and waste. This deprives much of the human family of health, robs persons of dignity, and hastens death.

## 3. The Healing Christ

Through Jesus Christ God has entered human suffering even to the point of dying on the cross. In the healing ministry and sacrificial death of Jesus Christ, God transforms suffering and death into wholeness and life. These realities call us to witness to God's presence in the midst of suffering by sharing compassionately in the tasks of healing the sick and comforting the dying.

## 4. Stewardship of Life

Life is given to us in trust: not that we "might be as gods" in absolute autonomy, but that we might exercise stewardship over life while seeking the purposes for which God made us. In this life we are called by God to develop and use the arts, sciences, technologies, and other resources within ethical limits defined by respect for human dignity, the creation of community, and the realization of love.

The care of the dying must always be informed by the principle of the loving stewardship of life. The direct, intentional termination of human life either of oneself or another generally has been treated in the history of Christian thought as contradictory to such stewardship because it is a claim to absolute dominion over human life.

Such stewardship, however, allows for the offering of one's life when a greater measure of love shall be realized through such action than otherwise would be possible, as in the case of sacrificing one's life for others or choosing martyrdom in the face of evil. When a person's suffering is unbearable and irreversible or when the burdens of living outweigh the benefits for a person suffering from a terminal or fatal illness, the cessation of life may be considered a relative good.

Christian theological and ethical reflection shows that the obligations to use life sustaining treatments cease when the physical, emotional, financial, or social burdens exceed the benefits for the dying patient and the caregivers.

## 5. Christian Hope

In the face of the ultimate mystery of why humans suffer and die, our hope rests in the God who brought again Jesus from the dead. God offers us, in the midst of our struggle and pain, the promise of wholeness within the unending community of the risen Christ. Nothing, neither life nor death, can separate us from the love of God in Jesus Christ.

## Part Two: Pastoral Care

## 1. Healing Ministry

Pastoral care should be an expression of the healing ministry of Christ, empowering persons in the experience of suffering and dying. Those who give pastoral care create a relationship wherein signs of God's presence are revealed. Pastoral care may come from the church and wider community of family, friends, neighbors, other patients, and the health care team. Suffering and dying persons remain autonomous and have a right to choose their relationships with pastoral care givers.

Persons offering pastoral care empathize with suffering patients and share in the wounds of their lives. In providing comfort, they point beyond pain to sources of strength, hope, and wholeness. They may join in prayer with a person who is facing death. Such prayer should focus on healing that points to wholeness of personhood, even in death. Healing implies affirmation of the goodness of life, while recognizing death is not always an enemy.

## 2. Reconciliation

In both the healing ministry and the death of Jesus Christ, God enters into our suffering, sustains us, and provides the resources for reconciliation and wholeness. This means assisting a person in reactivating broken or idle relationships with God and with others, and being at peace with oneself.

## 3. Relationships and Care

Pastoral care provides families and friends an opportunity to share their emotions, including hurt and anger as well as grief, and provides help for complex questions that frequently require difficult decisions. Religious, cultural and personal differences among family and friends must be considered with special sensitivity. Grieving persons need to be reminded that their feelings are normal human responses. Such feelings need not cause embarrassment or guilt. Families at the bedside usually act according to long-established patterns of relationships. Attention to the entire family as a unit must be incorporated into pastoral care.

Health care workers also need pastoral care. Doctors, and especially, support staff, have intimate contact with dying persons in ways experienced by few others. They live in the tension of giving compassionate care to patients while maintaining professional detachment. Pastoral care for health care workers means helping them to take loving care of themselves as well as their patients.

## 4. Specific Pastoral Concerns

### a. Communications with the dying person and family

Pastoral care persons are trained to help patients understand their illness. While they usually do not communicate medical information to patients, they can assist in assimilating information provided by medical personnel. Pastoral care persons are especially needed when illness is terminal and neither patients or family members are able to discuss this relatively freely.

The complexity of treatment options and requests by physicians for patient and family involvement in life-prolonging decisions require good communication. Pastoral care persons can bring the insights of Christian values and Christian hope to the decision making process. If advance directives for treatment, often called "living wills," are contemplated or are being interpreted, the pastoral care person can offer support and guidance to those involved in decision making. They can facilitate discussion of treatment options including home and hospice care.

### b. Suicide

Some persons, confronted with a terminal illness that promises prolonged suffering and anguish for themselves and for loved ones, may consider suicide as a means to hasten death. When the natural process of dying is extended by application of medical technology, the emotional, economic and relational consequences for self and others may lead a responsible person seriously to consider whether continued living is faithful stewardship of the gift of life. Some may ask care givers for assistance in taking their lives. Churches need to provide preparation in dealing with these complex issues.

Among the issues of stewardship to be considered in such a decision are: (1) God's sacred gift of life and the characteristics or boundaries of meaningful life; (2) the rights and responsibilities of the person in relationship to the community; (3) the exercise and limits of human freedom; (4) the burdens and benefits for both the person and the community. Engagement with these issues is necessary for persons considering suicide.

When possible, others who are related to and care about the dying person should be included in discussion. The loving presence of Christ as manifested in the church community should surround those contemplating suicide or assisted suicide, and the survivors of those who take their own lives. An important pastoral concern is the guilt and stigma often felt by survivors, particularly when they have not been included in prior considerations.

### c. Donation of organs for transplantation, or of one's body, after death to medical research.

The gift of life in organ donation allows patients and survivors to experience positive meaning in the midst of their grief. Donation is to be encouraged, assuming appropriate safeguards against hastening death and with determination of death by reliable criteria. Pastoral care persons would be willing to explore these options as a normal part of conversation with patients and their families.

### d. Holy Living

A major concern of pastors and chaplains is the sustaining ministry to and spiritual growth of patients, families and health-care personnel.

Pastoral care persons bear witness to God's grace, with words of comfort and salvation. In our United Methodist tradition spiritual growth is nurtured by persons who offer prayers and read the Scriptures with patients and loved ones, by Holy Communion, the laying on of hands, and by prayers of repentance, reconciliation and intercession. A ritual of prayer or anointing with oil after miscarriage, or after a death in a hospital, nursing home, or hospice are examples of means to bring comfort and grace to the participants. Rituals developed in connection with a diagnosis of terminal illness, of welcome to a hospice or nursing home, or of return to a local congregation by persons who have been absent for treatment or in the care of a loved one, may also enhance spiritual growth. Preparation of these rituals with and by the persons involved is strongly encouraged.

Pastoral care givers and the community of faith are called to be open to God's presence in the midst of pain and suffering,to engender hope and to enable the people of God to live and die in faith and in holiness.

## Part Three: The Social Dimension

Ethical decisions about death and dying are always made in a social context that includes policies and practices of legislative bodies, public agencies and institutions, and the social consensus that supports them. Therefore, it is important for Christians to be attentive to the social situations and policies that affect the dying. The social context of dying decisively affects individual decisions to continue or forego treatment or to accept death. Social policies and practices must protect the fundamental values of respect for persons, self-determination, and patient benefit in treatment.

### 1. Respect for Persons: Holy Dying

Dying with dignity calls for care that puts emphasis on compassion, personal interaction between patient and caregivers, respect for the patient as a whole person with social as well as medical needs.

To the extent that medical technology is used to sustain, support, and compensate for human functions, it supports the preservation of human dignity. Indeed, medical technology is a gift of our age supported by the will and resources of a society that values life and is willing to apply the measures necessary for extending life when possible. When technology becomes an end in itself, however, unduly prolonging the dying process, it creates a paradox in which human dignity may be undermined and the goals of treatment distorted in the interest of technology.

When a person is dying and medical intervention can at best prolong a minimal level of life at great cost to human dignity, the objective of medical care should be to give comfort and maximize the individual's capacity for awareness, feeling, and relationships with others. In some cases of patients who are without any doubt in an irreversibly comatose state, wherein cognitive functions and conscious relationships are no longer possible, decisions to withhold or withdraw mechanical devices which continue respiration and circulation may justly be made by family members or guardians, physicians, hospital ethics committees and chaplains.

## 2. Justice for All

All persons deserve to be able to die with dignity, regardless of age, race, social status, lifestyle, communicability of disease, or ability to pay for adequate care. The biblical witness to God's concern for justice, particularly for those most marginalized and powerless in society, demands such commitments. Equitable allocation of economic resources is necessary to assure the protection of individuals in their dying from neglect, social isolation, unnecessary pain and unreasonable expense.

## 3. Self Determination

The right of persons to accept or reject treatment is protected in a just society by norms and procedures that involve the patient as an active participant in medical decisions. In order to safeguard the right of self determination at a time when one may lack decision-making capacity due to dementia or unconsciousness, individuals are encouraged to designate a proxy or execute a durable power of attorney and to stipulate, in written advance directives, guidelines for their treatment in terminal illness.

All persons are endowed with the gift of freedom and are accountable to God and their covenant community for their decisions. Congregations and other church groups can play a particularly important role helping their members provide written guidance for their treatment in terminal illness and find support for implementing their own directives or those of others.

## 4. Pain and Dying

In spite of the belief held by some that euthanasia and suicide may be the humane solution for the problem of excruciating pain experienced by the terminally ill, use of these options is minimized by effective medical management of pain. Presently, the proper application of medical science, as demonstrated by hospice care, can in most cases enable patients to live and die without extreme physical suffering. Such methods of controlling pain, even when they risk or shorten life, can be used for terminally ill patients, provided the intention is to relieve pain and not to kill. The law should facilitate the use of drugs to relieve pain in such cases.

If adequate support by community, family and competent pastoral care givers is provided, the mental suffering of loneliness, fear and anguish, which is often more painful than physical suffering, can be alleviated. This support is particularly important in those patients who are without any physical pain but who suffer emotional trauma in knowing that they are in the early stages of certain diseases currently considered incurable, such as Alzheimer's disease, amyotrophic lateral sclerosis, Huntington's disease and HIV-related diseases.

## 5. Social Constraints

Certain social constraints militate against the ideals of holy dying.

### a. Attitudes toward dying

The attempt to deny death frequently results both in reluctance by individuals to plan ahead for their dying and unwillingness in professionals to "let go" even when a patient is beyond medical help or benefit. This denial is intensified by negative attitudes toward old age, poverty, and disability.

### b. Ethos of the medical profession

The emphasis on curing, healing, and restoration can contribute to uneasiness among physicians in making the transition from cure to care when possibilities of cure are exhausted. Members of the medical profession are to be commended when they accept the legitimacy of medicine oriented toward relief of suffering rather than extension of the inevitable process of dying. This is not easily done; institutional pressure encourages the use of sophisticated technology even when it can only prolong a patient's dying. This is heightened by the fear of physicians concerning legal liability for failing to use all available technologies.

## c. Failures in distributive justice

Budget allocations and reimbursement policies for medical care by both private and government health plans given priority to funding technologically sophisticated diagnosis and treatments. At the same time, they often deny or minimize payments for less costly services that are critical for humane dying.

In addition, medical professionals are often constrained in their efforts to implement health care plans that have patient benefit as their goal by payment policies of government and insurance companies that dictate the length and modalities of treatment. A society committed to helping every person realize a humane death will reverse these policies and give highest priorities to such services as hospice and home care, social services and pastoral resources. This will include an adequately funded national health plan that assures all persons access to these resources.

## d. Use of the legal system

Persons increasingly have sought to redress perceived injustices in medical treatment or to resolve difficult cases in the adversarial setting of the courtroom. As a result, the courts have become the site of medical decisions. The failure of society to provide effective support systems in health care facilities, including the use of ethics committees, leaves individuals and institutions vulnerable to outside interference. The resulting practice of defensive medicine has frequently increased the use of futile diagnostic and treatment procedures by physicians and added to the cost of patient care.

## 6. United Methodist Response

Churches need to work together to overcome these social constraints. It is recommended that United Methodists:

a. Acknowledge dying as part of human existence, without romanticizing it. In dying as in living, mercy and justice must shape corporate response to human need and vulnerability.

b. Accept relief of suffering as a goal for care of the dying person rather than focusing primarily on prolongation of life. It is within human and financial means, if made a priority, to provide pain control and comfort-giving measures in a setting of communal affection and support, such as a hospice.

c. Advocate equitable access for all persons to resources, including a national health care plan, needed to relieve the dying and their loved ones from financial crises created by extended terminal illness.

d. Promote effective personal support systems, such as pastoral care teams, ethics committees in hospitals and nursing facilities, and church groups, for medical personnel who must implement difficult decision on behalf of the dying person and their families.

e. Participate in congregational, ecumenical and community-wide dialogue to help shape consensus on treatment of the dying person.

f. Encourage persons to use advance directives for their treatment in terminal illness and dying. Congregations can be supportive by providing information, opportunities for considering alternatives and assistance in implementing the directive.

Holy dying, with loving, personal care and without efforts to prolong terminal illness, will be enhanced to the extent that the church and the human community embody mercy and justice for all persons.

# Chapter 13

---

# The Baptist Churches

---

## THE AMERICAN BAPTIST CHURCHES

Unlike many other religious organizations, Baptists pass resolutions and issue policy statements to which each independent congregation may respond either positively or negatively. The Rev. Thelma C. Mitchell, Director of Issue Development in the National Ministries of the American Baptist Convention, has spelled out the process in response to a request for information on euthanasia. She wrote:

> We appreciate your attempt at clarity when discussing the American Baptist Churches' position on euthanasia.
>
> Unfortunately, at this time it is not possible to comment specifically on the events you cite in your letter pertaining to euthanasia as our General Board has not voted on any resolution addressing or voiced an opinion on those issues. To help you understand our policy statements and resolutions, let me take a moment to explain our process. *A policy statement* represents the position of the ABC on a broad issue. Each policy statement lays down the principles on which ABC resolutions, programs, and/or actions will be based. A *resolution* represents the position of ABC on a specific issue and calls for some type of implementing action. All resolutions must be based on a policy statement. Both policy statements and resolutions are adopted by the ABC General Board. Their development includes a six-step process carried out by the Director of Issue Development and the Issue Development Council:

1. identifying and prioritizing issues;
2. staffing of the Board/staff task forces;
3. educating Board and staff about the issues;
4. shepherding the statements through the approval process;
5. educating Board, staff, and the constituency after the policy statement or resolution has been adopted; and
6. monitoring the use and implementation of policy statements and resolutions.

As you have probably gathered at this point, part of who we are as American Baptists does not give us a *denominationally representative* mechanism for immediate, specific response to the events you mentioned.

Among the numerous positive and supportive policy statements pertaining to Human Rights and to "Health, Healing and Wholeness" and resolutions regarding "Older Americans" is a "Resolution on Death and Dying." The traditional Baptist emphasis on personal freedom and the human community permeates the documents, but none deal directly with euthanasia and the individual right to choose death. The one that comes closest is the "Resolution on Death and Dying" (General Board Reference #8182:6/90) passed in 1990. It reads as follows:

## RESOLUTION ON DEATH AND DYING

The Christian faith affirms that life is a good gift of the Creator, who wills us to live our lives to the fullest. God has given us the ability to make choices, and calls us all to choose what is good, and right, and just. God's gift in Jesus Christ is that we might "have life, and have it abundantly" (John 10:10). While we believe there is a life beyond death, we also affirm that death is a natural part of this existence and there are choices and decisions we must make to prepare for our own or another's dying.

These choices and decisions have been made more complex with the advances made in recent years in expensive, sophisticated medical technology which have prolonged lives under circumstances which in earlier times would have resulted in death. In too many cases extraordinary measures have been taken to sustain a life with no apparent regard for the quality of that life nor for the wishes and desires of the dying person, and/or their family. In the worse scenario the extra years of the life saved may be spent in a chronically debilitated, demented or even an unconscious condition.

The legal, ethical and moral issues inherent in these situations received national attention with the Karen Ann Quinlan case, where the New Jersey Supreme Court ruled in 1976 that she had a constitutional and common-law right to have life sustaining medical treatment refused on her behalf. Subsequently, rulings by courts in other states have also recognized the right to refuse treatment as within the protection of the constitutionally derived right of privacy. Although in some decisions, most notably the Nancy Cruzan case in Missouri, the courts have held that in the absence of informed refusal, the state's interest in preserving life prevails. This would seem to indicate that the right of individuals to be in control of their own lives and bodies in the face of imminent death exists in those states only for the competent.

Advance directives, which are commonly known as living wills, do not provide a guarantee of self-determination for those who set forth their wishes concerning the use of life sustaining treatment if such a situation should arise. Even if written quite specifically, the terms in these documents are subject to different statutory definitions and judicial interpretations. For example, a terminal condition under the Montana statute is not identical under the Florida statute. Imperfect as they may be, living wills do provide an invaluable record of a person's informed choices in such situations. Currently, thirty-six states have adopted living will legislation.

Over the years care for the seriously ill or a dying person has shifted more and more from the family to the medical community where the concern has increasingly been for the preservation of life at all costs. There needs to be a balance restored between the caring and curing goals of medicine, where the concern for minimizing suffering and preserving dignity that caring entails is given equal status to curing especially in those situations where curing is not possible.

Some of the American Baptists related long-term care facilities have taken the lead in this area by adopting crisis care policies which stipulate categories of care available to residents and/or their families in order for them to make decisions as to what level of care will be given in advance of a life threatening crisis. Some American Baptist churches have developed congregational support systems designed to minister in a compassionate and caring way to the needs of dying persons. Other churches have become involved in hospice programs while still others have become advocates in community health care issues. These models of active concern for the dignity and worth of the individual in his/her most vulnerable time need to be affirmed and lifted up among American Baptists.

We therefore call upon American Baptist churches and related organizations:

1. to familiarize themselves with the statutes within their states regarding living wills, durable powers of attorney, and natural death acts and where appropriate, to lobby for legislation that enhances and facilitates the individual's right to make his/her own decisions regarding life sustaining treatment or measures.

2. to educate members of their congregations or residents/patients in their facilities regarding the issues involved and the options available in the treatment of terminal illnesses.

3. to establish support groups within their congregations to minister to the needs of the terminally ill and crisis care policies for the care and treatment of residents/patients in their facilities.

4. to advocate within the medical community for increased emphasis on the caring goals of medicine which preserve the dignity and minimize the suffering of the individual.

The Reverend Rodney Romney, Pastor of Seattle First Baptist Church wrote that in dealing with Initiative 119, a forum approach was used. "At one session we invited all the physicians of the congregation to present their views, which were both pro and con. We also invited representatives of the Washington Citizens for Death with Dignity to speak on two occasions to our congregation."

In a publication titled "The Pastor's Column," the Reverend Romney wrote on May 9, 1990:

Initiative 119 concerns itself with the right of terminally ill persons to make an intentional choice about their death. Opponents of it believe the initiative offers too much possibility of abuse and is morally wrong. Supporters believe that the initiative provides dying persons more protection than they have now, and that in situations where life is coming to an inevitable end, the patient in consultation with physicians should have the right to terminate a prolonged period of acute distress. This initiative poses new ethical questions for health care and society and needs to be carefully studied. I personally believe we ought to permit dying people the right to exercise their own choice for a humane and dignified death and trust physicians to act responsibly in this process. Prolonging life through heroic measures, when true life is no longer possible, works against a God who has designed a closure for all of us.

On October 30, 1991 he wrote:

Initiative 119 is known as the "Death With Dignity" measure. Controversy over this initiative centers on a provision that would allow terminally ill patients the right to request a physician's aid in dying. This would allow for more than just removal life support systems; the new law would allow physicians to provide information, supplies, and even medical services for helping a patient die. This turns the final decisions of death over to the patient, which is where it really belongs. I have supported the initiative since its inception. Medical science has made great gains in helping us live longer, often extending life beyond a place of meaning or usefulness. People who are opposed to this initiative have every right not to request aid in dying, if the measure is passed, and doctors can decide for themselves whether to be involved. But we should not deny the terminally ill person the right to have control over his or her death. That, it seems to me, can also be a celebration of life, since our Judeo-Christian belief system has long advanced the notion that death is the doorway to a fuller life and as much a part of God's plan as birth.

## THE BAPTIST GENERAL CONFERENCE

The Baptist General Conference is defined by Donald E. Anderson, Editor of *The Standard*, as a "fellowship of 800 autonomous Baptist churches, and each church is free to adopt a statement on euthanasia or on other questions." He pointed that "the Baptist General Conference is middle-of-the-road evangelical.

> Hence we believe in the creation of the soul by God, in the conscious afterlife, either in heaven or hell, and in divine judgement. Euthanasia (especially active) is probably considered a sin by most of our people. Sin will be judged by God; euthanasia does not affect the destiny of the soul of the patient or of the one participating in the act. . . .
>
> Counseling regarding passive euthanasia is prepared by our ministers, not by our denominational headquarters. The same is true with regards to content of counseling on active euthanasia. Our ministers would probably be reluctant to encourage participation in active euthanasia, and may be more open to participation in passive euthanasia.

An article by Dr. Robert V. Rakestraw, Associate Professor of Theology at Bethel Seminary, St. Paul, Minnesota (the BGC Seminary) entitled "When Does Death Come?" was published in *The Standard*, November, 1991. Professor Rakestraw referred to Nancy Cruzan who had been in a persistent vegetative state (PVS) for nearly eight years before the nutrition and hydration feeding tubes were removed and she was permitted to die in December, 1990. He wrote:

> Concerning the morality of withdrawing the mechanical feeding, two main positions have emerged, even within the evangelical Christian community.
>
> Typical of the one side is Rev. Joseph Foreman of Atlanta, a founder of the antiabortion group Operation Rescue. Foreman called Cruzan's death a tragedy. "I think in the next few years you will see an entire industry spring up around putting people to death whom family, friends and so forth have deemed to be no longer of use to anybody," he said. "There will be wings of hospitals devoted to putting people to death like this." This side considers Nancy Cruzan's death a case of euthanasia, and morally wrong.
>
> Typical of the other side is Kenneth Schemmer, a surgeon in Orange County, California, and a member of First Evangelical Free Church of Fullerton. A physician for twenty-five years, Schemmer stated his opinion before the Supreme Court

heard the case. He argued that the Court "should allow Nancy Cruzan's living corpse to die."

In Schemmer's view, "Nancy actually died on January 11, 1983, of anoxia," as the result of her car accident which produced cardio-respiratory arrest. Because Nancy's cerebral cortex—the seat of consciousness, reasoning, value decisions, and everything else we associate with personality—was so severely damaged that it no longer functions, only her living "animal" body remains. Her "mammalian body" should be allowed to die.

What is a proper Christian response to the issue of the PVS? Specifically, should Christians ever request the withdrawal of fluid and nutrition from individuals in this condition? According to the American Medical Association there are an estimated 10,000 PVS patients in the United States.

To disconnect food and water from those in the PVS will almost certainly result in dehydration and starvation within seven to fourteen days. To continue to supply food and water will ensure the maintenance of bodily processes for a time, often for years (the longest PVS case on record is thirty-seven years), but will almost certainly not lead to improvement in the patient.

Although much has been written on the PVS, there is little from a distinctly Christian view point. The purpose of this article is to examine the ethical question of withdrawing fluid and nutrition from the PVS patients, and to offer an answer consistent with a strong pro-life view, a high view of Scripture, and the medical realities of the situation.

Dr. Rakestraw then pointed out the importance of defining death:

We must next attempt to define death. Much of the argument over the withdrawal of artificial feeding revolves around the question of whether or not PVS patients are alive or in some sense "dead." Schemmer holds that Nancy Cruzan actually died in 1983. Others, such as Rita L. Marker, director of the International Anti-Euthanasia Task Force, have argued that Cruzan was alive.

Setting aside the specific case of Nancy Cruzan, in what sense can it be said that PVS individuals, correctly diagnosed as such, are dead? How do we know when death has come? If we can determine that the PVS individual is dead, then we need not hesitate to withdraw food and water. If, on the other hand, the patient is alive, we must not take his or her life.

Several concepts of death have been proposed. The permanent failure of heart and lungs traditionally has been understood to constitute death, but with the modern use of the respirator and other life-extending medical technologies, this concept of death is not always adequate.

In certain situations one's breathing (and, therefore, one's heartbeat) may indeed cease permanently without a respirator within a few minutes, but with the machine the person may be alive indefinitely.

Brain death (sometimes called "whole-brain death") is another understanding of death. With this concept, the brainstem (which controls breathing and the rate of the heartbeat) and the rest of the brain are destroyed. There is the irreversible loss of the capacity for both bodily integration and social interaction.

When brain death occurs, all other organ systems fail within days. It is not possible to keep the body alive indefinitely with machines in cases of brain death. No one with brain death—correctly diagnosed as such—has ever survived.

Practically all Christians agree that when brain death has occurred, whatever machines have been used to keep the body functioning may be disconnected. The "person" or "spirit" is clearly gone from the body even though the organ systems may be sustained artificially for several days after brain death. Thus, when brain death has occurred, it is correct to say "death" has occurred.

However, while whole brain death is a sufficient condition for declaring someone dead, is it a necessary condition? To be declared dead, is it necessary for all those with severe brain trauma to have lost the capacity for bodily integration and functioning, as well as the capacity for self-awareness and social interaction?

This leads to a third category—the most controversial—in seeking to define death.

Neocortical death (also called "cerebral death" or "higher brain death") has been described above under the definition of PVS. Because the neocortex appears to be the biological precondition for consciousness and self-awareness, when it is destroyed the basis for personal life is gone.

This concept of death differs from the previous category by accepting the permanent loss of the capacity for self-awareness, cognition, and social interaction, but not necessarily the loss of all bodily functioning, as signifying death of the person. Robert Veatch, director of the Kennedy Institute of Ethics at Georgetown University, has argued for neocortical death as an acceptable concept of death. Schemmer agrees with this conclusion.

While there is no uniform definition of death (and the diagnosis is still left to the judgment of the physician) the most widely accepted scientific definitions of death include the permanent loss of organ system integration, as well as the permanent loss of consciousness and the capacity for social interaction.

It would thus be unwise to try to redefine death scientifically. There is clearly a difference between a corpse and a PVS individual (no one advocates burying the PVS patient).

As Christians, however, we are not limited to scientific opinion in ethical decision-making. While we must not ignore valid scientific findings, we must consider scriptural revelation in formulating ethical judgments.

Does neocortical death constitute the death of the person theologically, even though it is not death of the body physiologically? This depends on how we understand the term "person." Although the Bible does not provide a definition of person, Christian ethicists are compelled to offer some definition because of the frequent use of the term in bioethics, sometimes in ways hostile to Christian positions.

In seeking to understand personhood and humanness, the key scriptural concept is undoubtedly the "image of God." The fact that human beings are made in (or as) the image of God is given as the reason they have rights of personhood. . . .

This pushes the issue back one question further: What is the image of God? Theologians have debated the matter exhaustively, and three main schools of thought may be identified.

The most common view is that the image is some inherent characteristic or characteristics—physical, psychological, or spiritual—within human nature, such as reason, self-consciousness, or self-determination (will). This position has been referred to as the substantive or structural view, and is based in part upon the marked innate difference between the animals and human beings (Gen. 1:24-28).

The relational view sees the image not as some quality within human nature itself but as the experiencing of relationships, either between oneself and God or between human beings. The relationship itself is the image of God. Some supporters of this view point to Genesis 1:26-27, where the male-female relationship is mentioned in close connection with creation in God's image, as if to mirror the internal communion within the Godhead.

A third position is the functional view, which maintains that the image of God is something that human beings do, not something they possess or something they experience. The function most commonly suggested is rulership or dominion over creation since this service is tied closely to the decision of God to create humans in His image (Gen. 1:26), and is repeated just after their creation (Gen. 1:27-28).

None of these views should be considered as totally without foundation, nor is it necessary to define the image in terms of only one view. A composite understanding of the image, incorporating each position, is not only possible but reasonable and harmonious with Scripture. . . .

We can propose, then, that to be "in the image of God" means that we exist as the representatives of God on earth, with certain inherent qualities and capacities, so we may experience vital relationships with God and others, and so we may exercise dominion over the earth.

As we study the Scriptures on the image of God concept, we find that to be the representatives of God on earth presupposes some capacity, either actual or potential, for self-awareness and self-direction, for relationships, and for the exercise of authority over creation.

Given this understanding of the image concept, we may now attempt a definition of the term "person." A human person is a unique individual, made as God's image, known and cared for by God at every stage of life, with the actual ability or potential to be aware of oneself, and to relate in some way to one's environment, to other human beings, and to God.

The earthly life of a person thus begins at conception and ends when this ability or potential ceases. . . .

It appears, then, that neocortical death equals the end of personal life. The PVS individual—correctly diagnosed as such—is a body of organs and systems, artificially sustained, without the personal human spirit that once enabled this body-soul unity to represent God on earth. . . .

What is essential about humanness, namely, the capacity to image God, is irreversibly gone. Neither the ability nor the potential to live as the personal representative of Another is any longer present in the physical remains of the person. For this reason, the discontinuance of nutrition and hydration appears to be justified. The Christian, then, has a theological basis for distinguishing between the death of the body, with its residual movements, and the death of the person.

The human body always must be respected—in death and dying as well as in life—because the person who was, while on earth, the image of God functioned as God's representative through that body. But the prolongation of biological life in the apparent absence of personal life is not mandated by the Christian principle of respect for life.

Because equipment is available to feed a body does not mean that it should always be used. Some who oppose withdrawal of artificial feeding tubes are unwilling to have such devices connected to themselves or their loved ones in the first place, if their prognosis should be for a prolonged and permanent vegetative state.

This unwillingness to connect feeding devices reveals that such persons actually agree that whatever may be used to prolong bodily existence is not always morally obligatory. If it were obligatory, no upright person should ever hesitate to connect artificial feeding equipment to a loved one who would, by this means, be enabled to live possibly many more years, if only in a vegetative state.

In Christian ethics one's intention is always a key factor in determining the morality of a given action. To disconnect the feeding tube from a PVS individual must never be done with the intention to kill—to take a person's life. Our attitude should be that of turning the individual over to God's providence, allowing the condition to take its course.

Yet—as with many conditions judged "hopeless" by human standards—we may hope beyond all reason for hope that God will yet quicken the loved one, if that would honor Him and be best for the patient. The position presented here is not euthanasia, which I oppose in either its "active" or "passive" forms.

We should be foolish to deny that there is some risk of error in bioethical decision-making. Our admittedly difficult but not (by God's grace) impossible task is to avoid the extremes of an excessive devotion to biological existence as the highest of all values, and the disrespect for human life that discards anyone—in the womb, newly born, or elderly—who does not measure up to an arbitrarily established level of intelligence or value to society.

Wisdom calls us to err on the side of keeping someone physically alive when the spirit may be gone, rather than risk killing a person. But if the PVS condition can be shown to be total and irreversible, and if the loss of personhood can be considered death in a theological sense, there appears to be strong support for disconnecting artificial feeding.

Those who intend to keep their PVS loved ones sustained by mechanical means are making one choice, and it should be respected. Similarly, those who, after prayerful and careful reflection upon the issues in the light of Scripture, in keeping with the law, decide to withdraw nutrition and hydration are making another choice. This, too, should be respected.

## THE GENERAL ASSOCIATION OF GENERAL BAPTISTS

Dr. Glen O. Spence, Denominational Executive Director, shared a copy of the denominational booklet "The Social Principles of General Baptists." The section on "Termination of Life" reads as follows:

Termination of Life: We believe life and death belong in the hands of God. Regardless of circumstances that befall man, he must know that God gave him existence and He holds him responsible for his stewardship of life. We are thankful to medical science for efforts and accomplishments made in preventing disease and illness and for the great advances in treatment which extend the life and usefulness of those affected. It is of deep Christian concern, however, when people suffer from incurable diseases to the point where the wisdom of God is questioned in continuing life. Questions arise as to whether a person has the right to die if it means release from suffering. The deliberate termination of life is a serious concern, whether it be done by the person himself, a friend, or the physician. We oppose euthanasia, sometimes referred to as mercy killing. We feel the answer is to be found in faith, endurance, and communication with God. We endorse the removal of pain by the use of drugs, even though consciousness may be lost because of it. We affirm the right of every person to die with dignity. We reject efforts made to prolong terminal illnesses merely because the technology is available to do so. At the same time we endorse the work and discoveries made by medical science through scientific experimentation based upon accepted procedures. However, the physician has the responsibility to insure that every precaution is taken so the patient is in no way victimized by such experimentation or its products.

## OTHER DENOMINATIONS

According to the Rev. W.P. Bauman, the Association of Regular Baptists (Canada) "have no governing body which speaks as a denomination. Each Baptist church is autonomous. It is possible for a Convention of Baptist Churches to pronounce on an issue but that would only be for that particular group of Baptists. If I may speak for our group, even though we have never entertained discussion on the topic, it would be fair to say that we take the position that life is a gift from God and we must do all to sustain that life until God is pleased to take it. However, we would not favour the prolonging of life unduly by artificial means."

The Rev. Leon Maltby, Chairman of the Christian Social Action Committee of the Seventh Day Baptist General Convention, wrote: "To the best of my knowledge euthanasia has not come up for serious study by our committee nor have there been conference pronouncements on the subject." He suggests that the reason the subject has not been discussed is that "practically none of our people favor it. It is too 'far out' to be seriously considered by Christians of the Seventh Day Baptist variety. We believe, I think, that only non-Christians favor it. If there is a real danger that the idea is gaining momentum and is likely to become prevalent, then we, as SDB's, should join with others in opposing it."

Mr. Maltby indicated that it would be difficult to respond on behalf of his denomination to the questionnaire: "Ours is a democratic (congregational) denomination. It is hard to get consensus on hard questions in one church, much less in all."

## THE SOUTHERN BAPTIST CHURCHES

From time to time statements are adopted at Southern Baptist Conventions that represent a general consensus on an issue. However, because each Southern Baptist Church constitutes an independent unit, these faith statements need not be binding upon members. This position is made clear in a tract published by the Sunday School Board and the Southern Baptist Convention titled "The Baptist Faith and Message":

> Such statements have never been regarded as complete, infallible statements of faith, nor as official creeds carrying mandatory authority. Thus this generation of Southern Baptists is in historic succession of intent and purpose as it endeavors to state for its time and theological climate those articles of the Christian faith which are most surely held among us.
>
> Baptists emphasize the soul's competency before God, freedom in religion, and the priesthood of the believer. However, this emphasis should not be interpreted to mean that there is an absence of certain definite doctrines that Baptists believe, cherish, and with which they have been and are now closely identified.

Dr. C. Ben Mitchell, Director of Biomedical and Life Issues for the Christian Life Commission of the Southern Baptist Convention, wrote:

> While I am not aware of any resolutions on euthanasia *per se*, Southern Baptists have expressed their general view on the issue. Nearly every year in the past decade Southern Baptists have affirmed their strong belief in the sanctity of human life. In a resolution passed at the convention in San Antonio, Texas, June 14-16, 1988, the "messengers" (the official designation for those who attend) affirmed that, "Human life, from fertilization until natural death, is sacred and should be pro-

tected, not destroyed." Furthermore, at that same convention, the messengers affirmed,

We recognize the validity of living wills and organ donor cards, along with the right of next of kin to make decisions regarding organ donations; and . . . that nothing in the resolution be construed to condone euthanasia, infanticide, abortion, or harvesting of fetal tissue for the procurement of organs.

The Christian Life Commission recently has published literature which is in keeping with a very strong sanctity of life or pro-life position. Our literature has been very well received by the vast majority of Southern Baptists and many pro-life non-Southern Baptists.

Our trustees, who give policy direction to our agency, have expressed their view on euthanasia in the following policy, "Efforts shall be undertaken by the Christian Life Commission staff to oppose infanticide and active euthanasia, including efforts to discourage any designation of food and/or water as 'extraordinary' medical care for some patients" (Christian Life Commission Annual Minutes, September 16, 1987, p.40).

We are in the process of producing materials on advance medical directives and living wills. . . .

In brief, I think you will find that the Christian Life Commission stands at the very heart of Southern Baptist life and thought. The majority of Southern Baptists are pro-life and are opposed to active euthanasia and doctor-assisted suicide.

The "Sanctity of Life" principle which is central in Southern Baptist discussions of abortion also impacts on the approach to euthanasia. In a publication titled "Sanctity of Human Life" published in 1991 by the Christian Life Commission, Dr. Richard D. Land, the Executive Director, has commented on the concept:

The phrase, Sanctity of Human Life, encompasses a host of issues—abortion, infanticide, Mercy-killing, "assisted" suicide, genetic engineering, fetal tissues experimentation—that have, or will, impact the life of every American. To believe in the sanctity of human life is to understand that God created human beings "in his own image" (Gen. 1:26), thus imparting to them a special sanctity, unique among all created life. The belief that life is sacred has serious personal, spiritual, moral, ethical, medical and legislative implications for all "life" issues. . . .

It was inevitable from the beginning that it would become a womb-to-tomb debate. Human life is now under relentless assault in our culture, from conception to natural death and everywhere in between. The debate has moved to the nursery where parents have been granted the legal right, as in Baby Doe case, to allow their child to die because he was mentally handicapped.

The debate also now includes the nursing home and the intensive care unit. As we witness our courts defining the administration of food and water to unconscious patients as "extraordinary" medical means which may be withheld in certain circumstances, and as we hear on the evening news the controversy over mercy-killing and assisted suicide, we see the consequences of the lethal quality-of-life ethic's assault on human life and its sanctity.

At the March, 1989 Christian Life Commission Seminar on "Life in the Balance" held in Kansas City, Missouri, Dr. Thomas B. Elkins, Professor of Medical Ethics at the University of Michigan Medical School in Ann Arbor, Michigan, presented a paper entitled "Ethics at the Edges of Life—Euthanasia." His paper has been published by the Christian Life Commission in the Seminar Proceedings "Life in the Balance." Professor Elkins discussed his observations as a member of the American Academy of Pediatrics Task Force (1983-1984) which looked at establishing a Bioethics Committee in hospitals to try to deal with ethical issues regarding euthanasia and newborns in the hospital nursery setting. He commented on the difficulties inherent in decision making and noted that the group tended to divide into "six or seven camps":

> One was the sanctity of life group. I think some of you feel very close to that organization that we call pro-life organizations today. I have sensed that throughout this meeting, and that certainly was one very forceful comment in all of the Baby Doe discussions of those organizations which urged treatment in every situation to maintain life at all costs.
>
> The next level in the argument was termed the relative sanctity of life group; that was our federal government stance that basically said we should be for life; protecting life; pro-

longing life unless it is futile; unless we are simply prolonging dying and it is, therefore, inhumane to continue; or unless death is imminent, and we are simply interrupting it for a brief period of time.

Then there was another level of concern, and that was termed "the best interest of the patient." This was held by the American Academy of Pediatrics. They looked upon each one of these situations as a time for there to be discussion about what would really be in the best interest of the handicapped newborn. That would separate them on occasion from the federal government and would place the decision-making more in the hands of the physician than what the federal government perhaps thought would be reasonable.

The next level was a concern for our burdens versus benefits. This was a fascinating concern because it entailed what would happen to the family more than the other concerns. It dropped back repeatedly to say, "This should be a family decision, and when a newborn with a severe handicap comes into a family, everyone else should back away and let the family decide." There was a problem with that. They never asked "us families" because those of us who had been in that situation realized very plainly that the grief that occurs when that anticipated, glorious, wonderful birth of a "normal" child does not happen, it prevents families from being bonded decision-makers. If anything, at that point in time, you want to back away. You want to find a quick solution to a sudden problem you didn't expect. You want help in any fashion. Sometimes you want to scream out with sorrow and agony and pain because that anticipated healthy child for whom you have brought gifts, for whom you've prepared a room, for whom grandparents are standing around waiting is not there, and instead, there is another child that right now you don't understand. The burdens-versus-benefits view said, "Let's let those families make the decision." But they hadn't asked those families. We in the National Down's Syndrome Congress who make up such families were very opposed to that view and stood in very strong opposition to it, and that is not the final view that has come about in the Baby Doe discussions.

Then there was another level of concern—a quality of life concern in which we were supposed to be interested as physicians. This came especially from the corner of the analytic philosophers. What is perhaps the classic story of the quality of life view takes us back to the University of Oklahoma and their quantitative way of trying to decide which newborns with meningomyelocele or spina bifida should be treated and nontreated. It all seemed very easy. It is easy for us to tabulate burdens in our society. We can put dollar signs on it. We can put all types of philosophic and psychologic quantitation on it. We can decide how much suffering we're going to have, and we can attach a number to it. We can talk about how much a community has available for special education needs, for needs of a handicapped person as they live and grow in a community, and we can attach a number to that.

In Oklahoma they had actually done this in a formula. The problem with formulas when used in conjunction with a utilitarian stance is that it occasionally overlooks individuals. So at the end of their program, which they boldly published about this time, they found out they were not overwhelmingly accepted in our society, but instead were harshly criticized. Some of the infants born with similar medical conditions were treated differently because of someone's quantitation of what a guess of quality of life would be—not a respect for life, but the quality of life. They went ahead and treated in different ways, hoping that one would die and one would live. Then as the Lord would always have it when we contrive things so carefully, He makes us fumble, stumble, and fall, and those who were supposed to die did not die but lived, and tragically lived damaged and in all sorts of poor quality of life ways that no one had anticipated. That program is still under discussion, and it will continue to be, but it scared all of us about quality of life normative values in terms of making decisions for any handicapped newborn in terms of ever thinking of euthanasia.

Then there was an economic utility view. This comes from those who point out to us at this point in time, especially for the very low-birth-weight infants, that there are those who will not have difficulty and will go ahead to become productive members of society, and when the balance sheet is all made at the end of life, will come out showing a dollar-sign value that they gave back to society rather than a negative value for having cost too much. It is amazing to watch this kind of thinking and process, and it is going on right now. We recently received a bulletin in medicine from Washington where this thinking is being put into place and where people are actually looking at the dollar value of very low-birth-weight infants, trying to give us guidance as to who we should treat aggressively, both in utero and just out of the uterus and where we should back off according to an economic end point.

Finally, there is the autonomy extreme that said that each individual mom, dad, or physician should be allowed to do whatever they want to do according to their setting, according to their hospital, and according to their community, and that everyone else should back away.

There was a pseudo victory that occurred over these Baby Doe discussions after all of these things were sorted out and after these positions were made clear, usually in multiple courtroom hearings. There was legislation that was passed by a 92-0 vote in the Senate that gave a welcoming hand to handicapped newborns in our society. This legislation said that treatment must be given unless it would be futile, or given only in the face of imminent death simply to prolong death (not life) which would thus appear inhumane. Furthermore, each state was to draw up a plan for reporting nontreatment cases to child abuse and neglect authorities, and Infant Care Review Committee systems were to be recommended to be used in large hospitals.

A lot of things happened, and on the surface it looked very good; however, some states such as California never got around to putting into effect any plans for reporting any problem cases, and at this point in time are openly standing in disobedience of what the federal legislation has required. . . .

Mandatory review was seen as another suspicious glance at the medical profession by most doctors—and I can tell you right now we are weary of that. We have been sued enough, and we are weary of you as a society. I can tell you that very plainly. So mandatory review to doctors meant just more people looking at them with a jaundiced eye. They missed the point of what mandatory review was all about.

There is an understanding that there must be more to the decision-making about euthanasia than a concern for physician or family welfare. It is an understanding that would require a knowledge of unconditional love, unmerited favor—what many of you theologians here today refer to as grace. . . .

It is a personal view of Matthew 25 that is required, and that's what mandatory review said—that there is a value in that handicapped life and that you cannot do away with it without distinct mandatory review of that life before the decision is ever made to stop a respirator or to stop that life. We can talk about burdens of handicapped people, but it is tough to talk about benefits, and it is hard to look at what it really means for us to welcome the handicapped person into our society.

As we look ahead, it is time for us to look also at what is happening with euthanasia in the elderly or the terminally ill patients in our society. We are in a time of change in process in the Baby Doe settings in the nursery, but what is happening in the older age group in our country today? There are some facts that underlie the current cry for euthanasia in our society. Over sixty percent of all medical dollars are spent on the first year and the last year of life, and the cost of health care has become higher than any of us ever dreamed. Technology has advanced from what was once "extraordinary" care, to become "ordinary" care in most centers in our country, such as a respirator in a newborn nursery. We can now do many great, wonderful, and tragic things to keep a body alive. Some say that over forty percent of our population may be over the age of 65 by the year 2020.

All of this concern stated about euthanasia with debates over what is extraordinary versus ordinary, and then overly burdensome versus routine care. It went from respirator usage to the concept of feeding tubes, from a concern over passive euthanasia to concern over active euthanasia. . . .

In every setting, our courts have spelled out reasons to withdraw tube feeding, to withdraw simple hydration and nutrition from patients who perhaps, as some authors have said, represent the wounded in our society. Our withdrawal of care from them may honestly be representing our inability to show love and concern till life's end point does come. We say "Well what about the Harvard brain death criteria? We thought that cleared it all up—that when you have flat EEG's, everything can stop and everybody agrees with that, and that is fine." The criteria leaves a tremendous number of people in what we would call a vegetative state today, and that is where the concern is coming in our country.

In some articles recently published, it seems that these patients are requesting this when terminal illness arises and is accompanied by such things as loss of strength, fatigue, pain, shortness of breath, incontinence, nausea and vomiting, sleeplessness, salivation, thirst, bed sores, itching that is intractable, coughing that is intractable or intractable hiccuping. We're seeing people who are looking at the end of life and are saying, "I don't want to go through this," and we're seeing a medical profession again responding as we have done in our own country in the past in ways that seem simple and quick. But perhaps underneath those simple, quick solutions should be the concern of a Christian community that says something about withdrawing of the very basics of care for one another may not always be a reasonable response.

I see this though as a time of interest in our society when there was an article written in the *Journal of the American Medical Association* during this past year in 1988 entitled "It's Over, Debbie." There was a great outcry. As a Christian physician, I see that as something wholesome and good. The article described a resident who was on call in the middle of the night seeing a young person in a great deal of pain and distress who was dying of ovarian cancer. The resident made the unilateral decision without consultation with anyone else or any type of process of decision-making to waltz back into that room and to give the patient a lethal dose of morphine. The fact that this article brought about a tremendous outcry from the medical community in America says that our country, even the nontheologically based among us, is not prepared for that kind of activity in our society. That outcry of physicians simply says to us that it is a time and opening for us as Christians to offer guidance in the area of euthanasia.

We must ask ourselves where the church is in the hospice movement in our society, and where the church is in helping AIDS patients live through their deaths. . . . Even in our own foreign missions among Southern Baptists, we must ask ourselves some hard questions. We have made a decision to prioritize money "for God" while we have put a lid on social spending in many of our areas of medical mission involvement worldwide. This is fine in areas of the world where governments can provide at least something to hungry, diseased, and suffering humanity, but I can take you to Baptist medical mission hospitals in African that offer the only health care to hundreds of thousands of people for hundreds of miles which are facing closure because of reprioritizing of funds by the Southern Baptist Convention in the name of evangelism "for God." There "euthanasia" will become common. Someone will look at you and you'll see the face of Christ whispering the word, "corban." So, I would suggest that we heed some of these concerns with a bit of warning as we jump into these issues. I am not saying don't be loud and forceful, but I am saying be cautious and reasonable as well. . . .

The time is right for a Christian voice to step into our society in a reasonable way. The Christian Life Commission can be that voice. The teaching of ethics is now for the first year being mandated in obstetrics and gynecology residencies throughout our country by the American Professors of Gynecology and Obstetrics in their board review or testing system. The time is right. . . .

You ask me about euthanasia, and I ask you about life. Our attitude about euthanasia is tied directly to our understanding of God and to our understanding of life. It is not tied to our understanding of death.

William M. Tillman who teaches at the Southwestern Baptist Technological Seminary in Fort Worth, Texas, commented on "Sanctity of Life - Quality of Life" in a chapter entitled "Behold a Pale Horse" in *Christian Ethics: A Primer* by William M. Tillman with Timothy D. Gilbert (Nashville: Broadman Press, 1986). He wrote:

These two concepts form the end points of a line. Between these two points, Christian decision making on issues of life and death is made.

From the sanctity of life perspective, life is seen as a sacred trust and a gift from the living God (Deut. 5:26; Josh. 3:10; Matt. 16:16; John 5:26). Genesis 2:7 says, "Then the Lord God formed man of the dust from the ground, and breathed into his nostrils the breath of life; and man became a living being."

Life is only once given and is irreplaceable. To throw it away or have it taken away would reflect improper stewardship of this God-given gift. . . .

Looking at the other end of the spectrum, the quality of

life perspective emphasizes the fullness of life. From this perspective, death is not the ultimate tragedy. Instead, purpose and direction of life become important.

When one is related to God, one's life is characterized by a better quality of living than when one is not related to God. This quality is not necessarily identified with financial blessing, although it could be. Rather, it is a quality of life where one's source of hope, faith, and reason for being is centered in God. . . .

For the most part, euthanasia has become an increasingly important issue because of medical technology. Patients can now be maintained well past what could have been considered permanent death. Now, *clinical* death (cessation of heartbeat and respiration) can be reversed. Most physicians now use brain wave reading as a means of determining irreversibility in the death process. Also, technology has provided pain-killing remedies to aid some terminal cancer patients.

As with all these bioethical issues considered, certain questions need to be asked for one to arrive at some moral conclusion. Does an individual or his family have the right to choose the when and how of his death? How much pain should one suffer? How much medical prolongation of existence should one or one's family endure?

This should cause us to reflect upon our cultural attitude toward death and dying. How does one prepare to meet death or live life in light of an inevitable death? . . .

Issues of life and death are so full of emotional overtones, of interplay, of moral values, and vagueness that it is difficult to grapple with them.

Most of them take us to the edge of our biblical, theological, and ethical understanding and ability. But, none of these hard things should be allowed to prevent us from using all the clarity and precision we can in dealing with them. Increasingly, it will be seen that this area of issues interlocking with the larger ones of family relations, citizenship, human relations, and economics is our ethical frontier.

In a chapter titled "Issues of Life and Death" in *Understanding Christian Ethics* edited by William E. Tillman (Nashville: Broadman Press, 1988), Dr. Daniel B. McGee wrote:

The Christian does not value human life because of qualities that humans possess. Human beings are valued simply because we are objects of God's love. Beginning at this point precludes the use of a definition of human life to determine who is more or less valuable. Rather, the purpose here is to identify the essential aspects of the human experience that we should seek to protect and enhance. If we love human lives as God does, what are the qualities or aspects of those lives that we are to guard and strengthen?

At the heart of any biblical view of human life must be the affirmation that our physical existence is an essential part of our being. Dualism makes a radical distinction between physical and spiritual aspects of human life. Dualism claims that the essence of any human life is some kind of nonphysical reality called soul or spirit.

The biblical perspective is very different and is usually called a holistic view. This outlook is reflected in Genesis 2:7 where God created a body from the ground, breathed life into the body, and it became a living soul or being. The human soul or being incorporates the living body. There is no radical division between body and spirit. The human is more than body.

A second essential element of human life is autonomy. A special feature of our existence that sets human life apart from the rest of creation is God's gift of His *own* image (Gen. 1:27). God gives human beings the ability to will and to decide, to say no even to God. In Christian history this capacity has often been referred to as freedom of the will.

Modern medicine imposes many powerful controls upon lives. The strength and frequency of these controls threaten the autonomy or freedom of everyone. At every turn, we seem threatened with the loss of personal control over our lives. Those who take seriously the Christian view that autonomy is a God-given capacity in every human life will protect that gift within this environment of control.

The biblical story of humanity not only points to human autonomy but also to human sociality. We are communal beings, created by God in such a way that each of us does not realize his or her full humanity except in fellowship with others. We become fully human only through the communities that nurture and enrich our individual lives. This sense of the communal nature of humanity is seen in the creation account in Genesis 2:21-25. By himself, Adam was incomplete. By nature, we are social and possess a need for community. If I say that I love human life, I will be committed to promoting that which unites people.

Dr. McGee commented on the problems associated with the human ability to control death. He stated:

No aspect of the human experience may be more provocative and compelling than death: It is inevitable, intimate, and mysterious. It forces us to deal with the most basic religious and ethical issues of the human experience.

Recent developments in controlling the end of life are forcing a reassessment of our attitudes and practices regarding death. Modern medicine has decreased the frequency of death from infectious diseases and, consequently, increased the frequency with which we die from senility and degenerative diseases. The result is that dying is increasingly a prolonged and torturous experience. As our capacity to control has increased, so has the necessity for assessment and reevaluation.

*General Assessment of Death.* In contemporary American culture, two attitudes toward death are held. One attitude essentially views death as the denial of life and all the values associated with human life. Death is the ultimate enemy of human life—to be avoided at all cost. From this perspective, nothing is worse than death: It is to be feared and prevented if at all possible.

In recent years people have reacted against this denial of death. Led by the writings of Elisabeth Kubler-Ross, an alternative view of death has become popular. Here, death is viewed as a natural event in the life cycle. Death is not to be greatly feared or shunned, but is to be accepted. Supportive of this sentiment is the life-after-life movement that seeks to prove scientifically that there is a meaningful existence beyond death.

Although dimensions of a Christian view of death may be found in both of these views, neither is on target in portraying a Christian view of death as seen from the resurrection. The Christian understanding of death involves both the cross and the resurrection. The cross affirms that death is cruel and shattering. It is not a masquerade that just appears to be tragic. The Christian answer to this destructive power of death is not denial, but resurrection. The resurrection event does not disguise or belittle death. It overcomes death. The Christian gospel claims that death is not unreal, but that God's loving power overcomes even the disaster of death. When seen from this perspective, death is not merely a "bump in life's road;" neither is it an ultimate calamity beyond which all is lost. Rather, it is seen as a tragedy that is overcome through God's loving sovereignty.

In commenting on euthanasia, Dr. McGee wrote:

Even though much progress has been made in controlling pain, people frequently face prolonged and intractable pain. Those who would choose death argue that suffering is at least useless and more commonly destructive of human life and values. Suffering robs its victims of joy and affirmation and turns life into an endurance race that cannot be won.

The alternative perspective contends that death is the only enemy. Suffering is a part of life and must be accepted. Indeed, suffering can be a source of meaning and strength, if the sufferer will have faith and will endure. The sufferer's character can be strengthened, and he can be an example of faith and hope to others.

Though the choice between death and suffering has a long history, new medical technologies have multiplied the options. Many times today suffering is not the issue; the issue is the choice between death and a demeaning or useless existence.

In the Karen Ann Quinlan case, the accounts often focused on a shriveled body drawn into a fetal position, hardly recognizable as the young woman of just a few months earlier. Alzheimer cases present a body and mind that have been ravaged by a disease that turns the patient into a shell of his or her former self. While the victim may not experience great pain, this condition is an affront to the memory of the formerly active and vital person. Many claim such continued existence repudiates human life. In such cases it is argued that the value of human life is better served by choosing death over demeaning existence.

These appeals are variations on the "quality-of-life" argument. In every case the central question is whether losing a certain quality of life justifies choosing death. Is existence, per se, worth having without those qualities? . . .

When choosing between death and one of these conditions of life, two competing value traditions influence us. One tradition very prominent in American culture places the highest value on the autonomy and freedom of individuals. To deprive someone of her right of self-control is to deprive that individual of the most precious of human possessions. The final expression of this freedom is the right to choose death is life is no longer tolerable or meaningful.

The other value tradition focuses not on the value of freedom, but on the value of life (i.e., the very condition of existence). Sometimes this position is supported by the theological claim that no one owns her own life. God owns each of us, and God alone decides when each would die. The emphasis is not on human freedom, but on the value of life and a power beyond us that affirms life. Thus, a life is to be preserved no matter what qualities may have been lost and no matter what the individual may personally desire. No one should choose against life. . . .

Some contend that there is no moral difference between active and passive euthanasia because the intent and result in both cases are the same. Nevertheless, on the American scene a clear precedent has been set in distinguishing between active and passive euthanasia in certain cases. Those who have maintained the distinction typically argue that passive euthanasia can be justified in some cases but that active euthanasia can never be justified. Several factors make the difference.

For one thing, passive euthanasia guards against an incorrect diagnosis. If there is a mistake in diagnosing a person as terminal, then the policy of passive euthanasia will allow that one to live, while active euthanasia will have unnecessarily and tragically taken a life. Also, passive euthanasia is much easier to regulate. A system of laws that allowed active euthanasia would require widespread and vigorous control procedures. Finally, a basic ethical distinction is made between allowing and causing a result. Allowing a person to die when there is good reason to do so is cooperating with God and nature.

In 1978, the Trustees of the Christian Life Commission adopted a "firm policy" opposing abortion in which it was stated that "Human life, from fertilization until natural death, is sacred and should be protected and not destroyed." Resolution No. 15 which dealt with human organ donation concluded with this statement: "That nothing in the resolution be construed to condone euthanasia, infanticide, abortion, or the harvesting of fetal tissue for the procurement of organs."

The Summer 1977 issue of *Perspectives in Religious Studies* published by the Baptist Professors of Religion, Southern Baptist Theological Seminary, Louisville, Kentucky, ran an article titled, "Death with Dignity: Christians Confront Euthanasia." The article concludes with the following statement:

> One can expect that any conclusion reached on the subject of the Christian's confronting euthanasia will also entail a degree of ambiguity. While this may seem indecisive to some, it will have the salutary effect of not simplistically resolving a complicated matter. Several things can be said by way of conclusion. First, the right to die with dignity can be supported with equal vigor as the responsibility for the medical care of the ill. The wishes of those who desire not to be sustained beyond responsive personhood are to be respected as firmly as the wishes of those who wish to be sustained as long as medically possible.
>
> Second, those who elect by "direct and voluntary" means may be seen as acting in the context of the Christian freedom to choose the terms under which they are to die. Suicide of this type is hardly to be regarded as a sin for which there is no forgiveness. On the contrary, such a decision may be based upon a commitment to the truth that "whether we live or whether we die, we are the Lord's" (Rom. 14:8).
>
> Third, Christians may well work to mollify the legal penalties that may be imposed upon those who act decisively to relieve loved ones of unbearable suffering. At the same time, they will work diligently to assure that such decisions must not be borne by one isolated from the physical-family health care team. No one person should have to bear the mental and spiritual burden of deciding when a patient should be enabled to die.
>
> Finally, Christians should be actively engaged in the discussions of the issues involved in euthanasia. The debate be-

tween a "sanctity of life ethic" and a "quality of life ethic" raises substantive questions for Christian theology. The biblical witness sustains a great hope in life that cannot be simply identified with biological functions. It is in the context of that hope that all discussions of death must be placed. For, as the Apostle reminded his readers "If for this life only we have hoped in Christ, we are of all men most to be pitied" (I Cor.15:19).

In his essay on "Baptist-Evangelical Biomedical Ethics" in the *Bioethics Yearbook* (Kluwer 1991), Professor Simmons wrote (text references have been omitted):

Those most opposed to "euthanasia" do not deal with the issue. The morality of assisted dying is based on either the notion of whole brain death or the absence of neocortical function.

Evangelicals and Baptists are virtually unanimous in supporting the right to refuse treatment when death is imminent. Further, there is no moral obligation to sustain life artificially when there is no reasonable hope for recovery or the patient is comatose or might otherwise reasonably be considered dead.

Biblical perspectives on suffering and death are important for evangelicals in the euthanasia debate. Theologically, however, wide differences of opinion can be found. Some believe death is "unnatural" as the consequence of sin, while others hold that it is a creation of God, the experience of which has been tainted by sin. The notion of "death as evil" is paired with the belief in the sanctity of life. The moral mandate becomes a simple application—preserve life, defeat death.

A more nuanced view of the evil that may accompany the experience of death allows and requires a more critical struggle with the moral issue of whether people are simply to be passive in the face of death. It is difficult, if not impossible, to sustain either the notion of death as evil or the idea of the sanctity of life on biblical grounds. Using the latter to settle the questions posed by advancing medical technology and the maintenance of patients far beyond the point at which death would typically have come is terribly problematic.

Two critical moral questions need to be addressed. First, what are the biblical/theological grounds for the right to refuse treatment? Second, might it not be more morally responsible and loving to assist a patient's dying painlessly and quicker rather than to adopt the morality of passive waiting for death to happen "naturally?" On these questions the literature is sparse among evangelicals.

Biblical anthropology is at the heart of the debate about elective death. Anti-euthanasia evangelicals seem more concerned to constrain by law what they regard as the impulse to kill than to discover the moral imperative of love in exceptional and tragic circumstances. A strong case can be made on Scriptural grounds that being made *imago Dei* requires not only anticipating death but participating in decisions about dying. Knowing that death belongs to human finitude is linked to the anticipatory and reflective capacities of being human. Knowledge about the causes and processes of death and the ability to calculate the course of the dying process underscore the moral responsibility for acting on the basis of such knowledge. Advocating passivity toward whatever happens by disease, accident, or medical technology seems more fatalism than faith. The question on the moral frontier is whether the artful uses of medical science now should be used in assisting death. Whether such "killing" is a "countervailing requirement of agape" or a malevolence disguised as mercy will generate considerable debate.

The publication of *Final Exit* by Derek Humphry prompted a strong statement against active euthanasia by the Arkansas Baptist Convention which met in Geyer Springs, November, 1991.

Resolution No. 7: Euthanasia
WHEREAS, God is the author of life and that the life made in His image is sacred; and
WHEREAS, the philosophy that attempts to permit an individual to usurp God's authority in the realm of life and death by justifying the arbitrary taking of an innocent human life based on some nebulous quality of life determination is humanistic in its origin and evil in its essence; and
WHEREAS, *Final Exit*, a how to book on how to commit suicide or assist another in the taking of his or her life by use of certain pharmaceuticals, has recently become a *New York Times* book list best-seller; and

WHEREAS, the "right to die" movement is not so subtly being euthanasia; and

WHEREAS, the parameters of what is acceptable in administering active euthanasia are ever-increasing.

THEREFORE BE IT RESOLVED, that we, the messengers to the Arkansas Baptist State Convention, meeting at Geyer Springs First Baptist Church, November 19-20, 1991, uphold the sanctity of human life in all its various stages; and

THEREFORE BE IT FURTHER RESOLVED, that we stand in opposition to the growing dependence on active euthanasia based on humanistic, arbitrary quality of life decisions, which serve only to cut short an individual's life and usurp God's authority in the context of human life and death situations.

## THE FREEWILL BAPTIST CHURCH

Dr. Laverne D. Miley, M.D., who is Professor of Bible and Science in the Freewill Baptist College, Nashville, Tennessee, responded to the request for information. He provided a copy of a pamphlet titled "Euthanasia: Mercy or Murder?" which he had written in 1981. Dr. Miley noted that the contents could not be interpreted as an "official denominational position on the subject, but I do believe that it represents a consensus of opinion of our people."

At the time when he wrote the pamphlet, Dr. Miley strongly opposed the Living Will. He feared that should it become legally binding it might "authorize the murder of virtually anyone who made out the Will, then for some reason lost consciousness for a period of time, and would consequently be expected to be in some way incapacitated upon regaining consciousness." He went on to state "Those who make wills such as this in actuality become candidates for 'mercy killing,' or euthanasia." However, Dr. Miley has maintained an open mind. He has watched what has taken place during the past ten years and today writes: "My personal opinion concerning the Living Will has changed somewhat over the past years, my fear of its being abused has diminished, and I now accept it as a valid option."

In the last section of this pamphlet, which provides a brief overview of the history of euthanasia, Dr. Miley presents his opposition to euthanasia:

## The Christian Attitude Toward Euthanasia

As Christians what should be our attitude toward euthanasia, or "mercy killing" as some prefer to call it? Many Christians feel that they can justify capital punishment and killing in time of war on the basis of God's Holy Word. But is there Scriptural justification for euthanasia? Joseph Fletcher would say "yes" when euthanasia is an act of mercy, to end human suffering, for Jesus said, "Blessed are the merciful" (Matthew 5:7a). But is this a valid application of Scripture?

In Genesis 3:19, we read that God said to Adam after his sin in the garden of Eden, "Dust thou art, and unto dust shalt thou return." The writer of Ecclesiastes remarked that "To every thing there is a season, and a time to every purpose under the heaven: A time to be born, and a time to die" (Ecclesiastes 3:1, 2a). The writer of Hebrews makes an even stronger statement in saying that "it is appointed unto men once to die, but after this the judgment" (Hebrews 9:27). The question we must face is this: Who makes man's appointment with death? Does man have the right to do so for himself, or even for another? Or is this God's prerogative only? God has said to man: Thou shalt not kill (Exodus 20:13).

Time and again during Christ's earthly ministry He alleviated human suffering and misery—He made the blind to see, the deaf to hear, the lame to walk; yea, He even made the dead to rise and live again, physically. But never once did He inflict death, not even as an act of mercy. "In him was life" (John 1:4a).

Death is man's enemy. In fact the Apostle Paul says: "The last enemy that shall be destroyed is death" (1 Corinthians 15:26). But Christ experienced death for us and came forth from the grave victorious over it. So now we can cry out with the Apostle Paul: "O death, where is thy sting? O grave, where is they victory? . . . Thanks be to God which giveth us the victory through our Lord Jesus Christ" (1 Corinthians 15:55, 57). In God's appointed time, for the child of God, death becomes the doorway to Heaven. But let us remember, God appoints the time; He does not give man the privilege of doing so, either for himself or for another.

The Christian view that life is sacred and that there is no such thing as a life not worthy to be lived, brings with it certain moral obligations. It is not enough to be against killing the elderly, the chronically ill, the incapacitated. We must be concerned about giving them real life, making life meaningful to them. We must be willing to sacrifice some of our own personal peace and affluence for the sake of those who have been made to question whether life is really worth living. If we oppose euthanasia, we must share the weight of caring for the lonely or incapacitated older people who are not terminally ill.

Those who are terminally ill and for whom death is imminent present a somewhat different problem. But we must remember that "caring for the dying must become an integral part of caring for the living, for the dying are living until they are dead." Often the physician finds himself in a dilemma, for he has dedicated himself not only to prolonging life but also to relieve suffering. Sometimes these two purposes appear entirely incompatible. In the case of a terminally ill patient, the use of extraordinary measures such as life-support systems to prolong life may at the same time increase suffering. To give adequate medication to relieve the suffering may certainly hasten death. What is the physician to do? It is at such a time as this that the Christian physician seeks that wisdom that is from above—wisdom to make the right decision, whether to attempt to prolong life or whether to let die. If the decision determined in this manner should be to let die, this is not euthanasia; as B.F. Colen has said, this is sound medicine.

## CONCLUSION

Our society seems to have lost its understanding of the sanctity of human life. More and more it insists that man assume God's prerogative to decide what life should be born and when life should end. Euthanasia may be presented in the guise of mercy, but in reality it is murder.

I am reminded of the words of a medical doctor, Henry A. Davidson, who said: "As a scientist I conclude that logic is all on the side of euthanasia. As a physician I will not take the power to put someone to death. 'Twilight and evening bell, and after that the dark. And there may be no sadness or farewell, when I embark.' I know this, but let me not push the boat. Let the weary river wind somewhere safe to sea without my help."

I personally would add: As a Christian I recognize the sacredness of human life and that God alone has the prerogative not only to give life but also to fix one's appointment with death.

# Chapter 14

## The Congregational Christian Churches

Michael S. Robertson, Executive Secretary for the denomination provided the following statement:

> The National Association of Congregational Christian Churches is composed of autonomous churches and cannot, therefore, speak for or on behalf of its constituent members. Each church must determine for itself what position, if any, it will take regarding the issue of euthanasia (or any other issue). Undoubtedly there would be a wide divergence of opinion within our fellowship. Most would affirm the sacredness of life, but how this is interpreted in terms of specific issues like euthanasia would vary widely.

He went on to note that inasmuch as each church speaks for itself, "Joining together in fellowship in no way confers on the Association any powers of representation."

Chapter 15

# The United Church of Christ

On June 25, 1972, the Synod of the United Church of Christ adopted "A Statement of Christian Concern Addressed to the Churches from the Ninth General Synod." It read, in part:

Nothing in Jewish or Christian traditions or in medical ethics presumes that a physician has a mandate to impose his or her wishes and skills upon patients for the sake of prolonging the length of their dying where those patients are diagnosed as terminally ill and do not wish the interventions of the physician. People who are dying have as much freedom as other living persons to accept or to refuse medical treatment where that treatment provides no cure for their ailment. Thus the freedom of the patient to choose his/her own style for the remainder of his/her life and the method and time for dying is enhanced. Here the illness, or, depending on one's theology, God, has already made death imminent.

The statement endorsed the Living Will and recognized that, "It is ethically and theologically proper for a person to wish to avoid artificial and/or painful prolongation of terminal illness and for him or her to execute a living will or similar document of instructions." The statement went on to note:

In another situation the patient may be in an irreversible terminal illness, perhaps with substantial pain or physical distress, but in no condition to give instructions and without a previously made living will or document of instructions. Again, life or death itself is no longer a question. The only question is "when." These are patients who would die reasonably soon if given only painkilling treatment but whose body could be kept alive, or at least with functioning organs (heart, lungs) by artificial means. The question is whether extraordinary measures should be used or whether the patient should be allowed to complete his or her natural death.

Every day in hospitals across the land, these decisions are made clinically. Too often they are made covertly. Too many hospitals, doctors and relatives feel vulnerable when facing the issue and so refuse to have the decision-making process open. Some are torn over their own motivation. Some fear they may be violating the will of God. Some fear malpractice suits by a money-seeking heir or ambitious prosecuting attorney.

We believe there comes a time in the course of an irreversible terminal illness when, in the interest of love, mercy and compassion, those who are caring for the patient should say: "Enough." We do not believe simply the continuance of mere physical existence is either morally defensible or socially desirable or is God's will.

Concerning suffering and miraculous cures, the statement read: "While we may learn from suffering, we do not believe it to be the intentional will of God that persons must be so tested," and, "Christians can and do affirm the miraculous acts of God; hope and pray for such acts and yet also know that God's will does not involve suffering beyond the limits of human endurance. God's miracles are beyond human power to control."

On June 27, 1979, the Twelfth General Synod reaffirmed the 1973 Statement and gave public support to and endorsement of the importance and legitimacy of Living Wills.

It was clear that the United Church of Christ supported passive euthanasia. However, in the query about a terminal patient unable to sign a Living Will the question was left open as to "whether the patient should be allowed to complete his or her natural death."

Clear support for euthanasia was stated in a resolution at the Eighteenth General Synod in Norfolk, Virginia, June 27 - July 2, 1991 in which seven hundred delegates affirmed the right of dying persons and their families to make their own decisions regarding euthanasia and suicide. The resolution titled "The Rights and Responsibilities of Christians Regarding Human Death" was preceded by a background statement:

> We all eventually must die. When death does come, we hope that it will be swift, that we will not experience prolonged suffering, and that our dignity will remain intact. There have always been possible circumstances involving death when these desires are not fulfilled. The concern has been intensified by recent medical advances in which medical machines can indefinitely keep people "alive" in critical care under conditions of intense, undignified suffering. Advanced Life Support measures such as cardio-pulmonary resuscitation, mechanical ventilators, renal dialysis, renal, cardiac, lung and bone marrow transplants, and artificial hearts are no longer futuristic treatments. It is in this context that euthanasia and suicide need to be examined.
>
> The term euthanasia now refers both to putting to death the incurably ill and to the withdrawing or withholding of artificial means used mainly to prolong life. A related concern is suicide, the taking of one's own life, as a response to a painful, lingering death or the prospect of a debilitating or terminal disease.
>
> Euthanasia legislation has been enacted in a number of states. There are two general kinds of legislation in effect or under consideration: validating provisions to permit instructions for terminal care, e.g. "Living Wills," and protecting the right of patients to refuse treatment. This legislation does not deal adequately with all contingencies.

## ETHICAL AND THEOLOGICAL ISSUES

More important are the ethical and theological issues. One of the underlying moral conflicts centers around the patients' desire to control what happens to his or her body and the family and health care professionals commitment to preserve life. For example, sometimes a dying person is in continuous pain, which cannot be alleviated by medication, except in amounts which may hasten death. Furthermore, improved diet and health care, disease prevention and health precautions have extended life expectancy for many into a much longer period of advanced years of utter helplessness.

## THE RELIGIOUS PERSPECTIVE

In light of these perplexities, what is our response? Our Christian perspective is that life is a gift, sourced in God, and that Christians are called to a life of freedom and responsibility as evidenced in the teachings and life of Christ. Our covenantal faith requires that we serve the ends of fullness of life—in body and spirit, mind and human relations—to the extent possible. Death is an inevitable part of every life process. It is not our enemy, but a part of the life cycle which we attribute to God as Creator. This present issue is about the manner of death and attitudes toward death when there is no hope for recovery to any significant degree. We affirm individual freedom and responsibility to make choices in these matters. It is not claimed that euthanasia is the Christian position, but that the right to choose is a legitimate Christian decision. It is contended that governmental powers and entrenched custom have made life and death decisions, closing off options which more properly belong to individuals and families.

Words from the 9th General Synod of the United Church of Christ are helpful as we consider issues which have arisen since 1973:

Theology is necessarily a being theology. It intends to relate our tradition to present and changing concerns. It searches for the will of God known and to be made known to us.

The supreme value in our religious heritage is derived from God the giver of personal wholeness, freedom, integrity and dignity. When illness takes away those abilities we associate with full personhood, leaving one so impaired that what is most valuable and precious is gone, we may feel that the mere continuance of the body by machines or drugs is a violation of the person.

## TEXT OF THE RESOLUTION

WHEREAS, we live in an era of complex biomedical technologies, with various means to maintain or prolong physical life and postpone inevitable death;

WHEREAS, there are ever-increasing anxieties about a prolonged dying process with irreversible deterioration, and its potentially devastating effects on the dignity of the dying person, the emotional and physical well-being of families, as well as the responsible Christian stewardship or resources;

WHEREAS, technology advances more quickly than public policy, and public opinion is often ahead of legislative enactment;

WHEREAS, individuals have increasing responsibilities in these life and death decisions, but often lack adequate information regarding available options;

WHEREAS, life is sourced in God, and the recognizing that our faith calls for commitment and work for the quality of human life with mercy, justice and truth;

WHEREAS, affirming that the gift of abundant life is more than the avoidance of death, and that over-regard for the body, without proper concern for the needs of the person or the human spirit, can become a kind of biological idolatry; we are convinced that what is required is a balanced appreciation of the whole person;

WHEREAS, General Synod 12 of the United Church of Christ has supported the legal recognition of living wills and General Synod 9 addressed the rights and responsibilities of Christians regarding human death; and

WHEREAS, we support the right and responsibility of individuals to choose their own destiny, and recognize the need for safeguards to protect persons who cannot make life and death choices for themselves.

THEREFORE, BE IT RESOLVED, the Eighteenth Synod supports the rights of individuals, their designees and their families to make decisions regarding human dying.

BE IT FURTHER RESOLVED, the Eighteenth General Synod affirms the right of individuals to die with dignity and not have their lives unnecessarily prolonged by extraordinary measures if so chosen.

BE IT FURTHER RESOLVED, the Eighteenth General

Synod calls on Christians to offer love, compassion and understanding to those who are faced with difficult life-ending decisions.

BE IT FURTHER RESOLVED, the Eighteenth General Synod calls upon the churches to study and discuss life-ending issues with resources provided by the United Church Board for Homeland Ministries, the United Church Board for World Ministries, the Office for Church in Society and the Council for Health and Human Service Ministries.

BE IT FURTHER RESOLVED, the Eighteenth General Synod calls upon the United Church Board for Homeland Ministries, the United Church Board for World Ministries, the Office for Church in Society and the Council for Health and Human Service Ministries to report to General Synod 19.

BE IT FURTHER RESOLVED, the Eighteenth General Synod encourages the enactment of legislation safeguarding these rights, including the rights of those who are unable to make decisions for themselves.

Subject to the availability of funds.

When Initiative 119 was placed on the ballot in the state of Washington, many United Church of Christ clergy brought the subject of euthanasia before their congregations. For example, the Rev. Jack Coates of Alki Congregational Church provided his parish with a summary statement concerning the Initiative and its safeguards. In his sermon "What Does Love Require?" he recognized the human concern for the preservation of life at all costs, but pointed out that so far as he was concerned some recent developments had caused reflection. The presence of those in a vegetative state, the "new" diseases like Alzheimer's and AIDS with their tragic endings, and the development of a medical science that "can prolong life without maintaining quality of life" have made euthanasia an issue for the Christian Church. In the face of Christian concern for the "worth and dignity of each person as a creation of God" and the person's "right to live with dignity" which includes "the right to die with dignity," the Rev. Coates asked, "What does love require?"

In response to his question, he stated that "love requires respect for those who disagree" even as love calls for "making available the widest range of options and choices for the terminally ill." One of those choices would include "the choice of making the passage from life to death without pain." He concluded that he, and many in his congregation, believed that Initiative 119 would accomplish these goals.

The Rev. Paul Flucke, Senior Minister of University Congregational Church in Seattle, Washington, preached a sermon titled "Whose Life Is It Anyway?" on July 1, 1990. He called attention to the death of Janet Adkins of Portland, who took her own life. She was in the early stages of Alzheimer's disease and feared the development of the ailment. She flew to Michigan to be provided the means for suicide by Dr. Jack Kevorkian. He referred to Marsha Harmer, a 44-year old Washington woman crippled with multiple sclerosis who took her own life. He discussed the case of Nancy Cruzan who, having slipped into an irreversible coma and a persistent vegetative state, was, for seven years, denied the right to die by "The Sovereign State of Missouri." There are, the Rev. Flucke noted, an estimated "10,000 Nancy Cruzans in our hospitals today. How many more will there be before we stop playing God in the face of death?" He challenged his congregation to support Initiative 119. "'I came that you might have life,' Jesus said, 'life in all its fullness' (John 10:10). Life is a gift—and when its fullness turns to emptiness, so is death. 'The Lord giveth and the Lord taketh away,' said Job. 'Blessed be the name of the Lord' (Job 1:21)." He concluded "Whose life is it anyway? It's yours—not the doctor's, not the hospital's, not the government's. It's yours! Take charge of it! But remember, it's God's life, too—and God is full of surprises!"

# Chapter 16

# The United Church of Canada

D r. Bonnie M. Greene, Director of Office of Church in Society for the United Church of Canada, responded to the request for information regarding the UCC stance on euthanasia. She pointed out that, to date, the UCC has not developed a statement. She stated, however:

The General Council in 1977 adopted a policy on certain aspects of medical ethics. That policy addressed the issue of euthanasia only with respect to infants born with hollow skulls. The debate took place in the context of a wider social debate on abortion, extraordinary medical intervention to save extremely premature foetuses, and the conflicting rights of the mother and the foetus. Hence, the question of policy on euthanasia was addressed by General Council only with respect to whether or not failure to use every possible means of intervention on every possible premature foetus constituted euthanasia. That General Council concluded that it was legitimate to place limits on the medical intervention.

The General Council has not subsequently addressed "euthanasia," except in 1990 to ask the Division of Mission in Canada to create the capacity to address matters of bio- and medical ethics. The key concern has been to address the ethical and social questions raised by the impact of modern technology on health care. In January 1991 a Commission on Reproductive Technologies presented a policy proposal to the

Division. At the moment, a policy on ethical questions of setting limits on technological intervention to prolong life is being developed for the Division. Although legislation tabled in the House of Commons has created some pressure for policy, the primary pressure has come from ministers trying to help people resolve the ethical dilemmas they face regarding treatment decisions for elderly parents.

The Brief directed to the Royal Commission on New Reproductive Technologies and developed on behalf of the UCC by the Division of Missions in Canada included pertinent information pertaining to the theological and ethical concerns of the church. Many of the statements are, according to Dr. Greene, reflective of the approach that the UCC may take in the future with regard to euthanasia. They have been reproduced here with the references to reproductive and child-bearing issues deleted.

The writers recognize that the Brief:

challenges the Commission to be consistent in emphasizing what it means to be human. It requires the Commission to be insistent and imaginative about the ways in which the discussion on what it means to be human can be fostered in every institution, every forum, every medium in Canada. That process of discussion is at least as important as the recommendations that may be made on particular issues.

The "Executive Summary" indicates that the Brief affirms that: Life is a gift of ultimate value and to be respected as such. It is an end in itself. The life and health of another person must never be treated as means to some other, or other person's ends.

That human beings are essentially relational rather than individual. This applies to professional as well as to personal situations and extends to national and world levels.

That justice and compassion are at the heart of being human. The measure of our humanity is our ability to create a society in which the rights of the weaker and the needy are protected.

That responsible use of the resources of the earth and its people requires the establishment of priorities that reflect these values.

That while the medical technologies offer hope to some,

they must be carefully scrutinized for their costs to human beings and their utilization of scarce resources. Clear guidelines must be established for their use.

Some of the general recommendations include the following (the numbers omitted refer specifically to child bearing and child rearing):

1. The Commission recognizes as a guiding principle in its Report that issues in new reproductive technologies are but one illustration of the wider concern in society regarding the relative distribution of scarce medical resources between individual and collective needs and call for a national review of medical priorities and the establishment of guidelines by which priorities may be determined.

An increasing proportion of medical resources is being devoted to costly procedures such as those designed to prolong life for the elderly or to provide children for those who feel they have a right to them. There is an increasing tendency to lean on technological solutions while not paying adequate attention to the many needs which can be met through a more just distribution of basic resources. Devoting, for example, a larger proportion of the national wealth to ensuring that children were properly fed would reduce the incidence of later illness and other problems. Much greater emphasis on preventive medicine and on responsible life styles would further reduce medical costs.

2. The Commission calls for a coordinated educational effort on the part of the federal and provincial governments, local education authorities and universities, medical associations and concerned bodies such as the churches and voluntary organizations. The goal is to provide the information necessary, first, for significant public debate on medical priorities and, secondly, as an aid to decision-making for all who are contemplating medical interventions.

Comment: At every level clear, accurate and complete information is essential, whether it be for the woman/man facing the far reaching decision whether to ask for a particular medical procedure, through the hospital or clinic seeking to determine its priorities, to the community or the nation as a whole deciding how to allocate funding. While it is not always easy to arouse public interest, an imaginative approach to presenting the alternatives together with a significant role in making the decisions will greatly increase involvement. Currently it would seem that priorities are determined largely by group pressures or by the market. Both are driven by the individualism which is more and more the dominant motivation of our society. . . .

[3. and 4. omitted]

5. The Commission accepts as a necessary principle that no person be used to meet another's need. . . .

6. The Commission recognizes that the role of government is not to protect individual privilege but rather through social policy and education to preserve those values that are most important in a just and caring society.

Comment: When this perspective is accepted as a guiding principle it provides a necessary key to the problems of deciding on priorities for research and treatment in our social and medical systems.

7. The Commission requests the medical community at all levels to institute a debate within its ranks regarding such issues as:

- How are clients involved in making the decisions that deeply affect their lives and how can professionals ensure that these are made freely and with full knowledge?
- What is the impact on the medical system and what are the costs of an approach which encourages the spending of public funds on procedures that are a matter of desire rather than need?
- How can the teaching of ethics in medical and nursing faculties be made more adequate in view of the complexity of the moral issues which must be faced by health professionals?

Comment: Decisions, whether individual or public, depend on information and information depends on those with power sharing it. The critical questions again and again are: who is really making the decision and how is the person helped to make it freely. Because so many medical issues are highly emotional for women and men, and even for society, it is most important that clear and complete information be provided and that medical staff be educated and given support in doing this.

8. The Commission strongly recommends the establishment of:

- A National Review Board on Medical and Bioethical Issues which would provide ongoing study and evaluation of advances in technology,
- in order to advise the government of Canada, and the provincial governments on needed legislation or regulation,
- to assist in the development of national standards for that purpose,
- to provide direction with regard to research grants. Such a Board would include medical researchers, practitioners and nurses, representatives of the disciplines of law, philosophy, ethics, religion and an equal number of lay persons and should be at least fifty percent women.
- Similar boards at provincial levels.
- An independent review board for every hospital and clinic to review its policies, procedures and case loads in relation to these issues. Membership would include a lay majority along with representatives of each professional group involved, whether nurses, physicians, technicians or hospital chaplains, representatives of other disciplines as suggested above, and have a majority of women. Part of the Board's responsibility would be to enable clients of the clinic or hospital to evaluate their experiences in the programs.

Comment: Mechanisms are necessary by which the knowledge and experience of the whole community, whether local, provincial or national, may be placed at the service of the health system. This can only happen effectively if established by law and regularly reviewed. At the national level it should focus on such issues as guidelines for research and experimentation; at the provincial level on the delivery of services and the standards to be met; and at the local level on evaluation, review and support of programs.

What is more significant is the extended "Theological and Ethical Framework" which sets forth basic theological and ethical assumptions. These "assumptions" are those that may be applicable in the consideration of euthanasia. References to human reproductive issues have been deleted.

## THEOLOGICAL ASSUMPTIONS

Underlying and informing any policy, strategy or decision we as individuals or institutions make are basic assumptions or beliefs as to what is important, what meaning things have and what value we give to persons. We are often unaware of these assumptions. At times we act without realizing that we are contradicting our stated beliefs. When we do not examine our basic assumptions critically or seek to apply them honestly to important issues we are likely to substitute self-interest for the rights of the person or the common good. Issues of reproductive technology are so complex and may be approached from such different perspectives that they require careful analysis of the assumptions on which policies and decisions are based.

Some at least of the assumptions drawn on by the United Church in policy formation in relation to new reproductive technologies issues are presented here.

## LIFE AS A GIFT

A modern creed developed by The United Church of Canada in 1968 and widely used in its congregations begins

We are not alone
We live in God's world
We believe in God who has created and is creating . . .

To believe thus is to act on the assumption that life is a gift from God, that it must be defined in relation to God's purposes, that we are stewards, responsible to God for how we live. Life is not to be seen as a right inherently belonging to humans but as a responsibility we hold for a time. This responsibility includes both how we live our individual lives and how we affect the lives of others. Life as a gift means that we do not possess others, including the children "given" to us. It means that we depreciate our own humanity when we treat others as things or as instruments for our purposes, including gain or reputation. *In non-theological terms it means that every human being is a person of ultimate worth, to be treated always as an end and not as a means to someone else's ends. When we acknowledge and live by that principle our relationship to all others changes . . .*

The understanding of life as of ultimate value means that it cannot be defined merely in relation to subjective wishes but only in relation to imperatives that transcend our short term and limited insights. Not everyone will define these ultimate insights in religious terms, and some will reject outright the concept of life as a gift. Nevertheless, for many the criteria for humanness that flow from the recognition of the ultimate value of human life will allow for common action. There will be differences because of our different starting points and there will be differences in emphasis, but what we hold in common makes a degree of common action possible.

## CREATIVITY IS AT THE HEART OF BEING HUMAN

God continues to be partner with us in the creation of life. In the words of the United Church creed, God "has created and is creating. . . ." This partnership is an awesome responsibility as well as a chief source of hope for human beings.

The Bible makes clear God's intention for individual human lives; that we be just, compassionate, creative; that we seek truth and new possibilities for wholeness. We are called to be co-creators with God, working for wholeness in our communities and in each person. This is in the proper sense "playing God" because it is set within the context of the search for full humanity and seeks to meet the conditions set out in God's intention. Anything less is to deny our worth and our role in world creation. It is the very opposite of any attempt at exploitation of another for one's own profit.

While a responsibility, our creativity can also be a great joy. It can enrich our lives, giving us a sense of unity with others and with the whole creation. It calls out deep resources in our nature as our abilities and our ideals combine in the challenge and satisfaction of seeking with God to create a new world. It requires that we remember that we are part of nature, not apart from it, and therefore must treat the world of nature, including our own bodies and those of others, with deep respect. It recognizes that as self-conscious creatures we seek to use the search for knowledge in order to create a more humane and more just world. Today justice must be seen not only as what is right for the individual but also as what is fair for all in a world of great need and limited resources.

## TO BE HUMAN IS TO BE IN COMMUNITY

We are not solitary beings, though in Western cultures the individualism of the nineteenth and twentieth centuries makes us think and act as if we were. The very words used above to describe God's intention for humanity are not individualistic; they are corporate terms that emphasize our relatedness. We cannot become whole persons except in community with other persons, all of us in our own ways and together seeking wholeness. To be human is to be a rational self. The quality of those relationships defines our humanity. This is as true of physician-client and politician-voter relationships as it is of the more intimate relationships of a family. To treat another person as merely the focus of a medical procedure is to objectify them in a way that robs both parties of their humanity.

From being seen in merely functional terms, relationships must be seen as expressions of our connectedness with other persons who also are ends in themselves. A person is never to be seen as merely a client, a patient, a bearer of children. Such an attitude of respect for others requires that we have a point of reference beyond ourselves, one that transcends, affirms or calls into question all our initiatives. For Christians that ultimate reference is God. At the heart of the Christian faith is the experience that love of God, self and others are three aspects of one reality. For any relationship to be fully human it must have that same shape of love towards oneself, others and God; or, to those who do not believe in God, towards whatever is recognized as ultimately life-giving. Without that reality we are simply using each other as means to our own ends. This is essentially an attitude of grace. It fully respects the other as a person with whom one is in relationship, seeks to affirm the other in meeting her/his needs, and is open to the new and life-giving possibilities that may flow from that relationship. In this way it is open to the energy, the powers of renewal and relationship which religious people experience as the grace of God. The question, therefore, that we must pose to ourselves in all relationships, whether professional or intimate, is, "What does love require in this context?"

Community must have shape and form, and so we are part of social systems and structures which we are allowed to make just, compassionate, truthful, creative—in a word, whole.

Central to these human-shaped systems is the family. The understanding of family today has changed, as indeed it is constantly in change. For most of this century the emphasis in family was on structure and form to the point where forms, images, roles in family life became oppressive, reflections of the values of a capitalist, consumerist society. As people rebel against these structures they try to create new forms which they feel to be more liberating. Clearly the search is still on and will be until humans learn that loving, caring, honest relationships are at the heart of genuine community.

This concern is far wider than individual families. If we have been shown anything by the image of planet earth it is that our possibilities and problems must be seen in planetary terms. Every significant issue demands that we ask what its world-wide implications are. The availability of reproductive technologies requires that we ask such questions as:

- Should something be done simply because it is technically possible?
- For whom should this technology be available?
- Who decides when a technology is to be used?
- Who profits from its use?
- Is it the best use of ever more scarce resources?
- What is the place of quality of life for all?

These are all questions of priority. They do not lead automatically to the cessation of research and practice in reproductive technologies. They do lead to questions about whether there are other concerns that should have higher priority, things which, if not addressed, call our humanity into question. These are questions not only for individuals but for the institutions in which our lives are organized: government, medicine, commerce, church. . . .

To be human, then, requires that each of us is continually aware of our relationship with others, critiquing our behaviour and our motives, and at every point of action asking ourselves how authentic relationship can best be expressed and nurtured. We avoid the demands of authentic relationship when we allow impersonal professionalism to replace compassion, or outdated beliefs and attitudes to make us deaf to the cries of those who long for the wholeness that new technologies may bring, or the overwhelming desire for a child of one's own body or genes to blind us to the needs of existing children who could benefit from our love through adoption, creating extended families or other support. All life is the interplay of relationships. The quality of these relationships is a measure of our humanity. We forget that at our peril.

## THE REALITY OF EVIL

At the heart of human creativity is the desire for knowledge. A two-edged sword, knowledge can be both the way forward into new life, better health and greater freedom or it may lead to more sophisticated exploitation and control. Knowledge is power and power must be used with full respect for the humanity, the needs and rights, of others. It can never be separated from the question of how it is used.

We believe God is calling humankind into ever expanding knowledge and truth but, as a report of the National Council of Churches of Christ in the USA put it, "We cannot agree with those who assert that scientific inquiry and research should acknowledge no limits."

When the goal of creativity is the wholeness and completeness of human life, then it becomes a partnership with God and a sign of hope to the world. On the surface it should seem that any technology which has as its goal the creation of new life or the enrichment of existing lives is an expression of such creativity. However, the matter is more complex and makes great demands on our ability to know ourselves as we are and use our creative skills with wisdom. . . .

No one should ever underestimate the human ability to rationalize our desires. What we want becomes what we may, and what we may becomes what we should. The very avail-

ability of a procedure is translated by many into a right to
have it.

## KNOWING AND DOING, MARKERS ON THE WAY

How then does anyone, or does society, arrive at an understanding of what is meant by wholeness and completeness
for human beings?

Each of us has to find our own answers. We do not do it
alone but discover them in community. There are many mark-
ers on the way.

In seeking to discover a faithful understanding of wholeness and completeness, and to act on it, we in the United
Church, like many other Christians, turn to four sources.

### The Bible

One source is the record of God's dealings as set out in
the Bible. God's covenant with the Hebrew people is described
in terms of justice and compassion. The arrogance of the powerful and wealthy is chastised and the rights of the poor and
the homeless upheld. God seeks to create a community in
which the rightful needs of all are met, a community of care
and support. Wholeness is seen in terms not only of spirit and
mind but of body also. Human beings are embodied spirits,
fully integrated, with no dichotomy between mind and body.
Beyond that, justice includes ecology: the earth has an ethical
demand on us.

This is portrayed clearly in the life of Jesus of Nazareth
whom Christians call Christ. His capacity to meet each person, be they tax collector, Samaritan, outcast women, blind,
lame or leper at the point of that person's deepest human need
(and not just their desires) and to open for them new possibilities of life, points the way to our understanding of full and
complete humanity. No one was a client or patient to him,
but a full person. He engages equally and with loving direct-
ness with Nicodemus as Nicodemus seeks to understand truth,
with the woman with an issue of blood whose condition
makes her feel rejected, with the lepers who felt their bodies

247

decaying. He did not discriminate on the basis of sex, position or race. He reserved his condemnation for those who used their positions to exploit others, who lived in the self-righteous conviction of their own goodness and religious systems that held people in thrall. He listened, he saw, and he responded to each as a person in the context of that person's total life. He pointed to a new kind of community which challenges the norms operating in our depersonalized, technological, commercialized society.

When we seek to apply these attitudes to our medical systems a number of things are required:

- Compassion requires that each person be met at the point of actual need, genuinely listened to and empowered to make a decision which is authentically theirs. This is very different from starting with the assumption that a particular technology is the needed answer.
- Justice requires that the benefits be available not only to those who are able to afford them or who live close to major medical centers but to all who genuinely need them. Accessibility is essential. But it may also require the decision by society that some technologies are too costly in a world as needy as this. This is a painful decision to make since it requires denying the hopes of some in order to meet the needs of a much larger number. It may be the decision required by the interests of justice.

Both compassion and justice require the fullest possible information about each procedure, its effects, its costs of all kinds, its hopes of success and so on. They also require that the professionals consider beyond the presenting need the factors that cause it. . . .

## Tradition

Because Christians believe that God has continued in every generation to work for human wholeness and completeness, we look also to the way the traditions of the faith have been understood and reinterpreted. This may be seen as the deepening understanding of what is just or compassionate or true as the Spirit opens our eyes to realities to which we have been blind. . . .

Tradition will be part of the process as we move to new conclusions. Tradition itself is dynamic and part of the dynamic. It reflects how we have arrived at other answers in other times and places and how, while limited, they have been helpful.

The re-interpretation of tradition may be seen as the refusal to slip into comfortable ways based on earlier attitudes. It represents the willingness to listen honestly to others and to question ourselves in order to rethink our assumptions and attitudes and challenge the status quo.

## Experience

A third source for insight is the experience of persons. In the past much Christian thinking has been done as if the experiences of ordinary Christians had little or no meaning. . . .

The Commission might recommend that local clinics and hospitals establish local review boards, including lay persons and those from other disciplines, to meet regularly to evaluate their practices, attitudes, results and so on. Membership would be small but must include an equal number of women. Clients of the program would be asked to submit their evaluations and suggestions. Similarly, provincial and national professional bodies involved with reproductive technologies need to be required to establish review boards which would include trained ethicists. These need have only advisory power to be very effective.

## The study of nature, the sciences

The fourth source is through the study of nature, the sciences. Participation in the creative process requires a continuing quest to unravel and understand the mysteries of life, but it too must have the goal of the wholeness and completeness of human life. We can be grateful for the insights and skills which have so enriched human life, while asking questions as to how they are being and will be applied.

Scientific knowledge is growing and changing at such a rate that it is almost impossible for lay people to keep informed. There is an obligation on scientists to provide information and assist society in understanding new knowledge. It is not acceptable for scientists to claim that technology is morally neutral and thus avoid responsibility for sharing in difficult decisions that result from their work. The use and application of technology is always a moral issue. This applies equally to researchers and practitioners. . . .

## SUMMARY

The new technologies are exciting and glamorous. They reflect the creative possibilities of the human mind, but that very excitement may blind us to their pitfalls. They require therefore very careful reflection about the goals and priorities of Canadian society.

Their use raises some fundamental questions:

- The relationship of persons to one another: how can we treat others as ends in themselves and not as means to our ends?
- The requirements of justice;
- Our relationship to nature: how should we use the world's resources with respect and care?

To be human is to be in relationship: with others near and far, with what is immediate and what is ultimate. The measure of our humanity is the measure of those relationships.

## ETHICAL FAMEWORK

What then is an appropriate framework for making moral decisions in the light of the above theological assumptions?

1. It will be contextual rather than the direct or simple application of one or more absolute principles. In other words, the matter is not to be decided *a priori* on the basis of any particular assumptions but through an attempt to identify and weigh all the interests, motives, outcomes and principles which are related to it. . . .

2. The fundamental issue has to do with the meaning of being human in this situation. When evaluating procedures we have to ask such questions as: does it contribute to human wholeness for the persons involved and for the common good? How is "humanity" defined or understood in this situation? Will it be enlarged or limited by this procedure?

3. Underlying all moral issues of this nature is the principle that no harm be done, or at least that any possible harm be limited in relation to the values hoped for. This raises the question of risk. What are the risks involved and how acceptable are they?

What constitutes adequate testing for a new drug and when should it no longer be regarded as experimental? What is the effect of the combination of these drugs, particularly in the dosages prescribed? Is anything known about their long term effects on the fetus?

Clearly a cost-benefit analysis of success and failure is not a proper basis for making such decisions. The relative "success" or "failure" of the procedure must not be the chief or only criterion for allowing it. Only the medical community can supply the information on which decisions about these questions can be based, though the decisions are not for the medical community to make alone. The Royal Commission must press these questions urgently on both the medical community and the government.

4. Central to weighing risks is the concern for informed consent or choice.

5. A contextual approach requires also looking at the broader social issues. . . . Prevention of a problem is much better than having to seek a cure. . . .

In a society and world where resources are not well shared and are becoming increasingly scarce, it should not be assumed that because a procedure can be carried out it therefore should be available. This raises again the issue of how our society sets its medical and other priorities. It would be better, for example, to spend more money preventing the illnesses and wasted lives caused by malnutrition and poverty, even if we have to spend less on the glamorous technologies. . . . It would seem that rising awareness of global warming, environmental degradation and similar issues is forcing society to recognize increasingly that we cannot go on exploiting the earth, appropriating its resources to ourselves in the western and northern lands, pursuing economic gain as the most important definition of humanness and destroying rather than creating community in the world. The same kind of awareness is needed in relation to medical issues.

Another view is provided by Marilynne Seguin in her book *A Gentle Death* (Toronto: Key-Porter Books, 1994) in which she quotes the Rev. Bruce McCleod, pastor of Bellefair United Church in Toronto, and the Rev. John Wesley Oldham, pastor of Donnelly United Church in Winnipeg, both of whom support the right of persons to die with dignity and both of whom recognize the validity of physician-assisted death for the terminally ill who request such help.

Chapter 17

# The Unitarian
# Universalist Association

At the twenty-seventh General Assembly of the Unitarian Universalist Association, convened on June 17, 1988 at Palm Springs,
California, the following general resolution was adopted by a
two-thirds vote:

## THE RIGHT TO DIE WITH DIGNITY—1988

Guided by our belief as Unitarian Universalists that human
life has inherent dignity, which may be compromised when
life is extended beyond the will or ability of a person to sustain that dignity; and believing that it is every person's invio-
lable right to determine in advance the course of action to be
taken in the event that there is no reasonable expectation of
recovery from extreme physical or mental disability; and

WHEREAS, medical knowledge and technology make
possible the mechanical prolongation of life; and

WHEREAS, such prolongation may cause unnecessary
suffering and/or loss of dignity while providing little or nothing of benefit to the individual; and

WHEREAS, such procedures have an impact upon a
health-care system in which services are limited and are ineq-
uitably distributed; and

WHEREAS, differences exist among people over religious, moral, and legal implications of administering aid in

dying when an individual of sound mind has voluntarily asked for such aid; and

WHEREAS, obstacles exist within our society against providing support for an individual's declared wish to die; and

WHEREAS, many counselors, clergy, and health-care personnel value prolongation of life regardless of the quality of life or will to live;

THEREFORE BE IT RESOLVED: That the Unitarian Universalist Association calls upon its congregations and individual Unitarian Universalists to examine attitudes and practices in our society relative to the ending of life, as well as those in other countries and cultures; and

BE IT FURTHER RESOLVED: That Unitarian Universalists reaffirm their support for the Living Will, as declared in a 1978 resolution of the General Assembly, declare support for the Durable Power of Attorney for Health Care, and seek assurance that both instruments will be honored; and

BE IT FURTHER RESOLVED: That Unitarian Universalists advocate the right to self-determination in dying, and the release from civil or criminal penalties of those who, under proper safeguards, act to honor the right of terminally ill patients to select the time of their own deaths; and

BE IT FURTHER RESOLVED: That Unitarian Universalists advocate safeguards against abuse by those who would hasten death contrary to an individual's desires; and

BE IT FINALLY RESOLVED: That Unitarian Universalists, acting through their congregations, memorial societies, and appropriate organizations, inform and petition legislators to support legislation that will create legal protection for the right to die with dignity, in accordance with one's own choice.

Members of the Association are not bound to support Assembly positions. Individual pastors tend to urge the members of their congregations to think and choose for themselves. For example, prompted by the June 17, 1988 resolution, the Rev. Edgar Peara spoke on "The Case for Euthanasia" at the Unitarian Universalist Community Church, Park Forest, Illinois, in November 1988. His presentation was designed to "make a case for" the resolution. He discussed terminal cases of illness where patients begged for surcease, and pointed out that some doctors have complied either by leaving large quantities of pain-relieving medications which, in overdose, could cause death, or by providing megadoses of morphine which resulted in death. He commented:

> We continue to voice theological and religious objections to mercy killings. The legal principle of individual self-determination does not include the right to formally ask a doctor to terminate a hopeless, pain-filled life. We say that is forbidden because we believe that human life is sacred. But think of all the ways we contradict that position. We condone warfare, killing in self-defense and in defense of others, and capital punishment.
>
> How sacred is life when we maintain an arsenal of nuclear weapons that could kill everyone on earth several times over? Is it a greater desecration to maintain a person in a vegetative state, or hopeless torment, than it is to kill him? We think of ourselves as being humane when we put to death painfully injured animals who can't be healed.
>
> People of other faiths condemn euthanasia because they think persons should die when God is ready to take them. They must not countervail the divine will. These religionists are not consistent. They don't deal that way with victims of other forms of suffering. For example, they don't say that people suffer hunger because God wants them to starve, and that they must not interfere with God's will. No, they send relief and food to the Ethiopians. Nor do they wait for the Lord to renovate slums. Instead they build habitats for humanity.
>
> If the anti-euthanasia people were consistent they would have to say that when patients first developed terminal cancer that they thwarted God's will, by seeking medical treatment without which they would have died. In other words, God was ready to take them. They would have died at that time if they hadn't frustrated the divine will by having surgery or chemotherapy. During that time, it was actually death that was natural. Existence maintained by an operation, respirator or heart pump was what was unnatural. Then after years of medical intervention which lengthened the patients' life, a time comes when nothing more can be done to help them. More years of suffering lie ahead. When the sick say they want to die, they are told they must be patient and stoic as they wait for God to take them by an exhausting, painful, natural

death. Isn't that thinking inconsistent, irrational and inhumane?

Those who administer euthanasia feel they are right and ethical in relieving patients of months or years of excruciating pain and desperate anxiety. The sufferers feel society is cruel, insensitive and immoral for sentencing them to misery without providing a panel or ombudsman who can grant them a legal death that is quick and painless.

In a practical sense we reject euthanasia because we can't decide who should have the authority and responsibility for deciding when human life is so wretched that it should not continue. If euthanasia were legal who might serve on such a committee? Not doctors, whose Hippocratic Oath commands them not to give any "deadly medicine, nor suggest any such counsel to anyone." Further, they shouldn't be placed in the double bind of representing society and their patient when there might be a conflict of interest. Likewise, clergy should be off the hook. The sufferers need to be confident that their physicians and ministers will act unequivocally for them. They must be competent to represent the miserable sick before the euthanasia panel and be committed to plead for their charges when they cannot speak for themselves. The advocates need to remind others that the terminally ill have previously said they wanted euthanasia if ever found in such a desperate, miserable situation.

He concluded his address with the following statements:

Until euthanasia is a public option what can we do to help the most desperate cases? We need to realize that their hopelessness flows from powerlessness and the melancholia of lost self-esteem. Patients benefit from open communication and disclosure about diagnosis, prognosis and the treatment that can be offered. Preserving personal dignity and encouraging participation in decisions about treatment are beneficial. The wonderful hospices that free terminally-ill patients from futile and uncomfortable life-extending therapies have been a blessing. In hospices patients are relieved of pain while being allowed to die comfortably without life-extending treatments.

What message should our society in general, and we, Unitarian Universalists, in particular, give to those who in increasing numbers are pleading for euthanasia? What should we do for those who have no mind with which to form a plea and no voice to utter it? We need to act as individuals, as congregations and as members of the other organizations to which we belong to create petitions and speak to our legislators. They need to be urged to create statutes that will make euthanasia legal. Then patients who are suffering excruciatingly, and who, when they were sound-minded, opted for euthanasia, if they found themselves in that pitiful state, might be able to have their lives ended painless and quickly. The life you thus help end with ease and dignity may be your own.

On the other hand, on September 22, 1991, the Rev. Don Beaudreault told his congregation at the Pacific Unitarian Church in Rancho Palos Verdes, California, that he did not support active euthanasia. He said:

I am in the minority when it comes to the issue of active euthanasia. My deep personal beliefs will not allow me to support our denominational resolution—and that is my right—and your right—as Unitarian Universalists. No creed, no dogma binds us. Rather, we are bonded by mutual consent to honor the differences (when there are differences) which unite us. And that means, that if you come to me to ask what I might think about your decision to take your own life because you have an incurable illness (physical or mental) and believe your life is no longer worth living—I shall tell you what I believe, but shall not judge you for your decision. I would not agree with your decision but I would not love you any less and I would hope you would honor me by returning your love.

Does this mean that I am not in favor of passive euthanasia—where the body is kept alive by machines? The answer is that I am in favor of this form of "mercy killing" because most of the time this form of "life" is certainly not a dignified one. . . .

Don't get me wrong. I am not in favor of physical or mental suffering. I have seen my share of it—in both a professional and personal way (and indeed the two join together). I have suffered along with all those who lay dying before me—including my father for those seven weeks it took him to die from the effects of a stroke. How helpless each of us is—as we see our loved ones perishing. How we would want to ease their suffering. And we might think: Is it cruel for us not to take such measures to help them die if that is their desire? Or we might ask ourselves: Is it cruel if we do assist their self-deliverance? And when it comes to our time to die—what would our choice be? . . .

What it is, I guess, is a strong passion within me along the lines of Albert Schweitzer's "reverence for life" principle—which respects an interconnection of all sentient existence. Rather than seeing the actual act of self-administered death as a peaceful release for me, I see it as a violent act.

As an agnostic who is forever seeking a divine purpose behind existence, I am also a person of vast curiosity—who refuses to go gently into that good night. I have experienced physical pain and will again and it eventually will be my death knell. Hopefully, the statistics are correct about pain medication: that ninety percent of suffering can be alleviated through the administration of the correct medication. But I, who am still somewhat of a brash young man, expect to learn about life from whatever pain there is at my time of death. The image of Christ's suffering on the cross is not one with which I identify. But the image created by Bertrand Russell of "those who bear the mark of pain" (meaning all of humanity) is one I as a religious humanist feel I must identify with. That is my choice and you are entitled to yours.

And if you are one of the sixty to sixty-five percent in our country who are in favor of a Death with Dignity Law, you are entitled to fight in favor of the initiative in the Washington State legislature and in our own state legislature, where within a year there will be a second attempt to put an initiative on the ballot. And, too, there will be battles on the topic in other states, notably in Oregon and Florida. . . .

The issue of Death With Dignity is one we as a people seeking truth and justice must address with much thought, for it could be the most crucial decision we will ever have to make for ourselves and those we love. And so, may we indeed speak the truth as we see it to each other. And may we do so with love.

Let me leave you with these words from Bertrand Russell's "A Free Man's Worship" taken from his book *Why I Am*

*Not a Christian:* "In the spectacle of death, in the endurance of pain, and in the irrevocableness of a vanished past, there is a sacredness, an overpowering awe, a feeling of the vastness, the depth, the inexhaustible mystery of existence, in which, as by some strange marriage of pain, the sufferer is bound to the world by bonds of sorrow. In these moments of insight, we lose all eagerness of temporary desire, all struggling and striving for petty ends, all care for the little trivial things that, to a superficial view, make up the common life of day by day; we see, surrounding the narrow raft illumined by the flickering light of human comradeship, the dark ocean on whose rolling waves we toss for a brief hour; from the great night without, a chill blast breaks in upon our refuge; all the loneliness of humanity amid hostile forces is concentrated upon the individual . . . which must struggle alone, with what of courage it can command, against the whole weight of a universe that cares nothing for its hopes and fears. Victory, in this struggle with the powers of darkness, is the true baptism into the glorious company of heroes, the true initiation into the overmastering beauty of human existence. From that awful encounter—with the outer world, renunciation, wisdom, and charity are born; and with their birth a new life begins. To take into the inmost shrine of (one's self) the irresistible forces whose puppets we seem to be—death and change, the irrevocableness of the past, and the powerlessness of (humanity) before the blind hurry of the universe from vanity to vanity—to feel these things and know them is to conquer them" (adapted).

In March, 1988, the Rev. Frank Rivas of the Unitarian Universalist Society of Daytona Beach area, Florida, discussed the ambivalence individuals feel when confronted with terminal illness. Does one fight the illness with every medical tool produced by our technological society, or does one accept the inevitability of death?

There are, then, two modes of dealing with a life-threatening situation: fighting and accepting. The problem is in knowing when each mode is appropriate. Physicians, hospitals, legislators, and medical ethicists have all attempted to identify the point at which it's appropriate to change from one mode to another, the point at which it's appropriate to stop fighting and begin to accept, but mostly they find blurry lines. When a person's condition slowly degenerates, there's no clear point of change, but rather slowly decreasing chances for survival.

I suspect that medical ethicists will never identify the ideal moment of acceptance. Instead, we may have to face the issue in an alternative way, by entering the suffering, allowing there to be mystery, surrendering to the unknown.

I have witnessed families who have surrendered, and I have been part of one, and I know that what happens is sacred when conflict and suffering are no longer avoided, but embraced. At once we can know the depth of our hope for recovery and the reality that it will probably never occur. At once we can feel the depth of our love and connection and at the same time know that we will survive without this person. At once we can give thanks that this person entered and transformed our lives and at the same time be angry that this life is being torn from us. It is a time of reverence, of tears, of silence, and of prayer. It is a time, finally, of transformation. As we surrender to the conflict, as we embrace it, as we allow it to transform our lives, suddenly we begin to cherish each moment of life more deeply than we had ever imagined and at the same time to accept the limits. Sacred and ephemeral no longer stand in contradiction, but become one.

This is the transformative power of the religious life, and it is, as Gordon McKeeman points out, a terrifying power. Knowing the sacredness and fragility of life we indeed are transformed; perhaps we will follow the path of Dorothy Day, who founded the Catholic Workers, or Sidhartha Gautama, later called the Buddha, or Mother Theresa, who ministers to the poor and dying of Calcutta. It is a transformation we both run from and are drawn to.

He stated that whichever decision one chose deserves respect. He did not call upon his listeners to follow either path. He closed with the following comments:

> We all want clear answers. We want laws, statutes, commandments to tell us when to stop the fight and allow ourselves to die. We may finally have to accept that there are no commandments, but only mystery, ambiguity. And reverence. And thanks.

May we be willing to enter that mystery and experience its transformative power. May we give thanks for the fullness of this mortal life.

The Rev. Marvin Evans, Minister Emeritus at the Bellingham Unitarian Fellowship in Bellingham, Washington, was the secretary of the "Washington Citizens for Death with Dignity" and on the Executive Board of "Unitarian Universalists for Death With Dignity." Mr. Evans, clearly, was in support of Initiative 119. He urged his fellow citizens, and in particular members of the Unitarian Universalists, to endorse efforts to get the initiative passed.

The Reverend Annie Foerster, Minister of the Evergreen Unitarian Universalist Fellowship in a newsletter column "The Foerst Word" noted that "Every UU minister in the state has signed a statement supporting the initiative [119]." However, when it came time to vote, she did not support the initiative. She wrote:

> My theology is somewhat different from many Unitarian Universalist ministers with whom I have spoken. Like them (and most UUs) I believe we should be allowed to make our own choices about our deaths—as well as our lives—and to be willing to assume the responsibility for those choices. That is pretty standard for the liberal religious who believe that the ultimate authority for religious decisions resides in the individual. However, I voted against the initiative because (1) it was not well written, and (2) I thought it was proposed for the wrong theological reasons. . . .
>
> Unitarian Universalists are more comfortable with material issues than with spiritual ones. They tend to look more toward technology and science to explain things than toward mysticism or "still small voices." Many life issues that were formerly the sole concern of theology have been relegated to technology. Death is one of these. In addition, since we are a this-world faith community, we tend not to worry about the afterlife. Thus death becomes not the responsibility or concern of the individual, but of the medical profession, researchers, fitness instructors, nursing homes, undertakers and such philosophers who want to bother with something we're only going to have to do once, at most. Fear of death is sublimated and fear of dying becomes mostly a fear of pain and loss of dignity.

This is where I part company with most. I believe that our social propensity to hide death in institutions has crippled us spiritually. We tend to look for dignity in death, when it can really only be found in the way we live. We tend to take responsibility for choosing an easy death, but want someone else (doctors, ministers) to be responsible for its happening. We cannot even talk with our families about our wishes, but institutionalize such personal matters by constructing "living wills."

When we can honestly acknowledge our mortality, to ourselves and to one another, we can truly celebrate the joy of life, even as we grieve its inevitable ending.

When we no longer fear the loss of youth and can appreciate the gifts of a wise old age, then we will no longer fear death or dying.

When we can learn to let go of the materialism, success and power that drives much of our lives, only then can we achieve the dignity necessary to let go of life when the time comes.

We need not live our lives in fear of eternal punishment in order to know morality, kindness and love. We need not give over our authority for decision-making nor our own generative power to effect transformation, just because we are finite creatures.

I do not believe suicide is immoral, nor that it is wrong to ask for assistance in ending one's life when that life becomes intolerable or useless. It is selfish to the extreme, however, to expect the right to do so without having done the work of living toward one's good death.

In Pasadena, California, the Rev. B.L. Lovely of Pasadena Neighborhood Church noted that in a vote taken in his congregation, 89.6 percent voted to actively support the "Death With Dignity Proposition proposed for the California, November, 1992 ballot." He, personally, would support voluntary "active euthanasia" for the comatose terminally ill whose lives are sustained by artificial means "on the grounds of preserving what remains of his/her human dignity as a person not as a vegetable." He believes that life "belongs to the adult person in his/her right mind. We should help one another. When we love them it does not violate our own integrity."

# Chapter 18

## Mennonite Churches

K ey persons in the Mennonite Churches provided answers to the questionnaire (see Appendix VIII). Dr. David Ewert has been a member of the Board of Reference and Counsel of the Mennonite Brethren Church. In answer to my first survey question he wrote:

> If the person who is dying, in consultation with family and physician, agrees to end the suffering by removing the life-support system, I believe that would be acceptable. Whereas technology is a gift of God to man, it is abused when it is used to sustain life artificially.

Vern Preheim, General Secretary of the General Conference Mennonite Church suggests that passive euthanasia would probably be accepted but "with mixed feelings."

John Stoner, who was formerly Executive Secretary of the Peace Committee of the Mennonite Central Committee, an inter-Mennonite Agency, wrote:

> In brief, my understanding of the generally held Mennonite position would be that most Mennonite groups would sanction the removal of life-support systems in the case of patients similar to the one described in example #1 [of the survey]. In other words, 'passive' euthanasia would be approved on the grounds that death is ultimately inevitable and is to be accepted.

The Mennonite Medical Association represents several major Mennonite groups, namely, The Mennonite Church, The General Council Mennonite Church, The Mennonite Brethren Church, and the Brethren in Christ Church. Dr. Erland Waltner, who was, until July, 1992, Executive Secretary of the Mennonite Medical Association, wrote:

> The Mennonite Medical Association, as a professional rather than an ecclesiastical organization, has taken no formal position on the issue of "passive euthanasia." "Positions" then would be taken in local congregations, by pastoral leaders, and more specifically by families consulting with their pastor and their doctor. My own position, shared by numerous others, would be open to what is above called "passive euthanasia" on the grounds that death can be accepted as God's own way of releasing persons from physical suffering while certain "heroic measures" of life-support may be undue resistance to normal/natural completion of life, even at the age of 22.

With regard to the second question and active euthanasia, Dr. Waltner wrote:

> Again, no formal positions have been taken, but especially because Mennonites affirm that human life is a sacred trust from God and thus take a formal position against destruction by active means, such as by war or by abortion, we would not approve participation in the hastening of the death process, though we accept death as a normal/natural process in human experience. Neither suicide nor active participation in suicide of a suffering patient would find general approval, though many would express a high level of compassion for those suffering in the way described above and would have a measure of "understanding" without approving "active euthanasia."

Vern Preheim suggests that active euthanasia would probably not be acceptable because it "is seen as killing." Dr. Ewert commented:

> It is one matter to remove the life-support system when a person is dying. It is another matter to inflict death or hurry it on. Suicide is viewed by us as a violation of the sacredness of life. Our denomination holds also that killing in war is con-

trary to the Scriptures, as is abortion. Active euthanasia would fall in the same category.

The effect of euthanasia on the after life "is not articulated in our beliefs," according to Dr. Waltner. He comments, "We understand the term 'soul' as used biblically to designate the SELF and not some 'fragment' of personhood. We do not believe that the SELF has an afterlife and that Divine Judgement is a part of eternal reality. . . . Eternal salvation is seen as a gift of Divine Grace." Nick Rempel, Secretary of the Mennonite Brethren Church, wrote, "The Afterlife is not based upon do's or don'ts—not a meritorious gain—but a gift of *grace* through faith in the person of Jesus Christ. Judgement belongs to God."

The funeral rites would not be affected by euthanasia. "Once the person is dead," wrote Dr. Ewert, "one is concerned with the living who are left behind and not with the corpse." Similarly, Nick Rempel states, "The funeral service would be in the Church—again, judgement belongs to God—we would not make a judgement about eternal destiny." Dr. Waltner does not believe that the fact of euthanasia would affect the ritual, but he qualifies his statement by pointing out that it may depend on the local pastor and/or congregation. "The burial of one who has committed suicide is generally handled with deep sensitivity for the grief being endured by the survivors and respect for the 'unknown factors' in 'cause of death.'"

Nick Rempel states that in the matter of counseling for passive euthanasia, "If the quality of life is such that only heroic measures will prolong it—and if prolonging has serious economic and emotional demands upon the family—we would probably counsel to take off the support system—allow death to come." Dr. Stoner wrote that, "Questions of the stewardship of limited funds and resources for the care of patients in extreme conditions would figure in. Many Mennonites would feel that it is unjust to spend thousands of dollars to prolong the life of a dying person for days or weeks when those dollars applied to basic health service for children in a needy country of the world could prevent brain damage and save lives." Dr. Waltner believes that the likely counsel would be "to continue to trust God. Prayer for 'release' (death) on the part of the patient and of the pastor may be appropriate."

Counseling for active euthanasia would tend to discourage such action. Dr. Waltner believes that, "In this case, more support would be given to 'patient endurance' with allowance for prayer that God may bring suffering to completion." According to Vern Preheim, the scriptural basis for the Mennonite position is the commandment "Thou shalt not kill." David Ewert adds: "Our view of the sacredness of life is based on the Bible's teaching that God is the Creator and therefore also the Lord over life."

The Rev. Ervin H. Hershberger responded to the questionnaire on behalf of the Beachy Amish Mennonite Churches. In response to the first question, he stated that his church would sanction the removal of life-support systems that sustain life in the terminally ill who would otherwise die. He notes, "God, the Author of Life, has a perfect right to terminate life when and how He chooses. To artificially maintain UNNATURAL functions after God has terminated all NATURAL functions is resisting God."

His church would not sanction suicide for the terminally ill patient referred to in the second question of the questionnaire. He wrote: "That would be actively terminating a human life, which ONLY GOD has a right to do! To those who honor God by trusting Him, and patiently waiting for His appointed time, God will provide sufficient grace to endure to the end. (Matthew 10:22b)."

He noted that his religious organization believes in an afterlife. He wrote, "YES! We believe in a living soul, afterlife, and divine judgement." With respect to the person who might participate in active euthanasia, The Rev. Hershberger quoted I John 3:15b ". . . ye know that no murderer hath eternal life abiding in him."

The fact that death resulted from "active euthanasia" would impact on the funeral ritual in the following way: "It would affect the funeral sermon, but not the burial rituals. Funeral rituals do not affect the destiny of the deceased, nor alter the mind of God. Burial rituals relate primarily to the body. The soul is committed to God in all cases."

For someone contemplating passive euthanasia he noted, "We would recommend total commitment to God, giving glory to Him Who does all things well. Man cannot improve on the will and perfect plan of God. 'Precious in the sight of the Lord is the death of His saints' (Psalm 116:15)." For someone considering active euthanasia, "We would warn against assuming any role whereby one might incur the guilt of taking human life. 'As I live, saith the Lord, I have no pleasure in the death of the wicked; but that the wicked turn from his way and live' (Ezekiel 33:11)." The Rev. Hershberger listed the following scriptural passages that he believes have importance for the discussion of euthanasia: Exodus 20:13; Matthew 19:18; I Peter 4:15 and I John 3:15.

# Chapter 19

---

# Church of the Brethren*

---

I
n the June, 1975, Church of the Brethren Annual Conference—"the highest decision-making body in the Church" according to then General Secretary Robert W. Neff, a "Life Stewardship" statement was passed. The statement began with comments on the "Biblical View of the Body":

> In the Creation account given to us in Genesis 2 we find that man is completely dependent upon the grace of God for his personal existence: *Then the Lord God formed man of dust from the ground, and breathed into his nostrils the breath of life; and man became a living being* (Gen. 2:7). Apart from the breath, or Spirit, of God, the human body is merely worthless dust.

The report goes on to note that in most of the Old Testament, there is no belief in any personal life beyond death, but that the New Testament proclaims there is a resurrection of the dead. The next portions review "Historical Positions Regarding the Funeral and Burial," "The Christian Funeral," "The Church as a Support Community," and "Christian Stewardship in Relation to Medical Need, the Funeral and Estate Planning." The importance of grief counseling is stressed, and the use of "heroic" medical measures is addressed from the point of view both of physicians and of laity.

---

*Several denominations employ the term "Brethren" in their identifications. To maintain clarity, each will be listed separately.

The query implies concern for "heroic medical measures that merely maintain life, but deny the terminally ill the dignity of dying in peace." This is a problem in some instances, though seldom intentional. According to a recent survey, the vast majority of doctors recognize no special duty to keep terminally ill patients alive. (The 1974 Annual Conference survey shows that fifty-five percent of the delegates who participated in it did not feel that "the doctor should keep you alive as long as possible.") However, in large, research-oriented institutions, it is more likely that "everything possible" will be tried, with no member of the treatment team being willing to admit defeat, or to take responsibility for the new phase of treatment of the person. Moreover, the patient is isolated from his home, thus cultural and community strengths cannot be utilized at this very important time. The dying patient is reduced to a set of complaints, symptoms, and physical findings, and the question is seldom asked, *Did the patient die peacefully, with self-esteem, dignity, and in control of his limited options?*

The patient often finds himself fed, bathed, sent for tests, X-rayed, intubated, awakened, sedated, medicated—sometimes without any active participation in the decisions. The patient—not the doctor, family, church, or society—has the right to be considered in these decisions, and acknowledging this right contributes to his dignity and humanity.

The problem of "heroic medical measures" at the time of death is not purely a problem for the physicians, for far too many people believe that something more can be done for the fatally ill when in reality nothing can. The ever-widening expectance of treatments for cancer, heart, and kidney diseases, for example, make the acceptance of death more and more difficult, not only for the physician, who feels some sense of obligation to maintain treatment until the very end, but also for the families, who fear the ensuing guilt when "everything possible" isn't done. Even patients who probably suspect that they are dying may not face the issue, but may fantasize potential breakthroughs for their particular disease.

There is justification for our concern about misapplication of "heroic medical measures." A few examples are truly horror stories of continued suffering, enormous expense, and the breakdown of the remaining family for the support of vegetative "life." Few, if any, are comfortable with this outcome, and many, through the signing of a "living will," hope to actively prevent such an occurrence. The Living Will is a signed and witnessed document which states that "at such time when there is no reasonable expectation of my recovering from physical or mental illness, I request that I not be kept alive by artificial means or heroic measures, and that I be allowed to die with dignity." A growing movement now asserts that there is a right to die, as well as a right to live, and that the right to die is often violated by the prolonged, excruciating, and expensive medical interventions that keep people alive who would be better off dead.

Unfortunately, it is still much more common that too little attention is given to the dying person, rather than too much, and it is here that we should focus our energies. We need to know more than we do about the care of the dying, with emphasis on the patient as a sensitive and sensible human being, and more about how best to help the anxious, strained, and suffering family and friends, during and after the event of dying. Ultimately, good care of the dying will be a test of the teamwork of all involved—family, pastor, medical personnel, et al., so that persons can live their last days with self-possession and self-respect whenever humanly possible. This is good stewardship of life.

Clearly the statement does not confront the issue of euthanasia, but perhaps it provides a groundwork for future discussions in harmony with the basic principles in the statement.

# Chapter 20

---

# Brethren in
# Christ Church

---

D r. R. Donald Shafer, General Secretary of the General
Conference of the denomination, wrote from Upland, California:

Basically, our denomination is pro-life in stance, but we do
not particularly make statements on every issue. The reason
for this is that, obviously, there are some differences of opinion across the denomination in North America, and we are
concerned that we care for one another and respect differing
opinions.

I think it is safe to say that we are a typical Pietistic and
Evangelical denomination with our roots in Anabaptism and
Holiness. This means that most of our people do not agree
with persons making their own decisions regarding euthanasia.
There is respect for decisions made in the context of community that includes family and friends and medical professionals
with decisions made within legal and accepted practices in the
midst of both the faith, community and society at large.

With the movement that is now taking place, we certainly do not support either a doctor alone or even a medical
group making a decision without taking in the context of the
person involved, the family, and friends. We also highly urge

the church to be an integral part of these dialogues regarding ethics and morality.

This may not be an easy response, but I believe it pretty much represents where our denomination stands without making specific, rigid statements.

Chapter 21

# Brethren Church
# in Ashland, Ohio

On behalf of the denomination, Ron Walters wrote, "We have taken no official position, but we would generally be opposed to active euthanasia."

## Chapter 22

# The Moravian Church

The Moravian Church adopted a statement concerning euthanasia at the 1974 Synod, Northern Province. The report, presented by the Committee on Church and Society, supported the use of the Living Will, the refusal by terminally ill patients to the use of heroic treatment, but rejected active euthanasia, which they labelled "mercy killing." The statement read as follows:

WHEREAS: God has conquered death through Christ, and
    WHEREAS: this belief is a central affirmation to the faith of a Christian, and is declared through our worship as the Church, the living body of Christ, and
    WHEREAS: the resulting resurrection faith of the Christian ought to exemplify a lack of fear in the face of death, therefore be it
    RESOLVED: (1) that members of the Moravian Church reaffirm God's message to man about death as spoken by Christ: "I am the resurrection and the life, he who believes in me, though he die, yet shall he live, and whosoever lives and believes in me shall never die." (John 11:25-26) and be it further
    RESOLVED: (2) that in handling the subject of the right to die with dignity without heroic life-prolonging measures, faith in Christ's victory shall be the setting in which one speaks of death, and through which we find its ultimate meaning; not as creators of life, but as creatures who believe in the eternal love of our creator.

WHEREAS: science is developing ever-increasing means to prolong life, and

WHEREAS: neither science nor religion have fully understood the mystery of when the physical life of an individual ends, and

WHEREAS: individuals should have the right to predetermine what will happen to them when their death becomes imminent, therefore be it

RESOLVED: (3) that this Synod approve of the practice of allowing an individual to die with dignity.

WHEREAS: it would be helpful to family and attending physician(s) to know the wishes of individuals facing death, therefore be it

RESOLVED: (4) that members of Moravian congregations be encouraged to study documents such as a "Living Will" regarding care when their own death will become imminent and prepare in written form their wishes; and be it further

RESOLVED: (5) that since there are certain diseases which are either deteriorating and/or cause intractable pain, and which will undoubtedly have no known cure at any given period in scientific discoveries, members of the Moravian Church do not condemn those who choose the right to die with dignity without heroic life-prolonging measures or those who are supportive of their decision; and be it further

RESOLVED: (6) that since the physically, mentally, and/or emotionally handicapped persons do receive definite satisfactions from life, this Synod disapproves of "mercy killing" as an appropriate means for dealing with any problems that may surround handicapped persons, and be it further

RESOLVED: (7) that the Board of Christian Education and Evangelism be responsible for the scheduling, planning, and programming of seminars on death and dying, including euthanasia, during the next inter-synodal period and provide adequate and appropriate materials and resources for use at the local congregational level.

Professor Will Horstine, Pastoral Department of the Moravian Theological Seminary, Bethany, Pennsylvania, wrote to say that "Apparently we have no more recent legislation on the matter [as of February 3, 1992]."

# Chapter 23

# The Society of Friends (Quaker)

harles Mylander, General Superintendent of Friends Church Southwest Yearly Meeting stated that although they have no "official position on euthanasia . . . we generally oppose it as part of our consistently pro-life position."

Mary Glenn Hadley, Associate Secretary for Meeting Ministries Commission of Friends United Meeting, the headquarters for one branch of Friends, wrote that she has been "struggling with the very questions you are raising. I come with a nursing background to this position so have wrestled with many questions of euthanasia in my nursing practice. One aspect of my commission is right now trying to address the very questions of medical ethics from our Christian Quaker perspective. However, we have not even begun to think in terms of making any statements. Instead, we are hoping to develop questions appropriate for people who face these kinds of decisions to ask that will help them consider God's overall plan in these circumstances. This is in character with our Quaker heritage that we ask queries that call us into a Divine center out of which decisions can be made. . . . We are encouraging our people to study a book called *Medical Ethics, Human Choices* edited by John Rogers and published through Herald Press, a Mennonite Publishing house. We hope this will at least allow us to think seriously in a Christian perspective so that we can know how to ask the right questions."

# Chapter 24

# The Christian and Missionary Alliance

M aurice R. Irvin, editor of *Alliance Life*, responded to our inquiry as follows:

> Our denomination is governed by a General Council that meets annually to elect officers of administration and to determine overall policy regarding the work of our group. From time to time the denomination has adopted positions concerning certain social issues, notably divorce, family life and abortion. However, we have never taken an official position as a denomination through our General Council on euthanasia. I suspect that if this continues to be a hotly debated issue, it will come up at one of our Councils. To date that has not been the case.
>
> Therefore it is not possible for any person associated with our denomination to say that the position of the C&MA is one thing or another on this matter. I can assure you that most of our leaders and pastors would take a very conservative view. Most, I am sure, would abhor what Dr. Jack Kevorkian has done. However, I do not know of any denominational literature, statements by clergymen or academicians that comment on this matter.

Dr. Bill W. Lampher, President of the Saint Paul Bible College in St. Boniface, Minnesota, wrote (in 1992) that he believed that the position of the C&MA stands as Dr. L.L. King stated it in 1985. At that time Dr. King wrote:

The Christian and Missionary Alliance has not taken an official position on euthanasia. Since, however, our denomination has taken an official anti-abortion stand, I assume our General Council would also vote against euthanasia.

Editor Maurice R. Irvin pointed out, no one person can speak for the denomination, and therefore the comments of hospital chaplain Gerald Oosterveen of Hickory Hills, Illinois, that were published in the "Readers Opinion" section of *Alliance Life* (1992) cannot be interpreted as representing that of the Christian and Missionary Alliance. Chaplain Oosterveen commented on problems raised by the "right-to-die" and "pulling-the-plug" issues. He then commented:

Today, despite modern medical miracles and a longer-than-ever life span, one thing has not changed: women, men and children still die. When death actually occurs, though, increasingly is open for debate. The common definition of death is when an individual has sustained either irreversible cessation of circulatory or respiratory functions or irreversible cessation of all functions of the entire brain, including the brain stem.

Doctors today do not have to guess when a person is dead because machines tell them what bodily functions remain. They know when a person has no pulse or when he has stopped breathing. They know when the brain shows no activity.

What of persons whose brain functions have not stopped entirely but who are so impaired that they are unlikely to regain the ability to think and speak? It will not do simply to say that we may not play God or that, as long as the doctor has not pronounced the patient dead, we must use all our resources to support the comatose person. We must instead decide whether we are supporting life or merely temporarily delaying death. More important, we must consider whether our decisions should be governed solely by a doctor's definition.

Answering these questions would be easier if the Bible gave us directions. In biblical times, just as today, someone was considered dead when a knowledgeable person said so.

But the Bible is silent about agonizing twilight in which a person is neither wholly dead nor truly alive. Our decisions, therefore, must be shaped by what we believe about life, about the function of death and about life after death.

I admit to a twofold bias that shaped my thinking. Almost twenty-five years ago I was painfully thrust into the life-support arena when doctors asked how we wanted to treat the cancer in our son. They offered no hope; it was a question of making him comfortable or subjecting him to experimental treatment. We chose comfort over chance, and he died at age nine.

Today, as a hospital chaplain, I frequently deal with families who must decide what to do about life support. When I stand at the bedside of these comatose loved ones, I often wonder if the joke is not on the living. Are we trying to sustain an empty shell while the person whose it was has long since returned to the Creator?

The Christian community must see death in a broader context than mere biological or brain death; life is more than the total of a human being's functions, more than heartbeat and breathing and brainflow combined. Life is relationships with God, human beings and creation. The Westminster Catechism says, "Man's chief and highest end is to glorify God, and fully to enjoy him forever."

On earth even the best life is, in James's words, "a mist that appears for a little while and then vanishes" (4:14, NIV). The apostle Paul said in Philippians 1:23, "I desire to depart and be with Christ, which is better by far." Death is not the end for believers; it is the entrance to unimpaired eternal life.

I have come to believe it is wrong to deny permanently brain-damaged, comatose Christians the opportunity to enjoy fellowship in heaven with God and the saints when he or she no longer can glorify God here and will never again have a meaningful relationship with another human being on earth. The lack of an official pronouncement of death cannot change the reality that for all practical purposes this person is now dead. God forbid that our frantic, fruitless life-support activity should affirm Satan's boast, "A man will give all he has for his own life" (Job 2:4) or that of a loved one, even if the life remaining is hardly life.

When my son was mere days from dying, I read the description of heaven in Revelation 21 and 22. It hints at such beauty, joy and happiness that my little boy exclaimed, "Dad, it will be so beautiful there. I can hardly wait to see it."

I believe Christians err when they bring to the bedside every possible machine, drug or procedure that cannot change the ultimate outcome but only prolongs the dying process. When all is said and done, it comes down to whether we love our family members enough to let their struggle end quickly, and whether we trust God enough to let them enter joyfully into His indescribably beautiful presence.

# Chapter 25

# The Christian Church (Disciples of Christ)

D r. Thomas R. McCormick is Senior Lecturer in Medical Ethics, Department of Medical History and Ethics, School of Medicine, University of Washington, Seattle, Washington. He is also an ordained minister in the Disciples of Christ denomination. He pointed out that:

> . . . the Disciples of Christ is a religious body which prizes the autonomy of local congregations. They also prize the doctrine of the "priesthood of all believers" and hold that persons ought to follow an informed conscience on ethical issues. (The conscience is informed by Scripture, Tradition, and the application of reason in the temporal context.) This same respect for autonomy also allows for a great deal of diversity of opinion within each congregation. In this sense issues such as "euthanasia" are usually considered matters of individual conscience.

His statement is underscored by Dr. D. Duane Cummins, President of Bethany College in Bethany, West Virginia. President Cummins wrote:

> Resolutions on moral ethical issues usually call the Church to study, but do not impose universally held positions on its members. One of the great hallmarks of discipledom is its tenacity in defending the freedom of individual opinion. Dis-

ciples are a people quick to challenge any source of authority that does not begin with an act of individual choice. An example of this continuing Disciples tradition is its stance on the controversial issue of abortion. The resolution passed by the General Assembly (1) affirmed the principle of individual liberty, freedom of individual conscious and the sacredness of life for all persons and (2) stated the respect for differences in religious beliefs concerning abortion and opposed, in accord with the principle of religious liberty, any attempt to legislate a specific religious opinion or belief concerning abortion upon all Americans.

While Disciples as a body may disapprove of the general practice of abortion, they recognize a greater danger of legislating a single moral opinion for all persons, thereby abridging the freedom of individual choice. This is a cherished part of Disciples heritage and it is my judgement that any action on Euthanasia would be almost identical to the action on abortion. Two discernable trends emerge through all the resolutions that have been passed over the last thirty years: (1) a clear protection of the individual right of decision, and (2) the absence of rigid pronouncements designed to govern individual lifestyles.

In seeking to assess the general opinion of Disciples of Christ regarding euthanasia, Dr. McCormick wrote:

I believe that in general the majority of Disciples are opposed to the practice of euthanasia, or the practice of physicians actively ending the lives of their patients. We hold a high regard for the sanctity and worth of each human life. We accept death as natural. We accept the application of medicine and technologies which are reasonably believed to restore health and function to life. We accept the fact that in some cases medical intervention will be "futile" in either preserving life or restoring health and in such cases are quite willing to forego life sustaining treatment. We further accept the position that individual patients have the moral and legal right to determine the nature and extent of their health care at the end of life, consistent with the available resources. We have supported the use of Advance Directives such as the Living Will, or Natural Death Act Directives which have been passed in forty-one states. We also support the use of Durable Power of Attorney For Health Care which allows the patient the right to delegate to a chosen surrogate the right and responsibility to make decisions for the patient should he or she lose consciousness or competency for decision making. We are committed to encouraging health care providers in learning the most effective pain control measures so that compassionate palliative care may be rendered to patients in the dying process. We have the utmost respect for the Hospice concept, which allows patients who have chosen to forego life sustaining treatment, to be cared for with primary emphasis on comfort measures and palliative care as opposed to aggressive medical intervention. This is in keeping with our belief that death is natural and is congruent with our belief in the human stewardship of life and its resources.

Every two years the Christian Church, Disciples of Christ, holds a General Assembly. During the business session resolutions may be passed indicating the sentiment of voting delegates. Robert Clarke Brock, President of the Northwest Regional Christian Church pointed out that in 1977, the General Assembly approved a "Resolution Concerning 'Death With Dignity.'" The Resolution, No. 7724, read as follows:

WHEREAS, modern biological technology has developed powerful means of intervening in and delaying the dying process, and

WHEREAS, increasing numbers of adult Americans are dying of chronic disease, prolonged over a period of months or years, and

WHEREAS, increasing numbers of dying persons are hospitalized or receive care in other institutions (seventy-three percent of the adults who died in 1963 received institutional care during the last year of their life and this percentage has grown steadily over the years from thirty-seven percent in 1937), and

WHEREAS, increasing numbers of persons institutionalized in the terminal stage of illness have their life prolonged through artificial means, even in the face of extreme suffering, irretrievable loss of consciousness, and

WHEREAS, the intervention in the dying process

through artificial means obscures the meaning of death, so that today it is more a matter of moral judgement than biological fact, and

WHEREAS, this situation has given rise to a number of ethical dilemmas, including the following:

1) patients frequently lose control over decisions affecting their death.

2) patient's dignity and quality of life may be sacrificed to the goal of cellular continuation.

3) grave financial burdens may accrue to families and to society in no hope of recovery, rehabilitation or mentation.

4) disagreement and confusion often persists with regard to the issue of who the decision maker(s) should be in determining the nature of the treatment, or the cessation of treatment for a dying person.

5) increasing legal issues have arisen which may threaten the protection of the physician, the right of survivors to collect insurance payments, the availability of organs for transplantation, and the right of the patient to refuse treatment.

THEREFORE BE IT RESOLVED, that the General Assembly of the Christian Church (Disciples of Christ) meeting in Kansas City, Missouri, October 21-26, 1977:

1) Encourage its congregations to study the issues related to dying with dignity.

2) Request the General Minister and President to appoint a person or persons to develop a theological statement to help our members reflect on the theological issues which surround the dying person in this time.

3) Encourage its members to engage in the dialogue pertaining to the formation of public policy toward the end that legislation which may develop in the various states is enriched by our concern for the moral issues at stake.

In 1991, at the General Assembly in Tulsa, Resolution No. 9146, "Concerning the End Stages of Life" was adopted. It reads as follows:

WHEREAS, God's gift of life requires our stewardship of every part of creation, including the end stages of life; and

WHEREAS, the Christian Church (Disciples of Christ) has a heritage of informed conscience and open dialogue on related issues, including the approval of Resolution 7724 concerning death with dignity; and

WHEREAS, increasing numbers of people are dying of chronic disease and debilitating injury, and their dying is prolonged over a period of months or years by technology; and

WHEREAS, the intervention in the dying process through artificial means has become a norm; and

WHEREAS, this situation has given rise to a number of ethical dilemmas, including the following:

1. Patients and families may lose control over decisions affecting the final days of individuals;

2. The individual's dignity and quality of life may be sacrificed;

3. Serious financial burdens may accrue to families and to society in situations where there are no reasonable expectations of recovery, rehabilitation, or mentation;

4. Lengthening of litigation may be used for political purposes, ignoring patient's rights;

THEREFORE BE IT RESOLVED, that the General Assembly of the Christian Church (Disciples of Christ) meeting in Tulsa, Oklahoma, October 25-30, 1991:

1. Support congregations as communities of faith who:
   a. Seek new insight from our Biblical and traditional heritage through prayerful study of these matters; and
   b. Prepare for possible extended durations of ethical, legal, and community debate surrounding some situations; and
   c. Encourage families to discuss possibilities openly and honestly before a decision must be faced; and
   d. Cultivate relationships with hospital social workers, chaplains, ethicists, and other caregivers so as to maintain current knowledge of medical developments.

2. Encourage congregations and pastors to recognize opportunities related to the end stages of life and to educate and to facilitate people finding a commonality of human experience by:
   a. Learning the terminology; and
   b. Becoming familiar with policies of local hospitals, nursing homes, and other care-giving institutions

regarding advance directives and exploring an individual's rights under the state, provincial and national laws; and

c. Developing a theological understanding of life and death; and

d. Recognizing the possibility of attention from the media, government officials, medical facility personnel and various issue-oriented groups which may seek to use these circumstances for purposes far beyond the immediate concerns of the individual, family, or health care workers.

3. Acknowledge that local pastors may be called to prophetic as well as pastoral leadership surrounding such issues and will require congregational support; and

BE IT FURTHER RESOLVED, that the General Assembly:

1. Encourage pastors and congregations to make their opinions known, recognizing that each situation is unique and offers a great opportunity for shared ministry and deeper spiritual growth; and

2. Encourage its members to engage in the dialogue pertaining to the formation of public policy that includes concern for moral issues; and

3. Request the General Minister and President to develop a process for creating a theological statement to help our members reflect on the theological, moral, and ethical issues related to the end stages of life.

# Chapter 26

---

# The Church
# of the Nazarene

---

The Rev. Donald D. Owens, Secretary of the Board of General Superintendents of the Church of the Nazarene General Headquarters noted that, "While we currently do not have a statement on this [euthanasia] in our official documents, we have research in process on the matter."

Dr. Albert L. Truesdale, Dean of the Faculty at the Nazarene Theological Seminary in Kansas City, Missouri, kindly provided a statement from his book, *A Matter of Life and Death: Bioethics and the Christian* (Kansas City: Nazarene Publishing House, 1990). He noted "I think the statement is fairly representative of the position the Church of the Nazarene will eventually adopt." The statement reads as follows:

> The Bible records only one instance of active euthanasia, the "mercy-killing" of King Saul by an unnamed Amalekite (2 Samuel 1:1-15). In this instance, the one who administered euthanasia was himself immediately struck down at David's command. However, the execution of the Amalekite occurred not primarily because of the *kind* of action taken, but because of the one ("the Lord's annointed," verse 14) to whom it was administered. So the Bible gives us no direct guidance on this matter, except its insistence that human life is sacred and must not be violated.
>
> The sixth commandment says, "You shall not murder." But the question arises, "Is euthanasia the same as violently and maliciously destroying the life of another?" At least by

intent and definition it is not. By what principle then are Christians to be guided? Does euthanasia violate a reverence for the sanctity of life? Members of the Hemlock Society who want to legalize euthanasia are prompted by humane and merciful interests. They believe that carefully monitored legalized euthanasia would demonstrate respect, rather than disrespect for life.

Nevertheless, there are two arguments that seem to rule out Christian support for euthanasia. The *first* is the Christian doctrine of humankind's fall into sin and the religious, moral, social and mental impairment it generated. Christians have a somber recognition of man's capacity for cruelty, deceit, and the misuse of other persons. Unlike some who attribute this to a lack of education or favorable social conditions, Christians know that it stems from a religious and moral depravity deep within the spirit of man, namely from his alienation from God. Many times in this century we have observed persons and nations committing monstrous evils by submitting civil law to evil ends. Even given the noble intentions that may prompt efforts to legalize euthanasia, such an option puts more responsibility on fallen man than he can successfully bear.

*Second,* human life is too sacred and delicate to be placed under the ultimate control of fallible men and women. Its general security is too vulnerable to trust the point of termination to the discretion of any one person or group of persons.

Both of these arguments have serious drawbacks, not the least of which is their uneven application in similar situations. If applied consistently, both arguments would appear to rule out capital punishment and all war. It may also be that they could be used successfully against "allowing to die" (withdrawal of artificial life support systems).

In a more personal comment he wrote:

Although I believe euthanasia to be religiously and morally unacceptable, I am also sensitive to the intense human agony that often drives a person either to seek medically assisted euthanasia or to support its legalization. The testimony of Marjorie Wantz, one of Dr. Kevorkian's most recent "patients," is an excellent example of the moral agony a person facing a terminal illness often experiences. I must say that if I were to state a position based solely on sensitivity to the trauma persons and families experience, I would likely become a supporter of legalized euthanasia.

My opposition to medically assisted euthanasia and to euthanasia in general comes from a different source. I believe that in the act of euthanasia, as opposed to "allowing to die," a person and those who assist him or her seizes an unjustifiably dangerous power; they set aside the sanctity of human life and take a responsibility which fallen humankind is not capable of shouldering. By intentionally ending a life in which a measure of meaning, love, and intentionality is still present, the act of euthanasia steps over a moral boundary; the immediate problem may be solved, but the "solution" threatens to plunge the race into a moral void from which there may be no return. In the act of euthanasia, it seems to me, a person arrogates himself or herself a power and knowledge that expresses the primordial idolatry Christians call original sin. My position appears to brush aside the legitimate compassion that prompts support for euthanasia. My response to the objection is that in this case compassion and the desire to relieve suffering must yield to higher values.

Dr. Millard Reed, President of Trevecca Nazarene College stated:

I will tell you that as a pastor of thirty-five years, I have come to appreciate the position of passive euthanasia and have often counseled and supported families to that difficult decision.

Again, I would never be in support of active euthanasia.

# Chapter 27

## Jehovah's Witness

In response to my request the Watchtower Bible and Tract Society of New York, Inc. (Jehovah's Witnesses) sent a copy of the magazine *Awake!* for October 22, 1991, which bore the caption "Help for the Dying" on the front cover. The first article, "Help for the Dying in our Modern Age," raised the question concerning the best help for "hopelessly ill in our technologically advanced age?" No specific response was given, perhaps because the magazine is published in sixty-four different languages and therefore must touch the needs of differing cultures. It was pointed out that:

> Some have the view that everything medically possible should be done for each person who is sick. This view is expressed by the Association of American Physicians and Surgeons: "The obligation of the physician to the comatose, vegetative, or developmentally disabled patient does not depend upon the prospect for recovery. The physician must always act on behalf of the patient's well-being." This means providing all the treatment or medical help that can possibly be applied. Do you feel that this is always best for a person who is gravely ill?
>
> To many people that course certainly sounds laudable. Yet, in the past few decades, experience with technologically advanced medicine has given rise to a new and different viewpoint. In a 1984 landmark paper entitled "The Physician's Responsibility Toward Hopelessly Ill Patients," a panel of ten experienced physicians concluded: "A decrease in aggressive treatment of the hopelessly ill patient is advisable when such

treatment would only prolong a difficult and uncomfortable process of dying." Five years later the same doctors published an article of the same title that was titled "A Second Look." Considering the same problem, they made an even plainer statement: "Many physicians and ethicists . . . have concluded, therefore, that it is ethical to withdraw nutrition and hydration (fluids) from certain dying, hopelessly ill, or permanently unconscious patients."

We cannot dismiss such comments as simple theorizing or as a mere debate that has no real bearing on us. Numerous Christians have been faced with agonizing decisions in this connection. Should a hopelessly ill loved one be kept alive on a respirator? Should intravenous feeding or other artificial feeding methods be applied to a terminally ill patient? When the situation is hopeless, should all the financial means of a relative or of an entire family, be expanded to pay for treatment, perhaps involving transportation to a distant center to receive the most advanced treatment?

You no doubt appreciate that such questions are not easy to answer. Much as you would want to help an ill friend or loved one, if you had to face these questions you might wonder: "What guidance does the Christian have? What resources are available for help? Most important, what do the Scriptures say on the subject?

A second item, "What Care for the Terminally Ill?" noted that because of the modern emphasis on "technology and cure, medical personnel have come to regard death as a failure or defeat" which in turn makes the primary aim of medical practice that of "preventing death at all costs." The article quotes one unnamed doctor:

Most physicians have lost the pearl that was once an intimate part of medicine, and that is humanism. Machinery, efficiency and precision have driven from the heart warmth, compassion, sympathy and concern for the individual. Medicine is now an icy science; its charm belongs to another age. The dying man can get little comfort from the mechanical doctor.

It is acknowledged that this statement represents only one person's point of view and that although it is not a "universal indictment of the medical profession . . . you have probably seen that many people have developed a fear of being kept alive on machines." The article continues:

> Gradually another view began to be heard. It was that in some cases people should be allowed to die naturally, with dignity, and without being subjected to the intervention of heartless technology. A poll recently conducted for *Time* magazine revealed that over three quarters of those contacted felt that a doctor should be allowed to withdraw life-sustaining treatment for a terminally ill patient. The study reached this conclusion: "Once reconciled to the inevitable, (people) want to die with dignity, not tethered to a battery of machines in an intensive-care unit like a laboratory specimen under glass." Do you agree?

The article notes that in response to the plight of the terminally ill DNR (Do Not Resuscitate) policies have come into use in hospitals together with living wills, which although not binding everywhere do provide guidance as to the individual's wishes. The important role of hospice care is also recognized.

The third article, "The Best Help Available!" directs the reader to the scripture for guidance. The "philosophy of preserving life at all costs" is described as a product of "modern secular philosophy" which teaches that "this life is all there is." For the Jehovah Witness, "the Bible teaches that life is sacred to Jehovah. 'With you is the source of life,' the inspired psalmist wrote (Psalm 36:9). Should, then, a true Christian agree to share in euthanasia?"

When King Saul's armor-bearer responded to the mortally wounded king's request to hasten his death and because the man complied he was put to death by King David (1 Samuel 31:3-4, 2 Samuel 1:2-16). "This biblical event, then, in no way justifies a Christian's having any part in euthanasia." The question is then raised:

> Does this mean, though, that a Christian must do everything that is technologically possible to prolong a life that is ending? Must one extend the dying process as long as possible? The Scriptures teach that death is not a friend of man, but an enemy. (1 Corinthians 15:26) Further, the dead are neither suffering nor in bliss, but they are in a sleeplike state. (Job 3:11, 13; Ecclesiastes 9:5, 10; John 11; 11-14; Acts 7:60). The future prospects of life for the dead are totally dependent on God's power to resurrect them through Jesus Christ (John

6:39, 40) so we find that God has provided us with this helpful knowledge: Death is not something to be longed for, but
neither is there an obligation to resort to desperate efforts to
prolong the dying process.

What guidelines do the Jehovah's Witnesses have when "a loved one
is in a terminal state?"

First, we must acknowledge that each situation involving a
terminal illness is different, tragically different, and there are
no universal rules. Furthermore, the Christian should be careful to consider the laws of the land in such cases. (Matthew
22:2) Keep in mind, too, that no loving Christian would advocate medical neglect.

Only when there is undeniably terminal disease (where
the situation has been clearly determined to be hopeless)
should consideration be given to asking that life-support technology be discontinued. In such cases there is no Scriptural
reason to insist on medical technology that would simply prolong a dying process that is far advanced.

These often are very difficult situations and may involve
agonizing decisions. How is one to know, for example, when a
situation is hopeless? Though no one can be absolutely certain,
reason needs to be exercised along with careful counsel.

One medical paper advising doctors comments: "If there
is disagreement concerning the diagnosis or prognosis or both,
the life-sustaining approach should be continued until reasonable agreement is reached. However, insistence on certainty
beyond a reasonable point can handicap the physician dealing
with treatment options in apparently hopeless cases. The rare
report of a patient with a similar condition who survived is
not an overriding reason to continue aggressive treatment.
Such negligible statistical possibilities do not outweigh the
reasonable expectations of outcome that will guide treatment
decisions."

In such a predicament, the Christian, whether patient or
relative, would rightfully expect some help from his physician.
This medical paper concludes: "In any case, it is unfair simply
to provide a mass of medical facts and options and leave the

patient adrift without any further guidance on the alternative courses of action and inaction."

Local Christian elders, being mature ministers, can also be of great value. Of course, the patient and his immediate family must make their own balanced decision in this very emotional situation.

Finally, reflect on these points. Christians very much want to stay alive so that they can enjoy serving God. They realize, though, that in the present system, all of us are dying; in this sense all of us are terminally ill. It is only through the ransoming blood of Jesus Christ that we have any hope of reversing that situation. (Ephesians 1:7)

This particular item refers readers to two articles that appeared in earlier editions of *Awake!* The first entitled "What About 'Mercy Killing'?" was published May 8, 1974, and the second, "Mercy Killing," on March 8, 1978. Both articles reflect an awareness of the inherent difficulties in cases where an individual is dying from a painful, incurable illness.

Active euthanasia is forbidden on three grounds. First, it violates the commandment "You must not murder" (Exodus 20:13). Second, it violates "the Bible's command that Christians 'hold a good conscience'" (1 Pet. 3:16). In discussing this point, the article refers to comments by Robert S. Morison in *Scientific American*, 1973, where he states that "an overwhelming majority of physicians, and certainly a substantial majority of laymen, instinctively recoil from such active measures as prescribing a known poison or injecting a large bubble into a vein." Third, Christians are required to "be in subjection to superior authorities" (Romans 13:1), and obey the laws of the land. And, in Jehovah's Witness thinking, active euthanasia is murder. Because they respect God's view of the sanctity of life, out of regard for their own consciences and in obedience to governmental laws, those desiring to conform their lives to Bible principles would never resort to positive euthanasia (*Awake!*, May 8, 1978, p. 28).

The Jehovah's Witnesses do not oppose passive euthanasia. "However, where there is clear evidence that death is imminent and unavoidable, the Scriptures do not require that extraordinary (and perhaps costly) means be employed to stretch out the dying process. In such a case, allowing death to take its course uninhibited would not violate any law of God. However, there is need for caution before people decide that a patient is beyond all hope of recovery" (*Awake!*, March 8, 1978, p.7).

It should be noted that Jehovah's Witnesses believe they "are now living in the 'conclusion' or 'the last days' of the present system of things

(Matt, 24:3-34, 2 Tim.3:1-5). This means that God's new order will become a reality within this generation." This "new order" means that "not only will people no longer become sick, but those who are now afflicted with infirmities will be permanently healed" (Isa. 33:24; 35:5-7) (*Awake!*, May 8, 1974, p. 28).

Although Jehovah's Witnesses do not shun medical assistance in time of illness, they do refuse blood transfusions outside of auto transfusions—blood donated by the person him/herself and frozen for possible use by the donor at a later date. The refusal to accept blood donated by others rests in the interpretation of biblical passages commanding that animal flesh with its blood not be eaten (Gen. 9:3-6; Leviticus 17:11-14; and the prohibition in Acts 15:28-29). For the Witnesses, intravenous injection is a form of feeding on blood. Witnesses do not interpret the refusal to accept transfusions as acts of martyrdom or, should the patient die, as suicide. According to William L. Barry, a Jehovah's Witness official: "They consider their integrity and witness to God's law more important. They have confidence in the resurrection and God's reward for them" (reported by Russell Chandler, "Rather Die Than Take Blood—Witnesses," *The Los Angeles Times*, August 20, 1977).

# Chapter 28

## The Seventh Day Adventists

A ccording to Dr. Mervyn G. Hardinge, Director of the Health and Temperance Department of the General Conference of Seventh Day Adventists, the denomination has undertaken no research to date on the subject of euthanasia. Indeed, Dr. Jim Walters, Professor of Christian Ethics at Loma Linda University, California, commented that "one would think that a denomination as heavily involved in health care as ours is" would have engaged in such a study. However, "an informal consensus appears to exist among S.D.A. clinicians and theologians in favor of passive euthanasia," according to Dr. David Larson of Loma Linda University. "The religious rationale is that it is both pointless and cruel to prolong the process of dying for no justifiable reasons."

Dr. Gerald R. Winslow, Professor of Ethics, Pacific Union College, Unwin, California, responded to the first question in the questionnaire (see Appendix VIII for a copy of the complete questionnaire):

> I know of no moral or theological positions espoused by Adventists that would prevent this patient's physician from ordering the termination of artificial life-support. I believe that most Adventist physicians would be willing to so act if they were reasonably certain that continuing artificial life-support would be futile. Personally, I would hope that the family could be involved in the decision to terminate what appear from this brief description to be unreasonable measures to sustain life. But assuming that this patient's brain is "gone," meaning a

295

persistent vegetative state is an accurate description of the facts, then there is no moral or theological obligation known to Adventists that would require further life-supporting effort.

Dr. Jack Provensha, a medical doctor and Professor Emeritus at the Loma Linda University, suggested that the Seventh Day Adventists would sanction the removal of life-support systems for someone whose brain "was gone" and who would die without the system:

> The person is defined functionally by SDA's. The above individual had suffered "personal death," even if he has not yet technically suffered brain death. The "meaning" of "active" and "passive" euthanasia differs for those who administer it. The difference being one of "causal" participation in the event. Letting nature take its course is not the same as giving nature a boost. We are concerned about protecting the sensitivities for life in the care provided but not meaninglessly. Heroics in the above case would be meaningless.

Concerning the case of M in the second question Professor Winslow wrote:

> Again, Adventists have not taken an official position. But my educated hunch is that Adventists do not differ from the mainstream of Christian thought on this subject. Most denominations, and Adventists are no exception, are against suicide. Suicide is viewed by Adventists as a breaking of one of God's commandments. But this still leaves open the question of whether or not every case of "active euthanasia" carried out with the patient's consent or carried out by the patient him/herself counts as wrongful suicide. My own position is that health care providers should not conduct active euthanasia, and I am quite sure that nearly all, if not all, Adventist practitioners would concur. No state in the union allows for active euthanasia, the AMA does not permit it, and there are good reasons beyond the conventions of laws or professional ethics to establish a strong moral presumption against active euthanasia being conducted by the medical profession. I believe that active euthanasia, if practiced by physicians and nurses, would seriously alter for the worse the ethos of medicine. I notice that those like Dame Saunders and Dr. Kubler-

Ross who have probably gained the most experience in helping the dying are generally opposed to active euthanasia. But what about the patient in your case who may take an overdose? Personally, I do not think that we should do all in our power to prevent such an occurrence. Nor should there be criminal penalties for attempting suicide in such cases.

Dr. Provensha believes also that his denomination would not favor M taking her own life:

Recognizing that pain can be depersonalizing as can drugs, the SDA physician would try to balance the drugs against the pain in such a way as to maximize insofar as possible what person-hood remains. The patient may still pull it off but the physician should be guided by his person-protective ideals in the care he prescribes. It is personal life that has value and as long as it persists it should be protected. The issue is the quality of life, not mere biological life. The health care provider who values personal existence will do what he can to preserve it. The alternative is open to all kinds of abuse.

Nor would Seventh Day Adventists approve of assisted suicide for the terminally ill. Dr. Larson comments, "There is a strong, though informal, presumption against deliberately destroying human life." Dr. Provensha expanded the idea. "Personal life is precious as a gift of God and must not be rejected casually. The patient has the right to do what we may think is wrong but not the right to have others violate their moral standards in assisting her." He continued: "Self destruction is wrong whether assisted or not and whether compassionate or not. Compassion should be directed toward supportive care and pain control."

Dr. Winslow also believes that the SDA church would not approve of assisted suicide or "compassionate murder." Concerning the latter, he wrote:

I believe that my church would oppose such action as wrongful on the grounds that human beings should not arrogate to themselves the power to end life which belongs only to God. (Adventists, it should be noted, tend to be pacifists for much the same reasons.) But I should hasten to add that physicians should be free to provide sufficient dosages of pain relievers so that the patients can be kept as free of pain as possible even if this results in the unintended shortening of life in some cases.

Adventists believe in an afterlife and in judgement. "SDA's do not believe in the Platonic immortal soul," wrote Dr. Provensha, "but do believe in a resurrection at the end of the world. They also believe in divine judgement based not on single acts such as compulsive suicide, however, but in the general relationship with God. A rational, calculated, self-destructive act would be considered to reflect an unfortunate and broken relationship with the life-giver." Professor Walters noted that, "If active euthanasia were deemed as murder (of the self) then this 'Sin' would obviously count against one in the judgement." Professor Winslow wrote: "Adventists do not believe in the immortality of the soul. The Adventist view is that human beings are souls in their wholeness. At death the person 'sleeps'—to use the biblical metaphor. So far as I know there is no Adventist position on what effect participation in euthanasia would have on eternal destiny. But it should be noted that Adventists believe in salvation by grace alone and not by works."

So far as euthanasia affecting the burial rituals, Professor Walters states, "Adventists are not heavily liturgical; and what liturgy pertains to a funeral service applies to saint and sinner alike. The difference would appear in what was said (or not said!) in the funeral sermon." Dr. Provensha suggests that, "It might condition the attitudes of mourners who might feel more sorrowful about the death. But no difference would be made in the rituals, etc."

Concerning counseling, Dr. Winslow wrote, "I hope and I believe that Adventists would seek to help those who, for example, want to sign a Living Will. My own counsel would be that we should never seek to end by direct action the life of any human being, but we should be willing to stop medical treatment that seems futile." Professor Walters thinks, "It would depend upon the local pastor. Possibly pastoral counseling—or psychological, and the direction it would take (pro or con euthanasia) would be decided by the pastor involved."

Dr. Larson suggests that four aspects of counseling would be important: to "listen," to "sort out as many options as possible," to "encourage deliberateness, not speed," and to "invite people to make up their own minds responsibly." Dr. Provensha thinks that the counseling "would be in the direction of helping the persons counseled to accept the true status of the one dying. This would apply to 'K.' For one still personally alive it would have to do with providing information requisite for deciding to reject treatment alternatives. Also some attempt to instil in such a person a sense of value for what life remained. It would allow the person to make his or her final judgement, however." With regard to counseling and "active euthanasia," Dr. Provensha believes it would counsel against it as an immoral act of self-destruction—and would try to instill a sense of respect for life—even if limited. The only biblical passage quoted by Dr. Provensha was "Thou shalt not kill."

In a more recent communiqué, dated March 2, 1992, Professor Walters revealed an important insight on the relationship of religious liberty and health:

> Please allow me to share how I see a couple of historic Adventist doctrinal emphases cutting in opposite ways on the active euthanasia question. The two doctrines are religious liberty and healthful living.
>
> Religious liberty's roots, for Adventists, spring from prudential concern for themselves as an often castigated group because of their unique beliefs. Hence, advocacy of religious liberty was, at the least, a struggle for survival. Later, Adventists applied this belief to others, and hence, the denomination has aided groups such as the Amish in contending for their right to unpopular religious practices.
>
> The second doctrinal point is that of health. A hundred years ago this emphasis led many Adventists to adopt a vegetarian diet and a lifestyle characterized by exercise and abstinence from substances such as alcohol and tobacco. At the turn of the century this emphasis also led to the establishment of Loma Linda University. Today the Adventist Church is heavily involved in running health care institutions around the world.
>
> What do these two doctrinal emphases have to do with euthanasia? I suggest that the two beliefs point in contradictory ways on euthanasia. On the one hand, concern for religious liberty lends credence to a patient's contending for his or her God-given liberty to make a personal decision about a topic so important as when and how death should come. On the other hand, the Adventist focus on health can tend to support an ethos of physical vitalism—keeping the body in operation as a good itself.

In an address titled "Christianity and the Right to Die" given at an ecumenical conference sponsored by the Center for Process Studies at the School of Theology at Claremont, California and the Center for Christian Bioethics at Loma Linda University, Dr. David Larson commented on the issues of "Freedom for Integrity," and "Intense and Intractable Pain." In the revised written document he stated:

> Although the so-called rule of double effect was probably initially developed in the late Middle Ages to justify some forms of self-defense, in subsequent generations it has been applied to other issues as well, including the problem of intense and intractable human suffering. This rule allows one to justify morally troubling outcomes of an honorable action providing four criteria are fulfilled: "(1) the act itself, prescinding from the evil caused, is good or at least indifferent; (2) the good effect of the act is what the agent intends directly, only permitting the evil effect; (3) the good effect must not come about by means of the evil effect; and (4) there must be some proportionately grave reason for permitting the evil effect to occur."

During the past quarter of a century, the historical development of the rule of double effect has been debated. The precise meaning of the four criteria, and especially the meaning of the third standard, has been a matter of controversy. And the general value of the rule as a whole has been questioned. But because it enables persons to justify the indirect termination of human life in specified circumstances while also underscoring the moral necessity of preserving human life in the vast majority of cases, it is likely that the rule of double effect will survive these challenges.

Imagine a dying patient whose discomfort is totally absorbing. Persons must be careful in such circumstances not to communicate Christian convictions about suffering in ways that add to the grief of those who are in agony. It is true that Christianity does believe that in general humans benefit from their ability to experience pain. It is also true that Christianity realizes that a certain amount of suffering is to be expected, particularly by those who do not always conform to custom. And yes, Christianity does teach that some forms and degrees of suffering can be redemptive, both for the sufferer and for those who emphatically observe. But it is not true that Christian convictions at their best prize suffering for its own sake. There is such a thing as preoccupying and pointless pain, a discomfort so wholly encompassing that it eclipses all human capacities to acknowledge and nurture relationships. Christianity has no vested interest in such agony.

The rule of double effect, or something like it, can be applied in such circumstances to provide relief. Building upon the distinction between "intended" and "merely foreseeable" consequences, it justifies the administration of pain-relieving medications even if these drugs have the unintended effect of shortening the patient's life somewhat, providing that only the relief of suffering is directly willed. Granted, it can be difficult to know how much more swiftly the patient dies, because unrelieved suffering can also have a debilitating effect. But in such circumstances the rule of double effect would justify actions that unquestionably shorten human life somewhat, providing that only the relief of suffering is directly intended.

Is this an empty verbal game that allows one to kill a sufferer without admitting it to oneself and others? Yes and no. From one point of view, the rule of double effect can be so viewed. A less severe and more accurate judgment might be that it is a game but not a vacuous or vicious one. It assuages the anxieties of those who administer the agents of pain-relief that hasten death. It also reinforces the sometimes conflicting obligations of relieving suffering and preserving life without wholly losing one in the other. The rule of double effect is also having a beneficial impact on discussions far beyond its original intellectual home. The President's Commission, for instance, did not find much help in the distinction between "intended" and "merely foreseeable" consequences when separating acceptable from unacceptable actions that lead to death, but it did find that the distinction pointed toward other important factors, such as the symbolic role of physicians as practicers of the healing arts. Most importantly, the rule of double effect has brought relief from suffering to many patients on the conviction that the Christian presumption in favor of prolonging human life can be overridden by intense and intractable pain. The rule of double effect may be a game; if so, we ought to continue playing it until a better one comes along.

In discussing "extraordinary medical" care, Dr. Larson pointed out:

> Several features of an "extraordinary medical means," as this
> has been understood by Christians and others, are worth un-
> derlining. First, it is burdensome. Second, it is burdensome
> from the patient's own point of view. Third, it can be burden-
> some to the patient's family and friends. Fourth, even if it is
> medically successful, it is "extraordinary" and therefore discre-
> tionary if it renders the person's life pointless to him or her.
> Fifth, the line between ordinary and extraordinary does vary
> from society to society, and it can vary from individual to in-
> dividual as well. Sixth, it is not necessary that the intervention
> be exotic or expensive or experimental to be considered ex-
> traordinary. And seventh, the overriding importance of the
> individual's relationships, and what the intervention will do to
> these relationships, informs the distinction. . . .
>
> In summary, then, an extraordinary and therefore discre-
> tionary treatment is any medical intervention that a free, in-
> formed and competent patient or his or her proper surrogate
> rejects as of negligible or negative net benefit, all things con-
> sidered. "Futility" does not refer to the absolute medical im-
> possibility of prolonging a particular human life. It refers to
> the intervention's net benefit or lack thereof when it is com-
> prehensively viewed by the patient himself or herself or by a
> proper surrogate. The distinction between ordinary and ex-
> traordinary treatments, particularly as understood lately, pre-
> serves an individual's right to refuse medical interventions of
> even the mildest forms if to that patient or to his or her
> proper decision maker the treatment is not worth the bother.
> This is a thorough expression of the right to die.

Should Christian ethical convictions be translated into social
policy? Dr. Larson wrote:

> It is neither possible nor prudent directly and immediately to
> translate Christianity's ethical convictions into social policy,
> whether legislative, executive or judicial. Those who influence
> the formation of social policy at the local, regional, national
> and global levels do well to attend to ethical considerations.
> But they also do well to attend to the constituents they serve.
> At its best, social policy is neither sheer conformity to moral

norms nor mere conformity to moral convention. Social policy is the best possible approximation of moral norms in a given cultural setting. As such, it neither imposes too much nor requires too little from the citizenry. As the society changes, its social policies must change as well so as to keep the tension between the "real" and the "ideal" as taut as possible without snapping the tie that binds them to each other.

A theological warrant for political discernment deserves notice. Christians are among those who believe that in all circumstances God works for good. This does not mean that every occurrence is good or that it will immediately or eventually prove beneficial. Neither does this mean that each event takes place precisely as it does because God willed that it occur exactly in that way and no other. But it does mean that in, with and under the other factors that make an event what it is God is also at work as One who nudges as much good out of a particular set of circumstances as possible without overwhelming the creatures by the Creator's presence. Divine omnipresence does not merely mean that "God is everywhere;" it also means that in every experience of every life God is an influence for good in ways that take into account the prospects that are genuinely available to each life at each juncture. Human political advocacy must therefore rest on human political analysis. The goal is to discern as clearly as possible the contours of a given set of circumstances, the contents of a given set of ethical possibilities and the optimal current convergence between them.

I offer the following comments on the four alternatives for social policy before us regarding the right to die as my own current reading of the "signs of the times" and the "Wind of the Spirit." Discernment of each is often more accurate when it is communal. I therefore welcome alternative or even opposing readings of our circumstances and prospects.

## ALLOWING VOLUNTARY DEATHS

I believe that our first and most important political priority should be to protect Option 1 ("allowing voluntary deaths"). We would do well to consolidate, preserve and extend the gains that have already been made in social policy that at this time do allow competent and informed persons voluntarily to refuse medical interventions even if these refusals result in their deaths. Although it has been debated and contested, this expression of the right to die now receives widespread, though not universal, approval. Because in the United States, and perhaps in other nations, additional forms of the right to die often depend conceptually and politically on this one, it seems essential to make certain that it is safe and secure before moving on to other possibilities. Much has been accomplished since the early 1980s. These advances deserve protection.

There are a number of encouraging omens. For one thing, the President's Commission concluded in 1983 after extensive study and discussion that competent and informed patients do have the right voluntarily to refuse medical interventions that may extend their lives. It added that "health care institutions and professionals should try to enhance patients' abilities to make decisions on their own behalf and to promote understanding of the available treatment options." The American Medical Association agrees. The 1989 Current Opinions of its Council of Ethical and Judicial Affairs states that "The social commitment of the physician is to sustain life and relieve suffering. Where the performance of one duty conflicts with the other, the preferences of the patient should prevail. . . . For humane reasons, with informed consent, a physician may do what is medically necessary to relieve severe pain, or cease or omit treatment to permit a terminally ill patient to die when death is imminent. However, the physician should not intentionally cause death."

The right of a competent and informed patient voluntarily to refuse life sustaining therapies has also been upheld in a series of decisions by courts across the nation regarding William Bartling, Elizabeth Bouvia and most importantly, Nancy Beth Cruzan. The courts often appeal to the common law's recognition that a competent citizen possesses individual autonomy over decisions relating to his or her health and welfare and that therefore battery occurs when a physician imposes a medical intervention without valid consent. The trends are not universally positive, especially in the courts, but they are encouraging.

Although the right of competent and informed citizens

voluntarily to forego life-sustaining therapies now seems established among policy makers, it does face some practical challenges. One of these is the all-too-pervasive impression that citizens of the United States do not possess this right. Another is the fear of legal liability on the part of some clinicians and institutions that are asked by patients to be allowed to die under their care. Still another is the attempt by some to limit the scope of this right by specifying that some kinds of medical care, such as artificially conveyed nutrition and hydration, must always be provided. A further difficulty is that some individuals and institutions are not willing to honor this right. The patient must then either accept the medical intervention or transfer to another facility.

The biggest challenge in clinical circumstances, however, is that of ascertaining with sufficient certainty that the person who is refusing a medical intervention is doing so as a competent, informed and voluntary citizen. Mistaken judgments regarding this are literally deadly. Increasingly, the notion of "decisional capacity" is used instead of that of "competency," because it has been discovered that persons who can easily establish their competency in other areas of their lives sometimes make decisions regarding medical matters they subsequently regret. The norm of "decisional capacity" can be prejudicially used to judge anyone who refuses a medical intervention "incompetent" merely because he or she is refusing. Sometimes this does happen. Most often, however, the idea of "decisional capacity" is appropriately used to protect the patient against temporary or localized deviations from his or her characteristic thinking.

## ALLOWING NONVOLUNTARY DEATHS

I believe that Option 2 ("allowing nonvoluntary deaths") is now taking precedence over Option 3 ("causing voluntary deaths") on the social policy agenda of the United States and that, given what is happening in medical facilities across the nation, it should do so. This political development is not entirely attractive from the point of view of conceptual ethical analysis because it would seem morally more appropriate to move from the right to allow voluntary deaths to the right to cause voluntary deaths before plunging into the discussion of what to do about those persons whose preferences, if they have any, are not knowable. This must be especially apparent to those who experience genuine doubts about the moral difference between allowing a human death and causing one. But even those who accept this distinction can admit that it may be less significant ethically than is the line between voluntary and involuntary deaths. We appear to be facing another trend in which the flow of human history exhibits a logic of its own that reflects the frustrations of personal and professional life more than it does the conceptual connections between various possibilities.

Although the efforts of the Hemlock Society and similar organizations have proposed policies that would approve of causing voluntary deaths, the pressure for change is not coming as powerfully from this quarter as it is from the relatives and friends of patients who have permanently lost all decisional capacity, as well as from the professionals and institutions that care for such patients. I am not now referring to persons with dementia from Alzheimers disease or other disorders. Neither am I now considering permanently comatose patients whose life expectancy is typically measured in weeks or months. I am referring to what some call the "persistent problem" of the persistent vegetative state. The 5,000 to 10,000 patients in the United States who are in this condition today at medical facilities that charge $2,000 to $10,000 a month are "awake" but not "aware." Unlike comatose patients, individuals in the persistent vegetative state do have sleep and awake cycles, their eyes do open, their throats will sometimes accept deeply positioned food, and they sometimes do respond to painful stimuli even though they lack the cortical capacity to experience suffering. They are permanently unconscious. If aggressively treated, and particularly if they are given artificial nutrition and hydration, they can have a life expectancy to be reckoned in decades. The annual cost of caring for such patients in the United States is estimated to range between $120 million and $1.2 billion, depending upon their number. One permanently unconscious persistent vegetative patient who lives for just one decade at a monthly cost of $5,000 will incur more than half a million dollars in charges even though it is known much earlier that he or she possesses no potential for acknowledging and nurturing relationships.

Beginning at least as early as the Karen Quinlan case, the courts have repeatedly addressed the problems posed by the persistent vegetative state. But their decisions have not been consistent in their conclusions or in their reasoning. Although it might be an exaggeration to call it a trend or a pattern, there is a noticeable tendency among the courts to allow guardians to discontinue medical interventions except for those that would assure an honorable and dignified death. Now and then, however, a court charts it own course with puzzling implications for all. The case of Nancy Cruzan of Missouri is such an instance.

On the one hand, in its decision regarding Nancy Beth Cruzan on June 25, 1990, the Supreme Court of the United States chose to "assume that a competent person would have a constitutionally protected right to refuse lifesaving hydration and nutrition." That the Court made this assumption might seem to fall short of formally ratifying a competent patient's right to refuse life-extending therapies. But if the Court had wanted to challenge the constitutionality of this alleged right, it could have. The impact of the Court's decision, therefore, was to lend the weight of its authority in behalf of the trend of legally allowing voluntary deaths.

On the other hand, the Supreme Court held that with respect to patients who are not able to refuse life extending therapies voluntarily because they are not competent, as was the circumstance of Nancy Beth Cruzan, a state may, if it chooses to do so, require "clear and convincing evidence" that such a refusal would be the patient's preference if he or she could make it. On this basis, the Supreme Court upheld the decision of the Supreme Court of Missouri.

If the Supreme Court's assumption that competent citizens possess a constitutional right to refuse life-extending therapies was a "victory" for "the right to die," its defense of Missouri's insistence on clear and convincing evidence in the case of incompetent patients has been seen by some as a defeat. But this defeat, if that is what it is, may be more apparent than real because the Supreme Court allowed but did not require states to employ the "clear and convincing evidence"

standard and because very few states other than Missouri utilized it in 1990.

There is no evidence that states will rush to accept it
either. If anything, the trend seems to be going the other way
with states being increasingly willing to allow proxies to make
decisions for incompetent patients with evidence that is less
than "clear and convincing." All in all, then, although it was
not everything I hoped for, and although some of the reasoning employed by some of the justices on the Supreme Court
struck me as questionable, I believe the Nancy Beth Cruzan
decision was a step in the right direction and deserves the support of Christians.

## CAUSING VOLUNTARY AND NONVOLUNTARY DEATHS

I do not believe that this is an opportune time for Christians in the United States actively and aggressively to promote
Option 3 ("causing voluntary deaths") or Option 4 ("causing
nonvoluntary deaths"). This is a political hunch and not a
moral judgment and should be evaluated as such. As previously indicated, my understanding of Christianity's strong presumption in favor of protecting each and every human life
leaves room for exceptional cases in which it would be permissible to choose death in order to preserve integrity, relieve pain
or avoid futile therapies. If I really work at it, I can imagine
circumstances in which one or the other of these three overriding considerations might justify causing the death of someone who truly chooses to die or causing the death of someone
for whom the choice between life and death is of no account.
So I can muster on Christian grounds no universal or absolute
prohibition of either. But neither can I find any reason at this
time in the United States to launch a campaign that would
transform Options 3 and 4 into formal social policy. I am
persuaded that such efforts are now unnecessary and that they
might prove counterproductive.

One consideration is that I believe a growing public acceptance of Options 1 and 2 is decreasing the number of instances in which Options 3 and 4 seem inviting and that this
trend should and will continue. If every competent and informed citizen who voluntarily chooses to die is allowed to die

and to do so comfortably, and if appropriate surrogate decision-makers are allowed to make similar decisions for those who are unable to decide for themselves, we can expect fewer and fewer calls for Options 3 and 4.

Another factor is that it seems to me that Options 1 and 2 are routinely practiced in medical facilities today and that this has been so for some time even though it engenders little fanfare. The media report the exceptional cases in which conflict emerges so forcefully that the impression may be conveyed that no one now actually exercises the right to refuse a medical intervention for himself or herself or for a person he or she serves as guardian. The situation today in most reputable medical facilities is nowhere near this grim. I have participated in numerous procedures that honored the wishes of patients or guardians to forego life-sustaining interventions at a number of hospitals in Southern California for the better part of a decade with no adverse consequences. It has also been my privilege to officiate at funerals for persons who died because of such decisions. It is necessary in such cases to proceed in a deliberate and collaborative fashion, but it is possible to do so with satisfactory results. This is being done daily throughout the nation.

A third factor is that the legal and cultural penalties for successfully committing suicide, or for enabling someone to do so in circumstances of medical extremity, are much lighter today than they may have been in previous generations. There was a time when suicide was viewed with such disesteem that those who were successful at it were denied burial in church graveyards. Other penalties were also imposed. This is rarely the case today in the United States. It is not difficult to acquire literature that tells one how to commit suicide, and it is not impossible to find a physician who will assist a patient in doing so. The *New England Journal of Medicine* recently reported that it is "certainly not rare" for physicians to assist patients who want to take their own lives by prescribing sleeping pills and by telling patients how many pills to take and how to take them if they really do not want to wake up. The same report indicated that "we know of no physician who has ever been prosecuted in the United States for prescribing sleeping pills in order to help a patient commit suicide."

A fourth factor is that physicians and other health professionals are overcoming some of their earlier reluctance to manage aggressively the discomfort of dying patients. Increasingly one reads in leading journals of medical opinion that "In the patient whose dying process is irreversible, the balance between minimizing pain and suffering and potentially hastening death should be struck clearly in favor of pain relief." Such recommendations are accompanied by a frank admission that pain-relieving measures too often have been inadequate.

A fifth consideration is that the legal and cultural penalties imposed upon those who actively cause the death of someone who is trapped in intolerable and intractable discomfort are so minimal today as to be virtually nonexistent. Now and then someone ends the life of a sufferer in a way that is so gory that law enforcers cannot pretend they did not notice, as in the recent Florida case where a man repeatedly shot his wife who was suffering from Alzheimers disease with a shotgun. Generally speaking, however, prosecuting attorneys don't like to take such cases to court. Juries don't like to convict persons accused of such crimes. And courts don't like to impose the full penalties allowed by law. Causing the death of someone who is sick and suffering is illegal in the United States. But with respect to this crime, the law usually says one thing and does another.

This brings us to the nub of the social policy issue. The question before us today in the United States is not, "Can a suffering patient acquire from physicians and other professionals the information and resources he or she needs to commit suicide?" The answer to this question is clearly, "yes!" Neither is the question before us, "Can a citizen cause the death of someone who is suffering intensely and irreversibly and escape adverse legal consequences?" The answer to this question is, "in the vast majority of cases, yes." The difficult social policy issue is that when the law says one thing and does another, as is so often the case in these circumstances, the possibility of selective and arbitrary enforcement is always present. Any policy that leaves the door open for such abuse should be a prime candidate for reconsideration.

I agree that the time may be nearing when official policies that forbid or discourage ending one's own life, or assisting others in doing so, or causing the death of someone who genuinely wants to die, should be reconsidered. We know that the present approach does leave the door open for abuse. But we also know that policies that officially approve of these practices also leave the door open for other kinds of abuses. We do not yet know which set of potential abuses is preferable, all things considered. This is why it strikes me as prudent to watch what is happening in the Netherlands for a few years before calling for fundamental change in the United States.

How can the churches contribute to the discussion of right-to-die issues? Dr. Larson has proposed the following:

The Christian churches of the United States, like the synagogues, temples and mosques of other communities of faith, can make at least five distinctive contributions to considerations of the right to die. To begin with, they can minister to those who face these questions in times of grief and perplexity. Working together, clergy and laity can enable congregations to be helpful and supportive when people are encountering choices regarding the end of human life. Such persons need the assurance of a caring and nonjudgmental presence. But they also need honest answers to their questions. It can be helpful for people to know, for instance, that their Christian faith does not require them to prolong medical interventions that only extend unending pain or have no net worth for their recipients. It can also be helpful for them to be told the stories of other Christians who have faced similar problems and resolved them with courage and conviction. It can also be helpful for them to know what the standard medical and legal alternatives are in given locations and institutions. These issues can begin to seem routine to those who meet them every day. But for those who are encountering them for the first time in circumstances that are far from ideal, they can seem almost overwhelming. This establishes an opportunity and an obligation for genuine ministry.

Christian churches can also help people to prepare themselves for making such decisions. There are a number of very practical things that individuals and families can do to plan well for their deaths. Financial plans need to be made. Wills need to be written. Agreements need to be formed as to what will be done when death is near and who will do what. We all know that death is the one deadline we all face irrespective of our other differences. We do well to prepare for it at least as carefully as we prepare for our annual vacations. Churches can encourage people to do so, not by nagging them but by sponsoring workshops and seminars in which very practical counsel is provided that enable persons to do what they know they should do and what they plan eventually to do. Perhaps the single most important thing the churches could do at this time in the United States would be to encourage each adult to execute a *Durable Power of Attorney for Health Care* that formally and with the full force of the law identifies someone who will be wholly authorized to make life-and-death decisions for oneself when one is no longer able to do so. These are far more effective than *Living Wills* and are readily available. The churches can promote their use with great benefit for all.

The churches can also educate people regarding the various issues that surround death and dying and the resources that are available for resolving them. Some of these matters are more ethical in nature. Some are more psychological. Some are historical and political. Some are Biblical. Such educational ventures step back from the specific and concrete matters associated with planning for one's own death, or for the death of a loved one, in hopes of addressing the issues in a more general, but not less important, way. How have people died in various times and places? How have Christians over the centuries addressed these matters? It is helpful to know something about Elisabeth Kubler-Ross's outline of the various stages of grief. It might also be interesting to learn something about Jeremy Taylor's rules for holy dying. One need not, indeed one could not and should not, endorse everything that even the most influential Christians throughout the ages have said about death and dying. But the churches serve well when they enable persons to sift through these comments for themselves and to be enriched by the process.

The churches can and should participate in the civic discourse that results in public policy for the whole nation. They can do so as denominations and institutions, and they can encourage individual Christians to do so as well. My own belief is that the churches serve the citizenry best on issues of this sort if, instead of seeking to impose their preferences on the population, they encourage public policy to extend the greatest possible liberties to all individuals and groups consistent with a secure but dynamic and just social order. Christians have a prudential interest in religious liberty for themselves because it provides room for their own beliefs and practices. Christians also have a prudential interest in religious liberty for other individuals and groups because Christians can learn from the beliefs and practices of other communities of faith. But the presumptive case for religious liberty in cases like these rests on moral principle as well as prudential calculation. It is right to extend to others the political freedoms one reserves for oneself. Barring morally relevant differences between oneself and others, it is wrong to do otherwise. The Golden Rule applies to Christians too.

Finally, but most importantly, the churches do well to bear in mind that first and last they are communities of theistic faith whose purpose is to increase love for God and neighbor. Attempts should therefore be made to connect Christian considerations of the right to die with recurring and pervasive theological themes that clarify and deepen Christian understanding of life and its purposes and death and its prospects in light of particular understandings and experiences of God. Christians do differ in their convictions regarding death to some extent. Some hold that those who die continue to live on in the memories of those who knew them, in the lives of subsequent generations and in the life of God. Others believe in the innate subjective immortality of the human soul. Still others look forward to the resurrection of the body and an apocalyptic transformation of all things. And some are able to combine more than one of these alternatives in a more comprehensive synthesis. But virtually all Christians agree that though Jesus the Christ God has overcome the sting of death and that this victory constitutes good news for every creature. Christian churches do well to remember that this good news does matter, and that for them it should matter most of all.

# Chapter 29

# The Latter-Day Saints (Mormon)

M
r. Glen Rowe, Manager of Public Services of the Historical
Department of the Church of Jesus Christ of Latter-Day
Saints, shared a statement from "the Church's current General
Handbook of Instructions, published in 1983, and intended as a book
of guidelines for local Church leadership," and another brief comment
on euthanasia, by Dr. James O. Mason, former Commissioner of Health
Services for the Church. The statement from the handbook is as follows:

> Because of its belief in the dignity of life, the Church opposes
> euthanasia. In addition to faith in the Lord, members should
> call upon recognized and licensed medical practitioners to as-
> sist in reversing conditions that threaten life. When dying be-
> comes inevitable, it should be considered a blessing and a
> purposeful part of mortality.

Dr. Mason's statement is in a list of items under the title "Attitudes
of The Church of Jesus Christ of Latter-Day Saints Toward Certain
Medical Problems." The section titled "Prolongation of Life and Right
to Die" reads:

> The Church does not look with favor upon any form of
> mercy killing. It believes in the dignity of life; faith in the
> Lord and medical science should be appropriately called upon
> and applied to reverse conditions that are a threat to life.
> There comes a time when dying becomes inevitable, when it

should be looked upon as a blessing, and as a purposeful part of mortality.

More recently, William S. Evans, Director of Special Affairs sent material from the recently published *Encyclopedia of Mormonism* (Macmillan Publishing Company, 1992, p. 971) that deals with suicide and euthanasia. The article was written for the encyclopedia by W. Cole Durham, Jr. and reads as follows:

> Suicide is regarded as self-murder and a grievous sin if committed by someone in full possession of his or her mental faculties. Because it is possible that a person who takes his or her own life may not be responsible for that action, only God can judge such a matter.
>
> A person who participates in euthanasia—the deliberate, intentional putting to death of a person suffering from incurable conditions or diseases—violates the commandments of God. There is a difference between allowing a terminally ill person to die of natural causes and the initiating of action that causes someone's death. The application or denial of life-support systems must be decided reverently, usually by competent and responsible family members through prayer and the consultation of competent medical authorities. It is not wrong to ask the Lord, if it be his will, to shorten the physical suffering of a person whose afflictions are terminal and irreversible.

# Chapter 30

---

# The Reorganized Church of Jesus Christ of Latter-Day Saints

---

Alan D. Tyson, the First President of the Reorganized LDS Church, wrote that recently "a study was undertaken by the Standing High Council, a formal body within the church which frequently expresses the church's position on various issues for the benefit of our membership. This recent study focused on questions relating to life prolonging decisions.

"On January 16, 1992 the Standing High Council approved the enclosed document, 'Preparation for Life-Prolonging Decisions,' for counsel and support to the church. We think that this statement touches directly on several of the questions which your own study raises. You are free to regard it as our official position at the present time." The statement reads as follows:

> Decision making for terminally ill or incompetent persons is an increasingly complex and pressing problem in today's society. In recent years, moral and ethical questions about withholding or withdrawing medical treatment from certain patients have been extensively debated. The Standing High Council offers this counsel for saints who will face such decisions for themselves and family members in the hope it will assist them in making informed and wise judgments.

## THE RIGHT TO REFUSE TREATMENT

All persons have the right to refuse life-sustaining treatment. Such a right is based on the principle that every autonomous individual may determine what care will be received or rejected. This basic right for all persons continues to be respected after they become nonautonomous and are no longer able to protect it themselves. (People who lack decision-making capacity may be considered nonautonomous, even if they have not yet been declared legally incompetent.) The common law right of self-determination has led to the development of the legal doctrine of informed consent to medical treatment, which includes, as well, the right to refuse treatment.

In a number of countries, including the United States, judicial decisions have protected the "dignity and equality" of all individuals by respecting the rights to self-determination and privacy of nonautonomous patients as well as patients who retain decision-making capacity. Courts have recognized that since incompetent individuals cannot exercise those rights themselves, the legal right to refuse medical treatment requires a surrogate to make decisions on the patient's behalf.

## THE FAMILY AS DECISION MAKER

A number of courts have recently concluded that the presence of caring, responsible family members is the key ingredient in surrogate decision-making. However, when illness or injury makes death a certainty unless life is artificially sustained through medical intervention, caring persons responsible for deciding the course of treatment are confronted with choices that are emotionally, legally, morally, and spiritually wrenching. Under what circumstances should "artificial" medical intervention be withheld or discontinued? Is "allowing a person to die" permissible from the standpoint of medical ethics, the law, or the spiritual imperatives of the gospel?

The act of putting to death painlessly a person suffering from an incurable disease has traditionally been called euthanasia. It entails *causing* death to occur. The Standing High Council, along with the preponderance of religious, medical

317

and legal opinion, opposes acts of what is now commonly referred to as "active euthanasia." This opposition extends to situations in which the patient requests death at the hands of family members, medical personnel, or others.

Allowing death to occur, on the other hand, may involve the withholding or withdrawing of life-sustaining medical treatment in circumstances where death is the natural outcome. We recognize that there are circumstances where it is more appropriate to allow individuals to die than to artificially keep their bodies alive. Allowing death to occur is permissible when death is the inevitable and natural outcome and the measures required to postpone it would rob the patient of the ability to relate meaningfully to others or to experience satisfaction with the quality of his or her existence. Such measures include artificially assisted nutrition and hydration.

When family members must become surrogate decision-makers, they will function best if they are qualified to represent the patient's desires and have some evidence regarding the nonautonomous patient's previously held views. Such evidence can take the form of a living will, an advance directive, or a durable power of attorney for health care. This can be most helpful to family members and medical professionals as they make the actual decisions. Lacking such evidence, the surrogate has a responsibility to follow guidance principles which have received strong legal consensus in recent years. One is the "substituted-judgment" standard, in which the patient's surrogate attempts to make the decision that the individual, if competent, would choose. Another is the "best interests" standard—acting to best promote the good of the individual in terms of the relative balance of benefits and burdens.

It is to be expected that whenever such difficult decisions are faced, there will be disagreements among conscientious persons. Mindful of this, we counsel those involved to remember that the decision to *allow* a person to die is not the moral equivalent of *causing* that person to die, and may be an expression of trust in the care of a loving God. All parties to these difficult decisions can find in them opportunities for understanding acceptance and forgiveness rather than blame or guilt. Confronting the mystery of death can lead to a fuller appreciation of our faith in eternal life.

## STEWARDSHIP OF SELF

We have indicated that American law and the laws of a number of other countries permit every competent adult to consent to or refuse any proposed medical treatment or intervention. It is unfortunate that many people are unwilling to confront their own mortality to the extent of giving advance thought and instruction about life support. Personal stewardship encompasses the responsibility of individuals to think ahead to the kind of care they may wish to receive at the end of their lives or after they become incapable of deciding for themselves. It greatly reduces the uncertainty and difficulty of treatment decisions if, sufficiently early in life's journey, planning has begun for an advance directive, a living will, or a durable power of attorney for health care. We place great value on the informed and reflective decision-making process in this life. It is wise to use this process to deal with the natural conclusion of life—our own death.

Chapter 31

# Christian Science

T he following statement was made available through the courtesy
of the office of the Christian Science Committee on Publication
for Southern California.

As Christian Scientists, we recognize that prolonged illness,
issues of aging, and euthanasia are widespread problems in
today's society.

As a rule, our Church does not establish official denominational positions on the broad range of social and personal
issues. The *Christian Science Monitor*, which is published by
The Christian Science Publishing Society, however, deals with
vital social questions on a continuing basis; but it does not
represent Church policy or official denominational stands.
Church members are free to determine their own positions on
such questions according to individual conscience, prayerful
striving, and sound moral judgment.

Rather than our returning a completed questionnaire, I
believe it would be most helpful to give some insight on how
a Christian Scientist would view this subject. In a sense, euthanasia is a subject that can be discussed only within the context of medical practice, since it involves acceptance of the
incurability of particular diseases and the assumption that an
individual is doomed in certain instances. On the other hand,
Christian Scientists view the question of living and dying from
a religious standpoint and rely on spiritual norms for healing.
A Christian Scientist does not consider any disease beyond the

power of God to heal. From this perspective, there is always hope, as evidenced in the countless healing through prayer of conditions that had been medically deemed incurable. It is because of Christian Science teachings regarding life, death, and illness, and this century-long experience of healing, that approaches like euthanasia and assisted suicide would not be considered part of the genuine practice of our religion.

In Christian Science, death is considered neither a friend nor a solution to illness or problems. Rather, as the Apostle Paul noted in the New Testament, death is seen as "the last enemy to overcome." If one takes this view, assisted suicide and euthanasia would be seen as a denial of the reality of God's presence and power—a reality, as most Christians believe, that Jesus' resurrection showed to be ultimately greater even than death.

As to a position on refusals of life-sustaining medical treatment, Christian Science starts from a different premise from many—i.e., that the very essence of man's life is spiritual rather than material, and hence that restoration of health and well-being comes best through spiritual regeneration rather than through material methods. So, in times of physical need, most practicing Christian Scientists continue to choose to rely on God to maintain and sustain their health and well-being rather than turning to medical intervention. This is an individual choice, however, one that is made not out of blind faith (and certainly not from any desire to hasten death or to become martyrs) but because, from their experience and that of their families, they've found that Christian Science treatment has effectively met their physical needs and has drawn them closer to God and their nature as children of God.

Death is neither the will of God nor the end of individual existence. Christian Scientists agree with Paul's teaching that "neither death, nor life . . . nor any other creature shall be able to separate us from the love of God, which is in Christ Jesus our Lord." It is this divine Love, they feel, which preserves individual identity both before and after the experience of death.

To Christian Scientists, then, death is not a special turning point for good or evil. Jesus spoke of the kingdom of heaven as "at hand" or "within." Thus, to a Christian Scientist heaven and hell are not physical locations, but ultimately mental states. Heaven is the spiritual consciousness gained through repentance and spiritual regeneration, striving to have the "mind which was also in Christ Jesus." Hell is a stricken state of the carnal mind undergoing the inevitable and purging self-destruction of evil. The need for spiritual growth continues. Life in the hereafter involves growth in holiness, repentance, and spiritual regeneration as does this life.

The Christian Science Church does not perform last rites, nor does it have ritual or doctrinal requirements regarding the bodily remains of the deceased. In many cases a simple memorial service would be given which might include reading from the Bible and the writings of Mary Baker Eddy, the founder of the Church, that lovingly acknowledge the ongoing meaning and spiritual nature of the individual's life and the promise that nothing can separate any individual—the deceased or those who remain—from "love of God."

Christian Scientists realize the complexity of this issue within the context of ordinary medical practice, and the driving agent this becomes for moral and ethical decisions from our various faith traditions. Far from ignoring or rationalizing suffering, they too are deeply moved by the dilemmas facing those struggling with pain and disease—which is why they put such emphasis on healing. While Christian Scientists strive to follow Jesus' commands and to fulfill his promise of abundant life, they recognize, like all Christians, how far they still have to go in this regard.

Chapter 32

# Swedenborgianism

The Church of the New Jerusalem (Swedenborgian) stands somewhat outside of traditional Western religions in that it recognizes a new "Divine revelation of truth given by the Lord Jesus Christ through His servant Emanuel Swedenborg" (*The General Church of the New Jerusalem: A Handbook of General Information*, 1952, p. 3). Swedenborg is recognized by the Church as an 18th century (1688-1722) "human instrument" of revelation.

The questionnaire (see Appendix VIII) was answered by the Rev. Michael D. Gladish, pastor of the Gabriel Church of the New Jerusalem in La Crescenta, California. Pastor Gladish wrote:

## OUR CHURCH'S STAND ON "PASSIVE" EUTHANASIA

From our doctrine we understand that all life is of and from God, and flows into the human "vessel" according to the organic, physiological and spiritual conditions that apply. Thus life flows into and is received by minerals, vegetables and animals each in a different way. The purpose of human life or consciousness is that God's love and wisdom be received AS IF THEY WERE our own, so that not only do we have consciousness but self-consciousness in the exercise of free will and rationality.

The faculties of will and understanding are opened and developed as a result of the interaction between sense experience and spiritual influx. Everything in the organic body corresponds to one or the other of these faculties, and the principal organs are the heart—which corresponds to the will—and the lungs—which correspond to the understanding. When the heart and the lungs can no longer function as of themselves and the brain no longer registers any responsiveness to either internal or external stimulation we take these as indications that the uniquely human quality of life has been withdrawn by God from that form; in other words, the spirit has departed and whatever life remains is not human life but life on a lower plane—with which we are relatively free to do as we like.

As a church organization we do not "sanction" much of anything on an external level, but try to represent the teachings about spiritual life as well as we can so that individuals in their best judgments can decide about issues of application. Thus an individual member of our organization might choose to sustain life in a human body by various "heroic" measures for various personal reasons (and I know of one such case), but on the other hand I do not know any ministers in our organization who would condemn the act of "passive euthanasia" as you have described it.

## OUR CHURCH'S STAND ON ACTIVE EUTHANASIA

I do not know of any ministers in our organization who would sanction any form of suicide or other "active euthanasia" such as you have described.

Human life does not consist of what happens to us but is rather a conscious response through the will and the understanding TO whatever happens to us. The experience of Norman Cousins (made famous in the book, *Anatomy of an Illness*) is a classic modern example of how the mind or spirit can overcome the adversities of the flesh. Jesus also taught that the spirit gives life, the flesh profits nothing (John 6:63) and that in the world we would have tribulation but through Him we might still have peace and be of good cheer (John 16:33). As tragic as human circumstances may be—and I am well aware that they may be terribly tragic—I believe an individual must persevere.

Now if the flesh "profits nothing" you may wonder why

we won't condone a deliberate rejection of it—for the enhanced spiritual life this might facilitate. . . . We are given the natural circumstances of our lives within which to grow spiritually, and we cannot become truly spiritual except through the effort—however feeble and restricted it may be—to exercise our faculties of choice in favor of whatever God-given virtue might be possible: I think of courage, for example, and honesty and optimism, not to mention faith, conscience, innocence and obedience of the ten commandments, which includes the law against murder.

Of course, we would not object to the use of medicines to ease pain or in other ways make hard circumstances easier to bear, but on the other hand I don't know of anyone in the church who would condone the use of drugs permanently to obstruct the exercise of the mental faculties. That would be much the same as taking the human life, since it would take the humanity out of that life.

Incidentally, one of the great difficulties in the decision about active euthanasia in any particular case is the very question of mental competence. I believe, and in my conscience I would have to advocate, that if we err we must err on the positive side, assuming there is truly human value not only to the suffering person but also through him to others in the continuation of his life. After all, human value is not determined by appearance.

And finally, once active euthanasia is condoned by law or conscience there is an awesome burden of responsibility to define justifiable circumstances. I don't think we can do this fairly ever and so must rest with the Word and Providence of God. Too much is at stake: too much that we in our limited perspective can't see.

By the way, in condemning the ACT of "active" euthanasia we do not condemn an individual who commits it. Though we believe the reasoning of someone who does this is impaired, false or misguided, we do not believe anyone but God can see the heart of another human being and we leave that judgment to Him. Spiritually speaking, the heart or motive of an act always qualifies it for the doer.

## BELIEF IN A SOUL OR AFTERLIFE

YES, with judgment according to the interior quality of the life, not by edict (Divine or otherwise) but according to the law of consequences: and spiritual association. An evil man, for instance, is already in hell, being influenced and surrounded by the evils he enjoys and the evil spirits who are like-minded. A good man is already in heaven, being in a heavenly state, and the transition from this world to the next is simply a matter of awakening consciousness on a new plane or level. We are not rewarded or punished for things we have done on earth, but the interior state of our life is simply continued, evil if evil, including the torments of frustration, the fires of anger and passion, jealousy, etc, and wonderful if good, including the sense of peace that can be cultivated even in spite of pain, through faith and humility.

With my conscience if I participated in euthanasia I would expect to bear the consequences in the form of spiritual torment; however, everything depends upon the interior quality of the motive, thus also the degree to which I have been able to exercise a truly free choice. If I have felt compelled by the pressure of outside circumstances so that I did not see even my own principles clearly any more, then I have hope that God's mercy will restore better judgment later and that being forgiven I may come to forgive myself and live in spiritual peace.

## FUNERAL CUSTOMS FOR THE VICTIMS OF MERCY KILLING

No differences from others. In the case of suicide we try to give the benefit of the doubt as to mental competence, not holding the individual responsible for a free and rational choice to commit murder. But in the last analysis who can place blame spiritually but God? As to our services we usually go to the site of burial (or cremation) first, and commit the body, then we proceed to the church for a "memorial" or "resurrection" service in which we focus on our teachings concerning the afterlife and on the positive qualities of the deceased person's life, eulogizing but not glorifying the individual and leaving judgment to God.

## COUNSELING FOR SOMEONE COMTEMPLATING EUTHANASIA/SUICIDE?

Focus first on acknowledgment and acceptance of the feelings expressed so that person gains a sense of worth through acceptance and real communication. Gradually and very gently try to instill some concepts of use, especially spiritual use, and a perspective of human values beyond (yet within the context of) the physical limitations that apply. Listening, active listening, would be the primary skill to exercise, for this more than anything highlights the value of continued life, which consists of nothing so much as communication. The essence of human life is love and if love cannot share it cannot go on.

## SCRIPTURAL OR DOCTRINAL REFERENCES?

I'm sorry but I do not have time for the extensive research that this would entail right now. However, our doctrinal point of view is taken specifically from the theological, exegetical and eschatological writings of Emanuel Swedenborg (1688-1722), some thirty volumes which may be found in many libraries. See especially the work on *Divine Providence* and the one on *Heaven and Hell* by Swedenborg. His work on *The New Jerusalem and Its Heavenly Doctrine* also provides insights into our understanding of the human spirit in relation to the body, as does the small treatment, *Divine Love and Divine Wisdom* found at the end of the 6th volume of *Apocalypse Explained.*

# Chapter 33

## The Unification Church

D r. David Carlson, who teaches Theology and World Religions at the Unification Theological Seminary in Barrytown, New York, shared material from *The Tradition: Book One* (New York: The Holy Spirit Association for the Unification of World Christianity, 1985). In the discussion about death, it was pointed out that:

> According to the Principle, death is the time when both the spiritual and physical bodies return to their original source. The Spiritual body goes to the world of the spirit. We can say that the physical body returns to the material world through its eventual decomposition.

The text next comments on euthanasia:

> *Importance of Physical Life.* The Principle shows us that Heavenly Father is involved in the creation of our lives, that His love is their main source . . . Until we reach perfection, in the truest sense, God owns our lives; we are only the stewards. After we reach perfection, He wants to bestow upon us the fullness of His love, creativity, and true life.
>
> *Relationship with Spiritual Life.* Our spiritual body grows through a reciprocal relationship with our physical body. Therefore, it is the Unification view that under the order of the universe, we should not willfully cut the connection existing between the body and spirit. Without the physical body, the spiritual body absolutely cannot grow.

*Accident victim.* When the question of euthanasia is raised in the case of accident victims, it is our view that everything possible should be done to keep the body alive. However, if it is known that severe brain damage is involved and there is absolutely no hope of recovery, we hold that it is not necessary to continue technological assistance to keep the body alive. Whether or not to unplug the life support system should be left to the discretion of the immediate family. If this is the decision reached, however, it is essential that death be allowed to occur naturally.

## TERMINAL ILLNESS

Members who become terminally ill and desire to prepare to go to the spiritual world should use the time they have left on the physical plane to re-examine themselves—their relationship with God, True Parents, spouse, children, other members, etc. Such a time would be especially appropriate for deep repentance. Members may wish to study the Principle and Father's words [the words of the Rev. Sun Myung Moon, the founder of the Unification Church] and meditate on the essence of their lives as well. Rather than focus on fulfilling any external desires, members would do well to strengthen their relationships in order to prepare for their rebirth into the spiritual world.

Dr. Carlson noted that the Unification Movement "is still a 'young' movement," consequently answers to all of the questions raised in the questionnaire have not been confronted. He stated that *"Generally speaking*, suicide as such is seen as wrong."

# Chapter 34

---

# The Theosophical Society

---

The teachings of the Theosophical Society rest primarily upon the works of Madame Helen P. Blavatsky who founded the organization in New York City in 1875. The organization did not respond directly to the questionnaire but sent a copy of *Report of the European Tour, May 20-July 15, 1980* (Theosophical University Press, 1980). This volume provides edited lectures and conversations of Grace F. Knoche, Leader of the Society, taped during a tour of Europe and Great Britain. Miss Knoche responds to questions concerning euthanasia and beliefs in the afterlife (among other things).

In her opening remarks in Munich, Miss Knoche delineated the Society's beliefs concerning the importance of Madame Blavatsky's teachings (p.6). She stated that, not only had the founder presented "ancient truths that had been given to mankind long ages ago . . . but she did so with the chief aim of restoring dignity to the human race." Miss Knoche continued:

> We had forgotten who we were; we had overlooked the fact that we are *gods in essence*. We had buried our heritage under creeds, and she restored to us the knowledge that we are transcendent beings, cosmic in power, using human vehicles for experience. When we realize what that means in our daily lives we see that there isn't a single avenue of experience or duty that cannot be viewed from the eyes of our cosmic self. This is extraordinarily important, because we recognize then that we are gods, first and foremost, divinities temporarily using hu-

man bodies. In other words, we are literally exiles from our real selves, and that puts quite a new perspective on our experience here on earth. We know that, whatever our karma, we need never be overwhelmed, because the long perspective, the long avenue of experience, gives us a sense of unlimited resources on which we can draw.

When she was asked a question about the destiny of the individual "divine being" after death, she replied:

Briefly put, when we die, the body is cast off and, the highest having gone to its own parent star, we are left with the spiritual essence of ourselves and our human attributes, both higher and lower, in an envelope, as it were. After a brief period of unconsciousness, we enter a purgation state, a cleansing process in which all that is heavy and material and low drops off, while the aroma or essence of all that was fine and noble in the life is drawn up into the spiritual self of us and enters a type of heaven-world—we call it devachan, which simply means "god-place"—there to enter the Elysian Fields, as the Greeks would say, in order to experience the fulfillment of its aspirations. This is a beautiful period in which all that has happened in the life, spiritually, has an opportunity to impress itself on the soul, while the spiritual monad in which the human entity is sleeping enters the planetary spheres for its own higher adventures. The old Latins made effective use of the epitaph: *Dormit in astris*, "he sleeps among the stars" and also: *Gaudeat in astris*, "he rejoices among the stars." In those two simple statements is an epitome of the theosophic teaching: a part of us is sleeping among the stars, and yet, during our dream-sleep, a still higher part of us is rejoicing in the freedom of sending forth its consciousness among the planetary and solar realms.

To return to your question: Where does our god-spark, or inner god, go when we die? It is a paradox: our god essence never leaves its own sphere and yet, because it is our essential self, it protects us from its own lofty sphere. We have to grow up as human beings into our godlike qualities; it is we who must approach their realm. But there is no separation unless we, through lives of direct deliberate evildoing, break the link.

331

In Manchester, England, she commented on "the right to die with dignity" (p. 146):

There is a movement abroad, among doctors and the general public, to allow people the "right to die in dignity," and the right to die when the soul is ready, and not keep the body going by artificial means. There is a moment when the soul knows that it is time to quit the body. We may not know the moment, it may be weeks in coming, but there should be an atmosphere of welcoming the change called death, recognizing that it is a beneficent process, that it is part of the pattern of the total life-experience that continues far longer than this immediate lifetime.

In response to a question concerning the use of the phrase "the right to die" by groups in Britain "who are claiming the right for euthanasia" she responded:

I am not referring to euthanasia. What I am speaking of is this: I believe that we should allow the soul to decide—by which I mean the higher soul, and not our brain-mind—because I believe it is wrong to take life. If we understood more we would know when to let go of our bodies, but we have lost that innate knowledge. There is a time to let the body go, and even in our Western culture there are many who do know this intuitively.

Some of the traditional peoples have retained this knowledge. In Nigeria they speak of death as "losing one's hold on mortality." I heard this story directly from the son of a chief who was over one hundred. The chief called together his large family or clan, and told them he would soon be leaving them. He gave them a long and beautiful talk about the spiritual principles that guided his life and the sacred tradition of his people. Then he entered the dying process: his consciousness went up and came down again, and he spoke to them. Three times this happened. Then he gave a final blessing and was gone. There is great beauty in this. He knew the time had come to "lose his hold on mortality."

Such intuitive knowledge hopefully will come back to us when we regain the "child state" that we have lost in our sophistication and in our hunger to live, to grasp, to gain. But this is not euthanasia. We should not take life. As Cicero and other Greek and Latin poets and philosophers always said, the soul is "the possession of the gods"—the divine within—and therefore is on a tour of duty; we have no right to dispose of our lives before the direction comes from above-within. This is the message that has been given by the wise of all ages.

At a Member's Meeting in London, Miss Knoche talked about the Society's belief in Karma and reincarnation. She was asked a question about the benefits of "healing circles" in which people ". . . sit and think and pray perhaps for particular people." She replied (p.179):

I am not so certain that it can do only good. I have experienced the illness and death of many close friends, and often I have thought to myself, "If only I had the power to heal; if only I could bring relief." As I have grown older, I have come to realize that that is not the most compassionate way to help another. I have come to understand that the most beautiful and effective way to sustain another is to help him find the courage and the love and the confidence to meet his karma creatively. Of course, we should use all the medical aids that are normally available, but let's allow our friend the honor and the dignity that belong to him, of recognizing that he has the capacity to meet his karma with full knowledge. Maybe his body will die earlier than the norm, but in so meeting the karma that is his, acting with full dignity as a man, he is accepting consciously the privilege of working through a heavy karmic experience for a beneficent purpose. I have seen this work; there is solace and strength in being able to take this attitude.

So, when someone you love dearly is facing death, I myself would not pray to have that one saved at all costs. Rather I would pray—and pray is a good word—for the strength and the love to assist and sustain that friend through his Gethsemane. He (or she) must be allowed to go through that Gethsemane alone, without interference, so that when he has succeeded, he is blessed in having come through in triumph; he has found a new birth of the soul which nothing can take from him henceforth. It is then his victory, not somebody else's.

Chapter 35

# The American
# Ethical Union

The following statement has been prepared by Judith E. Espenschied, an Ethical Culture Society Leader and Past President of the National Leaders Council of the American Ethical Union.

## COMMENTS ON EUTHANASIA

1. Ethical culture is a noncreedal religious fellowship, which means that we don't have unchangeable doctrinal positions. Rather each member is encouraged to take responsibility for making ethical choices in the situations that come to each of us in our lives, basing responsible choosing on some working hypotheses: human beings are worthy of respect and consideration regardless of their productivity or usefulness; ethical behavior is behavior that cultivates good, caring, relationships among people; the meaning of one's life cannot be attributed by someone else or some institution.

As a result of this nondogmatic basic stance, most Ethical Culturists would answer the euthanasia question by referring to the quality of life as perceived by the suffering person, not by referring to some rule or authority. In keeping with what we consider to be humane and merciful (and in accord with the positions of many mainstream religious groups), we would approve the removal of life-support systems and/or the cessation of heroic medical measures, even when such removal or

cessation would result in the death of someone, if that someone him or herself found life so reduced in meaning as to be
an entirely unrewarding burden (or in the case of someone not
conscious, if such an attitude could be assumed to be consistent with the person's life and history, or if specific intentions
about the situation had been expressed at an earlier time). In
other words, the continuation of life should be based on the
valuation of life by the person living it. Conversely, it would
seem to me that a person who finds positive value in his or
her life should be the judge of whether to exert continued
effort to preserve that life—rather than leaving the decision to
medical, psychological, or financial experts.

2. Ethical Culture has not taken a unified single position
with regard to active euthanasia. Nevertheless the above mentioned principles and attitudes of responsible decision-making
clearly include the possibility that active euthanasia would be
among the options. I am personally acquainted with a number
of people who have (for themselves or members of their family) participated in active euthanasia in a caring and merciful
way. Generally, they have been required to keep this secret. I
am also acquainted with one man who told me that he has
been tormented for many years by the fact that he *did not*
respond when his dying wife asked for release from her pain. I
believe that turning one's eyes and mind away from the issue
is hypocritical, playing dumb, and sometimes simple coward-
ice. The real decisions are hard enough to make without the
threat of legal dangers and medical authoritarianism (not to
mention theological authoritarianism). These decisions should
be made (and legally enabled) in an open social context, with
family, friends, and doctors as consultants. If a doctor's or
nurse's oath requires preservation of life at all costs, then it is
clear that medical expertise has limited applicability and
should be called on in some situations and not others. If our
laws define any active termination of life as crime-and-
violence, then our laws need to be changed. Our present state
of medical technology requires increasing numbers of options:
heroic measures for premature babies, elective plastic surgery,
sex change surgery, organ transplants, stomach stapling, etc. At
each decision point there is the possibility of not acting. There
is also, in extreme cases, the possibility of ending the suffering
for a person who wants to make meaning by limiting mean-

ingless pain. We need to be educated to understand that doing nothing is choosing to make something happen. (There are cases where the meaningless terminal pain is psychological but equally serious and real, as in early Alzheimer's disease and predicted fast-acting cancer.)

The fundamental answer from my personal and religious perspective is that these issues need to be addressed with the profoundest respect for the individual life that is to be extended or ended. The quality of life, the meaning of life, the value of life—these are to be known, if at all possible, from the point of view of the individual, not from the point of view of rules of thumb or laws of society. Wouldn't it be wonderful if the ending of our lives could be private and personally meaningful to us, not made public, ugly, and bureaucratic by general required procedures? Wouldn't it be wonderful if our experience of death could be as individual and as touched by love as our experiences of conception and birth?

Some Ethical Culture Leaders were discussing euthanasia nearly thirty years ago. Indeed, when *The Humanist* magazine published "A Plea for Beneficent Euthanasia" in 1974, Jerome Nathanson who was then Chairman of the Board of Leaders, New York Society for Ethical Culture, and Algernon Black, Fraternity of Leaders, American Ethical Union, were among the signers (The "Plea" is published in the next chapter). Algernon Black in an address to the New York Society for Ethical Culture said:

> If we had a more ethical world, we would be able to help one another live, and we would be able to help one another die. We would not be afraid, and we would trust one another because there would be love among us. When there is great love in life and great love at death, we may help one another face death without fear. When human beings have lived to the full, death may be less of a tragedy. And under certain circumstances, death may be a release and a blessing for ourselves or for those we love.
>
> The advocates of euthanasia are not callous to the value of human life. They are sensitive and care about safeguarding life. Indeed, because they treasure life, they believe that euthanasia is a problem concerning which human beings must not evade moral responsibility. We dare not be party to the need-

less and continued suffering of thousands who may wish for and be permitted to have release from suffering. Nor can we ignore the fact that some form of euthanasia is practiced every day by physicians with and without the approval of patients and relatives—where patients are permitted to die—and where the practice is carried on in accord with the physician's conscience and without the benefits of public knowledge or responsible social approval or permission.

We who are associated in the Ethical Movement, and many other people as well, do not look back 3,000 or 2,000 years for final answers on contemporary problems or specific questions of ethics. We know that there is wisdom there, and much of what is valid in our lives, much of our wisdom and sense of values has grown out of the Jewish-Christian tradition. But our whole approach is present-oriented and future-oriented. In addition to past experience, our own experience must help us grow and learn so that we understand better what it means to be human, and what it means to have responsible relations with other human beings and what it means to deal with such questions. This is difficult.

There is in the nature of the universe a being born and dying. It is part of the whole life cycle in this universe. Traditional religions will say God gives and God takes away. We should accept pregnancy and birth, and we should accept death as the will of the power which created and rules the world. Those of us who do not accept this interpretation of man's relation to the processes of existence have to find some way of thinking about this too. True, there may be a time for being born and a time for dying. We know that though man may prolong his life through science, we still have a limited existence and none of us will achieve immortal existence or life eternal, even though we can live longer than men did years ago. But when the time comes when a person is dying, we should not prolong his dying. There is a difference between prolonging life when it still has the qualities of life and prolonging the agony and the processes of death.

The issue is not merely that of the avoidance of pain. It is concerned with the deeper questions of man's attitude toward the responsibility for living and safeguarding life—and the issues involved with what men owe one another. The will to live carries with it the will to bear pain. . . . Men know

337

that they cannot live without pain any more than they can live without pleasure. . . . One can stand a great deal of pain if there is reason for wanting to live and a basis for hope.

We accept pain as an inevitable part of life. . . . Where there is great love, there can be a will to live that can carry people through great pain.

But there is a point where you and I might want to die, and there might be nothing cowardly or undignified about it because we know that pain from then on is pointless, and there is no hope. . . . We are speaking about freedom here, spiritual freedom . . . the right of an individual to decide how he lives and how he will die. Usually we do not have much control about when and where and how it will happen, but where possible, do we not owe it to one another to try to assure that right?

In a separate, and perhaps more recent statement, Algernon Black wrote:

The will to live is strong in human beings. The capacity to endure suffering is beyond belief. It is part of the human condition that men must endure pain and suffering. To summon strength and courage to endure and overcome such hardships is the test of character. Human dignity requires that men accept the hard realities of life and learn to live with them. Temporary suffering, even though extreme, we must all bear at times. We may hold ourselves to this viewpoint and hope we shall have the strength to withstand suffering.

Since the act of ending a life means the ending of a personality as a conscious, active, unique entity, no effort should be spared to encourage the will of the sufferer to live, to ease his pain by therapy and anesthesia, and to give the quality of nursing care and increased attention and love that will nourish the will to live and the feeling of being loved and wanted. Every possible device should be used to make certain that no one end his existence or be helped to do so because of fear or temporary depression.

Euthanasia originates in man's concern for his fellow man and his compassion for one who is suffering unbearably. For there are times when the margin of pleasure may lessen to the zero point and the margin of pain may increase to the unbearable point. Where the disease has permeated the entire body and the suffering is beyond relief, and the agony is such that the individual cannot function, cannot control himself physically or mentally—indeed, where he is reduced to nothingness; where medical science has no remedy and, as far as is known, the illness is terminal and hopeless—in such a case, who has the right to refuse to yield to the request that a person end his misery? As free men, we have a right to live and a right to die.

In many cases the medical profession feels the obligation to keep a human being alive, even when everything indicates the case to be hopeless. Thus life is prolonged when life is no life. Chemicals, food, oxygen, and drugs are pumped into patients, thus prolonging the agony of patients and relatives and adding expense and debts—to little purpose. To continue these efforts is no kindness.

When a relative or friend or professional person is party to an act of euthanasia, every effort should be made to remove this act from the category of criminal action subject to criminal punishment—provided the suffering is unbearable and the illness terminal and hopeless, and the sufferer has fervently requested such action in the presence of witnesses, and written and sworn affidavits are furnished.

Since euthanasia is an act that is irrevocable and irreparable, it must not be permitted without the safeguards that protect human beings from personal hostility or prejudices, religious, ethnic, national, and political. It must be protected from purposes of personal gain and fraud, from criminal purposes, and from personal hostility and destructiveness. Since it is born of compassion and love, it must be safeguarded as the deepest possible expression of such compassion—to spare a loved one unbearable and hopeless suffering.

Jean Kotkin, an AEU Leader indicated that, in her personal judgment, both passive and active euthanasia were permissible under the conditions outlined in the questionnaire. She wrote, "A person must be allowed to die with dignity, not live as a vegetable. We are responsible for ourselves and for our fellow human beings." There is no expressed belief in an afterlife. Indeed, Ms. Kotkin wrote, "If Ethical Culturists go anywhere after they die (which I don't believe), it would be to the library." So far as counseling is concerned, she believes that the aim would be "To try and get them to understand fully the reasons for the act and the consequences for the people left."

Dr. Matthew Ies Spetter, Leader of the Riverdale-Yonkers Society, wrote that involvement in euthanasia would not affect rituals associated with the deceased person because "the dignity of the person is paramount." He stated that in such terminal situations he does "explore the marital relationships deeply before offering any counsel."

At a meeting of the Board of Directors held on December 11, 1993, the American Ethical Union passed the following resolution:

> WHEREAS, the American Ethical Union supports the right of each individual to make critical decisions about his/her own life, including the right to terminate it when it is no longer bearable . . .
>
> *NOW, THEREFORE BE IT RESOLVED*, THAT THE Board of the American Ethical Union deplores the action of the State of Michigan with respect to Dr. Jack Kevorkian and urges that he be set free pending the disposition of the case challenging the constitutionality of the law he has refused to obey. The American Ethical Union further urges legislation be adopted to permit assisted suicide under appropriate conditions.

# Chapter 36

---

# The American
# Humanist Association

---

The following official statement has been provided through the
courtesy of Sidney M. Goetz, J.D. of Gulfport, Florida, a
member of the Board of Directors of the American Humanist
Association. It is important to note that although the Association is
listed as an "educational" organization, one of the AHA's family of
organizations is the Humanist Society of Friends, a religious organization that is responsible for the training and certification of Humanist
Counselors who serve in capacities analogous to clergy in other groups.

## STATEMENT OF EUTHANASIA ADOPTED BY THE BOARD
## OF DIRECTORS OF THE AMERICAN HUMANIST
## ASSOCIATION AT ITS MEEING ON NOVEMBER 21, 1991

### Preliminary Statement

In 1973, the American Humanist Association issued
Manifesto II. Succinctly stated therein is its position on Euthanasia. In a sentence listing the full range of civil liberties
every individual is entitled to possess in all societies, there is
included "recognition of an individual's right to die with dignity, euthanasia, and the right to suicide."
We now reaffirm that statement.
An effort to elaborate or perhaps to be more precise ap-

pears to have motivated the publication of "A Plea for Beneficent Euthanasia" in the July/August issue that year of *The
Humanist* magazine. It was signed by three Nobel Laureates,
five physicians, twelve religious leaders, five philosophers, five
lawyers and businessmen, five "academics," and five additional
signers, distinguished persons and Humanists, all.

Perhaps we should have left well enough alone.

The frontiers of ethical thought have advanced in the
eighteen years intervening between then and now.

Euthanasia was a term that fell harshly on the ear in
1973. Despite its literal translation from the Greek—"easy
death"—and the commonly accepted definitions of "good
death" and "painless death," the authors of the 1973 Plea felt
it necessary to ease the pain further by adding the word "beneficent," which is, in itself, defined as "doing good."

The tautology was, perhaps, excusable to soften the impact of the positions taken. They were, indeed, radical in
1973, a time before even "Living Wills"—now widely
accepted—were given official sanction by any state legislatures. Since 1976, we now have all but four or five states with
laws expressly permitting some form of written advance directive, such as living wills, durable powers of attorney, health
care proxies and appointments of health care surrogates.

Despite the recent defeat of Proposition #119 in the State
of Washington, an initiative which would have legalized physician assisted voluntary euthanasia under strictly controlled
conditions, medical, religious and popular perceptions of the
circumstances under which a certain form of euthanasia is
deemed to be an acceptable practice have advanced far beyond
the position expressed in the 1973 Plea. Of course, many of
the early Living Will statutes have also become obsolete. And
along with changing public and professional attitudes has
come substantial movement in the ethical debate.

In some aspects, the Plea was, indeed, far advanced beyond the then current mainstream expressions urging tolera-
tion for euthanasia. The medical profession as well as most
religious ethicists have come to accept the premise that an
individual has the right to refuse the application, or demand
the withdrawal, of extraordinary measures to prolong the semblance of life when all hope is gone.

For a long time, those measures were held *not* to include

forcibly applied nutrition or hydration, such as nasogastric or intravenous bodily intrusions. Finally the medical profession issued a dictum equating such interventions with other "extraordinary measures" to sustain the spark of life. Accordingly, though not without a last ditch fight from some quarters, nutrition and hydration may now be withheld or removed from a patient in most states if the patient so willed it in an advance directive.

The withdrawal of life support systems of any kind has been dubbed "passive" euthanasia, and it now enjoys general support in the ethical and religious community where the patient has made clear advance expression of his or her consent in the particular circumstances.

Active euthanasia is often distinguished from passive euthanasia by the fact that the intervention of a third person in the physical condition of the patient consists of an act *other than* the refusal to apply life sustaining technology or the withdrawal of such technology after it has been applied. Instead of being allowed to die because of the underlying condition, in active euthanasia the patient receives assistance in dying in order to shorten pain and suffering.

The Plea for Beneficent Euthanasia bravely suggests that the distinction is more rhetorical than real. It says: "On the basis of a compassionate approach to life and death it seems to us at times difficult to distinguish between passive and active approaches."

It is suggested that the ethical approach, rather than the compassionate approach, would completely obliterate any distinction between passive and active euthanasia, since in each case the third party actor is performing an act—staying away from the patient or "pulling the plug" on the one hand, and ministering to the patient in one form or another, on the other. The significant factor in both cases is that the third party actor is conducting himself, deliberately and intentionally, in a manner calculated to bring about the death of the patient. The Nature of his activity has no bearing on the righteousness of his conduct.

Perhaps the most significant development over the years in the evolving views about the ethics of euthanasia is the gradual emergence of public consensus that the autonomy of the individual is paramount and should prevail over the authority heretofore exercised by the medical profession or by government paternalism to control the time, manner and place of death. This is strongly illustrated by those cases—most notably the case of Elizabeth Bouvia in the state of California— in which the patient did not suffer from a terminal condition but sought simply to be in control of the ending of life. In an outstanding concurring opinion, Judge Crompton went beyond the prevailing publicly accepted ethic when he stated (referring to Ms. Bouvia's attempt to starve herself to death): "This state and the medical profession instead of frustrating her desire (to commit suicide), should be attempting to relieve her suffering by permitting and in fact assisting her to die with ease and dignity. The fact that she is forced to suffer the ordeal of self-starvation to achieve her objective is in itself inhumane. The right to die is an integral part of our right to control our own destinies. . . . That right should . . . include the ability to enlist assistance from others, including the medical profession, in making death as painless and quick as possible."

To effectuate control by the individual, there have been developed several varieties of advance directives. One such is called the "durable power of attorney." Another is the appointment of a "health care surrogate" or "health care proxy." And, of course, there is the "living will" under which a person may be designated to make decisions when the maker of the instrument is unable to do so. Each of these forms calls for the designation of a person or persons to carry out the directions of the individual executing the document when that person is unconscious, comatose or incompetent. Most importantly, such directives can be quite specific as to the medical occasions when a person wishes to be denied treatment. In the states in which court tests have arisen, most of such directives have been upheld even in the absence of specific validating legislation.

It is to be noted that such directives are honored not only in the case of patients deemed to be terminal, but also when the patient is in a persistent vegetative state or other condition from which recovery is unlikely. (There are an estimated 10,000 persons in a persistent vegetative state being sustained by feeding tubes as was Nancy Cruzan in the 1990 U.S. Supreme Court case.) It is important to note that we have moved beyond the 1973 Plea which is limited, by its terms, to cases of terminal illness. The right to individual autonomy and to insist upon freedom from intrusive medical interventions has now been recognized to apply when the patient is not terminally ill.

The narrow defeat of Proposition #119 in the State of Washington would indicate that the time of other-person assisted euthanasia, by medically trained personnel or otherwise, has not yet arrived. However, advances are being made in other directions.

On December 1, 1991, the federal Patient Self-Determination Act became effective throughout the land. From that date on, all hospitals, nursing homes and other health care facilities that participate in Medicare and Medicaid are required to advise patients, upon admission, of their right to refuse treatment and their right to sign advance directives for health care decisions. The public will be brought face-to-face with the concept of "death with dignity" and with the issues so long debated by philosophers, religionists and ethicists. The heightened consciousness of these issues among a population heretofore largely ignorant of them is bound to have a profound impact upon the future direction of legislation similar to Washington's Proposition #119.

## Statement

The human being is more than mere protoplasm, more than the sum of its body parts, more than its chemical components. Our genetic content and our unique life experiences make each human being different from any other that ever lived, that now lives, or that is yet to come.

Each of us develops a sense of self. As individuals, we know, deep down, who we are and what we are, apart from the public face we show to others. We may like or dislike what we know of ourselves, but I am I and no one can take that away from me.

When what I know as myself is no longer discernable to me, I want to die, because I am already dead. My sense of myself is gone.

I have lost my essence . . . only a body is left. Whether

345

it is breathing and its heart is beating is immaterial. My unique quality has disappeared.

I am in control of my life and my lifestyle. No religious authority, no government authority can exercise control over my manner of living unless I constitute a threat to my family or to the larger community. Dying is an integral part of living and I demand to exercise control over the manner and time of my dying, just as I was in control of my living. I am free to choose it. There is no principle of ethics or morality to justify imposing other or greater controls over my "deathstyle" than over my lifestyle.

Many people fear dependency, pain and disability more than they fear death. They do not want to be saved from massive strokes for a life of dependency and increasing disability. They do not want to have their lives prolonged by extensive periods of chemotherapy or intrusive life-support technologies. They do not wish to live for years in a state of advanced Alzheimer's disease or senile dementia, incontinent and no longer the persons they once were. To keep these individuals alive against their wishes is to do them great harm—just as it is to do great harm to allow those to die who want to go on living.

Of course, not all seriously ill patients are competent to choose or refuse life-sustaining treatment. But the same principles that guide decision-making for competent patients—autonomy and sense of self—will guide decision-making when the patient is comatose or otherwise incompetent by the execution of one of a variety of "advance directives" which empower another person to make medical treatment decisions for the patient, and contain explicit directives to carry out the patient's wishes.

If it is permissible to *let* some patients die, why is it not also permissible to *help* a patient to die? The fact is that simple cessation of life-sustaining treatment does not always result in a swift and painfree death. It may take the patient days or weeks to die and the suffering is often extreme, in spite of palliatives. Would it not be more in consonance with kindness and compassion for a fellow human being to help the patient die? Being *allowed* to die may mean that a patient is compelled to suffer more than he or she should be made to

bear. That is not "death with dignity." That is cruel and unusual punishment to the living.

We should also recognize that it is essential that laws permitting assisted suicide must contain adequate safeguards as-
suring that such actions are wholly voluntary and clinically
appropriate.

There can be no doubt that a greater harm to the individual can result from prolonging a life that is bereft of any
quality rather than permitting it to end, or, in the proper case,
ending it.

The basic question is—how do we respond to human
need? Do we fall back upon the concept of a deity who controls living and dying? Do we talk in terms of moral absolutes? As the distinguished Dr. Joseph Fletcher (AHA
Humanist of the Year in 1974) put it: ". . . to reject control
responsibility, to deny human beings the role of decision
makers . . . is to deny human beings their moral status. We
become puppets, cease to be people. Fatalism and ethical abso-
lutism are the religious forms of puppetry . . . I believe that
when love and concern for human need is our ideal, rather
than moral laws and rights, we then see that knowingly letting
a monster be born into the world, or knowingly letting a man
become a monster, is in any case not justifiable."

Following is the 1973 "Plea" mentioned by Judith Espenschied in
the previous chapter and by Sidney M. Goetz in this chapter.


## A PLEA FOR BENEFICENT EUTHANASIA

We, the undersigned, declare our support on ethical
grounds for beneficent euthanasia. We believe that reflective
ethical consciousness has developed to a point that makes it
possible for societies to work out a humane policy toward
death and dying. We deplore moral insensitivity and legal restrictions that impede and oppose consideration of the ethical
case for euthanasia. We appeal to an enlightened public opinion to transcend traditional taboos and to move in the direction of a compassionate view toward needless suffering in
dying.

We reject theories that imply that human suffering is

inevitable or that little can be done to improve the human condition. We hold that the tolerance, acceptance, or enforcement of the unnecessary suffering of others is immoral.

We believe in the value and dignity of the individual person. This requires respectful treatment, which entails the right to reasonable self-determination. No rational morality can categorically forbid the termination of life if it has been blighted by some horrible malady for which all known remedial measures are unavailing.

## Definition

Euthanasia, which literally means "good death," may be defined as "a mode or act of inducing or permitting death painlessly as a relief from suffering." It is an effort to make possible a "gentle and easy death" for those afflicted with an incurable disease or injury in its terminal stages. It is beneficent euthanasia if, and only if, it results in a painless and quick death, and if the act as a whole is beneficial to the recipient.

## Dying with Dignity

To require that a person be kept alive against his will and to deny his pleas for merciful release after the dignity, beauty, promise, and meaning of life have vanished, when he can only linger on in stages of agony or decay, is cruel and barbarous. The imposition of unnecessary suffering is an evil that should be avoided by civilized society.

We believe that our first commitment as human beings is to preserve, fulfill, and enhance life for ourselves and our fellow human beings. However, under certain conditions, a meaningful or significant life may no longer be possible. It is natural for human beings to hope that when that time comes they will be able to die peacefully and with dignity. When there is great distress and the end is inevitable, we advocate a humane effort to ease the suffering of ourselves and others, without moral or legal recriminations.

From an ethical viewpoint, death should be seen as part

of a life-continuum. Since every individual has the right to live with dignity—however often this right may in fact be violated—every individual has the right to die with dignity.

Euthanasia presents an ethical problem for patients who know that their condition is incurable or irremediable and their suffering unendurable only if their theology or philosophy has persuaded them that no human involvement in the termination of life is morally permissible. For ethical humanists, euthanasia should be no problem. Pain or suffering is to be endured with as much dignity as patients can summon, as long as there is present a possibility of relief or cure. It is not to be endured when it is completely pointless, as is the case in the final stages of incurable disease.

## Voluntary Euthanasia

We recommend that those individuals who believe as we do sign a "living will," preferably when they are in good health, stating unequivocally the expectation that the right to die with dignity should be respected. The individual's regular physician should be informed of this will and be given a copy of it; and, if the physician is not willing to comply, another, more sympathetic physician should be chosen. Family and close friends should have copies of the "living will" or, in its absence, be aware of the individual's desire, in the event that at a terminal stage the person is incapable of communicating with others.

When a living will has not been written or an intention stated before the onset of an incurable disease, the patient's expressed request for euthanasia should be respected. Preferably, this should be a reflective judgment stated over a period of time. In all of these cases, euthanasia is voluntary, and it follows from a person's own free conscience to control both his life and, to some extent, the time and manner of his death.

## Passive and Active Euthanasia

For those who have reached the point of such acceptance, there is yet another distinction of major importance: that between passive and active euthanasia. Passive euthanasia is the withdrawal of extraordinary life-prolonging techniques, such as intravenous feeding and resuscitation, or not initiating such treatment, when the situation is hopeless. Given the tremendous advances in medical science, it is now possible to keep terminal patients alive far beyond the time they might ordinarily die. Active euthanasia is the administration of increasing dosages of drugs (such as morphine) to relieve suffering, until the dosage, of necessity, reaches the lethal stage. On the basis of a compassionate approach to life and death, it seems to us at times difficult to distinguish between passive and active approaches. The acceptance of both forms of euthanasia seems to us implied by a fitting respect for the right to live and die with dignity.

## Cortical Death

The most difficult questions of euthanasia may arise when individuals are in an unconscious state or coma and are unable to convey their wishes. We believe that, when a medical pronouncement of cortical death has been made, the health-care delivery team in consultation with the patient's family and friends, and with proper legal protections, should suspend treatment calculated to prolong life. Euthanasia should here be administered only in carefully defined circumstances and as a last resort and with all possible legal safeguards against abuse.

## Attitudes of Physicians

Often physicians and families, unable to bear a terminal patient's torture, permit acts of euthanasia to occur, but with great fear and secrecy. It is time that society faced this moral dilemma openly.

For some physicians the problem of euthanasia arises primarily because of a certain ambivalence in the Hippocratic oath. We should point out that, by this oath, a physician is committed both to the treatment and cure of disease and to the relief of suffering. A physician's own theology or philosophy will often influence the decision about which horn of this "doctor's dilemma" to choose. Often, too, consciously or subconsciously, a doctor's choice will be determined by his unwillingness to "lose" a patient, especially in cases where there is close personal identification. But the physician has no moral right to frustrate the patient's reflective wishes in these circumstances. For an ethical humanist, the physician's primary concern in the terminal stages of incurable illness should be relief of suffering. If the attending physician rejects this attitude toward the patient, another doctor should be called in to take charge of the case.

## Conclusion

We believe that the practice of voluntary beneficent euthanasia will enhance the general welfare of human beings and, once legal safeguards are established, that such actions will encourage human beings to act courageously, out of kindness and justice. We believe that society has no genuine interest or need to preserve the terminally ill against their will and that the right to beneficent euthanasia, with proper procedural safeguards, can be protected against abuse.

## Signers

NOBEL PRIZE LAUREATES
Linus Pauling, *Stanford University*
Sir George Thomson, *Fellow of the Royal Society, England*
Jacques Monod, *Institut Pasteur, France*

PHYSICIANS
Maurice B. Visscher, M.D., *University of Minnesota Medical School*
Jules H. Masserman, *M.D., Pres., International Association of Social Psychiatry*
Louis Lasagna, *M.D., University of Rochester*
Thomas W. Furlow, *M.D., University of Virginia Medical Center*
Eliot Slater, *M.D., British Voluntary Euthanasia Society*

RELIGIOUS LEADERS
Jerome Nathanson, *Chairman, Board of Leaders, New York Society for Ethical Culture*

Joseph Fletcher, *Professor of Biomedical Ethics, University of Virginia School of Medicine*
Edna Ruth Johnson, *Editor, The Churchman*
Algernon D. *Black, Fraternity of Leaders, American Ethical Union*
Tilford E. Dudley, *Director, Washington Office, United Church of Christ*
Rev. John R. Scotford, *Former Editor of Advance* (the national journal of Congregational churches)
Rev. Richard Henry, *Unitarian Minister, President of Good Death Fellowship*
Rev. Edward L. Peet, *Glide Memorial Methodist Church, San Francisco, California*
Rev. Gardiner M. Day, *Rector Emeritus, Christ Episcopal Church, Cambridge, Massachusetts*
Rabbi Daniel Friedman, *Congregation Beth Or, Board of Directors, Society for Humanistic Judaism*
Rev. D. R. Sharpe, *Baptist Minister*
Rev. H. L. MacKenzie, *United Church of Christ*

PHILOSOPHERS
Marvin Kohl, *State University College, Fredonia, New York*
Paul Kurtz, *State University of New York at Buffalo*
Sidney Hook, *New York University*
Ernest Nagel, *Columbia University*
Charles Frankel, *Columbia University*
R. B. Brandt, *University of Michigan*

LAWYERS AND BUSINESSMEN
Cyril C. Means, Jr., *New York Law School*
Arval A. Morris, *School of Law, University of Washington*
Mary R. Barrington, *Solicitor of the Supreme Court of Judicature of England and Wales*
Lloyd Morain, *Vice President, International Society for General Semantics*
Stewart V. Pahl, *Counselor, American Humanist Association*

ACADEMICS
Daniel C. Maguire, *Marquette University*
O. Ruth Russell, *Western Maryland College*
Chauncey D. Leake, *University of California*
Roy P. Fairfield, *Coordinator, Union Graduate School*
Lee A. Belford, *New York University*

ADDITIONAL SIGNERS
James Farmer, *President, Council on Minority Planning and Strategy*
Mary Morain, *Board of Directors, Association for Voluntary Sterilization*
Bette Chambers, *President, American Humanist Association*
Sicco L. Mansholt, *Former President, Commission of the European Economic Community*
H. J. Blackham, *President, British Humanist Association*

# Chapter 37

## Islam

The discussion of euthanasia and Islam has been prepared by Dr. Hassan Hathout, M.D., Ph.D., who is an Islamic scholar with the Islamic Center of Southern California and a medical doctor. For those unfamiliar with Islamic literature, the references to "Bukhari" and "Muslim" indicate that the statements are drawn from the Hadith, which represent collections of sayings of the Prophet Muhammad preserved by "attestors" or "authorities" and gathered and edited during the ninth century of the Common Era by the Persian scholars Abu Abadallah Muhammad al-Bukhari, and Abul-Husain al-Muslim.

### BACKGROUND

Islam is the third of the monotheistic Abrahamic religions following Judaism and Christianity which Islam recognizes and shares the moral code. Islam, however, brought forth a comprehensive system, the Shari'a, that covers all aspects of individual or collective human life.

The primary sources of the Shari'a are the Qur'an (to Muslims God's very words) and the tradition (teachings and deeds) of Prophet Muhammad. Issues not specifically mentioned in those two sources are ruled on by Analogy (intelligent reasoning matching new issues with issues judged by Qur'an or Tradition) and the unanimous consensus of Muslim scholars. When an issue is clearly settled by the Qur'an or Tradition the verdict is final. "It is not fitting for a believer, man or woman, when a matter has been decided by Allah (arabic word for God) and His messenger, to have any option about their decision . . . if anyone disobeys Allah and His messenger, he is indeed on a clearly wrong path" (Qur'an 33:36).

These, however, are not the majority of issues and are concerned mainly with matters of creed, worship, morality and only a few legislative rulings. The major part of Islamic Jurisprudence is the product of human thinking to meet new events in new times and places, always heeding the five objectives of the Shari'a which are the protection of faith, life, mind, ownership and honour. A basic premise is the lawfulness of all things unless specified by the Qur'an and Tradition or conflicting with the objectives of the Shari'a.

## HUMAN LIFE

The sanctity of human life is a basic value, decreed by God even before the times of Moses, Jesus and Muhammad. Commenting on the killing of Abel by his brother Cain (the two sons of Adam), God says in the Qur'an: "On that account We ordained for the Children of Israel that if anyone slew a person—unless it be for murder or spreading mischief in the land—it would be as if he slew the whole people. And if anyone saved a life, it would be as if he saved the life of the whole people" (Qur'an 5:32). The Qur'an also says: "Take not life which Allah made sacred otherwise than in the course of justice" (Qur'an 6:151 and 17:33). The Shari'a went into great detail in defining the conditions where taking life is permissible whether in war or in peace (as an item of the criminal law), with rigorous prerequisites and precautions to minimize that event.

## IS THERE A RIGHT TO SUICIDE?

Not in Islam. Since we did not create ourselves we do not own ourselves but are entrusted with the self for care, nurture and safe upkeep. God is the owner and giver of life and His rights in giving and in taking are not to be violated. Attempting to kill oneself is a crime in Islam as well as a grave sin. The Qur'an says: "Do not kill (or destroy) yourselves . . . for verily Allah has been to you most merciful" (Qur'an: 4:29). To warn against suicide, Prophet Muhammad said: "Whoever kills himself with an iron instrument will be carrying it forever in hell. Whoever takes poison and kills himself will forever keep sipping that poison in hell. Whoever jumps off a mountain and kills himself will forever keep falling down in the depths of hell" (narrated by Bukhari and Muslim).

## EUTHANASIA—MERCY KILLING

The Shari'a listed and specified the bases for taking life (i.e. the exceptions to the general rule of sanctity of human life) and they do not include mercy killing or make allowance for it. Human life, per se, is a value to be respected unconditionally, irrespective of other circumstances. The concept of "a life not worth living" does not exist in Islam. No justification for taking life to escape suffering is acceptable in Islam. Prophet Muhammad taught: "There was a man in older times who had an affliction that taxed his patience, so he took a knife, cut his wrist and bled to death. Upon this God said: My subject hastened his end . . . I deny him paradise" (narrated by Bukhari). "During one of the military campaigns, one of the Muslims was killed and the companions of the Prophet kept praising his gallantry and efficiency in fighting, but to their surprise the Prophet commented 'His lot is hell.' Upon inquiry, the companions found out that the man had been seriously injured, so he supported the handle of his sword on the ground and plunged his chest onto its tip, committing suicide" (narrated by Muslim).

The Islamic Code of Medical Ethics, endorsed by the First International Conference on Islamic Medicine (Islamic Organization of Medical Sciences, Kuwait, 1981, p.65), states: "Mercy killing—like suicide—finds no support except in the atheistic way of thinking that believes that our life on this earth is followed by void. The claim of killing for painful hopeless illness is also refuted, for there is no human pain that cannot be largely conquered by medication or by suitable neurosurgery."

But there is another dimension to the question of pain and suffering. Patience and endurance are highly regarded and highly rewarded values in Islam. "Those who patiently persevere will truly receive a reward without measure" (Qur'an 39:10). "And bear in patience whatever (ill) may befall you this, behold, is something to set one's heart upon" (Qur'an 31:17). Prophet Muhammad taught "when the believer is afflicted with pain—even that of a prick of a thorn or more—God forgives his sins and his wrongdoings are discarded as a tree sheds off its leaves" (narrated by Bukhari and Muslim). When means of preventing or alleviating pain fall short, this spiritual dimension can be very effectively called upon to support the patient who believes that accepting and enduring unavoidable pain will be to his/her credit in the hereafter, the real and enduring life. To a person who does not believe in a hereafter, this might sound like nonsense, but to one who does, euthanasia is certainly nonsense.

## THE FINANCIAL FACTOR

There is no disagreement that the economic cost of maintaining the incurably ill and the senile are growing concerns, so much so that some groups have gone beyond the concept of the "right to die" to that of the "duty to die." They claim that when the human machine has outlived its productive span, its maintenance would be an unacceptable burden on the productive stratum of society and it should be disposed of, and—for that matter—abruptly rather than allowing it to deteriorate gradually (Jacques Atalli: "La Medecine en accusation"—in Michel Soloman, "*L'avenir de la vie*", Coll. Les visages de l'avenir. Ed. Seghers, Paris, 1981, p. 273-275).

This logic is completely alien to Islam. Values take priority over prices. Caring for the weak, old and helpless is a value in itself for which people willingly sacrifice time, effort and money, and this care starts, naturally, with one's own parents, "Your Lord decreed that you worship none but Him, and that you be kind to your parents. Whether one or both of them attain old age in your life, say not to them a word of contempt but address them in terms of honour. And lower to them the wing of humility out of compassion, and say: My

Lord, bestow on them Your mercy even as they cherished me in childhood" (Qur'an 17:24-25). Because such caring is a virtue ordained and rewarded by God in this world and in the hereafter, the believers don't take it as a debit but as an investment. In a materialistic dollar-centered community, this logic is meaningless, but not so in the value-oriented God-heeding community of the faithful.

When individual means cannot cover the needed care, it becomes, according to Islam, the collective responsibility of society, and financial priorities are reshuffled so that values take priority over pleasures. People derive more pleasure from heeding values than from pursuing other pleasantries. A prerequisite, of course, is a complete moral and spiritual reorientation of a society that does not hold to these premises.

## CLINICAL SITUATIONS

In an Islamic setting, the question of euthanasia does not arise, and if it does, it is dismissed as religiously unlawful. The patient should receive all possible psychological support and compassion from family and friends, including the recruitment of the patient's own spiritual (religious) stamina. The doctor also participates in this process, as well as providing the therapeutic measures for the relief of pain. A dilemma arises when the dose of the pain killer necessary to alleviate pain approximates or overlaps with the lethal dose that might bring about the patient's death. Ingenuity, on part of the doctor, is called to avoid this situation, but from a religious point of view the critical issue is the doctor's intention: is it to kill or alleviate pain? Intention is beyond verification by the law but, according to Islam, it cannot escape the everwatching eye of God who according to the Qur'an "knows the treachery of the eyes, and all that hearts conceal" (Qur'an 40:19). Sins that do not fulfill the criteria of a legal crime are beyond the domain of the judge but remain answerable to God.

The Islamic Code of Medical Ethics (1981, p.67), states: "In his/her defense of life, however, the doctor is well advised to realize his limit and not transgress it. If it is scientifically certain that life cannot be restored, then it is futile to diligently maintain the vegetative state of the patient by heroic

means of animation or to seek to preserve the patient by deep
freezing or other artificial methods. It is the process of life that
the doctor aims to maintain and not the process of dying. In
any case, the doctor shall not take a positive measure to terminate the patient's life."

The seeking of medical treatment for illness is mandatory
in Islam, according to two sayings of the Prophet: "Seek treatment, subjects of God, for to every illness God has made a
cure," and "Your body has claim on you." But when the treatment holds no promise it ceases to be mandatory. This applies
both to surgical and/or pharmaceutical measures, and—
according to a majority of scholars—to artificial animation
equipment. Ordinary life needs, which are the right of every
living person and which are not categorized as "treatment," are
regarded differently. These include food and drink and ordinary nursing care, and are not to be withheld as long as the
patient lives (an interesting development is the acceptance of
total brain death—including the brain stem—as a verdict that
a person has withdrawn from life even if artificially animated,
and certain rulings of the dead become applicable to him/her,
including removal of artificial maintenance and procuring his
fresh heart for transplantation, based on analogy to an old
juridical rule called "the movement of the slain" (in *Human
Life: Its Inception and End*, Islamic Organization of Medical
Sciences, Kuwait, 1989, p. 628-9).

## COMMENTARY

The discussion of euthanasia cannot be isolated from the
total ideological background of a certain community. Muslims,
believing in God, and in a divinely prescribed Shari'a, will
naturally have different views from others who neither believe
in God, nor acknowledge God, but deny Him any authority
to tell us what we should or shouldn't do. As Dostoevsky said,
"where there is no God, everything is possible." In much of
contemporary Christendom, the concept of separation of
church and state is being pushed to mean the exclusion of
God from human affairs, although they are not the same.

The experience of euthanasia in Nazi Germany earlier in

this century left us with some eye openers. Euthanasia was endorsed, pioneered and implemented by medical practitioners of the highest order of intelligence and professional status. Once having condoned the concept of "a life not worth living," the sliding slope led subtly to the horrors that followed. Now, fifty years later, the euthanasia lobby has regrouped and is launching a powerful second attempt, that has succeeded in the Netherlands and in targeting Europe and America. Euthanasia opponents question the validity of the alleged free consent of the patient and ask whether the consent is, in fact, authentic or whether it has been influenced by a morbid psychology, or given under the pressure of embarrassment on part of the patient who is made to feel a burden on the family both psychologically and financially. Consent given by the family is open to the possibility of conflict of interest. The battle draws near and the outcome remains to be seen; a battle which, in Islam, has no premise for arising in the first instance.

In an additional note, in response to a question as to whether or not there would be any change in burial rituals for a person who chose to die by active euthanasia, Dr. Hathout indicated that there would be no change. However, there could be effects in the after life, both for the person who assisted in the patient's death and for the patient who participated in euthanasia. Dr. Hathout noted that the act is "sinful" but that "it is up to God to dispense justice or grant forgiveness." Dr. Hathout's position received support from a news report of a meeting of Muslim theologians held in Jiddah, Saudi Arabia in May, 1992. The account was published in the *Trentonian*, Trenton, New Jersey on Sunday, May 17, 1992 and reads as follows:

Muslim theologians opposed to *right-to-die* policies forced last-minute changes in a document that earlier said ending life support did not violate Islamic law, an official said yesterday.

The final text of the statement by the Islamic High Academy asked Muslims to continue to provide medical care to terminally ill patients, said a spokesman for the academy, which offers interpretations and guidelines on Islamic tenets.

The Islamic academy official, who spoke on condition of anonymity, told The Associated Press the change was made after heated debate among the more than 110 theologians who ended a six-day meeting Thursday.

The fact that a debate occurred suggests that there are Muslim theologians who disagreed with the vote and who would support right-to-die policies in Islam.

# Chapter 38

## The Baha'is

In 1985, Anna Lee Strasburg, on behalf of the Office of the Secretary of the National Spiritual Assembly of the Baha'is of the United States, wrote:

> The Baha'i Writings do not contain specific guidance on euthanasia or on the subject of life support systems as used by the medical profession in cases of the terminally ill. Therefore Baha'is are free to make their own decisions about the termination of such treatment. The supreme governing body of the Baha'i Faith considers it untimely to make definitive rulings on certain matters to which no direct reference can be found in the Sacred Text. Rather it is the task of the individual believer to determine, according to his own understanding of the Writings, precisely what his course of conduct should be in relation to situations which he encounters in his daily life.
>
> However, concerning "active" euthanasia or "assisted suicide," the Baha'i teachings state that suicide is forbidden and that whoever commits suicide endangers his soul and will suffer spiritually in the afterlife.
>
> The manner in which a Baha'i dies not affect the application of the Baha'i burial laws.

In 1988, the Baha'i Publishing Trust, New Delhi, India published a revised and enlarged edition of Helen Hornby's *Lights of Guidance*. This book consists of responses given by the Baha'i Universal House of Justice to questions asked by Baha'is. Item 985 (p. 290) responds to a

362

question concerning euthanasia and item 987 (p. 291) deals with the removal of life-support equipment.

## EUTHANASIA (MERCY KILLING)

As to the questions relating to euthanasia . . . the House of Justice has asked us to share with you these two statements. . . .

"As to the Baha'i viewpoint on the removal of withholding of life support in medical cases where intervention prolongs life in disabling illnesses, nothing has been found in the Sacred Text specifically on this matter. In such cases decisions must be left to those responsible, including the patient."

*(From a letter dated 31 May 1979 written on behalf of the Universal House of Justice to an individual believer.)*

"We have received your letter of March 18, 1974 in which you asked for the Baha'i viewpoint on euthanasia and on the removal of life support in medical cases where physiological interventions prolong life in disabling illnesses. In general our teachings indicate that God, the Giver of life, can alone dispose of it as He deems best, and we have found nothing in the Sacred Text on these matters specifically but in a letter to an individual written on behalf of the beloved Guardian by his secretary regarding mercy killings, or legalized euthanasia, it is stated: '. . . this is also a matter which the Universal House of Justice will have to legislate.'

"Until such time as the Universal House of Justice considers legislation on Euthanasia, decisions in the matters to which you refer must be left to the conscience of those responsible."

*(From a letter dated 17 May 1974 from the Universal House of Justice to the National Spiritual Assembly of Alaska)* and *(From a letter written on behalf of the Universal House of Justice to the compiler, October 27, 1981)*

## LIFE SUPPORT

"With references to your letter of 1 July 1985, we are asked to say that, in general, our Teachings indicate that God, the Giver of life, can alone dispose of it as He deems best. The Universal House of Justice has found nothing in the Sacred Text about the matter of with-holding or removing life support in disabling or terminal illnesses where intervention prolongs life. Therefore, until such time as the House of Justice considers legislation on these matters, it is left to the conscience of the individual concerned whether or not to subscribe to a 'living will.'"

*(From a letter written on behalf of the Universal House of Justice to a Local Spiritual Assembly, July 23, 1985)*

# Chapter 39

## Hinduism

S wami Swahananda of the Vedanta Society of Southern California writes that there never has been "any official discussion" concerning euthanasia "here or in Ramakrishna Mission in India of which we are a branch." He notes that in Hinduism, in general, "The decision is left to the individual, subject to the laws of the country." He added:

> Recently a very famous incident happened. The well-known Vinobha Bhave, a great disciple of Mahatma Gandhi, and the organizer of the Bhoodan Movement, who became old, stopped taking food. So some newspapers announced. Of course the government did not take any position. Probably it was quietly done.
>
> Hinduism doesn't take any dogmatic positions based on theology. In ancient India, that is in very old days, there was occasionally cases of sadhus giving up their life in rivers or mountains. Of course, on very rare occasions.

V. D'Souza, Executive Secretary of the society for the Right to Die With Dignity (India), wrote:

> The classical Hindu tradition is that when a man has served his purpose in life, i.e., performed his functions required of him, brought up his family and has no direct obligations, it is time for him to retire. It is not expected that he should die, but he should retire from life. The term used is 'Sanyas' like the verse:

He's gone to the mountain
He is lost in the forest
Like a summer dried fountain
When our need was the sorest . . .

In other words, the man eclipses himself when he reaches a certain level of spiritual maturity and seeks self-deliverance.

In fact, Jainism, which is a Hindu sect . . . actually demands the most painful form of euthanasia, and such incidents take place time and again. Notable examples in India are a social worker Mr. Gapal Mandlik and Acharya Vinobha Bhave, a respected Ghandian disciple.

# Chapter 40

---

# Buddhism

---

The preciousness of the "life force" is a major feature in Buddhism. Buddhist commentaries contain warnings about the seriousness of taking life but most writers do not focus on the complex issues of euthanasia. For example, Geshe Tsultrim Gyeltsen, Director of Thubten Dhargye Ling, the Center for the Study of Buddhism and Tibetan Culture in Los Angeles, wrote simply:

> Regarding your question about euthanasia, we Buddhists do not accept this idea of killing oneself or others. For us, killing is always negative. We believe that killing will not remove suffering, because suffering is the result of karma. If the karmic influence still exists when a person dies, he will experience the suffering in the next life if it has not been finished. We also will not kill injured animals.

The concept of karma is related to the Buddhist doctrine of rebirth. In *The Joyful Path of Good Fortune*, Geshe Kelsang Gyatso quoted the Buddha:

> The actions of living beings are never wasted even though hundreds of aeons may pass before their effects are experienced. . . . If one thousand years pass between the time when we commit an action and the time when we experience its effect, during all of that time the potentialities of our action are carried within our mind. For example, if we commit the action of killing and all the causes for us to expe-

rience the effect of that action do not come together for one hundred lifetimes, still the potentialities of our action of killing remain within our mind throughout all of those lives. (p. 237)

In his discussion of non-virtuous actions, he lists killing as the first and points out that "The object of killing is any other being from the smallest insect to a Buddha." (p. 240) Although he does not address the issue of physician-assisted death, he writes that the employment of another to cause the killing does not excuse the person from the karmic consequences:

It is mistaken to think that the consequences of our non-virtuous actions can be avoided by employing someone else to commit them. In fact, if we use someone else as our agent, the total effect of our action will be twice as severe because two people will have to suffer bad results. In addition, we will have to experience the consequences of exploiting someone else for our own selfish purposes without having concern for their future welfare. (p. 241)

This same concept is emphasized by His Eminence Kalu Rinpoche in *The Gem Ornament of Manifold Oral Instructions* where he discusses the basic precept of lay ordination:

The first precept is a vow against the taking of life. When we take formal ordination, there is for each precept a single kind of action which violates the precept completely and terminates the ordination. In the case of taking the precept not to kill, if we consciously take the life of another human being, we have violated the precept completely. This is not to say that taking other forms of life is not harmful; it is in fact a very harmful thing to do, both to ourselves and the other creature. If we take a single act of killing and examine its results, without any mitigating factors, this act can produce rebirth for an infinitely long period of time in the hell realms, and five hundred lifetimes of the karmic retribution of being killed or experiencing a short life. So in no case could we say that the taking of the life of any creature is acceptable, but in the formal context of having taken the ordination not to kill, the only act which specifically destroys the ordination (rather than being a serious infraction of that ordination) is to take the life of a human being consciously. (pp. 87-88)

Nor may a Buddhist seek to persuade or enable another to choose death. Charles S. Prebish in *Buddhist Monastic Discipline: The Sanskrit Pratimoksa Sutras of the Mahasamghikas and Mulasarvastivadins* (Pennsylvania State University Press, 1975) quotes the third Parajika dharma:

> Whatever monk should intentionally, with his own hand, deprive a human or one that has human form of life, supply him with a knife, search for an assassin for him, instigate him to death, or praise the nature of death, saying, "O man, what use is this dreadful, impure, sinful life to you? O man, death is better than life for you"; should [the monk] purposefully, being of one opinion, instigate him in many ways to death, or recommend the nature of death to him, and he (i.e., that man) should die by that [means], this monk is parajika, expelled. (p. 53)

When the Dalai Lama of Tibet visited Harvard University (*The Dalai Lama at Harvard*. Ithaca, N.Y.: Snow Line Publications, 1988), he was asked about the ways that Buddhism could alleviate depression. The Dalai Lama related the question to suffering and pointed out that suffering had a karmic origin and that the knowledge of that fact and the awareness that suffering had a cyclic nature would be helpful. He emphasized the importance of will power, but what was even more important was to concentrate on the welfare of others. He said:

> Again, it is helpful to consider a Bodhisattva's way of thinking, emphasizing the welfare of the majority—everyone else—over one's own benefit. I am human, a monk, and in my case, the Dalai Lama, whom a number of people respect, but when the welfare of others and my own welfare are compared, I am just a single person and thus not worthy of my primary concern. Others' welfare is far more important. Then with such an attitude, it is helpful to think, "may the pain that I am experiencing serve as a substitute for the suffering that others have to undergo." This is called the practice of taking others' suffering and giving them your own happiness. It gives you inner strength.
>
> Through thinking along these lines, you will look on

your own pain as not unfortunate but a fortunate opportunity to practice these teachings. You will even think, "Even more problems *should* come; then, I will have more opportunities to practice." This gives you inner determination—a Bodhisattva's determination, like steel. (p. 98)

When he was asked if suicide would create greater suffering in subsequent karmas, he responded,

Suicide is described as being extremely harmful. In particular, it is said that for someone who has taken the tantric vows upon receiving initiation in either Yoga Tantra or Highest Yoga Tantra, killing oneself incurs the fault of killing a deity. (p. 114)

Some Buddhist scholars have dealt directly with euthanasia. When Arnold J. Toynbee engaged in dialogue with Daisaku Ikeda, who was president of the Buddhist lay organization Soko Gakkai, the discussion turned to the subject of suicide and euthanasia (*The Toynbee-Ikeda Dialogue.* Tokyo, N.Y. Kodansha International Ltd., n.d.) Dr. Ikeda objected to persons "sacrificing life for the sake of escape from pain." (p. 150). With regard to euthanasia he said that he could not condone the shortening of life by any means. He continued:

I do agree, however, that it is unnecessary to waste efforts on keeping alive hopelessly ill people—the so-called human vegetables whose brains no longer function or whose bodies cannot take in nourishment unaided—even though modern science has the ability to prolong such lives even when there is no longer a possibility of effective treatment. I agree with you on this point because I feel that a human being who has reached such a condition is no longer functioning as a human being and in a sense is dead already. In criticizing euthanasia, I am not thinking of truly hopeless people but of persons who, though in virtually unbearable suffering at the time, do have a period of life left to them, a period in which they can possibly achieve something worthwhile or maybe even brilliant. The person who is suffering may not see this possibility, and it is the duty of those around him to point it out to him as convincingly as possible. While recognizing that freedom to assist another to escape unbearable pain by taking his life or to seek

370

death for oneself is a logical conclusion of humanistic thought, I am afraid that, should this idea be regarded with less than maximum caution, it could degenerate into the kind of undervaluing of life I have often condemned.

For example, if people come to regard euthanasia as totally acceptable, it is not possible that the elderly who, as a result of illness are bedridden and dependent on the care of others for whom they can no longer do anything in return might feel guilty about simply remaining alive? In cases of this kind, recognizing euthanasia as born of a spirit of mercy might deprive all society of compassion.

I believe that whatever means are available ought to be applied in attempts to lessen suffering. Maximum efforts must be made to this end. But human agencies must not be allowed to affect the inherent rights of life itself to survive. Pleasure and pain have no intrinsic dignity, whereas life has a dignity for which there is no equivalent. Consequently, no pleasure and no pain can weigh as much in the scales of judgment as the dignity of life.

Dr. Ikeda suggested that the self-immolation of Vietnamese Buddhist monks which had occurred at that time might be explained, in part, by the "Southern Buddhist doctrine that flesh is fundamentally unclean." He pointed out that:

Northern Buddhism asserts that all life is a precious vessel containing the Buddha nature or the Buddha world. In other words, life itself is of value without equivalent, and above this value it is doubly precious because the Buddha nature is latent in it. The Buddha world may be briefly outlined in the following ways. It is the wisdom that has determined the ultimate nature of the universe and of the life force. It is the entity containing the boundless life force, which is one with individualized life. It is the wellspring of all true happiness. Though Buddhist literature contains nothing specifically prohibiting suicide and euthanasia, on the basis of Buddhist belief in the dignity of life it cannot be considered to condone it. (p. 156)

Toynbee stressed the importance of human dignity and said, "I feel that a human being's dignity is violated by other people when he is kept alive by them against his will, in accordance with principles in which these other people believe but in which the person primarily concerned perhaps does not believe. I also hold that a human being is violating his own dignity if he fails to commit suicide in certain instances." To this statement, Ikeda replied:

> I do not deny your assertion that human beings have the right to kill themselves, but I insist that the decisions of when life ought to end ought to be left to the life force itself. Intellect, reasoning, and emotion are superficial attributes of the life force and work to the end that the life force can manifest itself in loftier ways. Consequently, intellect, reason and emotions do not have the right to destroy total life or to decide when it shall terminate. Only life itself has this right. Life may terminate itself as the result of karma from the pastor perhaps as a consequence of some malfunction of the physical mechanism that supports its continuation. No matter which is the cause, the termination of life is determined at a level beyond human consciousness and is unrelated to intellect and emotion. (p. 157)

On April 6, 1991, the *Los Angeles Times* reported that in a lecture at Rice University, the Dalai Lama noted that euthanasia was a "very complicated" issue and that "from the Buddhist viewpoint generally speaking it is not good." It should only be performed, he said, where it is considered best for the "larger society," or for the patient himself.

Dr. Ronald Y. Nakasone, a priest of the Hongwanji Sect of Pure Land tradition, teaches Buddhist philosophy and ethics at the Institute of Buddhist Studies and the Graduate Theological Union in Berkeley, California. In 1989, he published two essays in *Wheel of Dharma*, the official monthly publication of the Buddhist Churches of America. The first, which appeared in the March issue (Vol. 16, Issue 3) was titled "Euthanasia: To Kill or Let Die." The essay was prompted by the failed effort of Americans Against Human Suffering to have the Humane and Dignified Death Act qualify for the November, 1988 ballot in California. Dr. Nakasone carefully defined "compulsory," "passive," and "voluntary euthanasia," the ethical issues of paternalism and autonomy, and the arguments for and against euthanasia. The second article, which appeared in the April, 1989, issue of the monthly publication, was titled "Euthanasia: A Buddhist Rejoinder." Both essays were later incorporated in his book *Ethics of Enlightenment* (1990). In the Rejoinder statement, Dr. Nakasone wrote:

My discussion on the Buddhist approach to the question of euthanasia is limited to two hypothetical sketches related in the *Samantapasadika.* Both sketches are of suicides, which are precipitated by a severe physical affliction. In these two accounts, it is the Buddha who is speaking. In the first account, the Buddha relates the encouragement of the death of a Bhikkhu or monk by his colleague.

There was a Bhikkhu who was very much distressed on account of a disease. The Bhikkhus saw this Bhikkhu suffering very acutely. Having pity upon him, they said, "Friend, you have been observing rules of good conduct. Being afraid of death you are now suffering so much. Friend, after death you are sure to be born among gods."

The Bhikkhus, moved by compassion for the plight of their colleague, believed that perhaps death, instead of prolonged suffering, was a preferable alternative. The monks simply wished to cheer their suffering friend by reviewing his life and looking beyond his immediate fear of death. The suffering monk, however, stirred by the assurance of birth among the gods, "abstained from taking food and died." The suffering monk interpreted the kind words of his fellow monks to be an encouragement to end his life. The commendation of death, however, is a *parajika* offense. Instead of encouraging death, the Buddha advised that a wise Bhikkhu should simply say:

Friend, you have been observing good conduct. Do not have any attachment for your place of residence, or for clothes, or for acquaintances and friends. Simply contemplate upon the three Jewels and reflect upon the unpleasant aspect of your body. In this threefold existence, be attentive, avoid sloth and torpor; one has to put in his life term, long or short.

In approaching a suffering monk, the Buddha instructed his disciples to remind him of his accomplishments and inspire him to continue his spiritual exercises. Despite suffering, death, however imminent should not be hurried. Life provides the opportunity for spiritual cultivation. Beside these more obvious details, one is left with a sense of fatalism in the statement "one has to put in his life term, long or short." But, perhaps, it may be more appropriate to interpret this last sentence to mean that one must make the most of life despite adversities. Note that the Buddha did not condemn the monk who chose euthanasia, rather he determined that the monks had erred, despite their best intentions, when they unwittingly urged their colleague to take his life.

Nevertheless, though the Buddha did not encourage suicide, he did not categorically reject it. On another occasion the Buddha said:

> "Do not commit suicide." . . . If, however, a Bhikkhu is very much afflicted with disease and sees the Sangha and other Bhikkhus attending upon him in his sickness put very much to trouble on account of nursing him, he thinks thus, "These people are very much put to trouble on account of me!" He then contemplates upon his life-span and finds that he is not going to live long and so he does not eat, does not clothe himself properly nor does he take any medicine, then it (i.e., suicide) may be excusable (lit. good).

According to this narrative, suicide was justifiable after the monk assessed the efforts that were being expended on his behalf, the severity of his affliction, and the immediacy of his death. The overriding motive for not living out one's life-span was the burden which the monk's illness was causing others and the imminence of death. To expedite his death, the monk resisted food and medicine and refused to care for himself.

To be sure, these two narratives do not address all of the issues that are generated by compulsory and voluntary euthanasia. Properly speaking, since the narratives only speak of the willful inducement of death or suicide, they are directly applicable only to voluntary euthanasia. In both instances, the monks, like Elizabeth, were mentally alert. But, unlike Elizabeth Bouvia, the monks were not prevented from carrying out their death wish. These two narratives avoid the problem of compulsory euthanasia. Further, no one made a decision to cause death by prescribing or administering a lethal poison or by withdrawing treatment.

What is significant for the present discussion is that the decision for death in both cases lay with the suffering monks. No others were involved. Both examples illustrate the principle of autonomy. While the principle of autonomy advocates an individual's right to self-determination and the right to choose a gentle death, this right is not absolute. Although an individual may be an autonomous being, there are limits to one's autonomy.

In an interdependent world, where our lives are intertwined with countless others, individuals do not have exclusive claim on their lives. We may have separate lives, but we must live in resonance with all others. We must accommodate the needs of others. Often we must acknowledge the wishes of others.

Further, an autonomous individual may infringe on the autonomy of another by inflicting grievous suffering and guilt on others, by committing suicide or by asking to have his life terminated. Even the monk who decided to end his life because he believed that his end was near and because he believed that he was causing others trouble, failed to take into account the wishes of his colleagues. The decision of both monks to end their lives demonstrated a degree of egoism.

What is more critical than the details (or lack thereof) of these two narratives, I believe, is the Buddha's attitude and approach toward the self-afflicted deaths. The Buddha's reproach, if one can even call it that, of the monks who unwittingly caused their fellow monk to commit suicide and his approval of the second monk's suicide, may seem contrary to the spirit of the Dharma. As we saw, the Buddha even supported the decision of the second monk to commit suicide. Instead of denying the Dharma, these two sketches reveal a premium on individual dignity and self-worth. Both affirm the individual right to determine his or her life.

The Buddha never meant, I venture to say, these sketches to be rules of thumb. These are only general guides from which to draw lessons in our own encounters with suffering and death. In the first narrative, the Buddha affirmed the reverence for life by asking his disciples not to encourage death. In the second, the Buddha supported the monk's suicide because of his selfless concern for others and his objective evaluation of the prospects for living. Within the confines of these two sketches, it is clear that the Buddha did not approach these two cases of willful euthanasia with some preconceived notion of right and wrong. More correctly, the Buddha considered each case within its immediate context.

Ethical codes rarely mesh with the realities of human experience and behavior. The question of euthanasia, for example, is a conflict between the respect for life and compassion to end continued suffering. Despite the prohibition of terminating life, there may be occasions when the continuation of life may not be the best alternative. Indeed, as we just saw, the Buddha even supported the suicide of a grievously ill monk.

But such an open ended approach is not without its burdens. The search for the proper decision which considers "all elements of suffering," demands careful deliberation. Sanghabhadra cautions in the *Samantapasadika* that the "violation" of the *patimokkha* rules must not be used for personal gain. In its overall spirit, Sanghabhadra does not condone killing nor does he pretend that the *patimokkha* codes are absolute. . . .

The ongoing euthanasia debate is a painful search for balancing individual rights and dignity, with societal concerns for the reverence of life and the protection of an individual's well being. Both sides of the debate are guided by a respect for life and human dignity. . . .

The willful termination of life is an especially irrevocable decision. The taking of life is a parajika offense, a defeat of the "holy life." Even the American criminal justice reserves its most severe punishment for killing another human being. It is no surprise, therefore, that there is great reluctance to legalize physician-assisted suicide. Condoning or acquiescing to the wishes of terminally ill individuals, even in the name of compassion, is believed by many to be equally reprehensible.

The evidence in the *Samantapasadika* suggests that Buddhists do not condone the willful termination of life, but it is clear that there may be occasions when the continuation of life may not be preferable. The passage of the Humane and Dignified Death Act or a similar law, with the proper safeguards against abuse, offers individuals, families and the physician an option to prolonged and unbearable suffering.

The four step method of decision making presented in the *Samantapasadika* is an exercise in judgement and accommodating exception. This method allows us to challenge time honored convictions and prescribed rules of conduct. Every situation is a novel event. Individual needs and wishes should be balanced in light of accepted norms of behavior. Life is never neatly patterned on prescribed rules, nor are rules totally reflective of life.

The process of weighing life and protracted pain against death and release from unnecessary suffering plummets the depth of our feelings. The decision to terminate life demands uncommon trust and understanding. On the other hand, such a decision presents an uncommon opportunity to explore our humanity and an occasion for spiritual flowering.

## SUDDEN DEATH TEMPLES (*POKKURI-DERA*)

In 1977, Winston Bradley Davis reported in a paper submitted to the East Asia Papers of Cornell University that since 1960, Sudden Death Temples in Japan had become popular with the aged ("Toward Modernity: A Developmental Typology of Popular Religious Affiliations in Japan"). He noted that as the number of aged people increase and as families decreased in size, traditional patterns that protected the elderly were set aside. Formerly, it was customary for elders to be cared for by their children. Today, more and more elderly Japanese now live apart from their children. Moreover, inasmuch as they live in a culture where the byword is "throw away after using" (*tsukai sutete bunka*), these older people tend to think that they have been used and cast aside. It is not surprising to find that the suicide rate among the elderly is on the increase. Some aged Japanese "turn to Amida Buddha and pray for a quick end to the sorrows of this life" (p.81). Tours to Sudden Death Temples provide opportunity to pray for a long life and good health, for protection against accidents and for a quick and easy death. Because diseases of the lower part of the body are a source of embarrassment, the elderly bring sets of underwear to be sprinkled with holy water and blessed by a priest who incantates a spell in the name of the toilet god Uzumasa, all for a fee. The priest also assures the visitors that death is not to be feared and that with simple effort one can be born into the Pure Land (p. 82).

# Chapter 41

## Sikh Dharma

The headquarters for the Sikh Dharma religion in the U.S.A., Canada, Mexico, Central and South America, Europe, Hong Kong and Australia is located in Los Angeles, California. The Secretary of Religion, Ram Das Kaur Khalsa, stated that "No official stand has been taken by Sikh Dharma, which is a world religion of fifteen million people. We also have not had any official discussions as such on the topic [of euthanasia]." He commented further:

We believe in keeping our bodies as God has created them, living healthy, happy and holy. We also believe in God's Will, and in being able to accept God's Will, whatever it may be. We do not believe in suicide, as we believe in reincarnation. We do use medicines and believe in surgery when necessary, so the line is very narrow between trying to save a life, and unnecessarily prolonging its stay here on earth. We are also not afraid of death.

This question would probably be left to the individual to decide, as the individual should have the choice how to live his life.

# Chapter 42

## Krishna Consciousness

Members of the International Society for Krishna Consciousness, whose followers are often identified as "Hare Krishnas," also believe in karma and reincarnation. These persons find their release from the wheel of life through their Lord Krishna and find guidance in the "timeless Vedic text Bhagavad-gita." In the book *Coming Back: The Science of Reincarnation* (Bhaktivedanta Book Trust, 1982) the editors explain:

> Everything we have thought and done during our life makes an impression on the mind, and the sum total of all these impressions influences our final thoughts at death. According to the quality of these thoughts, material nature awards us a suitable body. Therefore, the type of body that we have now is the expression of our consciousness at the time of our last death. (p. 16)

Clearly, the person's state at the moment of death has significance for the next incarnation. Hence, one looks for the perfect example of the way to die. For the members of the Hare Krishna group, that model was provided by Srila Prabhupada, the founder of the organization. According to Satsvarupa Dasa Goswami in *Prabhupada* (Bhaktivedanta Book Trust, 1983), Srila Prabhupada's "departure was exemplary" and "his 'last breathing' was glorious":

> . . . not because of any last-minute mystical demonstration, but because Srila Prabhupada remained in perfect Krishna

consciousness. . . . At the time of his departure, therefore, he was teaching how to die, by depending always on Krishna. Prabhupada's passing away was peaceful. During the evening of November 14, the *kaviraja* (an Ayur-Vedic doctor) asked him, "Is there anything you want?" and Prabhupada replied faintly, *Kuch iccha nahi*: "I have no desire." His passing away was in the perfect situation: in Vrndavana (a village that was Krishna's childhood home, but here it means the state of pure Krishna consciousness), with devotees. (p. 372)

Although there is no discussion of euthanasia, it is clear that, like the Buddhists, the members of this group prefer to avoid palliatives that might cloud the mind and would reject anything that might alter the natural dying trajectory.

# Chapter 43

# General Guidelines for Six Churches

**THE CHRISTIAN REFORMED CHURCH**
**THE ASSEMBLIES OF GOD**
**THE CHURCH OF GOD**
**THE CHRISTIAN REFORMED CHURCH IN**
  **NORTH AMERICA**
**THE UNITED PENTECOSTAL CHURCH INTERNATIONAL**
**METROPOLITAN COMMUNITY CHURCHES**

A number of denominations have not formulated statements on euthanasia. Some have guidelines that suggest the ways in which individual pastors and churches may react.

## THE CHRISTIAN REFORMED CHURCH

According to Dr. Calvin Van Reken, Assistant Professor of Moral Theology at Calvin Theological Seminary, Grand Rapids, Michigan, "the Christian Reformed Church has no official position regarding active or passive euthanasia. We are, however, generally opposed to both suicide and murder, and these prohibitions guide individuals in offering pastoral guidance."

## THE ASSEMBLIES OF GOD

Joseph R. Flower, General Secretary for the General Council of the Assemblies of God, Springfield, Missouri, wrote in 1985, and confirmed recently, that, "Our church has not officially addressed itself to this issue, but in general our people would be opposed to deliberately terminating life, or doing anything other than saving or preserving it." He provided as scriptural references Psalm 31:15 and Genesis 9:6, noting, "Only God has the right to terminate human life or to decree its termination. So highly does He evaluate it that any human who deliberately takes life will have his life terminated. The reason: man has been made in the image of God."

## THE CHURCH OF GOD

David L. Lawson, Associate Executive Secretary of the Executive Council of the Church of God, Anderson, Indiana responded as follows:

Since we are non-creedal and our polity does not allow any leader to speak for the total Church, we have some difficulty in being on record on issues of controversy. Our General Assembly does, periodically, review and vote a given stance with the understanding that this is representative of the majority of believers of our Church, but is not binding on any local congregation. Our congregations are autonomous bodies.

Nevertheless, I can draw from actions taken some stance in this matter. We believe life to be a sacred gift from God and therefore worthy of every effort to preserve it. In our 1981 General Assembly, we voted a stand against "abortion on demand." Part of the rationale for that stance was stated as "whereas, this opens the door to possible elimination of other unwanted or undesirable human beings."

In the resolve that followed, the General Assembly urged that "all congregations express our compassion and concern *not only to protect life before birth* but *to work to assure* that the lives that are preserved may receive care, attention, and help God wants for all persons; to provide *family life and marriage education that will foster a reverence for God-given life*. . . ."

The Church of God would be in basic agreement that we do not have the right to take life, either from another or on our own, and that would include those who might, for some reason wish to die. We watched with relief the defeat of Initiative 119.

382

As John Donne said, "any man's death diminishes me, because I am involved in mankind." Walt Whitman proclaimed "if anything is sacred, the human body is sacred." Paul, in his letter to Corinth wrote, "Do you not know that your body is a temple of the Holy Spirit?" (I Cor. 6:19).

Our Commission on Social Concern will do further work in this area.

# THE CHRISTIAN REFORMED CHURCH IN NORTH AMERICA

According to Leonard J. Hofman, General Secretary, "The Christian Reformed Church in North America (CRCNA) has not officially spoken to the issue of euthanasia." He went on to note that "the CRCNA has spoken to the issues of abortion and capital punishment. . . . Our polity provides that such issues are addressed when a local church or classes—a group of area churches—request a study. To date no such request has been received by the denomination through its member classes or churches."

# THE UNITED PENTECOSTAL CHURCH INTERNATIONAL

C.M. Becton, the General Secretary wrote, "Although I feel we are opposed to euthanasia, our organization, at this point, has made no official statement. By that I mean there has been no resolution presented to be formally voted on."

# METROPOLITAN COMMUNITY CHURCHES

The Rev. Troy Perry, founder of The Universal Fellowship of Metropolitan Community Churches, and pastor of the church in Santa Monica, California, noted ". . . our denomination has not taken a stance on the issue of euthanasia one way or the other. I am sure that in our denomination we have people who would be totally against euthanasia and we would have those who would view it as a humane alternative for the lot of the terminally ill."

Appendix I

---

# H-0814.1/91
# House Initiative 119

---

State of Washington
52nd Legislature
1991 Regular Session

By the People of the State of Washington.

Read first time January 18, 1991. Referred to Committee on Health Care.

AN ACT Relating to the natural death act; and amending RCW 70.122.010, 70.122.020, 70.122.030, 70.122.040, 70.122,050, 70.122.060, 70.122.070, 70.122.080, 70.122.090, 70.122.100, and 70.122.900.
BE IT ENACTED BY THE PEOPLE OF THE STATE OF WASHINGTON:
Sec. 1. RCW 70.122.010 and 1979 c 112 s 2 are each amended to read as follows:
The ((legislature)) *people* find ((s)) that adult persons have the fundamental right to control the decisions relating to the rendering of their own medical care, including the decision to have *all* life-sustaining procedures withheld or withdrawn in instances of a terminal condition, *and including the right to death with dignity through voluntary aid-in-dying if suffering from a terminal condition.*

The ((legislature)) *people* further find ((s)) that modern medical technology has made possible the artificial prolongation of human life beyond natural limits.

The ((legislature)) *people* further find ((s)) that, in the interest of protecting individual autonomy, such prolongation of life for persons with a terminal condition may cause loss of patient dignity, and unnecessary pain and suffering, while providing nothing medically necessary or beneficial to the patient.

The ((legislature)) *people* further find ((s)) that there exists considerable uncertainty in the medical and legal professions as to the legality of terminating the use or application of life-sustaining procedures where the patient has voluntarily and in sound mind evidenced a desire that such procedures be withheld or withdrawn.

*The people further find that existing law does not allow willing physicians to render aid-in-dying to qualified patients who request it.*

In recognition of the dignity and privacy which patients have a right to expect, the ((legislature)) *people* hereby declare ((s)) that the laws of the state of Washington shall recognize the right of an adult person to make a written directive instructing such person's physician to withhold or withdraw life-sustaining procedures in the event of a terminal condition, *and/or to request and receive aid-in-dying under the provisions of this chapter.*

Sec. 2. RCW 70.122.020 and 1979 c 112 s 3 are each amended to read as follows:

Unless the context clearly requires otherwise, the definitions contained in this section shall apply throughout this chapter.

(1) "Attending physician" means the physician selected by, or assigned to, the patient who has primary responsibility for the treatment and care of the patient.

(2) "Directive" means a written document voluntarily executed by the declarer in accordance with the requirements of RCW 70.122.030.

(3) "Health facility" means a hospital defined in RCW *70.41.020(2)*, a nursing home as defined in RCW *18.51.010, or a home health agency or hospice agency as defined in RCW 70.126.010.*

(4) "Life-sustaining procedure" means any medical or surgical procedure or intervention which utilizes mechanical or other artificial means to sustain, restore, or supplant a vital function, which, when applied to a qualified patient, would serve only to artificially prolong the moment of

death. "Life-sustaining procedure" *includes, but is not limited to, cardiac resuscitation, respiratory support, and artificially administered nutrition and hydration, but* shall not include the administration of medication *to relieve pain* or the performance of any medical procedure deemed necessary to alleviate pain.

(5) "Physician" means a person licensed under chapter 18.71 or 18.57 RCW.

(6) "Qualified patient" means a patient diagnosed and certified in writing to be afflicted with a terminal condition by two physicians one of whom shall be the attending physician, who have personally examined the patient.

(7) "Terminal condition" means an incurable *or irreversible condition which, in the written opinion of two physicians having examined the patient and exercising reasonable medical judgment, will result in death within six months, or a condition in which the patient has been determined in writing by two physicians as having no reasonable probability of recovery from an irreversible coma or persistent vegetative state.*

(8) "Adult person" means a person attaining the age of majority as defined in RCW 26.28.010 and 26.28.015.

(9) *"Aid-in-dying" means aid in the form of a medical service provided in person by a physician that will end the life of a conscious and mentally competent qualified patient in a dignified, painless and humane manner, when requested voluntarily by the patient, through a written directive in accordance with this chapter at the time the medical service is to be provided.*

Sec. 3. RCW 70.122.030 and 1979 c 112 s 4 are each amended to read as follows:

(1) Any adult person may execute *at any time* a directive directing the withholding or withdrawal of life-sustaining procedures *and/or requesting the provision of aid-in-dying when* in a terminal condition. The directive shall be signed by the declarer in the presence of two witnesses not related to the declarer by blood or marriage and who would not be entitled to any portion of the estate of the declarer upon declarer's decease under any will of the declarer or codicil thereto then existing or, at the time of the directive, by operation of law then existing. In addition, a witness to a directive shall not be the attending physician, an employee of the attending physician or a health facility in which the declarer is a patient, or any person who has a claim against any portion of the estate of the declarer upon declarer's decease at the time of the execution of the directive. The directive, or a copy thereof,

shall be made part of the patient's medical records retained by the attending physician, a copy of which shall be forwarded to the health facility upon the withdrawal of life-sustaining procedures, *and/or provision of aid-in-dying. No person shall be required to execute a directive in accordance with this chapter. Any person who has not executed such a directive is ineligible for aid-in-dying under any circumstances.* The directive shall be essentially in the following form, but in addition may include other specific directions:


## DIRECTIVE TO PHYSICIANS


Directive made this. . . . day of. . . . . . . (month, year).

I . . . . . . . . . . , being of sound mind, willfully, and voluntarily make known my desire that my life shall not be artificially prolonged under the circumstances set forth below, and do hereby declare that:

(a) If at any time I should have an incurable injury, disease, or illness certified to be a terminal condition by two physicians, and where the application of life-sustaining procedures would serve only to artificially prolong the moment of my death.

*Declarant must initial one or both of the following:*

. . . . . . . . . . *I direct that such procedures be withheld or withdrawn, and that I be permitted to die naturally.*

. . . . . . . . . *I direct that upon my request my physician provide aid-in-dying so that I might die in a dignified, painless and humane manner.*

(b) In the absence of my ability to give directions regarding the use of such life-sustaining procedures, *such as while in an irreversible coma or persistent vegetative state,* it is my intention that this directive shall be honored by my family and physician(s) as the final expression of my legal right to refuse medical or surgical treatment and I accept the consequences *of* such refusal.

(c) If I have been diagnosed as pregnant and that diagnosis is known to my physician, this directive shall have no force or effect during the course of my pregnancy.

(d) I understand the full import of this directive and I am emotionally and mentally competent to make this directive.

*(e) I understand that I may add or delete from or otherwise change the wording of this directive before I sign it, and that I may revoke this directive at any time.*

Signed . . . . . . . . . . . . . . . . . . . . . . . . .

City, County, and State of Residence

The declarer has been personally known to me and I believe him or her to be of sound mind.

Witness . . . . . . . . . . . . . . . . . . . . . . . . . . . .

Witness . . . . . . . . . . . . . . . . . . . . . . . . . . . .

(2) Prior to effectuating a directive the diagnosis of a terminal condition by two physicians shall be verified in writing, attached to the directive, and made a permanent part of the patient's medical records.

*(3) Similar directives to physicians lawfully executed in order states shall be recognized within Washington state as having the same authority as in the state where executed.*

Sec. 4. RCW 70.122.040 and 1979 c 112 s 5 are each amended to read as follows:

(1) A directive may be revoked at any time by the declarer, without regard to declarer's mental state or competency, by any of the following methods: (a) By being canceled, defaced, obliterated, burned, torn, or otherwise destroyed by the declarer or by some person in declarer's presence and by declarer's direction.

(b) By a written revocation of the declarer expressing declarer's intent to revoke, signed, and dated by the declarer. Such revocation shall become effective only upon communication to the attending physician by the declarer or by a person acting on behalf of the declarer. The attending physician shall record in the patient's medical record the time and date when said physician received notification of the written revocation.

(c) By a verbal expression by the declarer of declarer's intent to revoke the directive. Such revocation shall become effective only upon communication to the attending physician by the declarer or by a person acting on behalf of the declarer. The attending physician shall record in the patient's medical record the time, date, and place of the revocation and the time, date, and place, if different, of when said physician received notification of the revocation.

(2) There shall be no criminal, civil, *or administrative* liability on the part of any person for failure to act upon a revocation made pursuant to this section unless that person has actual or constructive knowledge of the revocation.

(3) If the declarer becomes comatose or is rendered incapable of communicating with the attending physician, the directive shall remain in effect for the duration of the comatose condition or until such time as the declarer's condition renders declarer able to communicate with the attending physician.

Sec. 5. RCW 70.122.050 and 1979 c 112 s 6 are amended to read as follows:

No physician or health facility which, acting in good faith in accordance with the requirements of this chapter, causes the withholding or withdrawal of life-sustaining procedures from a qualified patient, shall be subject to civil liability therefrom. No licensed health personnel, acting under the direction of a physician, who participates in good faith in the withholding or withdrawal of life-sustaining procedures in accordance with the provisions of this chapter shall be subject to any civil liability. No physician, or licensed health personnel acting under the direction of a physician, *or health facility ethics committee member* who participates in good faith in the withholding or withdrawal of life-sustaining procedures *and no physician who provides aid-in-dying to a qualified patient* in accordance with the provisions of this chapter shall be *subject to prosecution for or be* guilty of any criminal act or of unprofessional conduct.

Sec. 6. RCW 70.122.060 and 1979 c 112 s 7 are each amended to read as follows:

(1) Prior to effectuating a withholding or withdrawal of life-sustaining procedures from *or provision of aid-in-dying to* a qualified patient pursuant to the directive, the attending physician shall make a reasonable effort to determine that the directive complies with RCW 70.122.030 and, if the patient is mentally competent, that the directive and all steps proposed by the attending physician to be undertaken are currently in accord with the desires of the qualified patient.

(2) The directive shall be conclusively presumed, unless revoked, to be the directions of the patient regarding the withholding or withdrawal of life-sustaining procedures *and/or the provision of aid-in-dying*. No physician, and no licensed health personnel acting in good faith under the direction of a physician, shall be criminally or civilly liable for failing to effectuate the directive of the qualified patient pursuant to this subsection, *and no health facility may be required to permit the provision of aid-in-dying within its facility*. If the physician *or health care facility* refuses to effectuate the directive, such physician *or facility* shall make a good faith effort to transfer the qualified patient to another physician who will effectuate the directive of the qualified patient *or to another facility*.

Sec. 7. RCW 70.122.070 and 1979 c 112 s 8 are each amended to read as follows:

(1) The withholding or withdrawal of life-sustaining procedures from *or*

*the provision of aid-in-dying to* to a qualified patient pursuant to the patient's directive in accordance with the provisions of this chapter shall not, for any purpose, constitute a suicide.

(2) The making of a directive pursuant to RCW 70.122.030 shall not restrict, inhibit, or impair in any manner the sale, procurement, or insurance of any policy of life insurance, nor shall it be deemed to modify the terms of an existing policy of life insurance. No policy of life insurance shall be legally impaired or invalidated in any manner by the withholding or withdrawal of life-sustaining procedures from *or the provision of aid-in-dying to* an insured qualified patient, notwithstanding any term of the policy to the contrary.

(3) No physician, health facility, or other health provider, and no health service plan, insurer issuing disability insurance, self-insured employee welfare benefit plan, or nonprofit hospital service plan, shall require any person to execute a directive as a condition for being insured for, or receiving, health care services.

Sec. 8. RCW 70.122.080 and 1979 c 112 s 10 are each amended to read as follows:

The act of withholding or withdrawing life-sustaining procedures *or providing aid-in-dying,* when done pursuant to a directive described in RCW 70.122.030 and which causes the death of the declarer, shall not be construed to be an intervening force or to affect the chain of proximate cause between the conduct of any person that placed the declarer in a terminal condition and the death of the declarer.

Sec. 9. RCW 70.122.090 and 1979 c 112 s 9 are each amended to read as follows:

Any person who willfully conceals, cancels, defaces, obliterates, or damages the directive of another without such declarer's consent shall be guilty of a gross misdemeanor. Any person who falsifies or forges the directive or another((т)) or willfully conceals or withholds personal knowledge of a revocation as provided in RCW 70.122.040, with the intent to cause a withholding or withdrawal of life-sustaining procedures *or the provision of aid-in-dying* contrary to the wishes of the declarer((т)) and thereby, because of any such act, directly causes life- sustaining procedures to be withheld or withdrawn *or aid-in-dying to be provided* and death to thereby be hastened, shall be subject to prosecution for murder in the first degree as defined in RCW 9A.32.030.

Sec. 10. RCW 70.122.100 and 1979 c 112 s 11 are each amended to read as follows:

Nothing in this chapter shall be construed to condone, authorize, or approve mercy killing, or to permit any affirmative or deliberate act or omission to end life other than to permit the natural process of dying *and to permit death with dignity through the provision of aid-in-dying only by a physician when voluntarily requested in writing as provided in this chapter by a conscious and mentally competent qualified patient at the time aid-in-dying is to be provided.*

Sec. 11. RCW 70.122.900 and 1979 c 112 s 1 are each amended to read as follows:

This act shall be known and may be cited as the "Death *With Dignity* Act((–))."

*NEW SECTION.* Sec. 12. If any provision of this act or its application to any person or circumstance is held invalid, the remainder of the act or the application of the provision to other persons or circumstances is not affected.

# Initiative 119 and the Greater Seattle Council of Churches

When Initiative 119, the Initiative for Death with Dignity (see Appendix I) acquired enough signatures to place it on ballot in the state of Washington, the Greater Seattle Council of Churches created a task force, "to explore the various perspectives" of local religious groups. The final report was edited by Dr. Thomas R. McCormick who is an ordained minister of the Christian Church (Disciples of Christ) and Professor of Medical History and Ethics in the School of Medicine, University of Washington, in Seattle. The entire report is reproduced below.

Dr. McCormick was also the editor of an earlier document published by the Washington Association of Churches. This publication, entitled: "Decisions: Ethical and Religious Issues Involved in Decisions Related to Medical Treatment of Dying Patients," focused on the Washington Natural Death Act of 1979 and covered such subjects as "The Value of Life," "The Context of Dying in Modern America," "Fears," "Autonomy," and the roles of the physician, nurse and clergy. Some of the same issues are touched on in this new statement, but are confronted in a different context.

## PERSPECTIVES REGARDING DEATH WITH DIGNITY
A Task Force of the Greater Seattle Council of Churches
Dr. Thomas R. McCormick, Editor

A task force of the Church Council of Greater Seattle was formed to explore the various perspectives of religious groups in this region pertaining to the proposed Initiative for Death with Dignity (Initiative 119) which, if adopted, would amend the Washington Natural Death Act of 1979. The task force was appointed by Dr. William Cate and was composed of persons from differing denominations who were known by him to be interested and generally informed regarding these issues. Although the members of the task force were from a variety of religious traditions, none claimed to speak authoritatively for their denomination. All, however, were familiar with the theology and teachings of their tradition, and brought the richness of personal experience in working with dying patients and their families to these discussions.

This task force met monthly to discuss issues related to death and dying. Discussion focused on ethical issues and attitudes and values surrounding appropriate care of dying patients. After a time the task force determined that its task would be the development of a paper indicating the many elements around which there was consensus or agreement involving decisions related to the care and treatment of dying patients. The paper would also identify those issues where agreement could not be reached in order to foster discussion regarding the points of view leading to such persistent disagreement. The task force began its work in October, 1989 and over the months developed eight major draft revisions leading to the formulation of this document which was ratified by consensus on August 21, 1990 and respectfully submitted to the Greater Seattle Council of Churches.

## SECTION 1
## AREAS OF GENERAL AGREEMENT

1. The Value of Human Life
   The task force discovered there was general agreement on the high regard for and value of human life. Within the faith traditions, life is regarded as a gift from God and the stewardship of human life is generally considered a natural duty or expression of loving response to God's initial creation. Such stewardship encompasses care for one's self,

one's own health, and the provision of health care to others in need. The normal goals of health care are provision of health care to others in need. The normal goals of health care are to maintain good health, to restore health to those who are ill, to provide comfort for those who are in pain, to relieve suffering and, when possible and appropriate, to prolong the life of the individual. It was further recognized that efforts to prolong life may not be appropriate in certain situations.

2. The Recognition of Death as a Natural Phenomenon

There was general agreement among the task force members that death is a natural part of human life. Thus there is an imperative to assist members of the human community to recognize the naturalness of death, and to prepare them for the acceptance of both their own deaths and those of members of their own community of family and friends. A process of discernment is needed to enable individuals to determine when the application of medical technology is futile and when aggressive treatment should be discontinued. It was recognized that palliative care and comfort measures are always needed and appropriate.

3. Principles for the Appropriate Use of Medical Technology

It is appropriate to use technological and medical procedures to support and prolong life when the procedures offer likelihood of extending the normal goals of human life, and are desired by the patient. However, there are occasions when aggressive treatment conflicts with our moral sense and is inappropriate:

a) For example, it is ethically inappropriate to offer futile medical treatment, that is, treatment which does not reasonably hold a benefit for the patient.

b) It is usually inappropriate to provide aggressive treatment when the patient is in an irreversible coma or in a persistent vegetative state.

c) It is inappropriate to provide aggressive treatment when the benefit to the patient would be very minimal, but the pain and suffering incurred would be very great.

4. Removing Life-sustaining Procedures in Terminal Care

When a person is terminally ill and death is imminent, the patient has a right to forego life-sustaining procedures. Any competent adult may sign an advance directive indicating that it is in keeping with his or her will not to have such procedures initiated or continued when certain conditions are met. The patient should be able to define which life-sustaining procedures shall be withheld or withdrawn such as: cardiac resuscitation, respiratory support, and artificially administered nutrition and hydration.

5. The Treatment of Pain and Suffering

Individuals are usually willing to undergo a certain amount of pain and suffering resulting from treatment which they believe will be effective in restoring them to a reasonable level of health. However, it widely recognized that the goals of both health care providers and patients change when recovery becomes impossible. At that moment, treatment passes from "cure" to "care," and it becomes ethically desirable to provide the patient with as much pain relief as possible, even at levels which would not normally be provided to non-terminal patients. It is understood that the provision of medication such as opioids to alleviate pain may at times shorten life to some extent, through depression of the respiratory system. This is an ethically acceptable outcome of treatment intended to alleviate pain for gravely ill patients.

6. Summary Statement

The task force members found themselves in general agreement on the above concepts and distinctions. The next section will provide a brief discussion of the areas of disagreement and point toward some of the major reasons for such disagreement.

## SECTION 2
## AREAS OF DISAGREEMENT

After considerable discussion it became increasingly apparent that while there was agreement about many concepts of moral duty to the terminally ill, there were issues in which disagreement existed and could not be resolved by continuing discussion. These discussions did, however, sharpen our understanding of the kinds of values and justifying arguments which the various dissenting parties used in stating their positions. The basic disagreement focused around three questions which are listed below with subsequent commentary.

1. Is it ever ethically acceptable for an individual in a terminal condition to voluntarily end his or her own life? This involves consideration of the principle of autonomy and the issue of self-determined death or suicide in the context of an already existent process of dying.

2. Should it be permissible for such a terminally ill patient to seek and receive the assistance of his or her physician in facilitating or hastening the end of life? This involves both the principle of nonmaleficence (do not harm) and the principle of beneficence (to benefit) in considering the physician's duty to the individual and to society.

3. Should Initiative 119 be passed into law?

## ARGUMENTS FAVORING INITIATIVE 119

1. Is it ever ethically acceptable for an individual in a terminal condition to voluntarily end his or her own life?

Discussants differed on the nature and meaning of the voluntary ending of life by a dying individual. The proponents of Initiative 119 support the view that there is an ethical difference between suicide and intentional self-determined death by a person who is already dying, often in acute distress. The former is often the emotional action of a depressed person who spends life without full regard for the possibility of improvement in what may be a temporary, if anguishing, situation. The latter may be the rational decision of a person already in the irreversible process of dying who seeks a hastened death over continued suffering when there can be no recovery of health. The principle of autonomy, understood as the responsible use of human freedom, supports the right of persons to shape their destiny in so far as their actions do not injure others. The concept of human beings as co-creators undergirds this principle. The rights flowing from this principle are still held by patients who are terminally ill, and are interpreted by the proponents of Initiative 119 as broad enough to cover the act of self-determined death in a terminal situation.

We have no specific scriptural guidance regarding the decision to die by terminal persons. Biblical accounts of the deaths of King Saul and Judas, for example, relate to situations very different from modern health care for hopelessly ill patients. While there is scriptural encouragement to "choose life" in general, preservation of human life in all instances is not a part of the Christian understanding of our moral responsibility.

The issue of self-determined death can also be informed by the affirmation of life everlasting. Some persons in terminal conditions long for death as a means of being embraced by the divine and reconnected with loved ones who have died previously. It may be argued that to deny a voluntarily hastened death to dying persons is to deny those patients the right to profoundly exercise their faith when that may be the most meaningful act of creation available to them.

2. Should it be permissible for a terminally ill patient to seek and receive the assistance of his or her physician in facilitating or hastening the end of life? If it is accepted that persons in the process of dying may intentionally choose to die, either through aid-in-dying or withdrawal of artificial life supports, (including artificial nutrition and hydration), compassion suggests that such persons should have the resources to accomplish death in a peaceful and non-violent manner. Violent death

should not be the means of release for patients dying of cancer, AIDS, or other diseases. Because many patients in this situations are physically unable to obtain the means for a composed and pain-free death, assistance is necessary. Proponents of the Initiative believe that this must necessarily involved physicians, the professionals entrusted by our society with responsibility for diagnosis and treatment of medical conditions. It is not uncommon for dying patients to request an overdose of lethal drugs. Current statutes and regulations prohibit physicians from prescribing drugs for the purpose of self-determined death. Offering such a prescription would constitute "assisted suicide," a class D felony in our state. Physicians who do comply with these requests risk loss of license and possible prosecution. The principle of benevolence instructs physicians to act for the well-being of the patient over the interests of any other party, or at least to "do no harm." Since there are some situations in which suffering can be alleviated only by death, supporters of Initiative 119 contend that physicians should not be prohibited from facilitating death when this is the voluntary and repeated request of the patient, so long as the patient is able to make an informed and rational decision. This means that the patient must meet the criteria of being already in the process of dying, being conscious and mentally competent, and acting solely in a volitional manner. Supporters of the Initiative believe that only physicians should be permitted to provide aid-in-dying.

Supporters argue that decriminalizing aid-in-dying shows respect for human dignity by obviating the need for severe physical or emotional deterioration in the dying process. It allows the dying individual to obtain a gentle and humane death to a greater extent than would be the case if the patient's death is left to result from the withdrawal of life-sustaining treatment or progressive deterioration of organ systems.

Some discussants express concern that aid-in-dying will contribute to diminished respect for the medical profession and fears that patients will lose confidence in their doctors. It is the actual experience of others that just the opposite is the case and they argue that families who know that a physician has helped a struggling terminally ill loved one to have a gentle and humane death are exceptionally grateful for what is seen as a merciful and courageous act. There is no evidence that physicians in Holland, where aid-in-dying is permitted in regulated cases, are any less respected by patients or society than their counterparts in other countries.

Supporters of the Initiative also believe that the hospice concept is a desirable and primary resource for some terminal individuals, providing every effort to help dying patients live as fully as possible until death with companionship, home health care when possible, spiritual ministry, and the alleviation of pain. However, even when this concept has been applied with all of its support systems, there are instances of unbearable pain and suffering. Proponents believe that an individual so suffering should be able to request a hastened death through the medical channels outlined in Initiative 119, and that this is ethically different from the act of "killing" as used by opponents of the Initiative.

3. Should Initiative 119 be passed into law?

Some discussants felt even if self-determined death were potentially acceptable, and even if it required the assistance of a physician, Initiative 119 should not be enacted into law because of the possibility of abuse. Supporters of the Initiative point out specific safeguards built into the Initiative which they believe will provide dying persons more protection than they have now, when aid-in-dying must be accomplished in a clandestine manner. Under the Initiative, a patient requesting aid-in-dying must be in a terminal condition confirmed by two physicians, and must be expected to die within a six month period. The dying patient must voluntarily request in writing before independent witnesses that the physician provide aid-in-dying. This service may not be initiated by a surrogate or family member for a patient who lacks decision-making capacity. Only a physician may provide such aid, and any physician may decline to participate. No health care facility is required to permit aid-in-dying, although the patient may request a transfer to another physician or facility in order to accomplish the desired outcome. Initiative 119 defines aid-in-dying as follows: "Aid-in-dying means aid in the form of a medical procedure provided in person by a physician that will end the life of a qualified patient in a dignified, painless and humane manner, as requested voluntarily by the patient through a written directive in accordance with this chapter."

The main purpose of the Initiative as articulated by its supporters is to expand citizen rights in situations where life is coming to an inevitable end. Exercising these rights should be entirely voluntary for patients and optional for physicians.

Whether society should agree to expand these rights will be determined by assessing the benefits derived for individuals versus any negative consequences for society. Proponents of the Initiative claim that while a dying patient may claim the right to aid-in-dying on the basis of autonomy, society should be willing to honor that claim on the basis of compassion for patients dying in acute distress. So long as the medical service is voluntarily requested and provided, and does not cause harm to others, refusing the dying patient's right to choose the manner of death is equivalent to holding the patient's physical and spiritual reality hostage to the interests of the state.

It is acknowledged that Initiative 119 poses new ethical questions for health care and society. We have no precedent except the experience of Holland during the past five years. (The so-called "euthanasia" campaign of Nazi Germany was neither voluntary in nature nor grounded in compassion. It was rather an effort by the state to eliminate persons deemed socially or genetically undesirable.) Initiative 119 rests on an affirmation of the inherent worth of each individual, respect for the wishes of dying persons to die in a manner which they deem dignified, and recognition of the special status in which physicians are held.

The Initiative also recognizes that just as there are terminal situations in which it is ethically appropriate to forego use of life-sustaining procedures in order that death might result, so there are terminal situations in which the usual strictures against an individual's intentionally ending life, assisted or unassisted, are no longer compelling.

For many persons of faith, the decision of whether to endorse the Initiative will be tied to theological views of Christian responsibility. The proponents have confidence in dying patients and their physicians to make morally appropriate and responsible medical decisions. They trust the processes and safeguards of the Initiative to further the quality of human existence at the end of life.

The proponents believe that should the Initiative become law, hope will be more available to those fearful of a painful death. It is further hoped that due to having more control over their dying, terminal patients will more fully value and experience their living. As Christians, we are called to bring hope, comfort and compassion to those facing death. Proponents believe that Initiative 119 will contribute to that calling.

## ARGUMENTS IN OPPOSITION TO INITIATIVE 119

1. Is it ever ethically acceptable for an individual in a terminal condition to voluntarily end his or her own life?

In the Christian tradition, life is affirmed as a gift from God and as humans we are stewards of the gifts that God has given. Opponents of Initiative 119 argue that this implies a limitation upon any concept of absolute autonomy, for the very nature of stewardship involves seeking the purposes of God. Since we live in community, stewardship also implies a responsibility to other members of the community. We are reminded of this long tradition by a concise statement from the Methodist–Roman Catholic document, *Holy Living and Holy Dying*: "The direct intentional termination of innocent human life either of oneself or another has been generally treated in Christian tradition as contradictory to such stewardship because it is a claim to absolute dominion over human life." In this spirit, human autonomy is not an absolute principle. While recognizing that death is the natural end of life, the role of the community is to affirm the value of life, to promote healing, to alleviate suffering, and to be present with the dying. Opponents of Initiative 119 are concerned that many features of modern life tend to devalue the elderly, the sick and the dying. The needs of these persons often require the attention and assistance of family members, the care of health professionals, and the investment of society through the allocation of resources which will maximize the quality of their lives until death occurs. Those arguing against Initiative 119 are concerned that the adoption of a public policy which permits the deliberate and intentional termination of the life of dying patients will tend to encourage society to further retreat and withdraw from providing those resources which are intended to support the worth and value of human life until death occurs. Further, for many of us, our predominant experience at the beside confirms the belief that when adequate supportive attention is given to the relief of pain, as well as the physical, emotional and spiritual needs of dying patients, they are able to die naturally, with dignity, and do not seek to be killed by another.

We note that the proponents of Initiative 119 have attempted to change the meaning of the word "suicide." They declare that suicide is the taking of one's life in a moment of severe emotional turmoil. However, they argue, if a patient is believed to be within six months of dying and deliberately decides to end life, then that person is not committing suicide.

We argue, on the other hand, that the word suicide simply means the taking of one's own life, whether one does so out of emotional distress or in a premeditated way. Both kinds of suicide have been recognized and decried by the tradition of many Churches, but the responses of the Churches to the two kinds differed. When emotional turmoil was the source of the suicide, the Churches have seen this as mitigating the responsibility of the person. However, a rationally premeditated decision to terminate one's life has been viewed as a grievous misuse of human autonomy.

In this light, the Initiative 119 challenges much of the Christian tradition on this issue. Premeditated suicide, far from being decried, is here dignified and given legal permissibility provided that a single condition is fulfilled, namely, that two doctors judge that the person will probably die within six months.

2. Should it be permissible for a terminally ill patient to seek and receive the assistance of his or her physician in facilitating or hastening the end of life? Members of the task force arguing against Initiative 119 claim it is ethically wrong for a physician to take an active step in directly causing the death of the patient. In recent years there has been a shift in terminology which seems to reflect a change in expectations concerning the role of the physician. Increasingly the physician is called a "provider," the patient is called a 'consumer," and health care is considered a "commodity." The paradigm shift which is reflected by this changing terminology undermines the true meaning of the "profession" of medicine. In original usage of this term, the physician "professed" upon entering the practice of medicine, before God and the community, that a commitment was being made to serve the needs of the sick, the injured and the dying. The language of "health care consumerism" seems to imply that the patient-consumer can request and purchase any medical service whatsoever which he or she desires and can afford, whether or not that request is medically appropriate or in his or her best interest.

The discussants opposing Initiative 119 believe that the action of physician assisted suicide is wrong, even though it may be done at the request of a terminally ill patient, and carried out in a painless manner with respect for the patient's wishes. The current goals of medicine are to heal when possible and to provide comfort and relief from pain in caring for the patient.

Changing this long tradition to involve the physician in direct actions designed to end the life of the patient would be a radical shift in the underlying philosophy of Western medicine. Such a course is contrary to the principles of practice upon which modern medical education and clinical training is founded.

Those not in support of the Initiative contend there is a moral distinction between the patient dying from an underlying disease and the patient dying from an action of the attending physician. They argue that this is one of the chief drawbacks to the Initiative. It will accustom the medical profession to the permissibility of killing patients, albeit it limited circumstances. We cannot know the psychological effects of such authority on either individual physicians or the profession as a whole. However, it is clear that law has a formative influence upon the morals of the community. The proposed change in social policy toward a more permissive view regarding either killing a terminally ill patient, or assisting such a patient in suicide is contrary to the ethics of the medical profession. There is a powerful moral responsibility for physicians to relieve the pain and suffering of patients to the greatest extent possible. There is also a duty to respect the patient's wishes in refusing any form of life prolonging treatment; however, opponents feel that a physician ought not to take an active step in killing the patient. Rather, the duty of the medical profession is to provide comfort, palliation, and to care for the patient until death occurs.

3. Should Initiative 119 be passed into law?

Discussants opposed to the Initiative believe that both the title and the summary of the initiative as prepared by the office of the Attorney-General are misleading. The *title: "Shall patients who are in a medically terminal condition be permitted to request and receive from a physician aid-in-dying?" The summary: "This initiative expands the right of adult persons with terminal conditions to have their wishes, expressed in a written directive, regarding life respected."*

The language of the title and summary do not convey to those who have not read the proposed law just what it contains. No reasonable person would oppose giving a terminally ill patient *aid-in-dying.* Who would not support having *their wishes, expressed in a written directive, regarding life respected?* It is claimed that a more accurate *title* would be: "Shall terminally ill adults be permitted to request and receive from a physician assistance in taking their own lives?" A more accurate *summary* would be: "This initiative grants terminally ill adults the right, expressed in writing, to have a physician assist them in taking their lives or to kill them if they are unable to act on their own behalf."

Moreover, opponents of Initiative 119 maintain that the language and content of the initiative are problematic. Present law in Washington State, the Natural Death Act, was designed to preserve the right of patients to die with dignity. It allows individuals to instruct their physicians to withhold or withdraw life sustaining procedures so that the process of dying may not be artificially extended by technology. The current law specifically prohibits any kind of active euthanasia. Initiative 119 amends the law to allow individuals to request physicians to kill them, thus attaching active euthanasia to a law designed to permit only the *natural* process of dying. Opponents believe that confusion is also created because in Section 2(7) the definition of terminal condition is amended to include irreversible coma and persistent vegetative state (PVS). In section 2(9) the Initiative adds the concept of aid-in-dying. The Initiative both declares that individuals must be conscious and mentally competent to request aid-in-dying, and states that a person's advance directives should be carried out while in irreversible coma or PVS. Though the framers of the Initiative state that they believe it is clear that persons in irreversible coma or PVS are not candidates for aid-in-dying, opponents believe that the wording is confusing, and increases at least two risks: that people will be afraid to sign a living will, and that aid-in-dying might be administered to unconsenting patients.

The issue of "assisted suicide" was a substantive issue on which the task force could not reach an agreement. Those who oppose the Initiative, while respecting patient autonomy, feel that other considerations provide limits to autonomy. First, they deny the presupposition of this law, namely, that the individual has a right to decide when to die. In Christian thought one's stewardship over life has a communal aspect. Also, those opposing the law fear that the legal endorsement of the concept of a terminally ill patient taking his or her life may put subtle and undue pressure on vulnerable patients, their families, physicians, and society as a whole, and that what "can" be done may eventually be perceived as what "ought" to be done. The effect of this so-called technological imperative in medical care has been documented in other circumstances. These discussions believe this possibility is too dangerous to risk in these circumstances. Finally, providing legal access to assisted death for terminally ill patients may further isolate those who face the end of life.

From a community context, a more desirable goal is the extension and expansion of hospice care which is emerging with growing strength in our society. Hospice makes every effort to help dying patients to live as fully as possible until they die, providing companionship, home health care, spiritual ministry, and the alleviation of pain so that individuals can remain as connected as possible within the community until death occurs.

# Appendix III

---

# The European
# Parliament and
# Euthanasia

---

Efforts to legalize medically assisted euthanasia have brought the issue before the public in new and unprecedented ways. In November 1988, Americans Against Human Suffering sought to place a Death With Dignity initiative on the ballot in California for the general election. Prior to that time, outside of the Netherlands (see Appendix IV), no physician aid-in-dying concept had ever been placed before the public for consideration. Despite efforts of a large group of volunteers, the initiative failed to qualify because too few signatures were obtained. In November, 1992, the unsuccessful Initiative 119 was placed on the ballot in the state of Washington.

Despite the fact that the California Initiative included more safeguards than Washington's Initiative 119, it was confronted with almost identical opposition from its opponents who utilized public forums and the media to present their views. As we have noted, the California Initiative was also defeated by an 8% majority. Response to anticipated objections were discussed in the book *Death With Dignity: A New Law Permitting Physician Aid-in-Dying* (National Hemlock Society, 1989), by Robert L. Risley, who helped draft the proposed law. On Nov. 8, 1994, the people of Oregon passed the first Death With Dignity Bill in the United States. Unfortunately, at the time of this writing, the enactment of the provisions in the bill have been held up for months in court. [Other states where the legalization of euthanasia is under consideration include Iowa, Maine, Michigan, New Hampshire and Florida.]

Meanwhile, in the Northern Territory of Australia, a "Rights of the Terminally Ill" bill was passed in May, 1995 over the vigorous protests of Right-to-Life groups and opposition by Islamic and Roman Catholic clergy. The legislation requires that

- The patient must be over 18 years of age and of "sound mind."
- The patient must be in pain and suffering
- Two doctors, each with five years medical experience must diagnose the patient as terminally ill
- The second doctor, who holds a psychiatric diploma, must state that the patient does not have a treatable clinical depression
- There must be an initial "cooling off" period of seven days before a certificate of authorization is signed

A further 48-hour "cooling off" period must elapse before the patient is killed.

Meanwhile, in Europe some dramatic steps have been taken towards the legalization of euthanasia. In September 1989, the President of the European Parliament announced that he had forwarded a motion for a resolution on counseling for the terminally ill to the Committee on the Environment, Public Health and Consumer Protection. Reviews were held on November 27, 1990, March 20, 1991, and April 25, 1991 when the resolution was adopted by 16 supportive votes over 11 objections with three abstentions. Four days later, on April 29, 1991, the report was tabled for presentation before the full European Parliament. The resolution, "Care for the Terminally Ill," the report by the European Parliament's Committee on the Environment, Public Health and Consumer Protection, reads as follows:

## A. MOTION FOR RESOLUTION

### On care of the terminally ill

The European Parliament,

—having regard to the motion for a resolution by Mrs. Van Hemeldoneck on counseling for the terminally ill (Doc. B3-0006/89).

—having regard to its resolution of 19 January 1984[1] on a European Charter on the Rights of Patients.
—having regard to its resolution of 13 May 1986[2].
—having regard to the report of the Committee on the Environment, Public Health and Consumer Protection (A3-0109/91).

A. whereas human life is founded on dignity and spirituality, and cannot therefore be reduced to merely natural functions, i.e., the functions of vegetative existence,

B. whereas the death of an individual is determined by the cessation of cerebral function, even where biological functions continue,

C. whereas cerebral function determines the level of consciousness which in turn defines a human being.

D. whereas attempts to cure at all costs, even though an illness is incurable at the present state of medical knowledge, must be avoided, as must inexorable treatment, which offends against the dignity of the individual.

E. whereas it is proposed that the European Charter on the Rights of Patients should enshrine 'the right to a dignified death,' (paragraph 3[o]).

F. whereas it is proposed that the European Charter for Children in Hospital should include "the right to be protected from unnecesssary medical treatment and physical or emotional distress" (paragraph 4[1]).

G. whereas physical pain is useless and destructive, and may offend against human dignity.

H. whereas every means available should be used to combat pain, in particular the use of appropriate drugs such as morphine and its derivatives, administered according to the rules in force.

I. whereas a lonely death in hospital has now sadly become a frequent occurrence.

J. whereas it is essential for all forms of palliative care to be provided to patients once a cure has become impossible and specific medical treatment is no longer effective.

K. whereas the provision of palliative care is not the responsibility of the medical institution alone but also of family, friends and acquaintances and society in general.

L. whereas the desire for eternal sleep is not a negation of life but a request for an end to an existence while illness has robbed of all dignity.

---

[1] ().1 No. C 46, 20.2 1984, p. 104
[2] ().1 No. C 148, 16.6 1986, p. 37

1. Considers that, in the interests of sound medical practice, it is necessary for medical staff, doctors, nurses and nursing auxiliaries to be trained so as to enable them to:
   a) treat and cure patients suffering from curable acute conditions;
   b) treat and give the best possible support to patients suffering from chronic conditions;
   c) provide appropriate care for incurable patients whose illness has become refractory to any specific treatment;
   d) have an understanding and caring attitude towards patients nearing death;

2. To this end, calls on the Commission to encourage exchanges both of experiences and of staff under existing programmes with a view of widening knowledge of palliative care and improving techniques;

3. Calls for the rapid establishment in every hospital service in the European Community of palliative care units, and the subsequent establishment of rooms for palliative or continuing care in all departments dealing with the seriously ill;

4. Calls upon the Commission to carry out a study of hospitals in the European Community with particular reference to this type of care;

5. Calls for account to be taken, in the allocation of hospital building aid from the European Regional Development Fund, of the creation of palliative care rooms and subsequently units and of the existence of structures to enable seriously ill patients to be with their family and/or those they love until the end of their lives;

6. Calls for all possible steps to be taken to promote treatment at home wherever medically possible;

7. Calls for encouragement and aid to be given to voluntary associations like those in Italy, the United Kingdom and Belgium which effectively support the medical profession by helping to care for patients in the terminal stages of their lives;

8. Considers that, in the absence of any curative treatment and following the failure of palliative care correctly provided at both psychological and medical level, each time a fully conscious patient insistently and repeatedly requests an end to an existence which has for him been robbed of all dignity and each time a team of doctors created for that purpose establishes the impossibility of providing further specific care, the request should be satisfied without thereby involving any breach of respect for human life;

9. Calls on the European Community to initiate a wide-ranging round-table discussion among those with ethical, political and medical authority on the respect due to the patient at the end of his life;

10. Instructs its President to forward this resolution to the Commission and Council.

## B. EXPLANATORY STATEMENT

In spite of the remarkable progress in medicine over the last forty years, some diseases still remain incurable.

Care of the terminally ill, an area long neglected, should be considered as one of the objectives of modern high-technology medicine, which must not forget that it is exclusively concerned with people, whose lives are defined by dignity.

Any debate on care of the terminally ill should be based on the following premises:

— The life of a human being cannot be reduced to its merely natural functions: the beating of the heart, the circulation of blood, the breathing of the lungs, . . . it is the functioning of the brain which determines the level of consciousness, and it is in turn the level of consciousness which defines human existence. The cessation of cerebral function means the death of the individual, even when his biological functions continue.

— The desire to cure at all costs even when an illness is incurable at the current stage of medical knowledge must be avoided, as must inexorable treatment, a medical failing related to intellectual stubbornness which has led in some cases to unreasonable suffering being inflicted in the name of political expediency.

— Pain is useless and destructive, and can in most cases be overcome by the administration of appropriate drugs. There is no reason to be afraid of using powerful pain-killers, principally morphine and its derivatives.

Among the medical profession, care of the terminally ill hides behind the term 'palliative care'[3]: such care should be opted for when a cure has become impossible because specific treatment has become ineffective.

---

[3] The value and effectiveness of 'palliative care,' that is the treatment of symptoms to the exclusions of any specific treatment of the disease, has very recently begun to be recognized, but the term seems to imply a limitation of medical aid to the patient. It deliberately ignores the possibility of further treatment, and could well be replaced by the term 'continuing care,' though a majority of the committee did not see fit to retain this term.

Palliative care consists in reducing the symptoms of the disease without acting on its cause. It makes it possible to fight against pain, discomfort and fear.

Experimental palliative care units have been set up, first in Britain, and later in Canada, the USA and France. These units play a pilot role, instead of being rare exceptions.

Each hospital department should include a few palliative care rooms for patients of this kind, who should not be grouped together in specialized, ghetto-like wards.

If the Commission were to carry out a study on the situation of palliative (or continuing) care units in hospitals throughout the Community, this could serve as a basis for a wider Community project, which could result in the setting up of a structure for the exchange of experiences involving all hospital departments.

It is undeniable that in the interests of sound medical practice and proper palliative (or continuing) care, all medical staff must be trained to enable them to:

— treat and cure patients suffering from acute curable conditions;
— treat and give the best possible support to patients suffering from chronic conditions;
— provide appropriate care for incurable patients who are 'no longer responding' to any specific treatment;
— have an understanding and caring attitude towards patients approaching death.

This provision of palliative care for the terminally ill is not the responsibility of the medical institution alone but also of family, friends, acquaintances and society in general.

In Italy and the United Kingdom, voluntary associations (Vidas and the Hospice movement) have developed aid structures for the seriously ill; regular hospital visits, premises to receive patients who have been permitted to leave hospital, etc. Such initiatives should be encouraged and developed throughout the Community.

Now that a lonely death in hospital has sadly become all too frequent, everything ought to be done to encourage caring for the terminally ill at home. It is highly desirable that hospitals in the EEC should set up reception structures to enable the seriously ill to be with their family and those they love until they die.

It is dignity which defines a human life. When, at the end of a long illness against which he has fought courageously, the patient asks the doctor to terminate an existence which has lost all dignity for him, and the doctor decides in all conscience to assist him and ease the final hours of his life by allowing him to fall asleep peacefully and finally, this medical and humane assistance (sometimes called euthanasia) is respect for human life.

The most important aspects of the document are the recognition of brain death as constituting the death of the person, the call for palliative care units or hospice centers in every hospital, and the endorsement of physician assisted euthanasia. Strong opposition from Roman Catholic clergy was published in Catholic International (Vol. 2, No. 19, November 1–14, 1991). Charles Amarin Brand, Archbishop of Strasbourg and President of the Commission of the Episcopal Conferences of the European Community, produced a statement titled "The Inalienable Dignity of the Human Person" (p. 908). Archbishop Brand protested the definition of personhood and human dignity in terms of "level of consciousness." He pointed out that the notion of "a human life not worthy of being lived" could be extended to include the mentally ill or the handicapped and argued that the resolution calls for the rejection of the "natural law principle—You shall not kill." He expressed concern that the resolution introduced rights that could become obligations. He wrote, "The divine origin of the life of a human being, who is made in the image of God, grounds the inalienable dignity of man independently of his condition at any given moment. No medical, social, legal or political authority may threaten human life and its inalienable dignity."

On September 23, 1991, the Permanent Council of the French Episcopal Conference produced a statement "Respecting the Person Close to Death," which was published in translation in the *Catholic International* (Vol. 2, No. 19, pp. 909–916). The statement supported the abandonment of treatments "which will bring little benefit in proportion to the discomfort, constraints, harmful effects and deprivations which they will inevitably bring." (p. 910). The use of analgesics, including narcotics in exceptional cases, was accepted, provided there was medical necessity for their use. What was preferred was the kind of palliative care offered by hospice programs. The presence of supportive persons was encouraged to enable the dying to talk and be heard, to "break out of their loneliness and find relief from their anxieties . . . With such support, the seriously ill experience reconciliation, both human and religious, which lets them accept themselves, with their real existence such as it has been until then, and opens new horizons for them in the days they still have left to live" (p. 911). Although induced sleep from which the person might not awaken was accepted for extreme instances, no acceptance of medically induced euthanasia was to be tolerated. Such action would violate the "You shall not kill" biblical commandment and would destroy "the indispensable trust needed for human relationships, those of the sick with their families, those of the sick and their families with the team offering care." (p. 914f). Euthanasia provided at the request of the dying person or out of pity would reflect the dulling of conscience. "We are firmly convinced that the law should not accept, much less justify euthanasia." (p. 916).

Catholic International also published a letter by Dame Cicely Saunders, sent on June 3, 1991 and addressed to all United Kingdom Members of the European Parliament (p. 914). (For further comment see "Euthanasia and Hospice" 70). This was the letter:

Dear Sir,

My attention has been drawn to a recent proposal to the European Parliament which may well lead to a serious and retrograde confusion between the accepted medical practice of palliative care and the campaign for legalized euthanasia. I write personally because the proposed National Hospice Council has not yet been formally constituted, and so cannot express an opinion on the matter which closely concerns the hospice movement as a whole.

The proposal, reported to the Environment Commission of the European Parliament by M. Leon Schwartzenberg, is contained in a document (PE 146:486) which one is bound to welcome for its encouragement of palliative care that is, pain control, spiritual comfort and measures to support the quality of life for the dying person and the family. But the document also says, and repeats, that a suffering patient has the right to choose a medically assisted death, and claims that this is merely an extension of the more general right to measures which can ease the final weeks or days of life. In a phrase that I can only describe as verbal juggling, the document claims that "if a doctor allows a patient to sleep peacefully and finally, this medical and human aid (sometimes called euthanasia) is respect for life." Such a paradox uses the rhetoric of respect for life to justify terminating it; and it glosses over all the problems of moral, civil and even criminal law which must be faced in any serious discussion of euthanasia and, indeed, of social pressures.

It is, moreover, most damaging to the public image of palliative care. Advocates of euthanasia especially in Germany and Holland have seriously hindered the establishment of hospices by creating the impression that they are "houses of death," and similar problems would arise everywhere if this proposal were to be endorsed, unamended by the European Parliament. There is no way in which care by a hospice team could change into direct and intended killing without causing unacceptable anxiety among patients, families and staff. I am sure if you visited on of your local hospices, you would see what a major difference of direction this would be.

I am now writing to all British MEPs asking them to scrutinize this document carefully, if it is brought forward, and to seek the elimination of the controversial clauses from a resolution which is otherwise most positive. I hope others, who may be equally concerned at this attempt to present euthanasia as an extension of the widely accepted hospice movement, will do the same.

Yours Sincerely,

Dame Cicely Saunders, OM., DBE., FRCP.
Chairman, Saint Christopher's Hospice

# Appendix IV

---

# Physician-Assisted
# Euthanasia in Holland

---

The legal setting for euthanasia in the Netherlands is unique. Up until February, 1993, Netherlands' law prohibited euthanasia. Presently voluntary euthanasia is still illegal, but medical doctors who follow guidelines (report the euthanasia to the municipal pathologist and the public prosecutor and provide medical records, living will statements, etc.) will not be prosecuted. The old prohibitory law was based on Article 293 of the Netherlands Penal Code which was enacted in 1986. The prohibition reads as follows: "He who robs another of life at his express and serious wish is published with a prison sentence of at most twelve years or of a fine of the fifth category." The code continues in Article 294, "He who deliberately incites another to suicide, assists him therein or provides him with the means is punished, if the suicide follows, with a prison sentence of at most three years or a fine of the fourth category." The term "category" refers to the fine in guilders; for example, "the fifth category" includes fines to a maximum of 100,000 guilders which amounts to about $50,000. "The fourth category" maximum is 25,000 guilders, which is the equivalent of $12,500. Despite the presence of these century-old laws, physician-assisted suicide has occurred regularly and physicians were "rarely prosecuted and even more rarely punished." Today physicians who follow the guidelines which are listed in full below will not be prosecuted.

413

## BY ORDER OF PARLIAMENT

Guidelines for the attending physician in reporting euthanasia to the municipal pathologist in the Netherlands: The following list of points is intended as a guideline in reporting euthanasia or assistance provided to a patient in taking his or her own life to the municipal pathologist. A full written report supplying motives for your action is required.

### I. Case history

A. What was the nature of the illness and what was the main diagnosis?

B. How long had the patient been suffering from the illness?

C. What was the nature of the medical treatment provided (medication, curative, surgical, etc.)?

D. Please provide the names, addresses and telephone numbers of the attending physicians. What were their diagnoses?

E. Was the patient's mental and/or physical suffering so great that he or she perceived it, or could have perceived it, to be unbearable?

F. Was the patient in a desperate situation with no prospect of relief and was his/her death inevitable?

1. Was the situation at the end such that the prognosis was increasing lack of dignity for the patient and/or such as to exacerbate suffering which the patient already experienced as unbearable?

2. Was there no longer any prospect of the patient being able to die with dignity?

3. When in your opinion would the patient have died if euthanasia had not been performed.

G. What measures, if any, did you consider or use to prevent the patient experiencing his/her suffering as unbearable (was there indeed any possibility of alleviating the suffering) and did you discuss these with the patient?

### II. Request for Euthanasia

A. Did the patient of his/her own free will make a very explicit and deliberate request for euthanasia to be performed:

1. On the basis of adequate information which you had provided on the course of the illness and the method of terminating life, and

2. after discussion of the measures referred to at 1G?

B. If the patient made such a request, when and to whom was it made? Who else was present at the time?

C. Is there a living will? If so, please pass this on to the municipal pathologist.

D. At the time of the request was the patient fully aware of the consequences thereof and of his/her physical and mental condition? What evidence of this can you provide?

E. Did the patient consider options other than euthanasia? If so, which options, and if not, why not?

F. Could anyone else have influenced either the patient or yourself in the decision? If so, how did this manifest itself?

### III. Second Opinion

A. Did you consult another doctor? If so, please supply all the names, addresses and telephone numbers. If you consulted more than one colleague, please supply all the names, addresses and telephone numbers.

B. What conclusions did the other doctors(s) reach, at least with respect to questions 1F and 1G?

C. Did this doctor/these doctors see the patient? If so, on what date? If not, on what were his/her/their conclusions based?

### IV. Euthanasia

A. Who performed the euthanasia and how?

B. Did the person concerned obtain information on the method used in advance? If so, where and from whom?

C. Was it reasonable to expect that the administration of the euthanasia-producing agent in question would result in death?

D. Who was present when euthanasia was performed? Please supply names, addresses and telephone numbers.

(From the *World Right-To-Die Newsletter*, Issue No. 22, Spring/ Summer 1993, p. 1.)

The reported number of deaths by doctor assisted euthanasia in Holland differs according to individual estimates. Within the population of about 1.5 million, about 127,000 deaths from all causes are reported each year. Of these only 1.5% or about 2,000 deaths involve physician assistance. Previous estimates ran as high as 5,000 but the new figures are based on a survey conducted by the medical examiner for North Holland who is a professor of general medicine and editor of Medisch Contact, the journal of the Royal Dutch Medical Association in which the report was published (Hemlock Quarterly, July 1991, p.1).[1]

The criteria that have guided Netherlands physicians in physician-assisted-euthanasia for more than a decade are as follows (Admiraal, 1986):

- The patient must be competent (which excludes patients in the advanced stages of Alzheimer's disease or those in a persistent vegetative state).
- The act is voluntary.
- The request for aid in dying is enduring, consistent, well-documented and made repeatedly (as opposed to being a sudden impulse).
- The patient experiences intolerable mental and/or physical suffering, which is to say the patient need not be terminal. Depression alone would not be an acceptable reason for euthanasia.
- The physician has tried all alternatives acceptable to the patient to relieve the suffering.
- Both patient and doctor acknowledge the cognitive deterioration that can come with end-stages of the illness.
- Euthanasia must be performed by the attending doctor in consultation with another physician not involved in the case.

The procedure involves the ingestion of a barbiturate (to induce sleep) mixed with powdered orphenadrine combined with yogurt and sugar to mask the bitter taste. The patient dies within 20 minutes (Admiraal, "Drug Combinations," 1988). On other occasions the barbiturate is followed by a lethal injection of curare (Angell). Although euthanasia often takes place within nursing homes or hospitals, it is commonly performed in homes where the patient can be with members of the family.

Because Holland is a small country, the potential for long-term relationships between family and physicians is enhanced. The provision for euthanasia in a home setting is, in a sense, the return to pre-institutionalizing patterns of patient care. Death at home provides a warmer and more comfortable setting for patient and family than death in an institution. The doctor does not act until the patient is ready and

---

[1]See References, page 42, for bibliographic information in this appendix.

until farewells have been expressed. Then, usually in the presence of the family, the doctor administers the lethal medication that produces a rapid and painless death. The patient dies with the family close at hand. The long, drawn out, pain-filled death that could result from "letting nature take its course" is avoided and an easy painless death results. In Holland, it is believed that doctor-assisted-euthanasia, which places the patient in control of living and dying to the last breath, provides for dignified dying and dignified death.

It is possible that abuses may occur. As with any law, there will always be those who are willing to test its limits and exceed its boundaries. Should they be discovered, those involved are subject to prosecution.

On September 28, 1991, Dutch psychiatrist Dr. Boudewijn Chabot provided Hilly Bosscher, a severely depressed 50-year-old social worker, with a lethal mixture that enabled the severely depressed woman to take her own life. Her depression stemmed from 25 years of beating by an alcoholic husband, the death of two sons, one from lung cancer and the other by suicide—both at the age of 20. Clearly, this was not a case of a patient with a terminal illness or suffering intractable, unbearable physical pain; Bosscher's pain was psychic. The case came to trial and in June, 1994 the court ruled that although Chabot had neglected to have another physician examine the woman, he would not be punished. Chabot contended that "Intolerable psychological suffering is not different from intolerable physical suffering . . . I do not know if I made the right choice, but I believe I opted for the lesser of two evils." His attorney, Eugene Sutorius, stated that "The ruling recognizes the right of patients experiencing severe psychic pain to choose to die with dignity." (Toufexis, p. 61)

Euthanasia in the Netherlands cannot provide a model for euthanasia in the United States. Those proposing the legalization of physician-assisted-euthanasia in the United States may learn much from the Dutch experience, but it is clear that within the complex society of the United States (and of Canada and other large countries) different codes will have to be developed. For those opposed to active voluntary euthanasia on religious grounds, the ways in which religious communities in the Netherlands deal with this complex issue may be important. I regret that it was not possible for me to acquire adequate data on this subject for this book. However, inasmuch as the religious bodies who have shared their stance in this volume are, for the most part, universal in outreach, it can be assumed that the same theological bases reported here will apply in the religious communities in Holland.

# Appendix V

## The Oregon Death With Dignity Act

**BALLOT MEASURE 16**
**Ballot Title:**
**ALLOWS TERMINALLY ILL**
**ADULTS TO OBTAIN**
**PRESCRIPTION FOR LETHAL DRUGS**

### QUESTION:

Shall law allow terminally ill adult patients voluntary informed choice to obtain physician's prescription for drugs to end life?

### SUMMARY:

Adopts law. Allows terminally ill adult Oregon residents voluntary informed choice to obtain physician's prescription for drugs to end life. Removes criminal penalties for qualifying physician-assisted suicide. Applies when physicians predict patient's death within 6 months. Requires:

- 15-day waiting period;
- 2 oral, 1 written request;
- second physician's opinion;
- counseling if either physician believes patient has mental disorder, impaired judgment from depression.

Person has choice whether to notify next of kin. Health care providers immune from civil, criminal liability for good faith compliance.

**Estimate of Financial Impact:** No financial effect on state or local government expenditures or revenues.

**Explanation:** The following is the official explanatory statement for Measure 16—

This measure would allow an informed and capable adult resident of Oregon, who is terminally ill and within six months of death, to voluntarily request a prescription for medication to take his or her life. The measure allows a physician to prescribe a lethal dose of medication when conditions of the measure are met. The physician and others may be present if the medication is taken.

The process begins when the patient makes the request of his or her physician, who shall:

- Determine if the patient is terminally ill, is capable of making health care decisions, and has made the request voluntarily.
- Inform the patient of his or her diagnosis and prognosis; the risks and results of taking the medication; and alternatives, including comfort care, hospice care, and pain control.
- Ask that the patient notify next of kin, but not deny the request if the patient declines or is unable to notify the next of kin.
- Inform the patient that he or she has an opportunity to rescind the request at any time, in any manner.
- Refer the patient for counseling, if appropriate.
- Refer the patient to a consulting physician. A consulting physician, who is qualified by specialty or experience, must confirm the diagnosis and determine that the patient is capable and acting voluntarily.

If either physician believes that the patient might be suffering from a psychiatric or psychological disorder, or from depression causing impaired judgment, the physician must refer the patient to a licensed psychiatrist or psychologist for counseling. The psychiatrist or psychologist must determine that the patient does not suffer from such a disorder before medication may be prescribed.

The measure requires two oral and one written request. The written request requires two witnesses attesting that the patient is acting voluntarily. At least one witness must not be a relative or heir of the patient.

At least fifteen days must pass from the time of the initial oral request and 48 hours must pass from the time of the written request before the prescription may be written.

Before writing the prescription, the attending physician must again verify the patient is making a voluntary and informed request, and offer the patient the opportunity to rescind the request.

Additional provisions of the measure are:

- Participating physicians must be licensed in Oregon.
- The physician must document in the patient's medical record that all requirements have been met. The State Health Division must review sample of those records and make statistical reports available to the public.
- Those who comply with the requirements of the measure are protected from prosecution and professional discipline.
- Any physician or health care provider may decline to participate.

This measure does not authorize lethal injection, mercy killing or active euthanasia. Actions taken in accordance with this measure shall not constitute suicide, assisted suicide, mercy killing or homicide, under the law.

Anyone coercing or exerting undue influence on a patient to request medication, or altering or forging a request for medication, is guilty of a Class A felony.

## Argument in Favor of Ballot Measure 16

For 16 years I have worked with dying people and their families as parish minister, hospital and hospice chaplain, and counselor to elders.

I have seen more death than most people see in a lifetime, and I believe we need to pass Measure 16—the Oregon Death with Dignity Act.

In the Bible, five people are reported to have ended their own lives (I Sam 31, II Sam 17, I Kings 16, Matt 27), and the fact of their action is simply reported with no moral judgment implied; at no point is condemnation expressed for their having done so.

Knowing the authorities were eager to silence Him, Jesus was, in effect, choosing death by returning there that fateful Passover season. When finally He was crucified, His dying took six hours, an agonizing death but one that normally took 24 hours or more to accomplish.

I have sat at the bedside of people suffering days, weeks, even months before their inevitable deaths, wondering about the duration of Jesus' agony. Whether it was an act of will, an intervention of God or perhaps even the Roman centurion's spear, Jesus' agony was cut unusually and mercifully short, a fact for which I am deeply grateful.

There is nothing shameful about death; it is the natural order of things as created by God. Neither Jesus nor the Bible espouse physical life as always being the highest good.

It is a fine line between reverence for life and idolatry of life.

*Information about the Oregon Death with Dignity Act*

Measure 16 allows dying patients who are rational, capable of making health care decisions, and acting voluntarily, the right to request a prescription for life-ending medication.

Under Measure 16, only the dying person may self-administer the medication.

Measure 16 does not allow lethal injection, mercy killing, or "suicide machines."

Measure 16 allows family members and physicians to be present when the medication is taken.

*Requirements under Measure 16:*

The process begins when an adult Oregon patient in the last six months of life makes a voluntary, oral request to the physician.

The physician must:

- Determine the patient is mentally competent and acting voluntarily.
- Get second physician's opinion on diagnosis, life expectancy and mental competency of the patient.
- Inform patient of all options including hospice, comfort care and pain control.
- Encourage patient of all options including hospice, comfort care and pain control.
- Encourage patient to notify family.
- Refer patient for counseling if either physician believes the patient may suffer from mental illness or depression causing impaired judgment.

Safeguards:
- 15-day waiting period.
- Written requests by the patient, witnessed by two persons, at least one who is not a blood relative or heir to the person's estate.
- 48-hour waiting period from filing the written request to writing the prescription.
- Establishes reporting requirements to the Health Department.

Punishes as Class A felony attempts to force or coerce someone to request medication to end life.

Reverend Sallierae Henderson
Oregon Death with
Dignity Campaign

**Argument in Opposition to Ballot Measure 16**

"I have worked first hand in developing a wide variety of health care policies. Many proposed policies at first sound like good ideas, but in fact are very dangerous. Measure 16 is one of those policies. I urge you to vote no." (C. Everett Koop, M.D., U.S. Surgeon General, 1981–1989).

Measure 16 confuses the role of physicians in our society. Doctors have an ethical and professional responsibility to sustain life when possible. Measure 16 would create an environment where physician-assisted suicide becomes the first line of defense against terminal diseases, resulting in final and fatal decisions. The medical profession cannot be society's healer and killer at the same time.

Measure 16 prescribes suicide as a treatment for disease. A patient's request for suicide is a signal that certain needs are not being met. Most likely, the patient is suffering from unnecessary pain or treatable depression. Medical doctors are not always trained to recognize the symptoms of depression. Doctors too often fail to dispense adequate pain management. The solution is to provide mental health treatment or better pain management, not drugs for suicide.

Hospice care and advanced directives should be emphasized. Measure 16 is a careless response to fears of dying alone or in pain. This does not need to be the case. Hospice provides comfort and support through the dying process. We must not abandon the terminally ill, but rather promote hospice as a means for support at the end of life's journey. Oregon has some of the strongest advance directive laws in the country allowing individuals complete control over treatment at the end of life. We should stress patient control by emphasizing the importance of living wills and advance directives.

Doctors can be wrong. According to a study by two prominent pathologists reported in *The Oregonian* (1/31/94), autopsies were wrong in 10 to 15 percent of all hospital cases where deaths occur. Under Measure 16, a misdiagnosis could cost a patient his or her life.

Measure 16 is ripe for abuse. The so-called safeguards built into Measure 16 are inadequate. Patients remain vulnerable to outside pressures to choose suicide. Physicians are required only to suggest the patient notify family members, leaving many to choose suicide without the support of loved ones.

Measure 16 strikes at the most vulnerable. Cost containment is a positive and necessary step towards reforming our health care system. However, in this environment Measure 16 is dangerous. Poor, elderly, frail and disabled patients will be the victims if the "choice" to die becomes the "duty" to die.

Passing Measure 16 would make Oregon the first jurisdiction in the world to legalize physician-assisted suicide. Even in Holland where assisted suicide is out of control, it is still illegal. It is bad policy that could have deadly results.

Vote no on Measure 16.

Coalition for Compassionate Care

### Legislative Ministries Commission Recommendation
### Majority Report

Vote "No."

Ballot Measure 16 crosses an important moral and ethical boundary line. Measure 16 would make Oregon the first jurisdiction in the world to decriminalize physician-assisted suicide and permit physicians to write prescriptions for a lethal dose of drugs for the terminally ill. Measure 16 would radically change medical, social and legal ethics.

Medical, social and legal ethics have drawn a clear line of distinction between "allowing death to occur" and "causing death." "Allowing death to occur" accepts that death is a part of life, part of being human. "Allowing death to occur" includes support for an individual's decision to forgo extraordinary medical means when the burdens outweigh the benefits of a particular course of medical conduct. Withholding or withdrawing life support systems and "allowing death to occur" are part of current ethical medical practice and supported by law.

The 1993 Oregon Health Care Decisions Act offers an Advance Directive for adults to indicate their preferences for end-of-life medical decisions. Ballot Measure 16 adds an additional preference for terminally ill patients. It allows them to request a prescription for a lethal drug, and it permits a physician to prescribe it.

Measure 16 is unwise and dangerous public policy. Measure 16 does not require a mental evaluation of the patient before a prescription for lethal drugs is written. Measure 16 does not require family notification before the prescription for lethal drugs is given to the patient. The possibility for abuse of patients under Measure 16 is real and poses greatest risks to those who are poor, elderly, or without access to good medical care.

Measure 16 is bad law and should be rejected by the people of Oregon. Instead of offering people who are terminally ill a prescription for lethal drugs, our society is called upon to provide loving and compassionate care. Modern means of pain control are extremely effective; hospice care and community support can surround a loved one with the necessary comfort to bear the patient through the terminal illness.

The Legislative Commission, mindful of the Biblical edict to "choose life so that you and your descendants may live," recommends a "No" vote on Measure 16.

In addition to the Legislative Committee, the Health and Human Ministries Committee also opposes Ballot Measure 16. Vote "NO" on Ballot Measure 16.

## Legislative Ministries Commission
## Minority Statement

As the Legislative Ministries Commission minority, we wish to advance our belief that a non-recommendation would have been the most appropriate decision on Measure 16. We have come to appreciate that there are doctrinal and theological differences among us within the faith community. We do not wish to diminish the morality and/or Christianity of the most ardent advocate or foe of Measure 16. Rather, we wish to encourage individual reflection and family and congregational dialogue on this initiative. An appropriate beginning for this decision journey would be to study and come to understand the existing choices available under Oregon's Advance Directive. The directive is available from your physician, hospital or Oregon Health Decisions. We also encourage you to contact the respective campaigns.

## Appendix VI

---

# California Death
# With Dignity Act

---

**INITIATIVE MEASURE
TO BE SUBMITTED DIRECTLY TO THE VOTERS**

The Attorney General of California has prepared the following
official title and summary of the chief purpose and points
of the proposed measure:

**TERMINAL ILLNESS. ASSISTANCE IN DYING. INITIATIVE
STATUTE.** Permits revocable written directive authorizing physician to
terminate life in "painless, humane and dignified manner" by mentally
competent adult after terminal illness diagnosed. States procedures for
witnessing and revoking directive, and requesting medical assistance in
dying. Precludes physicians, health professionals, and facilities from civil
or criminal liability if initiative's provisions followed. Provides requesting
or receiving authorized aid not suicide. Allows physicians and health
professionals to refuse to end life if religiously, morally or ethically
opposed. Prohibits existence or non-existence of directive from affecting
sale, renewal, cancellation, terms, or premiums of insurance policies.
Estimate by Legislative Analyst and Director of Finance of fiscal impact
on state and local governments: This measure would result in some
unknown savings due to decreased utilization of the state Medi-Cal
program and other public programs, including county programs.

**To the Honorable Secretary of State of California**

We, the undersigned, registered, qualified voters of California, residents
of _____ County (or City and County), hereby propose

amendments to the Civil and Penal Codes, relating to the rights of terminal patients and petition the Secretary of State to submit the same to the voters of California for their adoption or rejection at the next succeeding general election or at any special statewide election held prior to that general election or otherwise provided by law. The proposed statutory amendments read as follows:

## THE CALIFORNIA DEATH WITH DIGNITY ACT

California Civil Code, Title 10.5

Sec. 1. Title 10.5 (commencing with Section 2525.) is added to Division 3 of part 4 of the Civil Code, to read:

### 2525. TITLE

This title shall be known and may be cited as the Death With Dignity Act.

### 2525.1. DECLARATION OF PURPOSE.

The people of California declare:

Current state laws do not adequately protect the rights of terminally ill patients. The purpose of this Act is to provide mentally competent terminally ill adults the legal right to voluntarily request and receive physician aid-in-dying. This Act protects physicians who voluntarily comply with the request and provides strong safeguards against abuse. The Act requires the signing of a witnessed revocable Directive in advance and then requires a terminally ill patient to communicate his or her request directly to the treating physician.

Self-determination is the most basic of freedoms. The right to choose to eliminate pain and suffering, and to die with dignity at the time and place of our own choosing when we are terminally ill is an integral part of our right to control our own destinies. That right is hereby established in law, but limited to ensure that the rights of others are not affected. The right should include the ability to make a conscious and informed choice to enlist the assistance of the medical profession in making death as painless, humane, and dignified as possible.

Modern medical technology has made possible the artificial prolongation of human life beyond natural limits. This prolongation of life for persons with terminal conditions may cause loss of patient dignity and unnecessary pain and suffering, for both the patient and the family, while providing nothing medically necessary or beneficial to the patient.

In recognition of the dignity which patients have a right to expect, the State of California recognizes the right of mentally competent terminally ill adults to make a voluntary revocable written Directive instructing their physician to administer aid-in-dying to end their life in a painless, humane and dignified manner.

The Act is voluntary. Accordingly, no one shall be required to take advantage of this legal right or to participate if they are religiously, morally or ethically opposed.

### 2525.2 DEFINITIONS

The following definitions shall govern the construction of this title:

(a) "Attending physician" means the physician selected by, or assigned to, the patient who has primary responsibility for the treatment and care of the patient.

(b) "Directive" means a revocable written document voluntarily executed by the declarant in accordance with the requirements of Section 2525.3 in substantially the form set forth in Section 2525.24.

(c) "Declarant" means a person who executes a Directive, in accordance with this title.

(d) "Life-sustaining procedure" means any medical procedure or intervention which utilizes mechanical or other artificial means to sustain, restore, or supplant a vital function, including nourishment and hydration which, when applied to a qualified patient, would serve only to prolong artificially the moment of death. "Life-sustaining procedure" shall not include the administration of medication or the performance of any medical procedure deemed necessary to alleviate pain or reverse any condition.

(e) "Physician" means a physician and surgeon licensed by the Medical Board of California.

(f) "Health care provider" and "Health care professional" mean a person or facility or employee of a health care facility licensed, certified, or otherwise authorized by the law of this state to administer health care in the ordinary course of business or practice of a profession.

(g) "Community care facility" means a community care facility as defined in Section 1502 of the Health and Safety Code.

(h) "Qualified patient" means a mentally competent adult patient who has voluntarily executed a currently valid revocable Directive as defined in this section, who has been diagnosed and certified in writing by two physicians to be afflicted with a terminal condition, and who has expressed an enduring request for aid-in-dying. One of said physicians shall be the attending physician as defined in subsection (a). Both physicians shall have personally examined the patient.

(i) "Enduring request" means a request for aid-in-dying, expressed on more than one occasion.

(j) "Terminal condition" means an incurable or irreversible condition which will, in the opinion of two certifying physicians exercising reasonable medical judgment, result in death within six months or less. One of said physicians shall be the attending physicians as defined in subsection (a).

(k) "Aid-in-dying" means a medical procedure that will terminate the life of the qualified patient in a painless, humane and dignified manner whether administered by the physician at the patient's choice or direction or whether the physician provides means to the patient for self-administration.

## 2525.3 WITNESSED DIRECTIVE

A mentally competent adult individual may at any time voluntarily execute a revocable Directive governing the administration of aid-indying. The Directive shall be signed by the declarant and witnessed by two adults who at the time of witnessing, meet the following requirements:

(a) Are not related to the declarant by blood or marriage, or adoption;

(b) Are not entitled to any portion of the estate of the declarant upon his/her death under any will of the delcarant or codicil thereto then existing, or, at the time of the Directive, by operation of law then existing;

(c) Have no creditor's claim against the delcarant, or anticipate making such claim against any portion of the estate of the declarant upon his or her death.

(d) Are not the attending physician, an employee of the attending physician, a health care provider, or an employee of a health care provider;

(e) Are not the operator of a community care facility or an employee of a community care facility.

The Directive shall be substantially in the form contained in Section 2525.24.

## 2525.4 SKILLED NURSING FACILITIES

A Directive shall have no force or effect if the declarant is a patient in a skilled nursing facility as defined in subdivision (c) of Section 1250 of the Health and Safety Code and intermediate care facility or community care facility at the time the Directive is executed unless one of the two witnesses to the Directive is a Patient Advocate or Ombudsman designated by the Department of Aging for this purpose pursuant to any other applicable provision of law. The Patient Advocate or Ombudsman shall have the same qualifications as a witness under Section 2525.3.

The intent of this paragraph is to recognize that some patients in skilled nursing facilities may be so insulated from a voluntary decision-making role, by virtue of the custodial nature of their care, as to require special assurance that they are capable of willingly and voluntarily executing a Directive.

## 2525.5 REVOCATION

A Directive may be revoked at any time by the declarant, without regard to his or her mental state or competency, by any of the following methods:

(a) By being canceled, defaced, obliterated, burned, torn, or otherwise destroyed by or at the direction of the declarant with the intent to revoke the Directive.

(b) By a written revocation of the declarant expressing his or her intent to revoke the Directive, signed and dated by the declarant. If the declarant is in a health care facility and under the care and management of a physician, the physician shall record in the patient's medical record the time and date when he or she received notification of the written revocation.

(c) By verbal expression by the declarant of his or her intent to revoke the Directive. The revocation shall become effective only upon communication to the attending physician by the declarant. The attending physician shall confirm with the patient that he or she wishes to revoke, and shall record in the patient's medical record the time, date and place of the revocation.

There shall be no criminal, civil or adiministrative liability on the part of the health care provider for following a Directive that has been revoked unless that person has actual knowledge of the revocation.

## 2525.6 TERM OF DIRECTIVE

A Directive shall be effective unless and until revoked in the manner described in Section 2525.5. This title shall not prevent a declarant from reexecuting a Directive at any time in accordance with Section 2525.3, including execution subsequent to a diagnosis of a terminal condition.

## 2525.7 ADMINISTRATION OF AID-IN-DYING

When, and only when, a qualified patient determines that the time for physician aid-in-dying has arrived and has made an enduring request, the patient will communicate that determination directly to the attending physician who will administer aid-in-dying in accordance with this Act.

## 2525.8 NO COMPULSION

Nothing herein requires a physician to administer aid-in-dying, or a licensed health care professional, such as a nurse, to participate in administering aid-in-dying under the direction of a physician, if he or she is religiously, morally or ethically opposed. Neither shall privately owned hospitals be required to permit administration of physician aid-in-dying in their facilities if they are religiously, morally or ethically opposed.

## 2525.9 PROTECTION OF HEALTH CARE PROFESSIONALS

No physician, health care facility or employee of a health care facility who, acting in accordance with the requirements of this title, administers aid-in-dying to a qualified patient shall be subject to civil, criminal, or administrative liability herefore. No licensed health care professional, such as a nurse, acting under the direction of a physician, who participates in the administration of aid-in-dying to a qualified patient in accordance with this title shall be subject to any civil, criminal, or administrative liability. No physician, or licensed health care professional acting under the direction of a physician, who acts in accordance with the provisions of this chapter, shall be guilty of any criminal act or of unprofessional conduct because he or she administers aid-in-dying.

## 2525.10 TRANSFER OF PATIENT

No physician, or health care professional or health care provider acting under the direction of a physician, shall be criminally, civilly, or administratively liable for failing to effectuate the Directive of the qualified patient, unless there is willful failure to transfer the patient to any physician, health care professional, or health care provider upon request of the patient.

## 2525.11 FEES

Fees, if any, for administering aid-in-dying shall be fair and reasonable.

## 2525.12 INDEPENDENT PHYSICIANS

The certifying physicians shall not be partners or shareholders in the same medical practice.

## 2525.13 CONSULTATIONS

An attending physician who is requested to give aid-in-dying may request psychiatric or psychological consultation if that physician has any concern about the patient's competence, with the consent of a qualified patient.

## 2525.14 DIRECTIVE COMPLIANCE

Prior to administering aid-in-dying to a qualified patient, the attending physician shall take reasonable steps to determine that the Directive has been signed and witnessed, and all steps are in accord with the desires of the patient, expressed in the Directive and in their personal discussions. Absent knowledge to the contrary, a physician or other health care provider may presume the Directive complies with this title and is valid.

## 2525.15 MEDICAL STANDARDS

No physician shall be required to take any action contrary to reasonable medical standards in administering aid-in-dying.

## 2525.16 NOT SUICIDE

Requesting and receiving aid-in-dying by a qualified patient in accordance with this title shall not, for any purpose, constitute a suicide.

### 2525.17 INSURANCE

(a) No insurer doing business in California shall refuse to insure, cancel, refuse to renew, re-assess the risk of an insured, or raise premiums on the basis of whether or not the insured has considered or completed a Directive. No insurer may require or request the insured to disclose whether he or she has executed a Directive.

(b) The making of a Directive pursuant to Section 2525.3 shall not restrict, inhibit, or impair in any manner the sale, procurement, issuance or rates of any policy of life, health or disability insurance, nor shall it affect in any way the terms of an existing policy of life, health, or disability insurance. No policy of life, health, or disability insurance shall be legally impaired or invalidated in any manner by the administration of aid-in-dying to an insured qualified patient, notwithstanding any term of the policy to the contrary.

(c) No physician, health care facility, or other health care provider, and no health care service plan, insurer issuing disability insurance, other insurer, self-insured employee welfare benefit plan, or non-profit hospital service plan shall require any person to execute or prohibit any person from executing a Directive as a condition for being insured for, or receiving, health care services, nor refuse service because of the execution, the existence, or the revocation of a Directive.

(d) A person who, or a corporation, or other business which, requires or prohibits the execution of a Directive as a condition for being insured for, or receiving, health care services is guilty of a misdemeanor.

(e) No life insurer doing business in California may refuse to pay sums due upon the death of the insured whose death was assisted in accordance with this Act.

### 2525.18 INDUCEMENT

No patient may be pressured to make a decision to seek aid-in-dying because that patient is a financial, emotional or other burden to his or her family, other persons, or the state. A person who coerces, pressures or fraudulently induces another to execute a Directive under this chapter is guilty of a misdemeanor, or if death occurs as a result of said coercion, pressure or fraud, is guilty of a felony.

### 2525.19 TAMPERING

Any person who willfully conceals, cancels, defaces, obliterates, or damages the Directive of another without the declarant's consent shall be guilty of a misdemeanor. Any person who falsifies or forges the Directive of another, or willfully conceals or withholds personal knowledge of a revocation as provided in Section 2525.5, with the intent to induce aid-in-dying procedures contrary to the wishes of the declarant, and thereby, because of such act, directly causes aid-in-dying to be administered, shall be subject to prosecution for unlawful homicide as provided in Chapter 1 (commencing with Section 187) of Title 8 of Part 1 of the Penal Code.

### 2525.20 OTHER RIGHTS

This Act shall not impair or supersede any right or legal responsibility which any person may have regarding the withholding or withdrawal of life-sustaining procedures in any lawful manner.

### 2525.21 REPORTING

Hospitals and other health care providers who carry out the Directive of a qualified patient shall keep a record of the number of these cases, and report annually to the State Department of Health Services the patient's age, type of illness, and the date the Directive was carried out. In all cases, the identity of the patient shall be strictly confidential and shall not be reported.

### 2525.22 RECORDING

The Directive, or a copy of the Directive, shall be made a part of a patient's medical record in each institution involved in the patient's medical care.

### 2525.23 MERCY KILLING DISAPPROVED

Nothing in this Act shall be construed to condone, authorize, or approve mercy killing.

### 2525.24 FORM OF DIRECTIVE

In order for a Directive to be valid under this title, the Directive shall be substantially the following form:

## VOLUNTARY DIRECTIVE TO PHYSICIANS

*NOTICE TO PATIENT:*

*This document will exist until it is revoked by you. This document revokes any prior Directive to administer aid-in-dying but does not revoke a durable power of attorney for health care or living will. You must follow the witnessing procedures described at the end of this form or the document will not be valid. You may wish to give your doctor a signed copy.*

### INSTRUCTIONS FOR PHYSICIANS

*ADMINISTRATION OF A MEDICAL PROCEDURE TO END MY LIFE IN A PAINLESS, HUMANE, AND DIGNIFIED MANNER*

*This Directive is made this _____ day of _____ (month) _____ (year).*

*I, _____, being of sound mind, do voluntarily make known my desire that my life shall be ended with the aid of a physician in a painless, humane, and dignified manner when I have a terminal condition or illness, certified to be terminal by two physicians, and they determine that my death will occur within six months or less.*

*When the terminal diagnosis is made and confirmed, and this Directive is in effect, I may then ask my attending physician for aid-in-dying. I trust and hope that he or she will comply. If he or she refuses to comply, which is his or her right, then I urge that he or she assist in locating a colleague who will comply.*

*Determining the time and place of my death shall be in my sole discretion. The manner of my death shall be determined jointly by my attending physician and myself.*

*This Directive shall remain valid until revoked by me. I may revoke this Directive at any time.*

*I recognize that a physician's judgment is not always certain, and that medical science continues to make progress in extending life, but in spite of these facts, I nevertheless wish aid-in-dying rather than letting my terminal condition take its natural course.*

*I will endeavor to inform my family of this Directive, and my intention to request the aid of my physician to help me to die when I am in a terminal condition, and take those opinions into consideration. But the final decision remains mine. I acknowledge that it is solely my responsibility to inform my family of my intentions.*

*I have given full consideration to and understand the full import of this Directive, and I am emotionally and mentally competent to make this Directive. I accept the moral and legal responsibility for receiving aid-in-dying.*

*This Directive will not be valid unless it is signed by two qualified witnesses who are present when you sign or acknowledge your signature. The witnesses must not be related to you by blood, marriage, or adoption; they must not be entitled to any part of your estate or at the time of execution of the Directive have no claim against any portion of your estate, nor anticipate making such claim against any portion of your estate; and they must not include: your attending physician, an employee of the attending physician; a health care provider; an employee of a health care provider; the operator of the community care facility or an employee of an operator of a community care facility.*

*If you have additional pages to this form, you must sign and date each of the additional pages at the same time you date and sign this Directive.*

*Signed:* _____


_____
*City, County, and State of Residence*

## STATEMENT OF WITNESSES

*I declare under penalty of perjury under the laws of California that the person who signed or acknowledged this document is personally known to me (or proved to me on the basis of satisfactory evidence) to be the declarant of this Directive; that he or she signed and acknowledged this Directive in my presence, that he or she appears to be of sound mind and under no duress, fraud, or undue influence; that I am not the attending physician, an employee of the attending physician, a health care provider, an employee of a health care provider, the operator of a community care facility, or an employee of an operator of a community care facility.*

*I further declare under penalty of perjury under the laws of California that I am not related to the declarant by blood, marriage, or adoption, and, to the best of my knowledge, I am not entitled to any part of the estate of the principal upon the death of the principal under a will now existing or by operation of law, and have no claim nor anticipate making a claim against any portion of the estate of the declarant upon his or her death.*

*Dated:* _____

*Witness's Signature:* _____

*Print Name:* _____

*Residence Address:* _____

*Dated:* _____

*Witness's Signature:* _____

*Print Name:* _____

*Residence Address:* _____

---

## STATEMENT OF PATIENT ADVOCATE OR OMBUDSMAN

*(If you are a patient in a skilled nursing facility, one of the witnesses must be a Patient Advocate or Ombudsman. The following statement is required only if you are a patient in a skilled nursing facility, a health care facility that provides the following basic services: skilled nursing care and supportive care to patients whose primary need is for availability of skilled nursing care on an extended basis. The Patient Advocate or Ombudsman must sign the "Statement of Witnesses" above AND must also sign the following statement.)*

*I further declare under penalty of perjury under laws of California that I am a Patient Advocate or Ombudsman as designated by the State Department of Aging and that I am serving as a witness as required by Section 2525.4 of the California Civil Code.*

*Signed:* _____

---

### SEC. 2. PENAL CODE AMENDMENT

Section 401 of the Penal Code is amended to read:

401. Suicide, aiding, advising or encouraging. Every person who deliberately aids, or advises, or encourages another to commit suicide, is guilty of a felony. Death resulting from a request for aid-in-dying pursuant to Title 10.5 (commencing with Section 2525) of Division 3 of Part 4 of the Civil Code shall not constitute suicide, nor is a licensed physician who lawfully administers aid-in-dying or a health care provider or licensed health care professional acting under the direction of a physician, liable under this section. Death resulting from aid-in-dying pursuant to a Directive in accordance with the Death With Dignity Act does not, for any purpose, constitute a homicide.

## SEC. 3. AMENDMENT OF INITIATIVE

This Act may be amended only by statute passed by a two-thirds vote of each house of the legislature and signed by the Governor.

# A Living Will
# And
# Durable Power of Attorney
# for Health Care

To my family, my relatives, my friends, my physicians, my employers, and all others whom it may concern: Directive made this _____ day of _____ 199 ___ I, _____ (name), being of sound mind, willfully, and voluntarily make known my desire that my life shall not be prolonged artificially under the circumstances set forth below, do hereby declare:

   **1.** If at any time I should have an incurable injury, disease, illness or condition certified to be terminal by two medical doctors who have examined me, and where the application of life-sustaining procedures of any kind would serve only to prolong artificially the moment of my death, and where a medical doctor determines that my death is imminent, whether or not life-sustaining procedures are utilized, I direct that such procedures be withheld or withdrawn and that I be permitted to die naturally, and that I receive whatever quantity of whatever drugs may be required to keep me free of pain or distress even if the moment of death is hastened.

   **2.** I hereby appoint _____ (name) currently residing at _____ , as my attorney-in-fact (i.e., proxy or agent) for the making of decisions relating to my health care in my place; and it is my intention that this appointment shall be honored by him/her, by my family, relatives, friends, physicians and lawyer as the final expression of my legal right to refuse medical or surgical treatment; and I accept the consequences of such a decision. I have duly executed a Durable Power of Attorney for health care decisions on this date.[1]

**3.** In the absence of my ability to give further directions regarding my treatment, including life-sustaining procedures, it is my intention that this directive shall be honoured by my family and physicians as the final expression of my legal right to refuse or accept medical and surgical treatment, and I accept the consequences of such refusal.

**4.** If I have been diagnosed as pregnant and that diagnosis is known to any interested person, this directive shall have no force during the course of my pregnancy.[2]

**5.** I have been diagnosed, and notified at least 14 days ago, as being in a terminal condition by, _____ M.D., whose address is _____ and whose telephone number is _____ . I understand that if I have not filled in the physician's name and address, it shall be presumed that I did not have a terminal condition when I made out this directive.[3]

**6.** This directive shall have no force and effect after five years from the date (above) of its execution, nor, if sooner, after revocation by me, either orally or in writing.[4]

**7.** I understand the full importance of this directive and am emotionally and mentally competent to make this directive. No participant in the making of this directive or in its being carried into effect, whether it be a medical doctor, my spouse, a relative, friend or any other person shall be held responsible in any way, legally, professionally or socially, for complying with my directions.

Signed _____

City, County and State of Residence _____

The declarant has been known to me personally and I believe her/him to be of sound mind.

Witness _____     Witness _____

Address _____     Address _____

_____     _____

[1]Under California law, for such an appointment to be as fully effective as the law will permit, it must be in the form included on page one under the title "DURABLE POWER OF ATTORNEY FOR HEALTH CARE DECISIONS." Persons living in other states and executing this "Living Will" also might wish to execute that form (Durable Power of Attorney), as it might well be honored by the medical practitioners and courts of any particular state. If you do not in fact execute a Durable Power of Attorney, strike out the last sentence of this paragraph.

[2]This is an explicit requirement of the California statute. However, even a woman of child-bearing age in another state should leave it in, in order to avoid the implication that this problem has not been considered, with the possible effect of voiding the instrument.

[3]If you are not a resident of California, strike out Paragraph 5 in its entirety.

[4]The five-year limit is a California legal requirement. If a different one exists in your state, strike out the 5 and insert the proper limit. If no limit is imposed in your state, strike out Paragraph 6 entirely.

## A DURABLE POWER OF ATTORNEY FOR HEALTH CARE

This is California's legal document. If you live in another state fill in that state's name.

Before signing you must first read and sign the warning printed on page 5 of this document.

### 1. DESIGNATION OF HEALTH CARE AGENT

I, _____
(Insert your name and address)

_____

do hereby designate and appoint _____

_____

_____

(Insert name, address, and telephone number of one individual only as your agent to make health care decisions for you. None of the following may be designated as your agent: (1) your treating health care provider, (2) a nonrelative employee of your treating health care provider, (3) an operator of a community care facility, or (4) a nonrelative employee of an operator of a community care facility).

as my attorney in fact (agent) to make health care decisions for me as authorized in this document. For the purposes of this document, "health care decision" means consent, refusal of consent, or withdrawal of consent to any care, treatment, service, or procedure to maintain, diagnose, or treat an individual's physical or mental condition.

2. CREATION OF DURABLE POWER OF ATTORNEY FOR HEALTH CARE. By this document I intend to create a durable power of attorney for health care. (Under Sections 2430 to 2443, inclusive, of the California Civil Code. This power of attorney is authorized by the Keene Health Care Agent Act and shall be construed in accordance with the provisions of Sections 2500 to 2506, inclusive, of the California Civil Code.) This power of attorney shall not be affected by my subsequent capacity.

3. GENERAL STATEMENT OF AUTHORITY GRANTED. Subject to any limitations in this document, I hereby grant to my agent full power and authority to make health care decisions for me to the same extent that I could make such decisions for myself if I had the capacity to do so. In exercising this authority, my agent shall make health care decisions that are consistent with my desires as stated in this document or otherwise made known to my agent, including, but not limited to, my desires concerning obtaining or refusing or withdrawing life-prolonging care, treatment, services, and procedures.
(If you want to limit the authority of your agent to make health care decisions for you, you can state the limitations in paragraph 4 ("Statement of Desires, Special Provisions, and Limitations") below. You can indicate your desires by including a statement of your desires in the same paragraph.

4. STATEMENT OF DESIRES, SPECIAL PROVISIONS, AND LIMITATIONS
(Your agent must make health care decisions that are consistent with your known desires. You can, but are not required to, state your desires in the space provided below. You should consider whether you want to include a statement of your desires concerning life-prolonging care, treatment, services, and procedures. You can also include a statement of your desires concerning other matters relating to your health care. You can also make your desires known to your agency by discussing your desires with your agent or by some other means. If there are any types of treatment that you do not want to be used, you should state them in the space below. If you do not state any limits, your agent will have broader powers to make health care decisions for you, except to the extent that there are limits provided by law.)

In exercising the authority under this durable power of attorney for health care, my agent shall act consistently with my desires as stated below and is subject to the special provisions and limitations stated below:

(a) Statement of desires concerning life-prolonging care, treatment, services, and procedures:

_____

_____

_____

_____

_____

_____

_____

_____

_____

_____

_____

_____

_____

_____

_____

_____

_____

(b) Additional statement of desires, special provisions, and limitations:

_____

_____

_____

_____

_____

_____

_____

_____

_____

_____

_____

_____

_____

_____

_____

_____

(You may attach additional pages if you need more space to complete your statement. If you attach additional pages, you must date and sign each of the additional pages at the same time you date and sign this document.)

## 5. INSPECTION AND DISCLOSURE OF INFORMATION RELATING TO MY PHYSICAL OR MENTAL HEALTH.

Subject to any limitations in this document, my agent has the power and authority to do all of the following:

(a) Request, review, and receive any information, verbal or written, regarding my physical or mental health, including, but not limited to, medical and hospital records.

(b) Execute on my behalf any releases or other documents that may be required in order to obtain this information.

(c) Consent to the disclosure of this information.

(If you want to limit the authority of your agent to receive and disclose information relating to your health, you must state the limitations in paragraph 4 ("Statement of Desires, Special Provisions, and Limitations") above.)

## 6. SIGNING DOCUMENTS, WAIVERS, AND RELEASES.

Where necessary to implement the health care decisions that my agent is authorized by this document to make, my agent has the power and authority to execute on my behalf all of the following:

(a) Documents titled or purporting to be a "Refusal to Permit Treatment" and "Leaving Hospital Against Medical Advice."

(b) Any necessary waiver or release form liability required by a hospital or physician.

## 7. UNIFORM ANATOMICAL GIFT ACT.

Subject to any limitations in this document, my agent has the power and authority to make a disposition of a part or parts of my body under the Uniform Anatomical Gift Act (Chapter 3.5 (commencing with Section 7150) of Part 1 of Division 7 of the Health and Safety Code).

(If you want to limit the authority of your agent to make a disposition under the Uniform Anatomical Gift Act, you must state the limitations in paragraph 4 ("Statement of Desires, Special Provisions, and Limitations") above.)

## 8. DURATION

(Unless you specify a shorter period in the space below, this power of attorney will exist for seven years from the date you execute this document and, if you are unable to make health care decisions for yourself at the time when this seven-year period ends, the power will continue to exist until the time when you become able to make health care decisions for yourself.)

This durable power of attorney for health care expires on _____

_____.

(Fill in this space ONLY if you want the authority of your agent to end earlier than the seven-year period described above.)

## 9. DESIGNATION OF ALTERNATE AGENTS

(You are not required to designate any alternate agents but you may do so. Any alternate agent you designate will be able to make the same health care decisions as the agent you designated in paragraph 1, above, in the event that agent is unable or ineligible to act as your agent. If the agent you designated is your spouse, he or she becomes ineligible to act as your agent if your marriage is dissolved.)

If the person designated as my agent in paragraph 1 is not available or becomes ineligible to act as my agent to make a health care decision for me or loses the mental capacity to make health care decisions for me, or if I revoke that person's appointment or authority to act as my agent to make health care decisions for me, then I designate and appoint the following persons to serve as my agent to make health care decisions for me as authorized in this document, such persons to serve in the order listed below.

A. First Alternate Agent _____

_____

_____

_____

(Insert name, address, and telephone number of first alternate agent)

B. Second Alternate Agent _____

_____

_____

_____

(Insert name, address, and telephone number of second alternate agent)

## 10. NOMINATION OF CONSERVATOR OF PERSON.

(A conservator of the person may be appointed for you if a court decides that one should be appointed. The conservator is responsible for your physical care, which under some circumstances includes making health care decisions for you. You are not required to nominate a conservator but you may do so. The court will appoint the person you nominate unless that would be contrary to your best interests. You may, but are not required to, nominate as your conservator the same persons you named in paragraph 1 as your health care agent. You can nominate an individual as your conservator by completing the space below.)

If a conservator of the person is to be appointed for me, I nominate the following individual to serve as conservator of the person

_____

_____

_____

(Insert name and address of person nominated as conservator of the person)

11. PRIOR DESIGNATIONS REVOKED. I revoke any prior durable power of attorney for health care.

### DATE AND SIGNATURE OF PRINCIPAL
(You Must Date and Sign This Power of Attorney)

I sign my name to this Statutory Form Durable Power of Attorney for Health Care on _____
at _____ , _____
     (City)         (State)

_____

(You sign here)

(This Power of Attorney will not be valid unless it is signed by two qualified witnesses who are present when you sign or acknowledge your signature. If you have attached any additional pages to this form, you must date and sign each of the additional pages at the same time you date and sign this Power of Attorney.)

### STATEMENT OF WITNESSES

(This document must be witnessed by two qualified adult witnesses. None of the following may be used as a witness: (1) a person you designate as your agent or alternate agent, (2) a health care provider, (3) an employee of a health care provider, (4) the operator of a community care facility, (5) an employee of an operator of a community care facility. At least one of the witnesses must make the additional declaration set out following the place where the witnesses sign.)

I declare under penalty of perjury under the laws of California _____ that the person who signed or
        other state
acknowledged this document is personally known to me (or proved to me on the basis of convincing evidence) to be the principal, that the principal signed or acknowledged this durable power of attorney in my presence, that the principal appears to be of sound mind and under no duress, fraud, or

undue influence, that I am not the person appointed as attorney in fact by this document, and that I am not a health care provider, an employee of a health care provider, the operator of a community care facility, nor an employee of an operator of a community care facility.

Signature: _____

Print name: _____

Date: _____

Residence address: _____

_____

_____

Signature: _____

Print name: _____

Date: _____

Residence address: _____

(AT LEAST ONE OF THE ABOVE WITNESSES MUST ALSO SIGN THE FOLLOWING DECLARATION.)

I further declare under penalty of perjury under the laws of California _____ that I am not related to the
other state
principal by blood, marriage, or adoption, and, to be best of my knowledge, I am not entitled to any part of the estate of the principal upon the death of the principal under a will now existing or by operation of law.

Signature: _____

Signature: _____

STATEMENT OF PATIENT ADVOCATE OR OMBUDSMAN
(If you are a patient in a skilled nursing facility, one of the witnesses must be a patient advocate or ombudsman. The following statement is required only if you are a patient in a skilled nursing facility—a health care facility that provides the following basic services: skilled nursing care and supportive care to patients whose primary need is for availability of skilled nursing care on an extended basis. The patient advocate or ombudsman must sign both parts of the "Statement of Witnesses" above AND must also sign the following statement.)

I further declare under penalty of perjury under the laws of California _____ that I am a patient advocate
other state
or ombudsman as designated by the State Department of Aging and that

I am serving as a witness as required by subdivision (f) of Section 2432 of the Civil Code.

Signature: _____

## NOTARY

(Signer of instrument may either have it witnessed as above or have his/her signature notarized as below, to legalize this instrument.)

State of California _____
                              other state

County of _____ ss

On this _____ day of _____ 199 ____

before me personally appeared _____
                                        (full name of signer of instrument)

to me known (or proved to me on basis of satisfactory evidence) to be the person whose name is subscribed to this instrument, and acknowledged that he/she executed it. I declare under penalty of perjury that the person whose name is subscribed to this instrument appears to be of sound mind and under no duress, fraud or undue influence.

_____
(Signature of Notary)

NOTARY SEAL

**Warning to Person Executing this Document**

This is an important legal document. It creates a durable power of attorney for health care. Before executing this document, you should know these important facts:

 This document gives the person you designate as your attorney in fact the power to make health care decisions for you, subject to any limitations or statement of your desires that you include in this document. The power to make health care decisions for you may include consent, refusal of consent, or withdrawal of consent to any care, treatment, service, or procedure to maintain, diagnose, or treat a physical or mental condition. You may state in this document any types of treatment or placements that you do not desire.

The person you designate in this document has a duty to act consistent with your desires as stated in this document or otherwise made known or, if your desires are unknown, to act in your best interests.

Except as you otherwise specify in this document, the power of the person you designate to make health care decisions for you may include the power to consent to your doctor not giving treatment or stopping treatment which would keep you alive.

Unless you specify a shorter period in this document, this power will exist for seven years from the date you execute this document and, if you are unable to make health care decisions for yourself at the time when this seven-year period ends, this power will continue to exist until the time when you become able to make health care decisions for yourself.

Notwithstanding this document, you have the right to make medical and other health care decisions for yourself so long as you can give informed consent with respect to the particular decision. In addition, no treatment may be given to you over your objection, and health care necessary to keep you alive may not be stopped if you object.

You have the right to revoke the appointment of the person designated in this document by notifying that person of the revocation orally or in writing.

You have the right to revoke the authority granted to the person designated in this document to make health care decisions for you by notifying the treating physician, hospital, or other health care provider orally or in writing.

The person designated in this document to make health care decisions for you has the right to examine your medical records and to consent to their disclosure unless you limit this right in this document.

If there is anything in this document that you do not understand, you should ask a lawyer to explain it to you.

(b) The printed form described in subdivision (a) shall also include the following notice: "This power of attorney will not be valid for making health care decisions unless it is either (1) signed by two qualified witnesses who are personally known to you and who are present when you sign or acknowledge your signature or (2) acknowledged before a notary public in California."

(c) A durable power of attorney prepared in this state that permits the attorney in fact to make health care decisions and that is not a printed form shall include one of the following:

(1) The substance of the statements provided for in subdivision (a) in capital letters.

(2) A certificate signed by the principal's lawyer stating: "I am a lawyer authorized to practice law in the state where this power of attorney was executed, and the principal was my client at the time this power of attorney was executed. I have advised my client concerning his or her rights in connection with this power of attorney and the applicable law and the consequences of signing or not signing this power of attorney, and my client, after being so advised, has executed this power of attorney."

(d) If a durable power of attorney includes the certificate provided for in paragraph (2) of subdivision (c) and permits the attorney in fact to make health care decisions for the principal, the applicable law of which the client is to be advised by the lawyer signing the certificate includes; but is not limited to, the matters listed in subdivision (a).

SEC. 6. Section 2434 of the Civil Code is amended to read:

2434. (a) Unless the durable power of attorney provides otherwise, the attorney in fact designated in a durable power of attorney for health care who is known to the health care provider to be available and willing to make health care decisions has priority over any other person to act for the principal in all matters of health care decisions, but the attorney in fact does not have authority to make a particular health care decision if the principal is able to give informed consent with respect to that decision.

(b) Subject to any limitations in the durable power of attorney, the attorney in fact designated in a durable power of attorney for health care may make health care decisions for the principal, before or after the death of the principal, to the same extent as the principal could make health care decisions for himself or herself if the principal had the capacity to do so, including: (1) making a disposition under the Uniform Anatomical Gift Act, Chapter 3.5 (commencing with Section 7150.5) of Part 1 of Division 7 of the Health and Safety Code, (2) authorizing an autopsy under Section 7113 of the Health and Safety Code, and (3) directing the disposition of remains under Section 7100 of the Health and Safety Code. In exercising the authority under the durable power of attorney for health care, the attorney in fact has a duty to act consistent with the desires of the principal as expressed in the durable power of attorney or otherwise made known to the attorney in fact at any time or, if the principal's desires are unknown, to act in the best interests of the principal.

(c) Nothing in this article affects any right the person designated as attorney in fact may have, apart from the durable power of attorney for health care, to make or participate in the making of health care decisions on behalf of the principal.

Read on (date) _____

Signed _____

## NATURAL DEATH ACT, 1976
### Guidelines for Signers in California

The DIRECTIVE allows you to instruct your doctor not to use artificial methods to extend the natural process of dying.

Before signing the DIRECTIVE, you may ask advice from anyone you wish, but you do not have to see a lawyer or have the DIRECTIVE certified by a notary public.

If you sign the DIRECTIVE, talk it over with your doctor and ask that it be made part of your medical record.

The DIRECTIVE must be WITNESSED by two adults who 1) are not related to you by blood or marriage, 2) are not mentioned in your will, and 3) would have no claim on your estate.

The DIRECTIVE may NOT be witnessed by your doctor or by anyone working for your doctor. If you are in a HOSPITAL at the time you sign the DIRECTIVE, none of its employees may be a witness. If you are in a SKILLED NURSING FACILITY, one of your two witnesses MUST be a "patient advocate" or "ombudsman" designated by the State Department of Aging.

You may sign a DIRECTIVE if you are at least 18 years old and of sound mind, acting of your own free will in the presence of two qualified witnesses.

No one may force you to sign the DIRECTIVE. No one may deny you insurance or health care services because you have chosen not to sign it. If you do sign the DIRECTIVE, it will not affect your insurance or any other rights you may have to accept or reject medical treatment.

Your doctor is bound by the DIRECTIVE only 1) if he/she is satisfied that your DIRECTIVE is valid, 2) if another doctor has certified your condition as terminal, and 3) at least 14 days have gone by since you were informed of your condition. (California only.)

If you sign a DIRECTIVE while in good health, your doctor may respect your wishes but is not bound by the DIRECTIVE.

The DIRECTIVE is valid for a period of five years, at which time you may sign a new one.

The DIRECTIVE is not valid during pregnancy.

### Revocation

You may revoke the DIRECTIVE at any time, even in the final stages of a terminal illness, by 1) destroying it, 2) signing and dating a written statement, or 3) by informing your doctor. No matter how you revoke the DIRECTIVE, be sure your doctor is told of your decision.

# Questionaire Prepared by Gerald A. Larue

1. What stand or position (if any) has your religious organization taken regarding so-called "passive" euthanasia? By "passive" euthanasia I refer to the removal of life-support systems or the cessation of what have been called "heroic measures" to continue life when the patient is in intractable pain with a terminal illness, or is in irreversible coma, and when the removal of the support system will result in the death of the patient?

*For example:* K, 22 years old, is suffering from "a rapidly fulminating type of multiple sclerosis." He has been in a coma for 2 months and does not respond to any attention. He is immobile and body wastes are excreted involuntarily into plastic receptacles. According to his physician, his brain "is gone," his nervous system is rapidly degenerating. He will never recover and, indeed, if it were not for the artificial support system, both heart and breathing would cease to function. (Case drawn from David Hendin: *Death as a Fact of Life*, New York, 1973, pp. 17f.)

In such a situation would your religious organization sanction the removal of the life-support system and permit K to die? If so: Why and on what ethical and theological grounds? If not: Why not?

2. What stand or position (if any) has your religious organization taken with regard to so-called "active" euthanasia? By "active" euthanasia I refer to the deliberate intervention into the life process by the patient who is terminally ill and in intractable pain, or by the patient acting with the assistance of some other person, or by some person acting on behalf of a patient.

*For example:* M is 69 years old and is suffering from a virulent form of cancer that will, according to her doctors, terminate her life within a period of weeks. Her pain is excruciating; and although it is somewhat relieved by drugs, the medications leave her in a semi-comatose state which she resents. She has saved dozens of sleeping pills and other potentially lethal medications which she has hidden away. She knows she is terminal and does not want to live her remaining days in pain and in a semi-comatose state.

In such a situation would your religious organization sanction her taking the medicine and thereby shorten her time of suffering and end her life, in other words—commit suicide?

Yes _____        No _____

If "yes": Why and on what ethical and theological grounds? If "no": Why not?

Suppose M was not able to collect the lethal medications, but persuaded her doctor or a friend or a relative *to provide her* with the lethal dosage. In such a situation would your religious organization sanction the participation of her associates in her taking of her own life to end suffering? (Assisted suicide)

Yes _____        No _____

If "yes": Why and on what ethical and theological grounds? If "no": Why not?

Suppose the doctor or a friend or relative, acting in accord with M's expresses wishes, *administered* the lethal medications that shortened the time of suffering and caused death. In such a situation would your religious organization sanction this act which can be labeled "homicide" or "murder" or even "compassionate murder"?

Yes _____     No _____

If "yes": Why and on what ethical and theological grounds? If "no": Why not?

3. Does your religious organizations espouse belief in a soul or afterlife or in divine judgement or karma? If "yes," circle appropriate terms.

Yes _____     No _____

If "yes": What effect would participation in active euthanasia have upon the afterlife of the deceased and/or the one who participated in the termination of the patient's life?

4. Would the fact that death came by "active" euthanasia affect the rituals or burial patterns of the deceased person? If "yes": How and why? If not: Why not?

5. What sort of counseling would your religious organization provide for someone contemplating "passive" euthanasia for the self or for another (as in the case of K)?

For "active" euthanasia?

6. Will you please provide me with references in Scripture or other religious writings, or to ethical or moral doctrines or statements made

by your religious organization or its members pertaining to euthanasia?


7. Are there other persons in your religious organization with whom you think I might communicate for further information about this important subject?


Your name? _____ Organization: _____

# Index

ment, 141; and euthanasia, 142–
147; repudiation of Luther's anti-
Judaism, 28
Evans, Marvin, 261
Evans, William S., 315
Evil, reality of, 246–247
Ewert, David, 262, 263
*Exile in the Fatherland* (M. Niemoller), 24–25
Extraordinary measures of treatment:
definition of, 302; and economic
factors, 214; misapplication of,
268–269, 339; withdrawal of, 70,
87–89, 99–101, 107, 109, 124,
132, 231. *See also* Treatment, refusal or withholding of

**F**
Family, as central to human life, 245
Family members: and decisions about
babies with birth defects, 211; and
end-of-life decisions, 20, 350–351;
and home care of patient, 40; and
hospice care, 39, 41; pain of in
presence of patient in vegetative
state, 84–85; presence of in euthanasia, 416–417; and requests for
active euthanasia, 335; support and
pastoral care for, 187–188, 192; as
surrogate decision makers, 317–
318
Feeding tubes, *see* Nutrition, artificial
Feinstein, Moshe, 59
*Final Exit* (D. Humphry), 4, 37, 224
Fletcher, Joseph, 226, 347
Flower, Joseph R., 382
Flucke, Paul, 236
Fluids, *see* Hydration
Foerster, Annie, 261–262

Foreman, Joseph, 200
Fox, Joseph, and right to die naturally,
18–19
Freewill Baptist Church, 225–228

**G**
Galland, Les, 148
Gandhi, Mahatma, 365
*Gem Ornament of Manifold Oral In-
structions, The* (K. Rinpoche), 368–
369
General Baptists, Association of, 206–
207
Geneva Declaration (1957), 83
*Gentle Death, A* (M. Seguin), 252
George, Francis E., 71
Germany: anti-Semitism in, 27; euthanasia in Nazi era, 21–22, 24–
25, 27–28, 359–360
Geronticide: and demographic considerations, 29–30; difference from
suicide, 35; and health care coverage, 32; and protection against involuntary euthanasia, 31; warnings
about, 28–29, 75, 76
Gladish, Michael D., 323
God: belief in as working for good in
all circumstances, 303; belief that
suffering is required by, 9; concept
of life as gift of, 49, 57, 59, 70, 72,
95, 101, 108, 116, 130, 137, 184–
185, 188, 196, 206, 207, 216, 221,
233, 242–243, 323, 355, 382,
393; covenant relationship with,
53, 61, 247; death as return to,
278; denial that suffering is God's
will, 255; euthanasia as playing role
of, 9–10, 147; futile treatment as
playing role of, 147, 162–163,